AFRICA'S ROLE AND CONTRIBUTION TO INTERNATIONAL CRIMINAL JUSTICE

Series Supranational Criminal Law: Capita Selecta, Volume 26

Recently published in the series:

10. *The Implementation of the European Arrest Warrant in the European Union: Law, Policy and Practice*, Massimo Fichera
11. *The Principle of Mutual Recognition in Cooperation in Criminal Matters: A Study of the Principle in Four Framework Decisions and in the Implementation Legislation in the Nordic Member States*, Annika Suominen
12. *The European Public Prosecutor's Office: Analysis of a Multilevel Criminal Justice System*, Martijn Willem Zwiers
13. *Victimological Approaches to International Crimes: Africa*, Rianne Letschert Roelof Haveman, Anne-Marie de Brouwer and Antony Pemberton *(eds.)*
14. *The United States and International Criminal Tribunals: An Introduction*, Harry M. Rhea
15. *EU Sanctions: Law and Policy Issues Concerning Restrictive Measures*, Iai Cameron *(ed.)*
16. *Whose Responsibility? A Study of Transnational Defence Rights and Mutual Recognition of Judicial Decisions within the EU*, Malin Thunberg Schunke
17. *Genocidal Gender and Sexual Violence: The Legacy of the ICTR, Rwanda's Ordinary Courts and Gacaca Courts*, Usta Kaitesi
18. *Addressing the Intentional Destruction of the Environment during Warfare under the Rome Statute of the International Criminal Court*, Steven Freeland
19. *Individual Criminal Liability for the International Crime of Aggression*, Gerhard Kemp
20. *Selective Enforcement and International Criminal Law: The International Criminal Court and Africa*, James Nyawo
21. *The Governance of Complementary Global Regimes and the Pursuit of Human Security: The Interaction between the United Nations and the International Criminal Court*, Andrea Marrone
22. *The Rationality of Dictators: Towards a More Effective Implementation of the Responsibility to Protect*, Maartje Weerdesteijn
23. *Extended Confiscation in Criminal Law*, Malin Thunberg Schunke
24. *Convergences and Divergences Between International Human Rights, International Humanitarian and International Criminal Law*, Paul de Hert, Stefaan Smis and Mathias Holvoet *(eds.)*
25. *The Independence of the International Criminal Court: Between a Rock and a Hard Place*, Alphonse Muleefu

AFRICA'S ROLE AND CONTRIBUTION TO INTERNATIONAL CRIMINAL JUSTICE

Edited by
Jeremy Sarkin
Ellah T.M. Siang'andu

INTERSENTIA
Cambridge – Antwerp – Chicago

Intersentia Ltd
8 Wellington Mews
Wellington Street | Cambridge
CB1 1HW | United Kingdom
Tel: +44 1223 736 170
Email: mail@intersentia.co.uk
www.intersentia.com | www.intersentia.co.uk

Distribution for the UK and
Rest of the World (incl. Eastern Europe)
NBN International
1 Deltic Avenue, Rooksley
Milton Keynes MK13 8LD
United Kingdom
Tel: +44 1752 202 301 | Fax: +44 1752 202 331
Email: orders@nbninternational.com

Distribution for Europe
Lefebvre Sarrut Belgium NV
Hoogstraat 139/6
1000 Brussels
Belgium
Tel: +32 (0)800 39 067
Email: mail@intersentia.be

Distribution for the USA and Canada
Independent Publishers Group
Order Department
814 North Franklin Street
Chicago, IL 60610
USA
Tel: +1 800 888 4741 (toll free) | Fax: +1 312 337 5985
Email: orders@ipgbook.com

Africa's Role and Contribution to International Criminal Justice

ISBN 978-1-78068-907-4
D/2020/7849/100
NUR 828

British Library Cataloguing in Publication Data. A catalogue record for this book is available from the British Library.

ACKNOWLEDGEMENTS

This volume is the culmination of a long process. It began when Jeremy Sarkin was invited by Ellah T.M. Siang'andu to come to Zambia be the keynote speaker and deliver a public address on the topic 'Why Africa Needs, and Must Cooperate with, the ICC: Avoiding Impunity, Promoting Peace, Democratic Advancement and Human Rights Protection'. This paper was delivered at the 2017 International Multi-Disciplinary Conference held in Lusaka, Zambia in August 2017.

At this conference, a number of the contributors were present. It was recognised that few of the contributions of African law and African justice processes are recognised or understood outside Africa and that Africans need to take up these challenges themselves more often. It was further agreed that often the emphasis of African legal issues is squarely on issues relating to the International Criminal Court (ICC). It was recognised that while that is an important issue, there was a lot more that needed delineation. Thus, the idea of this book was born.

The process then began to work out what each potential contributor would write about. Chapters were then finalised and an internal review process occurred with content editing by Jeremy Sarkin. A language review of all the chapters was also carried out. The editors of the Intersentia Supranational Criminal Law book series then oversaw the review process of the draft chapters. The chapters were then finalised.

There are many to thank for their assistance in this process. NOVA University of Lisbon supported the process of publishing this book. The research centre CEDIS was very helpful in various ways. The Portuguese national funding agency for science, research and technology (FCT) assisted with funding. The University of the Free State where Jeremy Sarkin has been appointed a Research Fellow in the Department of Criminology also supported the publication of this book.

Intersentia have been wonderful to work with and their professionalism helps to ensure books of high quality. Our thanks particularly to Tom Scheirs and Rebecca Moffat.

Jeremy Sarkin and Ellah T.M. Siang'andu
Lisbon/Lusaka, February 2020

CONTENTS

LIST OF CONTRIBUTORS

Evelyne Owiye Asaala is a lecturer of law at the University of Nairobi. She holds a PhD from the University of Witwatersrand (South Africa), a Master of Laws degree from the University of Pretoria (South Africa) and a Bachelor of Laws degree from the University of Nairobi (Kenya). She has previously consulted with the Trust Fund for Victims of the International Criminal Court, Safer World International, the International Nuremberg Principles Academy, Truth Justice and Reconciliation Commission of Kenya (TJRC) and the Bail and Bond Task Force in Kenya.

Max du Plessis is an advocate in South Africa (Senior Counsel), Honorary Research Fellow of the University of KwaZulu-Natal in Durban, a senior research associate at the Institute for Security Studies, Pretoria, and fellow at Chatham House, London (UK). As an advocate in South Africa and associate tenant, Doughty Street Chambers, London, he has an extensive practice in public law, human rights and international law. As an international criminal lawyer, he has advised states before the ICC and has worked on domestic cases, especially regarding complementarity and universal jurisdiction, dealing with arrest warrants for senior government officials implicated in international crimes and litigating and advising on them in South Africa and other countries. He has published extensively on international criminal law topics and is a frequent panelist at conferences and events around the world.

Christopher Gevers teaches international law and legal theory in the School of Law, University of KwaZulu-Natal (South Africa). His research focuses on Black Internationalism, Third World Approaches to International Law, Critical Race Theory, and Law and Literature. Since 2015 he has been a faculty member of the Institute for Global Law and Policy at Harvard Law School, and has been a visiting Fellow at the University of Oxford and Harvard Law School. His most recent publications appear in *International Law and the Cold War* (2019), *Oxford Handbook of International Criminal Law* (2019) and the *London Review of International Law*.

O'Brien Kaaba is a lecturer in the School of Law at the University of Zambia and is a Senior Research Fellow at the Southern African Institute for Policy and Research (SAIPAR). He holds a Bachelor of Laws degree (LLB) from the University of London, LLM from the University of Zambia and LLD from the University of South Africa. He has formerly served as Elections Manager for the National Democratic Institute for International Affairs (NDI) in Zambia, the Political Specialist for the US Department of State at the American Embassy in Lusaka (Zambia) and as the Human Rights and Rule of Law Advisor for the Germany Development Cooperation (GIZ) in Zambia.

Godfrey Mupanga teaches undergraduate courses in the Faculty of Law at the University of Zimbabwe and runs the human rights practice in the law firm Mupanga Bhatasara Attorneys, which he set up with a colleague in 2012 in Harare. Previously, he served in various positions as Consultant, Director and Chief of Party for programmes on human rights, access to justice, rule of law and protection in countries that include Sudan – Darfur, South Sudan, Ethiopia, Kenya and Somaliland. He holds degrees in law that include a Doctor of Laws (LLD) from the University of Fort Hare, Master of Laws (LLM from the University of Leeds and Bachelor of Laws Honours (LLB (Hons)) from the University of Zimbabwe.

Felix Mukwiza Ndahinda is Director of Research, Policy and Higher Education (RPHE) at the Aegis Trust, Honorary Associate Professor at the University of Rwanda's College of Arts and Social Sciences and a Research Fellow at INTERVICT (Tilburg University, the Netherlands). He holds a PhD from Tilburg University (2009) and an LLM from the Raoul Wallenberg Institute of Human Rights (Sweden, 2006). He was formerly Assistant Professor at the International Victimology Institute Tilburg of Tilburg University from 2009 to 2017 and worked as Associate Legal Officer for the International Criminal Tribunal for Rwanda in Arusha-Tanzania (2009). He has authored several publications, including *Indigenousness in Africa: A Contested Legal Framework for Empowerment of 'Marginalized' Communities* (Springer/Asser Press, 2011).

Lydia A. Nkansah LLB, LLM, PhD is Dean and Associate Professor of Law at the Faculty of Law, Kwame Nkrumah University of Science and Technology in Kumasi (Ghana). Previously, she was a lecturer at the Ghana Institute of Management and Public Administration, where she helped to establish a third public law school in Ghana. She was also instrumental in the setting up of the law school in Ondo State University in Nigeria. She has facilitated courses at the Kofi Annan International Peacekeeping Training Centre. She was a senior legal officer at the Commission on Human Rights and Administrative Justice of Ghana, Head of the Research Unit and Leader of Evidence of the Truth and Reconciliation Commission for Sierra Leone. She also served as the international expert advisor to the Transitional Legislative Assembly of Liberia on a Truth and Reconciliation Bill.

Juan Pablo Perez-Leon-Acevedo is a researcher at the Faculty of Humanities and Social Sciences, University of Jyväskylä (Finland). He was a researcher at PluriCourts (Research Council of Norway, Project No 223274), in the Faculty of Law at the University of Oslo (Norway) where he also taught international law classes (lecturer) and supervised various master's theses in international law and related areas. He is currently a guest researcher at PluriCourts and is also Visiting Professor of international law at the Faculty of Law and Humanities of the Technological University of Peru. He served in different capacities at the Center for Human Rights of the University of Pretoria (South Africa), the Institute of Human Rights of Åbo Akademi University (Finland), the International Criminal Court and the International Criminal Tribunal for the former Yugoslavia. His contribution in this book is funded by the Research Council of Norway.

Jeremy Sarkin is Distinguished Visiting Professor of Law at Nova University of Lisbon (Portugal) and a Research Fellow in the Department of Criminology at the University of the Free State (South Africa). He has undergraduate and postgraduate law degrees from South Africa, a Master of Laws degree from Harvard Law School and a Doctor of Laws degree on comparative and international law. He is admitted to practice as an attorney in the USA and South Africa. He was Chairperson-Rapporteur of the United Nations Working Group on Enforced or Involuntary Disappearances. He served as an acting judge in 2002 and 2003 in the High Court in South Africa. He is also a member of a number of journal editorial boards. He has published 18 books and more than 300 articles. Some of his books are *The Global Impact and Legacy of Truth Commissions* (Intersentia 2019); *Germany's Genocide of the Herero* (UCT Press 2011); *Reparations for Colonial Genocides* (Praeger 2009); *Human Rights in African Prisons* (Ohio University Press 2008); *Reconciliation in Divided Societies: Finding Common Ground* (University of Pennsylvania Press 2007); and *Carrots and Sticks: The TRC and the South African Amnesty Process* (Intersentia 2004).

Ellah T.M. Siang'andu is a lecturer of law at the University of Zambia, School of Law. She is also a Research Fellow at the Southern African Institute for Policy and Research (SAIPAR). She holds a Doctor of Laws degree from the University of South Africa, a Master of Laws in Public International Law from the University of Nottingham (United Kingdom) and a Bachelor of Laws degree from the University of Hull (United Kingdom). She is currently a post-doctoral fellow under the Norwegian Programme for Capacity Development in Higher Education and Research for Development (*NORHED*)/University of Zambia, where she has been working on a project on women in prison with children.

INTRODUCTION

Understanding the Meaning, Context, Role and Importance of African Criminal Justice on the Continent and Beyond

Jeremy Sarkin and Ellah T.M. Siang'andu

Justice is the foundation of governance. This means that the very reason for the existence of a state as a centralized authority is to ensure justice for persons under its jurisdiction by investigating and prosecuting serious crimes and human rights violations and upholding the rule of law as the only way to live in peace.

Kebreab Isaac Weldesellasie

1. INTRODUCTION

The purpose of this book, which focuses on African criminal justice matters, is to examine a range of issues related to the development and the use of international criminal justice in Africa and on Africa. Thus, the book also seeks to understand the reach of the issues beyond Africa in ways that affect the continent. Adopting African perspectives, it provides details relating to the development, application and enforcement of international criminal law in Africa.

This book is timely as it is intended to provide a basis for examining African criminal justice issues. Therefore, engaging in theoretical and policy discourses on the substantive, as well as the procedural, features of criminal justice in Africa can contribute towards inculcating values about the need to ensure that perpetrators of international crimes are held responsible. We argue that a book focusing on criminal justice matters should assist in the understanding of these issues in Africa and around the world, and should also assist in improving the teaching of international criminal justice by providing more of an African perspective. Thus, the book adopts an expansive approach that is intended to allow for the exploration of ideas, themes, institutions and practices related to Africa's role and involvement in international criminal justice generally. It aims to explore concepts, patterns of convergence of criminal justice systems in Africa and how they have responded to international criminal justice issues generally. The continent's responses to international crime will be analysed on the basis of assumptions and expectations underlying international crimes.

This book therefore seeks to articulate issues concerning African criminal justice and to assess how its various component parts can be reformed in order to improve its effectiveness. It enunciates what have been the experiences of a range of institutions in and outside Africa, as well as African states, in holding individuals accountable for international crimes. It provides solutions on how African states can enhance their fight against impunity for the most serious offences of international concern. It addresses fundamental issues of criminal justice, which includes institutions that have been established in order to hold persons suspected of the commission of international crimes responsible. So far, the response of African states to the egregious atrocities on the continent includes the establishment of institutions such as the Extraordinary African Chambers (EAC), the International Criminal Tribunal for Rwanda (ICTR) and other criminal courts established in Sierra Leone, the Central African Republic and South Sudan for the purpose of holding suspected persons accountable for their crimes. In addition, a number of other indigenous approaches have been adopted, such as the *gacaca* courts and the *mato oput* in Rwanda and Uganda respectively.

These are important issues for the continent, as a large percentage of the mass human rights violations that have occurred around the world have taken place in Africa. This is examined later in this chapter, which contextualises the extensive human rights problems that exist on the continent and why viable criminal justice processes are sorely needed. This is important because using (international) criminal law is vital for the African continent for two main reasons. First, the continent has witnessed the most serious crimes, particularly genocide, war crimes and crimes against humanity. These have been committed in many African countries, including Burundi, the Central African Republic, Chad, the Democratic Republic of the Congo, Kenya, Mali, Libya, Liberia, Rwanda, Sierra Leone, Sudan and Uganda, to mention but a few (Sarkin 2016b). Second, it is also important for African states to ensure that there are adequate laws and institutions to hold persons suspected of committing the most serious atrocities criminally liable in national courts. Allowing individuals to escape with impunity will not in any way deter the commission of further atrocities on the continent (Sarkin 2018). Steps to deal with these issues are thus essential in order to deter others from doing similar things in the future (Sarkin 2009b, 2011). It is also imperative because African people have suffered severely because of these acts (Monageng 2014: 13) and ways of addressing their need for accountability are necessary.

This book also evaluates Africa's role and contributions to the development of international criminal justice. It highlights Africa's contribution to international criminal justice so far and how its role in establishing individual criminal responsibility for international crimes can be enhanced. It also evaluates why criminal justice issues are important in the African context, particularly from a human rights perspective, and deals with issues across the continent that make taking up such matters in a criminal justice context so important.

This book also explores existing laws intended to combat international crimes, as well as how they have been used and applied. Significantly, it examines a number of themes around the move to give the African Court on Human and Peoples' Rights (Sarkin 2011) criminal jurisdiction. This point is mentioned throughout the book as it is an issue that has deep significance for the continent as far as a number of different matters are concerned. The role that the reformed court could play and a range of human rights abuses that are occurring across the continent are also discussed to provide context for the examination of the role of the Court.

It must be noted that the administration of criminal justice generally is linked to politics. As Sumner (1979: 267–268) observes, the law 'lies in the cradle of political practice and is therefore subject to the pressures and imperatives of politics'. This implies that the existence of an effective and legitimate criminal justice system will depend on the nature of the government in power and whether it is in its interests to ensure that relevant legislation is adopted to enable the prosecution of suspects of international crime. This is a problem that has resulted in impunity for the most serious offences of international concern.

In this chapter, a number of issues related to the broad themes of the book are examined. At the end of the chapter, an overview is provided of the coverage of each of the subsequent chapters. However, first some of the theoretical perspectives relating to African criminal justice matters are explored. Some of the rationales advanced for African criminal justice at both the regional and domestic law levels are considered. In addition, the philosophical doubts surrounding African criminal justice and Africa's response so far to international crimes and their implications are examined.

2. UNDERSTANDING THE CONTEXT OF AFRICAN CRIMINAL JUSTICE

We understand African criminal justice as including processes in Africa and beyond that promote the use of criminal justice. It is also about initiatives and measures adopted by African states as a response to international crimes. It involves the application of international criminal law, which is the substantive law that provides for the prosecution of what the preamble to the Rome Statute of the International Criminal Court (ICC) refers to as the most serious offences of international concern. These are as follows: genocide, war crimes, crimes against humanity and crimes of aggression (Articles 6, 7, 8 and 8 *bis* of the Rome Statute and the Elements of Crimes 2002 and 2010). The African continent has witnessed some of the worst human rights atrocities, including genocide, crimes against humanity and war crimes (Mbazira 2011; Sarkin 2009a, 2009b). These atrocities have continued to reoccur on the continent as it has faced a series of armed conflicts (Nkansah 2014). Despite a number of individuals being suspected of having committed such atrocities on the continent, African states have been reluctant to prosecute suspects of international crimes (Cryer et al. 2007; McCormack 2003). However, the problem of states not prosecuting suspects of international crimes has not been restricted to Africa, but has also been prevalent elsewhere. The limited number of prosecutions has been due to the challenges of conducting trials for international crimes, including difficulties in gathering evidence as well as issues of fairness (Glueck 1944). As a result, many suspects have escaped prosecution.

In the context of Africa, there has been a debate about what to do about human rights abuses that plague the continent and whether prosecutions are the best way to address them, as was the case in Sierra Leone, where many suspects were children (Schabas 2004).

As far as the different schools of thought regarding punishment are concerned, the neo-Kantian retributionists argue that punishment is a useful means to reintegrate the offender into the society and for that to occur in harmony with the logic and contemplation of the social contract (Alemika 2009). It is thus intended to be an inevitable consequence of criminality (ibid.). As such, punishment is viewed as only reasonable to ensure that individuals who violate the rules of international criminal law are held responsible. According to the retributionists, it is vital to secure justice by punishing suspects of international crimes, on the grounds that they deserve to be punished for their actions, by imposing a penalty that is proportional to the harms caused by their crimes (von Hirsch 1976). In this context, later on in this chapter, we will examine some of the human rights atrocities and related problems that need to be addressed in various ways, including through the use of criminal justice. On the other hand, utilitarians justify punishment on the grounds of deterrence, social defence, incapacitation, crime prevention, reformation and rehabilitation. They are forward-looking in nature by focusing on the future conduct of the offenders and the benefits resulting from punishments. The utilitarian philosophy of punishment is that offenders ought to be punished if doing so will deter the population from committing crimes, protect society or reform and rehabilitate convicts. The assumption is that those who violate criminal law do so because of biological, psychological, socio-economic, political and cultural deficiencies. Thus, perpetrators are seen to be sick and in need of treatment and rehabilitation.

2.1. THE HISTORICAL CONTEXT

Until 1945, there were no prosecutions conducted at an international level due to an absence of international mechanisms to prosecute international crimes (Sarkin 2009a). Mass atrocities were first tried after the Second World War between 1945 and 1946, in Nuremberg and Tokyo respectively, on the basis of the statutes of the Nuremberg Tribunal and the International Military Tribunal for the Far East in 1945–1947 (Cassese and Gaeta 2013). This is despite the fact that some of the crimes that were tried at Nuremberg, emanated from customary law and the preambles to the 1899 and 1907 Hague Conventions and the Martens Clause. On this basis, Sarkin (2009a) argues that the origins of these crimes pre-date the conventions. However, the fundamental legal principles that are drawn from the trials have been recognised as the Principles of International Law documented in the Charter of the Nuremberg Tribunals and in the Judgement of the Tribunals.

2.2. THE INTERNATIONAL CRIMINAL TRIBUNAL FOR RWANDA

The Nuremberg Principles have been reaffirmed with the development of ad hoc tribunals like the International Criminal Tribunal for the Former Yugoslavia (ICTY) and the International Criminal Tribunal for Rwanda (ICTR) (UN Doc. S/RES/955 (1994)). The ICTR has been a major development and forms part of the foundation of African criminal justice. In fact, some see the ICTR as constituting Africa's most notable criminal justice initiative (du Plessis 2008: 1). The ICTR was set up in order to establish individual responsibility for the atrocities that were committed in the territory of Rwanda between 1 January and 31 December 1994. The ICTR managed to secure convictions of high-profile suspects, such as Jean Kambanda, Rwanda's Prime Minister from April to July 1994 (United Nations 1994: 6). Another important landmark decision of the ICTR was in the *Nahimana* case, which was the first post-Nuremberg decision to scrutinise the role of the media in the context of mass crimes, taking into account the freedom of expression and notion of incitement to international crime (Jallow and Bensouda 2008: 37). The ICTR has also played a vital role in contributing to the development of the jurisprudence of international criminal justice, particularly with reference to rape as an international crime for the first time in history of international criminal justice, as illustrated in the landmark decision of *Prosecutor v. Jean-Paul Akayesu.*

2.3. THE SPECIAL COURT FOR SIERRA LEONE

The United Nations has often played a key role in investigating or prosecuting human rights abuses in Africa (Sarkin 2009b). One key institution it established, together with the country concerned, was the hybrid court in Sierra Leone. The Special Court for Sierra Leone (SCSL) was created through an agreement between the United Nations and Sierra Leone on 16 January 2002 (SC Res. 1315 of 14 August 2000). It was established in order to prosecute serious violations of international humanitarian law and Sierra Leonean law committed in Sierra Leone since 30 November 1996 (United Nations 2000). Like the ICTR, the SCSL has contributed significantly to the development of international criminal law. More remarkable are its decisions relating to the recruitment of child solders, such as *Prosecutor v. Sam Hinga Norman*. The accused, Sam Norman, was arrested and charged under the Statute of the SCSL with the crime of conscripting or enlisting children under the age of 15 years into armed forces or groups for the purpose of using them in active hostilities. The SCSL concluded that the act of recruitment of child solders was a criminal act (a war crime) and contrary to international humanitarian law. The judgment is notable for being rendered well before the prosecution of the offence within the ICC framework, as in the later decision of *Prosecutor v. Thomas Lubanga Dyilo*.

2.4. THE INTERNATIONAL CRIMINAL COURT

However, it is the role of the ICC that has most affected Africa in a variety of ways, some positive and others more negative (Sarkin 2017). Most importantly, Africans played a vital role in the establishment of the Court (ibid.). African states actively participated in the creation of the ICC before 1998. They participated in the negotiation and adoption of the Rome Statute, which establishes a permanent international criminal court. In fact, African states constitute the largest regional bloc under the Rome Statute. An African state, Senegal, was the first to ratify the Statute on 2 February 1999 (Udombana 2014: 59). As argued by Mochochoko (2005: 243), 'the historical developments leading up to the establishment of the court portray an international will of which Africa was a part, to enforce humanitarian norms and to bring justice to those responsible for the most serious crimes of concern to the international community'. He also argues quite rightly that:

> No other continent has paid more dearly than Africa for the absence of legitimate institutions of law and accountability, resulting in a culture of impunity. Events in Rwanda were a grim reminder that such atrocities could be repeated anytime. This serves to strengthen Africa's determination and commitment to the creation of a permanent, impartial, effective and independent judicial mechanism to try and punish the perpetrators of these types of crimes whenever they occur (ibid.: 249).

The high number of ratifications by African states indicates the support that the ICC enjoyed in its early years. By 24 April 2008, 30 African states had signed and ratified the Rome Statute (Jallow and Bensouda 2008: 41). It is important to bear in mind that the ICC was meant to ensure that it did not replace domestic criminal justice systems, but rather empower them. Thus, the ICC operates on the basis of complementarity. This means that it grants primacy to national courts by only intervening where states are unwilling or unable to investigate, prosecute and establish individual responsibility for those suspected of having committed offences under the Rome Statute (Article 17 of and the preamble to the Rome Statute). This implies that African states have primacy over the ICC, which means that they can adopt measures to prosecute international crimes in domestic courts. However, Africa's response to international crimes has been scanty, as evidenced by the limited examples where African states responded to international crimes by conducting prosecutions in domestic courts. This is further illustrated by the large number of self-referrals of situations by African states to the ICC. Consequently, most situations and cases before the Court are from Africa. The first situations before the ICC were from three African states – Uganda, the Democratic Republic of the Congo and the Central African Republic – and the ICC has since continued to focus its work on African countries. Clearly, there is a need to interrogate the mechanisms that states have in place and ascertain how they can be improved in order to ensure processes of establishing individual accountability.

2.5. THE EXTRAORDINARY AFRICAN CHAMBERS

More recently, the EAC, a hybrid court was established in Senegal in order to prosecute Hissène Habré on the basis of universal jurisdiction for the crimes committed in Chad during his time as head of state (1982–1990). Habré was prosecuted in the EAC established by Senegal with the assistance of the African Union (AU) to ensure that prosecution was undertaken in Africa. He was eventually convicted of war crimes and sentenced to life in prison on the basis of Senegalese law (Jallow and Bensouda 2008: 26–27). Senegal was the first state in Africa to exercise the principle of universal jurisdiction (ibid.: 43).

2.6. DOMESTIC CRIMINAL JUSTICE SYSTEMS

While the international dimension of African criminal justice is important, when we talk of African criminal justice, we also need to include and examine the role that the various criminal justice systems that exist across the continent have played. In this context, we are referring to the norms, processes and decisions relating to the enactment and implementation of criminal laws, the determination of the guilt of crime suspects, and the distribution and administration of punishment (Alemika 2009: 11), usually but not exclusively in the domestic context, especially in the light of the move to create a regional criminal court. African criminal justice also refers to both the substantive and procedural measures that have been put in place, again usually by African states, to address international crimes by ensuring that those guilty of committing international crimes are held accountable.

At the national level, African states such as Ethiopia have shown a keenness to ensure that individuals are held criminally liable for international crimes (du Plessis 2008: 1). Mengistu Haile Mariam, the President of the military junta of the Dergue that ruled over Ethiopia from 1974 to 1987, was prosecuted for offences committed during his time in power (Jallow and Bensouda 2008: 28). He was convicted of genocide and crimes against humanity in December 2006 (ibid.). However, such processes have also been used against political opponents over the years.

3. THE ABUSE OF CRIMINAL JUSTICE SYSTEMS AND CRIMINAL LAW

Criminal justice systems in Africa have at times been abused for political purposes. On many occasions, they have been used as dangerous tools in the hands of regimes and governments in order to deal with their political opponents (Kinnes 2009: 3). While there is not always direct control over these systems, criminal justice institutions in Africa are often not independent and are easily influenced by other organs within a state, particularly the executive. Criminal justice processes have instead been used inappropriately by the ruling elites, who prefer to remain in power, as is the case, for example, in Uganda and Rwanda. Thus, criminal justice systems are used as a means of preserving the powers of the ruling elites.

Disputed elections, civil wars, conflicts and the displacement of people are the order of the day in Africa. Because of underfunding and the way in which the systems are used, perpetrators of crimes, especially those with a political dimension, often escape with impunity. This is partly because the processes, institutions and officials of justice have been described as ineffective, corrupt and repressive (Alemika 2009: 25). These problems have often been attributed to the colonial origins of these systems. However, while some problems can be blamed on the past, much responsibility must be placed at the feet of those who have been in power in the years after independence.

4. THE DEVELOPMENT OF THE APPLICATION OF CRIMINAL LAW AND OTHER PROCESSES IN AFRICA

Criminal justice systems and processes in Africa are evolving. However, many systems remain fragile. African criminal justice systems are often characterised by a lack of funding and personnel shortages (Bowd 2009: 1). The effective implementation of criminal justice will depend on the nature of governance within an African state. It must be noted that there is a nexus between criminal justice and democracy. For this reason, its application and implementation can be used as an indicator of democratic practices (Kinnes 2009: 1). This is despite the fact that it does not guarantee democratic governance. Criminal justice theory in fact provides a lens for scrutinising the practices and how the laid-down principles and standards are observed (ibid.: 2). Unfortunately, the continent has suffered adversities, including colonialism, poor leadership, dictatorships, armed conflict, oppression and unstable states that are still in the process of recovering. Consequently, the theory and practice of criminal justice in Africa produce results that either impede or endorse the political legitimacy of such states. The contention is that the criminal justice system is usually undermined in events of intra-state conflict or a coup d'état experienced by a state (ibid.: 3), particularly when used to deal with political opponents of the governments that have usurped democratic power. This has been the case in some countries such as Zimbabwe and Zambia, where excessive charges like treason have been imposed on individuals, only for the charges to be dropped later on.

African states have proceeded to introduce various measures in order to address the challenges created by the prosecution of perpetrators of international crimes. Thus, truth commissions and restorative justice measures, such as the *gacaca* courts, have been adopted in various places. The roles of commissions of inquiry in Africa for criminal conduct and the AU in promoting accountability, as well as issues concerning deterrence for international crimes, is scrutinised, as is the role of the ICC in Africa. So far, a majority of the situations and cases before the ICC are based in Africa, which clearly constitutes a problem.

5. WHY CRIMINAL JUSTICE PROCESSES ARE NEEDED IN AFRICA

Despite the numerous human rights atrocities that have been committed in Africa, impunity remains the order of the day (Sarkin 2016b). On the African continent, gross human rights abuses, including unlawful killings, torture and rape, are common (Manga 2013). Many states remain undemocratic and barely uphold human rights values (Sarkin 2017). Numerous countries are far from democratic (Human Rights Watch 2015). They do not sufficiently respect the human rights of their citizens (Sarkin 2019). There are limited instances when suspected persons have been held accountable (Sarkin 2018). More needs to be done in order to inculcate a culture that respects the rule of law and human rights by ensuring that those suspected of having committed international crimes are held accountable.

To deal with this, criminal law ought to be a tool that is used more often to prosecute those people who have committed these abuses. This is because human rights violations are usually crimes, but are not often prosecuted, especially by nation states. This could change when (and if) the African Court takes up the criminal jurisdiction that has been given to it under the terms of the Malabo Protocol. Crucially, when the Court is operational it will be able to prosecute the commission of genocide, crimes against humanity, war crimes, unconstitutional change of government, piracy, terrorism, use of mercenaries, corruption, money laundering, trafficking in persons, trafficking in drugs, trafficking in hazardous waste, illicit exploitation of natural resources and the crime of aggression. The African Union Assembly, with the consent of the state parties, may add crimes to this list. Thus, the Court could have a massive impact on the numerous and ongoing human rights violations committed on the continent. However, this is a long way off yet, as little progress has been made in getting states to ratify the Malabo Protocol.

The abuses that are occurring across the African continent need to be understood in the context in which they take place. There is a critical link between the type of state that exists and the abuses that are carried out. Crucially, many African states are far from democratic, and abuses are tolerated and in fact are often carried out by the state (Sarkin 2017). Thus, the Human

Freedom Index (HFI) finds that there is a strong correlation between freedom and democracy. Freedom is influenced by 'political regimes [and] economic development', along with a variety of other factors (Vasquez and Porcnik 2017: 8–10). As such, it is not surprising that African countries are only ranked between 63 and 157 out of the 159 countries included in the HFI (ibid.: 8–10). The largest deteriorations in freedom that have occurred recently took place in North Africa (ibid.: 27). Many of these states often do not tolerate dissent and many restrict freedom of expression (Kurt and Karp 2015). Most cooperate with international human rights institutions formally, but do little in practice to act on the issues raised by these mechanisms.

Of the 49 countries in the world to which the Index of Freedom in the World (FITW) has attributed the classification 'not free', the Central African Republic, Eritrea, Equatorial Guinea, Libya, Somalia, South Sudan, Sudan and Syria feature among the 12 worst 'aggregate scores for political rights and civil liberties' (Freedom House 2018: 6). Sub-Saharan Africa, with a total of 49 countries and a population of 1.02 billion people, is regarded as 39% not free, 43% partially free and 18% free (ibid.: 19), and North Africa, with a population of 424.8 million (Middle East and North Africa (MENA) total), is 67% not free, 22% partially free and 11% free (ibid.: 17).

Similarly (and having a dramatic effect on the human rights situation), overall global levels of peace have continued to decline. In general, conflicts have continued to rage all over the world. Conflicts in Africa have left hundreds of thousands people displaced (Amnesty International 2015: 12). Severely bloody conflicts have played out in the Central African Republic, South Sudan and Nigeria, and armed violence has continued in the Democratic Republic of the Congo, Sudan and Somalia (ibid.: 6). The effect has been to ensure that many people have been left with limited access to basic human rights necessities such as health, water, food and education (Amnesty International 2015: 12). Refugees in African countries have reportedly suffered xenophobia, abuses and violations (Amnesty International 2017: 21), as well as killings, sexual violence, torture and religious persecution (ibid.: 20). Even though the number of improving countries outnumbers the deteriorating countries (by 81 to 79) (ibid.: 8), the deteriorations were larger by size than the improvements, thus leading to a decline in the average country score (ibid.: 8).

In fact, the world has seen a 10-year deterioration in peace, which has been largely driven by the intensification of conflicts in the MENA region (ibid.: 3, 26). The main fields in which we can see deterioration are terrorism, refugees and internally displaced persons, and internal versus external conflict. In this regard, the Global Peace Index (GPI) indicates that in the MENA region and in Sub-Saharan Africa, peace levels have deteriorated. In Sub-Saharan Africa, 24 out of the 44 countries became less peaceful, with the greatest decline seen in Ethiopia, Mali, Burundi and Lesotho (Institute for Economics and Peace 2017a: 14). This deterioration in Sub-Saharan Africa can be attributed to the increasing threat of Islamic extremist terrorist groups, political instability – as evidenced by the military coup of 2014 in Lesotho – and internal conflicts fuelled by rising ethnic tensions (ibid.: 18). This decline in levels of peace seems to be attributed to an increase in political terror, perceived criminality and the involvement of police forces, organised internal conflict and the subsequent deaths, violent crimes and military expenditure as a percentage of GDP (ibid.: 23–24).

On rule of law matters, the Rule of Law Index (ROLI) is created by examining countries on issues concerning 'constraints on government powers, absence of corruption, open government, fundamental rights, order and security, regulatory enforcement, civil justice, and criminal justice' (World Justice Project 2018: 2). In this regard, African countries have a weak adherence to the rule of law (ibid.: 16–17).

In the Democracy Index (DI), 160 countries were ranked, based on 60 indicators. African countries scored between 7.24 – a 'flawed democracy' (South Africa) – and 1.50 – an 'authoritarian regime' (Chad) – with the majority of the countries falling into the authoritarian regime bracket in 2017. This marked a decline from 2006, which saw South Africa at 7.91 and Chad at 1.65 (Economist Intelligence Unit 2017). In 2007, across the various regions in Africa, MENA held a DI average of 3.53, with 16 authoritarian regimes, two hybrid regimes and two flawed democracies out of a total of 20 countries. Sub-Saharan Africa, with a total of 44 countries, had 23 authoritarian regimes, 13 hybrid regimes, seven flawed democracies and only one full democracy, thus attaining an average score of 4.24 (ibid.: 7). However, in 2017, MENA's DI average was 3.54, down 0.02 from 2016, with 14 authoritarian regimes, four hybrid regimes and two flawed democracies. Sub-Saharan Africa had a score of 4.35, down 0.02 from 2016, with 22 authoritarian regimes, 14 hybrid regimes and seven flawed democracies. Both regions thus show a decrease compared to the previous year, yet a slight increase in democratic readings since 2007 (Economist Intelligence Unit 2018: 18).

The DI highlights significant factors that contributed to the decline in Sub-Saharan Africa's score; electoral processes remain an area of conflict and contestation, with disputes resolved by military intervention and not domestic institutions (ibid.: 34). Civil liberties also decreased in 2017, characterised by attacks on the media and freedom of speech, and thus 'functioning government' remains the weakest score in Sub-Saharan Africa (ibid.: 35). Thus, the Sub-Saharan Africa region saw a score of 4.8, which is the second-worst regional performance after MENA with 3.6 (ibid.: 58–59). Media freedom is refused, often in contexts of 'authoritarian regimes', which are often seen as refusing dissent and protest (ibid.: 57). Governments in Sub-Saharan African have been seen to crack down on media freedom, from increasing regulatory powers to 'wholesale internet shutdowns' (ibid.: 59).

The decline in MENA's score in 2017 can be accredited to the presence of absolute monarchs, authoritarian regimes and military conflicts. In the wake of the Arab Spring of 2011, there has been a lack of 'genuine progress towards democracy' and this power vacuum has subsequently been filled by civil wars, as is evident in Egypt and Libya (ibid.: 35).

According to the Global Terrorism Index (GTI), terrorism is at an all-time high. Deaths from terrorism have increased by 286% since 2008 (Institute for Economics and Peace 2017b: 24). The impact of terrorism has grown over the past decade, with the number of incidents have almost tripled since 2011 (ibid.: 29). Terrorism also seems to be becoming more common across the globe, with every region seeing an increase in terrorist activities (ibid.: 29). The majority of terrorist attacks have occurred in MENA and Sub-Saharan Africa. These regions, together with South Asia, account for 84% of all terrorist attacks and 94% of deaths caused by terrorism (ibid.: 19). Sub-Saharan Africa 'has been the most deadly region in terms of fatalities per attack, with an average of 4.8 deaths per attack in 2016' (ibid.). In Africa as a whole, most attacks were conducted against civilians (60% in MENA and 56% in Sub-Saharan Africa) and not members of government and infrastructure (ibid.). Of the 10 countries most impacted by terrorism, African countries (Nigeria, Somalia and Libya) claim the three highest places. However, the increase in terrorism experienced by these countries in the period 2006–2016 is attributed to different things: in Libya, this rise follows the destabilisation of the government, while in Nigeria it is interesting to note that the rise in terrorism is not solely due to the presence of Boko Haram, as this group pre-dates the rise in terrorism (ibid.: 21).

What all the problems in the Sub-Saharan region reflect are the struggles countries face in terms of political problems. This triggers violence and is a setback for democracy (ibid.: 11). When it comes to safety and the rule of law, no country seems to have made much progress. The majority of African citizens (64%) now reside in countries where safety and the rule of law have deteriorated over the last 10 years (ibid.: 19).

As far as participation and human rights are concerned, performance in this category has improved overall, with the progress driven by the sub-categories of gender (which showed an overall positive trend in the last decade (GTI 2017: 45)) and participation. The majority of African countries (37) have made progress, but 15 countries showed a deterioration in this category. The rights sub-category registered a marginal deterioration in general (ibid.: 38), with 28 countries showing a drop (ibid.: 44). What is interesting in terms of this category is the fact that 70% of African citizens live in a country that has experienced a change in head of state and have seen improvements in terms of democratic participation and human rights. Linked to this are seven countries that still have the same head of state as previously and have registered a decline in this category (ibid.: 38). At the same time, Africa's average score in overall governance went up by one point (Mo Ibrahim Foundation 2014: 24). The scores of 37 out of 64 countries, representing 70% of African citizens, have gone up since 2006 (Mo Ibrahim Foundation 2016: 18). However, the scores for 16 countries went down, representing a negative trend in overall governance.

Various reports note how African governments do not pay much attention to the rights of civilians (Amnesty International 2015: 8). An issue emphasised is the fact that civilians bear the heavy burden of armed conflicts (ibid.: 2). Explosive weapons cause the most civilian casualties (Human Rights Watch 2015: ix). Many deaths and woundings of individuals could be avoided if the use of these weapons were subject to more regulation and if there were to be accountability for what was done (Amnesty International 2015: 3).

Other issues include continued impunity in many parts of Africa (ibid.: 6), including continuing unequal treatment of and violence against women, ongoing torture and further use of the death penalty, crackdowns on freedom of expression and assembly, pressure on civil society, and threats against human rights defenders and media workers. Threats to the human rights system is also a massive issue. The crises of refugees and displaced people, among others, showed that 'the brutal repression of dissent and the denial of people's basic rights – including economic, social and cultural rights – as well as the failure by states to protect the human rights of all, often spawn societal tensions, the by-products of which, in turn, stretch international protection systems beyond their limits' (ibid.: 16).

6. OVERVIEW OF THE CHAPTERS

In 'Types of International Criminal Courts in Africa', Lydia A. Nkansah examines the different types of international criminal courts that have been created in Africa. There is the ICTR, a purely international court that was established and administered as an organ of the United Nations. There is also the SCSL, a hybrid international court not part of the UN. In addition, there are courts that are divisions of existing national judicial systems. Within this group are those courts facilitated by the AU, namely the EAC of Senegal and the Hybrid Court for South Sudan (HCSS). There are also those facilitated by the ICC on the basis of the complementarity principle: the International Crimes Division (ICD) of Uganda's High Court and the Special Criminal Court for the Central African Republic. Each of these courts is a type of international criminal court with its own unique features and dynamism. The chapter notes that there is no one-size-fits-all juridical structure for the pursuit of international criminal justice in Africa. The choice and design of a juridical structure for international justice is dictated by the prevailing social, economic and political conditions at the time of the court's creation. Although the driving actors – the United Nations, the

AU, the ICC and civil society organisations – as well as the countries involved themselves have played a critical role in enforcing international criminal justice in Africa, the choice of juridical structure should also be informed by victims' engagement and the justice concerns of the state involved.

In 'The Extraordinary African Chambers in the Senegalese Courts and the Development of International Criminal Law in Africa', Juan Pablo Perez-Leon-Acevedo seeks to identify and examine the main characteristics, innovative features and/or contributions of the law and practice of the EAC in the Senegalese courts to international criminal law and international criminal justice, particularly in Africa. The EAC was established via an agreement between the AU and Senegal, and convicted former Chadian dictator Hissène Habré of international crimes. Despite its short existence and limitations, the specific features of the EAC are related to its (potential) contributions to the development of international criminal law in Africa and beyond in four areas. First, concerning institutional innovations, the EAC constitutes a *sui generis* option to design and establish criminal courts at the international level in Africa and elsewhere, namely a hybrid criminal court supported by a regional organisation. Second, in terms of ways to ensure accountability, the EAC (besides *mutatis mutandis* the ICC) is the first international criminal justice institution to exercise its jurisdiction based on universal jurisdiction grounds. In addition, the inadmissibility of immunities at the EAC is consistent with international standards. Third, in terms of substantive criminal law, the EAC's law and practice on legal elements of crimes against humanity, war crimes and torture have overall been consistent with international criminal justice standards, especially normative instruments and jurisprudence. Fourth, concerning international criminal procedure, the EAC's law and practice overall followed international standards on the rights of the accused to guarantee impartial, independent, effective and fair proceedings for the defendant Habré, despite some practical challenges. As for the victims' procedural role, the EAC's law and practice are consistent with international criminal justice trends of allowing victims to properly participate in the proceedings. Therefore, the law and practice of the EAC present important and innovative institutional, procedural and substantive features that arguably contribute to the development of international criminal law in Africa and beyond.

In 'The Use of International Criminal Law in African Countries', Ellah T.M. Siang'andu considers how international criminal law is used in African states, as well as the incorporation of the Rome Statute crimes into the domestic laws of African countries. It considers examples of instances where African states have applied international criminal law in the national courts before and after the adoption of the Rome Statute. Focusing on selected countries, the various approaches used in the implementation of the Rome Statute are considered. The chapter reveals that while African states have the relevant requisite laws that establish criminal liability for international crimes, states are still reluctant to effectively apply international criminal law by prosecuting persons suspected of committing international crimes. In order to enhance the combating of international crimes in Africa, more needs to be done in terms of inculcating the ideas of accountability in institutions of higher learning education. While most prosecution of international crimes on the continent have been hindered due to reasons such as a lack of political will to prosecute, incompetence and a lack of resources, there is need to go beyond the mere domestication of the Rome Statute in the national legal systems. Values relating to the importance of establishing individual responsibility for international crimes are instilled as part of the legal education for key players in the criminal justice system. The culture of impunity can be addressed by intensifying the dissemination of international criminal law as part of the standard education so that it is offered as part of the education and training for law students, political science students, magistrates, judges, the police, as well as all those in security and defence services. It is only by educating the masses on the importance of establishing accountability for international crimes that international criminal law will be better realised and enforced on the continent.

In 'The Nuremberg Principles in the Context of Africa: The Theory and Practice of Individual Criminal Responsibility', Evelyne Owiye Asaala argues that the Nuremberg Principles have played a foundational role in developing the principles of individual criminal liability and corporate criminal liability for international crimes. It traces the origins of these principles from the Charter of the International Military Tribunals and then analyses their manifestation in Africa. It is observed that within Africa, there are two levels at which these doctrines can be conceptualised: the traditional African conception and the AU conceptualisation. Traditional African approaches have played a key role in the fight against impunity in most post-conflict African societies. Despite their perceived flaws, traditional approaches to justice have been taken in seeking accountability for historic crimes in post-conflict African states. The chapter refers to the *gacaca* process in Rwanda and *mato oput* in Uganda. After a conceptual analysis of the doctrine of individual criminal liability within the AU and traditional African approaches, it then provides a general critique of African state practices on individual criminal responsibility for international crimes. Uganda, the Democratic Republic of the Congo and Senegal (via the EAC) are the only regional states with practices that demonstrate visible effort in enforcing individual criminal responsibility for international crimes and in a manner that resembles the Nuremberg practice and the practice of the ad hoc tribunals and the ICC. Finally, it analyses the doctrine of corporate criminal liability for international crimes, with a particular focus on the Malabo Protocol.

In 'The Application of Universal Jurisdiction in Africa', O'Brien Kaaba asks whether universal jurisdiction exists in international law and whether it is recognised in Africa, both at the regional and the national levels. The chapter notes that some scholars doubt the existence of the doctrine of universal jurisdiction and consider it as no more than a hollow doctrine lacking a basis in the practice of the community of states. According to this line of thinking, the idea of universal jurisdiction is a misconceived claim that arose in the post-Second World War era perpetuated by scholars, human rights activists and leaders of international non-governmental human rights organisations. The doctrine has been drawn into further controversy following the indictment of some sitting African heads of state and government, such as President Omar al-Bashir in Sudan and President Uhuru Kenyatta in Kenya, by the ICC, as well as by the assertion of universal jurisdiction by some European states over African leaders. This has invariably led to a strong reaction by African leaders, accusing the ICC and European countries that have asserted universal jurisdiction over crimes committed in Africa of unfairly targeting African leaders. This chapter demonstrates that universal jurisdiction is recognised in international law by both international and domestic courts, as well as by scholars, as arising from customary international law and that it is actually backed by state practice. In the African context, the doctrine has been given some authority by the regional integration mechanism under the AU, as it has drafted a Model Law on universal jurisdiction that member states should adopt and implement domestically. This is despite the fact that the Organisation of African Unity (OAU), the predecessor of the AU, adopted and practised the approach of non-interference in domestic matters of member states, a practice that has largely been abandoned by the AU, at least in principle. Although the chapter argues for the existence of universal jurisdiction and highlights its application in Africa, it also demonstrates the challenges that accompany its implementation, leading to its limited use judging from the paucity of cases applying the doctrine.

In 'African Victims of Mass Atrocities before Domestic Jurisdictions and the International Criminal Court: Bargaining for Justice', Felix Mukwiza Ndahinda seeks to comparatively examine the agency of African victims of mass atrocities within domestic and international transitional justice processes. It is a widely documented fact that several post-conflict societies in Africa and beyond carry a heavy burden in terms of addressing calls for justice and reparation from large numbers of victims of atrocities committed during the conflict. Socio-political contestations and competing reconstruction priorities in post-conflict landscapes often leave victims with unfulfilled promises of redress. The emergent international victims' rights movement is contributing to a rethinking of dominant state-centric justice processes that have long sidelined victims. The adoption and growing domestication of victims' rights are creating more space for victims to voice their suffering and formulate their demands. This analysis focuses on four African post-conflict societies – the Central African Republic, Côte d'Ivoire, the Democratic Republic of the Congo and Uganda – in an attempt to understand how victims navigate proceedings before domestic bodies and the ICC. The examination of victims' rights in domestic and international contexts, where dialogue (if any) between the two forums of justice is still limited, shows both the potential and the current limits of reparative justice for African victims of mass atrocities.

In 'The Role of the International Criminal Court in Africa: The Epic Fails?', Max du Plessis and Christopher Gevers examine the role of the ICC in Africa. The chapter notes that to date, the ICC has only prosecuted Africans. While in 2016 the Prosecutor took the momentous step of formally opening an *investigation* outside of Africa (in respect of crimes committed in Georgia), it is yet to bring any cases in relation to that situation. Thus, all the remaining 10 situations and all the pending cases concern Africa and Africans. While there is a debate on whether the Office of the Prosecutor (OTP) has 'targeted' Africans, there is growing concern that the OTP has failed to pursue merit-worthy cases outside of Africa and that the OTP has failed to adequately address the *perception* that it has targeted African states, compounding matters further. The authors argue that while threats of a mass withdrawal have simmered – in the end only Burundi followed through, while South Africa demurred – there seems to be little hope of a rapprochement between the Court and Africa. The authors note that the fractures within the relationship between member states and the Court have come about as the result of the actions and inactions of the ICC and its supporters. The authors consider the role that the ICC has played in Africa in the light of hopes and fears raised by African states at Rome regarding the impartiality of the Prosecutor, the influence of the 'Great Powers', the relationship between supranational and domestic prosecutions, and the Court's role in the pursuit of lasting peace and security. The authors contend that these general concerns that African states had in relation to the ICC were present in 1998 – and have come to be realised, for the worse, with each passing year.

In 'Is the African Court on Human and Peoples' Rights with Criminal Jurisdiction an African Solution to an African Problem?', Jeremy Sarkin seeks to understand the reasons for giving the African Court criminal jurisdiction and whether the creation of this Court will achieve the goals articulated and even unarticulated. The chapter first reviews the process the regional system has adopted with regards to creating courts. It briefly discusses the historical development of institutions such as the African Court of Justice and the African Court on Human and Peoples' Rights (ACHPR). The role of the African Court is examined, as well as why the Court is being reformed first to merge with the African Court of Justice and then to give it criminal jurisdiction. Thus, the process of adopting the Malabo Protocol is reviewed, as well as why the AU wishes the Court to have criminal jurisdiction. The content of the Malabo Protocol is then examined in order to determine what the issues are concerning the jurisdiction, structure and role of the Court when it has criminal jurisdiction, in addition to what its human rights and general international law jurisdiction will be.

The crimes over which the Court will have jurisdiction are reviewed to determine what role it may play in dealing with the massive problems that exist on the continent. The issue of who is given immunity from prosecution in the Malabo Protocol is discussed, not only because this will be one of the most controversial features of the Court's jurisdiction, but also because it undermines Africa's claim that the Court will play the role that has been envisaged for it. In this context, the chapter discusses whether the Court will play a positive role and whether issues such as resources and capacity will undermine the role it might play.

In 'Head of State Immunity in the African Context', Godfrey Mupanga analyses the immunity clause of the Malabo Protocol with a view to establishing whether it is consistent with customary international law on head of state immunity, the trajectory of the AU and the organising principles of the AU. Suggestions for amendments to the Protocol are given. Extracted almost word for word from one of the resolutions of the AU on its relationship with the ICC, Article 46A *bis* of the Malabo Protocol provides blanket immunity from prosecution to sitting heads of state or any individuals acting as such during their tenure. The author argues that, characterised by poor draftsmanship, the immunity clause of the Malabo Protocol betrays a lack of understanding of the application of immunity at two levels – that is, as between the head of state and the court, and immunity from arrest by a foreign state for them to be surrendered to the court. It is argued that by seeking to place incumbent state officials beyond the reach of the African Court of Justice and Human and Peoples' Rights, which is an international court, the immunity clause of the Malabo Protocol misses the point of state immunity and thereby contradicts the objects and purposes of customary international law on head of state immunity. Most African states have signed the Rome Statute, thereby assuming the obligation to refrain from acts that would defeat its objects. If these states ratify the Malabo Protocol, which contradicts the Rome Statute and customary international, they risk breaching Article 18 of the Vienna Convention on the Law of Treaties. By way of reform, it is recommended that an amendment of the immunity clause of the Malabo Protocol that separates immunity as a matter of substantive law, that is, from prosecution by the court, and immunity as a procedural matter, that protects a sitting head of state from arrest by any foreign state is required.

BIBLIOGRAPHY

Alemika, E.E.O. (2003) 'Police, Policing and Rule of Law in Transitional Countries' in L. Lindholt, et al. (eds), *Human Rights and the Police in Transitional Countries*. The Hague: Kluwer Law International, pp. 63–96.

Alemika, E.E.O. (2009) 'Criminal Justice Norms, Politics, Institutions, Processes and Constraints' in *The Theory and Practice of Criminal Justice in Africa*, Monograph 161. Pretoria: African Human Security Initiative, pp. 11–33.

Amnesty International Report 2014/2015: The State of the World's Human Rights (2015) *Amnesty International World Report 2014/15*, https://www.amnesty.org/en/documents/pol10/0001/2015/en/.
Amnesty International Report 2015/2016: The State of the World's Human Rights (2016) *Amnesty International World Report 2015/2016*, https://www.amnesty.org/download/Documents/POL1025522016ENGLISH.PDF.
Amnesty International Report 2016/2017: The State of the World's Human Rights (2017) *Amnesty International World Report 2016/17*, https://www.amnesty.org/download/Documents/POL1048002017ENGLISH.PDF.
Amnesty International Public Statement (2018) *Amnesty International Report 2017/18*, https://www.amnesty.org/en/countries/africa/report-africa.
Anya, J. (2009) *International Human Rights and Indigenous Peoples*. New York: Aspen Publishers.
Arnot, M., Casely-Hayford, L. and Yeboah, T. (2018) 'Post-colonial Dilemmas in the Construction of Ghanaian Citizenship Education: National Unity, Human Rights and Social Inequalities', *International Journal of Educational Development* 61: 117–126.
Baker, B. (2005) 'Multi-choice Policing in Uganda', *Policing and Society* 15(1): 19–41.
Bales, K. (2012) *Disposable People: New Slavery in the Global Economy*. Berkeley: University of California Press.
Bowd, R. (2009) 'The Theory and Practice of Criminal Justice in Africa', *Policy Brief Nr* 07. Pretoria: Institute for Security Studies, pp. 35–55.
Branch, A. (2004) 'Global Justice, Local Injustice', *Dissent* 51(3): 22–26.
Branch, A. (2007) 'Uganda's Civil War and the Politics of ICC Intervention', *Ethics and International Affairs* 21(2): 179–198.
Brinkerhoff, J.M. (2011) 'Diasporas and Conflict Societies: Conflict Entrepreneurs, Competing Interests or Contributors to Stability and Development?', *Conflict, Security and Development* 11(2): 115–143.
Carey, S.C. (2004) 'Domestic Threat and Repression: An Analysis of State Responses to Different Forms of Dissent' in S.C. Carey and S.C. Poe (eds), *Understanding Human Rights Violations: New Systematic Studies*. Aldershot: Ashgate, pp. 202–220.
Cassese, A. (2003) *International Criminal Law*. Oxford: Oxford University Press.
Cassese, A. et al. (2013) *Cassese's International Criminal Law*. 3rd ed. Oxford: Oxford University Press.
Coldman, S. (2000) 'Criminal Justice Policies in Commonwealth Africa: Trends and Prospects', *Journal of African Law* 44(2): 218–238.
Crush, J. (2001) 'The Dark Side of Democracy: Migration, Xenophobia and Human Rights in South Africa', *International Migration* 38(6): 103–133.
Cryer, R., Friman, H., Robinson, D. and Wilmshurst, E. (2007) *International Criminal Law and Procedure*. Cambridge: Cambridge University Press.
Deflem, M. (1994) 'Law Enforcement in British Colonial Africa', *Police Studies* 17(1): 45–64.
Du Plessis, M. (2008) 'The African Guide to International Criminal Justice: Purpose and Overview' in M. du Plessis (ed.), *African Guide to International Criminal Justice*. Pretoria: Institute for Security Studies, pp. 1–13.
Economist Intelligence Unit (2018) *Democracy Index 2017: Free Speech under Attack*, https://infographics.economist.com/2018/DemocracyIndex.

Englund, H. (2006) 'Rights as Freedoms: Translating Human Rights' in *Prisoners of Freedom: Human Rights and the African Poor*. Berkeley: University of California Press, pp. 202–220.

Epprecht, M. (1998) 'The "Unsaying" of Indigenous Homosexuality: Mapping a Blindspot in African Masculinity', *Journal of Southern African Studies* 28(4): 631–651.

Fombad, C.M. (2013) 'The Context of Justice in Africa: Emerging Trends and Prospects', in *The Role Of Law And Justice In Africa's Development*. Addis Ababa: UNDP, pp. 3–23.

Freedom House (2019) Annual Report on Political Rights and Civil Liberties. *Freedom in the World 2018*, https://freedomhouse.org/sites/default/files/2020-02/FH_FIW_Report_2018_Final.pdf.

Glueck, S. (1944) *War Criminals: Their Prosecutions and Punishment*. New York: A.A. Knopf.

Hills, A. (2000) *Policing Africa: Internal Security and the Limits of Liberalization*. Boulder, CO: Lynne Reiner.

Institute for Economics and Peace (2017a) *Global Peace Index 2017*, http://visionofhumanity.org/app/uploads/2017/06/GPI-2017-Report-1.pdf.

Institute for Economics and Peace (2017b) *Global Terrorism Index 2017: Measuring and understanding the impact of terrorism*, http://visionofhumanity.org/app/uploads/2017/11/Global-Terrorism-Index-2017.pdf.

Jalloh, C.C. and Bantekas, I. (eds) (2017) *The International Criminal Court and Africa*. Oxford: Oxford University Press.

Jallow, H. and Bensouda, F. (2008) 'International Criminal Law in an African Context' in M. du Plessis (ed.), *African Guide to International Criminal Justice*. Pretoria: Institute for Security Studies, pp. 15–53.

Joireman, S.F. (2001) 'Inherited Legal Systems and Effective Rule of Law: Africa and the Colonial Legacy', *Journal of Modern African Studies* 39(4): 571–596.

Kanogo, T. (2005) 'Becoming Kavirondo: Cliterodectomy, Ethnicity and Womanhood' in *African Womanhood in Colonial Kenya 1900–1950*. Oxford: James Currey, pp. 73–103.

Kebreab, I.W. (2017) 'The Development of Criminal Law and Criminal Justice in Africa from Pre-colonial Rule to the Present Day' in C.C. Jalloh and I. Bantekas (eds), *The International Criminal Court and Africa*. Oxford: Oxford University Press, pp. 247–271.

Kekic, L. and the Economist Intelligence Unit (2007) *The World in 2007: The Economist Intelligence Unit's Index of Democracy*, https://www.economist.com/media/pdf/DEMOCRACY_INDEX_2007_v3.pdf.

Kinnes, I. (2009) 'Criminal Justice in Africa: An Introduction to the Theory and Practice of Criminal Justice' in *The Theory and Practice of Criminal Justice in Africa*, Monograph 161. Pretoria: African Human Security Initiative, pp. 1–10.

Kirsch, P. (2007) 'The Role of the International Criminal Court in Enforcing International Criminal Law', *American University International Law Review* 22(4): 539–547.

Kurt, M. and Karp, D. (eds) (2015) *Human Rights Protection in Global Politics: Responsibilities of States and Non-state Actors*. Dordrecht: Springer.

Lyons, T. (2002) 'Guerrilla Girls and Women in the Zimbabwean National Liberation Struggle' in *Women in African Colonial Histories*. Bloomington: Indiana University Press, pp. 305–326.

Lyons, T. (2004) 'Women in the Second *Chimurenga*' in *Guns and Guerrilla Girls: Women in the Zimbabwean National Liberation Struggle*. Trenton: Africa World Press, pp. 301–324.

Mahmoud, M. (2016) 'Religious Extremism, Insurgent Violence and the Transformations of a New African Security Landscape' in P. Aall and C. Crocker (eds), *Minding the Gap: African Conflict Management in a Time of Change*. Montreal: McGill-Queen's University Press, pp. 79–90.

Mbazira, C. (2011) 'Prosecuting International Crimes Committed by the LRA in Uganda' in C. Murungu and J. Biegon (eds), *Prosecuting International Crimes in Africa*. Pretoria: Pretoria University Law Press, pp. 197–220.

McCormack, T.L.H. (2003) 'Their Atrocities and Our Misdemeanours the Reticence of States to Try Their "Own Nationals" for International Crimes' in M. Lattimer and P. Sands (eds), *Justice for Crimes against Humanity*. Oxford: Hart Publishing, pp. 107–142.

Ministry of Legal Affairs – Government of the Republic of Zambia (1995) 'The Public Order Act', http://www.parliament.gov.zm/sites/default/files/documents/acts/Public%20Order%20Act.pdf.

Mo Ibrahim Foundation (2016) *Ibrahim Index of African Governance Report*, https://mo.ibrahim.foundation/iiag.

Monageng, S.M. (2014) 'Africa and the International Criminal Court: Then and Now' in G. Werle et al. (eds), *African and the International Criminal Court*. The Hague: T.M.C. Asser Press, pp. 13–20.

Morreira, S. (2016) 'Introduction: The Rise of Rights Talk in Zimbabwe' in *Rights after Wrongs: Local Knowledge and Human Rights in Zimbabwe*. Stanford: Stanford University Press, pp. 1–24.

Msibi, T. (2009) 'The Lies We Have Been Told: On (Homo) Sexuality in Africa', *Africa Today* 58(1): 54–77.

Nasong'o, S.W. (2005) *Contending Political Paradigms in Africa: Rationality and the Politics of Democratization in Kenya and Zambia*. New York: Routledge.

Nkansah, L. (2014) 'International Criminal Court in the Trenches of Africa', *African Journal of International Criminal Justice* (1)1: 8–36.

Nsongurua, J. and Udombana, N.J. (2014) '"Can These Dry Bones Live?" In Search of a Lasting Therapy for AU and ICC Toxic Relationship', *African Journal of International Criminal Justice* 1(1): 57–76.

Roth, K. (2015) 'Why Rights aren't Wrong in Tough Times', in *World Report 2015: Events of 2014*, https://www.hrw.org/report/2015/01/29/world-report-2015/events-2014.

Roth K. (2018) 'The Pushback Against the Populist Challenge Human Rights Watch' in *World Report 2018: Events of 2017*, https://www.hrw.org/sites/default/files/world_report_download/201801world_report_web.pdf.

Salehyan, I. and Gleditsch K.A. (2006) 'Refugees and the Spread of Civil War', *International Organisation* 60(2): 335–366.

Sarkin, J. (2009a) 'The Origins of International Criminal Law: Its Connection to and Convergence with Other Branches of International Law', *Hague Justice Journal* 4(1): 5–41.

Sarkin, J. (2009b) 'Dealing with Africa's Human Rights Problems: The Role of the United Nations, the African Union and Africa's Sub-regional Organisations in Dealing with Africa's Human Rights Problems Connecting Humanitarian Intervention and the Responsibility to Protect', *Journal of African Law* 53(1): 1–33.

Sarkin, J. (2011) 'The African Commission on Human and Peoples' Rights and the Future African Court of Justice and Human Rights: Comparative Lessons from the European Court of Human Rights', *South African Journal of International Affairs* 18(3): 281–293.

Sarkin, J. (2016a) 'A Critique of the Decision of the African Commission on Human and Peoples' Rights Permitting the Demolition of the SADC Tribunal: Politics versus Economics and Human Rights', *African Journal of International and Comparative Law* 24(2): 215–241.

Sarkin, J. (2016b) 'Is the African Union's Position on Non-indifference Making a Difference? The Implementation of the Responsibility to Protect (R2P) in Africa in Theory and Practice', *Journal of African Union Studies* 5(1): 5–37.

Sarkin, J. (2017) 'Understanding the Changing Relationship of South Africa and the International Criminal Court: Towards a Culture of Greater Impunity in Africa?', *Revista Themis* XVIII (32): 7–33.

Sarkin, J. (2018) 'The Need to Reform the Political Role of the African Union (AU) in Promoting Democracy and Human Rights in Domestic States: Making States More Accountable and Less Able to Avoid Scrutiny at the United Nations and at the AU, Using Swaziland to Spotlight the Issues', *African Journal of International and Comparative Law* 26(1): 84–107.

Sarkin, J. (2019) 'Why the Role of the African Commission on Human and Peoples' Rights in Advancing Democratic Principles and Human Rights in African Countries Needs to Be Reformed: An Examination Using the Lens of Swaziland/eSwatini', *Southern African Public Law* 34(2): 1–56.

Schabas, W.A. (2004) 'Internationalized Courts and Their Relationship with Alternative Accountability Mechanisms: The Case of Sierra Leone' in C.P.R. Romano, A. Nollkaemper and J.K. Kleffner (eds), *Internationalized Criminal Courts: Sierra Leone, East Timor, Kosovo and Cambodia*. Oxford: Oxford University Press, pp. 157–180.

Sharp, J. (2008) '"Fortress SA": Xenophobic Violence in South Africa', *Anthropology Today* 24(4): 1–3.

Sichone, O. (2008) 'Xenophobia and Xenophilia in South Africa: African Migrants in Cape Town' in P. Werbner (ed.), *Anthropology and the New Cosmopolitanism: Rooted, Feminist and Vernacular Perspectives*. Oxford: Berg, pp. 309–324.

Ssebagga, R. (2011) 'Straight Talk on the Gay Question in Uganda', *Transition* 106: 150.

Stein, V.J. (2015) 'Making Promises, Keeping Promises: Democracy, Ratification and Compliance in International Human Rights Law', *British Journal of Political Science* 46: 655–679.

Sumner, C. (1979) *Reading Ideologies*. New York: Academic Press.

Sumner, C. (ed.) (1982) *Crime, Justice and Underdevelopment*. London: Heinemann.

Tandon, Y. (2000) 'Root Causes of Peacelessness and Approaches to Peace in Africa', *Peace & Change* 25(2): 166–187.

Tsing, A.L. (2005) *Friction: An Ethnography of Global Connection*. Princeton: Princeton University Press.

United Nations (1994) Security Council Resolution 955 of 8 November. UN Doc. S/RES/955.

United Nations (2000) Security Council Resolution 1315 of 14 August. UN Doc. S/RES/1315.

Van der Merwe, H.J. and Kemp, G. (eds) (2018) *International Criminal Justice in Africa 2017*. Nairobi: Strathmore University Press.

Vasquez, I. and Porcnik, T. (2017) *The Human Freedom Index 2017: A Global Measurement of Personal, Civil and Economic Freedom*, https://www.cato.org/human-freedom-index-new.

Von Hirsch, A. (1976) *Doing Justice: The Choice of Punishments*. New York: Hill & Wan.
Von Hirsch, A. (1993) *Censure and Sanctions*. Oxford: Oxford University Press.
Weldesellasie, K.I. (2017) 'The Development of Criminal Law and Criminal Justice in Africa from Pre-colonial Rule to the Present Day' in C.C. Jalloh and I. Bantekas (eds), *The International Criminal Court and Africa*. Oxford: Oxford University Press, pp. 247–271.
World Justice Project (2018) *Rule of Law Index 2017–18*, https://worldjusticeproject.org/news/2017-2018-wjp-rule-law-index-global-press-release.

CASE LAW

Ferdinand Nahimana, Jean-Bosco Barayagwiza, Hassan Ngeze v. The Prosecutor ICTR-99-52-A.
Prosecutor v. Jean-Paul Akayesu ICTR-96-4-T, Trial Chamber 1, 2 September 1998.
Prosecutor v. Thomas Lubanga Dyilo, case no. ICC-01/04-01/06, Decision on Sentence Pursuant to Article 76 of the Statute, 10 July 2012.
Special Court of Sierra Leone, Prosecutor v. Sam Hinga Norman, case no. SCSL-2004-14-AR72 (E), Decision on preliminary motion based on lack of jurisdiction (child recruitment), 31 May 2004.

TYPES OF INTERNATIONAL CRIMINAL COURTS IN AFRICA

Lydia A. NKANSAH*

* I wish to acknowledge the contribution of Jeremy Sarkin for giving generous time to review this chapter and providing very useful comments and feedback that helped to strengthen the chapter. I am also grateful to Westcott Wereko-Bobby for assisting in the research for the chapter.

1. INTRODUCTION

The establishment of the Nuremberg and the Tokyo tribunals in 1945 by the Allied Forces to prosecute German and Japanese war criminals for abuses carried out during the Second World War marked the beginning of formalised international criminal justice at the global level. Until then, breaches of international criminal law, whether treaty-based or custom-based, had been prosecuted by states through national courts to the extent that such breaches were incorporated into national laws (Damrosch et al. 2001). Subsequent efforts by the United Nations (UN) to establish an international criminal tribunal after Nuremberg and Tokyo to prosecute genocide and other war crimes proved futile due to the Cold War (Hobbs 2016: 500; Roht-Arriaza 1999: 477). Thus, after the Nuremberg and Tokyo tribunals, there were no such trials until 1992, when the UN Security Council established the International Criminal Tribunal for the former Yugoslavia (ICTY) in response to the genocide that took place in that country from the beginning of 1991. Shortly afterwards, a civil war broke out between the Hutus and the Tutsis of Rwanda, which led to the establishment of the International Criminal Tribunal for Rwanda (ICTR) by the Security Council in 1994. In the same year, 1994, the UN revived its earlier initiatives towards a permanent mechanism for the prosecution of war crimes, culminating in the establishment of the International Criminal Court (ICC) (Damrosch et al. 2001). Following the creation of the ICTY, the ICTR and the ICC, the international community sought to establish domesticated international courts – international criminal mechanisms with national components.[1]

Various forms of international criminal courts have been established in Africa since the 1990s to prosecute breaches of international humanitarian law and human rights in certain conflict situations. The international criminal courts in Africa can be grouped into three categories. The first is a purely international court established and administered as an organ of the UN, i.e. the ICTR.[2] The second category is an independent hybrid international court not anchored in the UN or the national judicial system, i.e. the Special Court for Sierra Leone (SCSL).[3] The third category consists of courts that are divisions of existing national judicial systems. These are further grouped into two sub-categories: those facilitated by the African Union (AU), namely the Extraordinary African

1 These include the Special Court for Sierra Leone (SCSL); the Special Tribunal for Cambodia (STC), instituted by virtue of an agreement between the UN and the government of Cambodia; the Serious Crimes Investigation Unit (SCIU) set up by the UN Transitional Administration in East Timor (UNTAET); and the Iraqi Special Tribunal established by the Coalition Provisional Authority.

2 Statute of the International Criminal Tribunal for Rwanda, 1994.

3 Statute of the Special Court for Sierra Leone, 2002.

Chambers (EAC) of Senegal and the Hybrid Court for South Sudan (HCSS);[4] and those facilitated by the ICC on the basis of complementarity, namely the International Crimes Division of Uganda's High Court (ICD) and the Special Criminal Court for the Central African Republic (SSC).[5] Each of these courts is a type of international criminal court with its own unique features and dynamism.

International criminal courts are thus booming in Africa. Studies have been conducted into some aspects of the courts in terms of the justification for them and how they resonated within the local settings of Africa, among other issues (Apori-Nkansah 2009; Dougherty 2004; Evenson 2004). However, there have been few or no in-depth studies into the juridical creation or design and constitution of the courts themselves and the underlying conditions that have led to a given juridical design. However, it is important to study the juridical constitution of the courts, since there are different types of such courts, each with its own unique form and features that to a large extent determine its operations and impact, and for that matter the unique texture of justice it offers, among other things. In addition, as part of their juridical nature, these courts share concurrent jurisdiction with national courts and/or the ICC, whether expressly or impliedly, which requires effective coordination so that the two (or three) levels are not pitted against each other as they carry out their plans. There are also the legal and political consequences of concurrent jurisdiction, since the same related war crimes tried in different legal systems could lead to different legal outcomes due to the uniqueness of the respective system. Therefore, understanding existing courts is necessary to inform choices about a given juridical structure going forward.

Against this background, this chapter examines the various types of international criminal courts in Africa in terms of the socio-political conditions that resulted in their creation, descriptive analyses of their juridical nature and constitution, as well as the benefits and challenges associated with each type of court (if any). The chapter maintains that the juridical nature of an international criminal court in Africa is largely influenced by the prevailing socio-economic and political conditions at the time of its creation and particularly the actors involved in its creation.

---

4 Statute of the Extraordinary African Chambers within the courts of Senegal created to prosecute international crimes committed in Chad between 7 June 1982 and 1 December 1990; Chapter V of the Agreement on the Resolution of the Conflict in the Republic of South Sudan (ARCSS) on 17 August 2015, which provides for the HCSS.

5 The International Criminal Court Act, 2010 (Act No. 11 of 2010); High Court (International Crimes Division) Practice Direction, 2011 (Legal Notice No. 10 of 2011); Statute of the Special Criminal Court for Central African Republic.

2. THE ICTR: AN ORGAN OF THE UN

2.1. BACKGROUND TO THE ESTABLISHMENT OF THE ICTR

The ICTR was an ad hoc international criminal court established by the UN to deal with atrocity crimes related to the conflict in Rwanda. A civil war broke out in Rwanda between the Hutus and the Tutsis in 1994. The conflict, which lasted from 7 April to 15 July, resulted in around 800,000–1,000,000 deaths. It is estimated that about 150,000–250,000 women were raped during that period.[6] In 1993, the total Rwandan refugee population displaced across Burundi, the Democratic Republic of the Congo, Uganda and Tanzania was 447,900, but this had increased[7] by 1994 to 2,254,100.[8] The government of Rwanda asked the UN to set up an international tribunal to prosecute the genocide and other abuses of international humanitarian law that had occurred during the conflict in Rwanda.[9] In 1994, the UN Security Council passed Resolution 955 in response to the carnage to establish the ICTR by virtue of the Chapter VII powers of the UN Charter. The Security Council unanimously voted for the ICTR, with the exception of Rwanda dissenting. The Security Council determined to end impunity in Rwanda through the prosecutorial platform of the ICTR. However, the view is strongly held that the UN responded to the genocide by establishing the ICTR because of its failure to act in a timely manner to in fact prevent the genocide, and hence felt obliged to act to deal with the situation, rather than in the pursuit of justice. In fact, Erik Mose, a former President of the ICTR, observes: 'There were strong incentives to act, and to do fast. It is regrettable that the United Nations and its Member States did not prevent the genocide. It has later been established that more should have been done. But a failure of the organization in 1994 cannot be held against the Tribunal' (Mose 2005: 940). Yet he maintains that as a result, the legitimacy of the ICTR may have or and has been questioned.

In any case, Rwanda voted against the establishment of the ICTR because it did not fit the idea of the court it had anticipated. For one thing, the government considered 'The composition and structure of the Tribunal inappropriate and ineffective' (Mose 2005: 939). Also, the temporal jurisdiction was fixed to the period between 1 January 1994 and 31 December 1994, as opposed to the

---

6 United Nations, 'Outreach Programme on the Rwanda Genocide and the United Nations', https://www.un.org/en/preventgenocide/rwanda/historical-background.shtml.

7 UNHCR, 'State of the World's Refugees 2000: Fifty Years of Humanitarian Action,' p. 250, https://www.unhcr.org/publications/sowr/4a4c754a9/state-worlds-refugees-2000-fifty-years-humanitarian-action.html.

8 Ibid.

9 S/1994/1115.

government's proposal of 1 October 1990 to 17 July 1994 in order to cover previous attacks. In addition, the tribunal's subject-matter jurisdiction included crimes that should or could be tried by the national courts. The government also wanted the seat of the tribunal to be in Kigali as opposed to being located outside the jurisdiction of Rwanda. In addition, it objected to the possible absence of capital punishment for convicts and the possibility of the convicts serving their sentences outside Rwanda.[10] The UN did not oblige the government of Rwanda in these requests and imposed its own juridical structure for the ICTR, which is discussed in the next section.

2.2. THE JURIDICAL NATURE OF THE ICTR

The ICTR was an ad hoc international court mandated to 'prosecute persons responsible for serious violations of international humanitarian law committed in the territory of Rwanda and Rwandan citizens responsible for such violations committed in the territory of neighbouring States between 1 January 1994 and 31 December 1994' (Article 1 of the ICTR Statute). The subject-matter jurisdiction only covered international crimes (Articles 2–4 of the ICTR Statute). The ICTR had concurrent jurisdiction with the national court, but had primacy over it (Article 8(1)); thus, it could request the national court to defer a case to its competency (Article 8(2)). A person prosecuted by the ICTR could not be tried again by a national court (Article 9(1)). However, the ICTR could try a case that had been tried by a national court where the crimes had been treated as ordinary crimes, where the trial was not independent or impartial, or the national court used the trial as a smokescreen to shield a perpetrator from 'international criminal responsibility', or where the case had not been prosecuted diligently (Article 9(2)).

Sentences handed down by the ICTR were to be served in Rwanda or in any state on a list drawn up by the Security Council that had expressed its readiness to allow convicted prisoners of the ICTR to serve prison sentence in their jurisdiction provided that the sentence would be served in accordance with the laws on imprisonment of the state concerned (Article 26 of the ICTR Statute). In a situation where the hosting state was required by its own law to grant the prisoner a pardon or commute his/her sentence, the state would have to do so with the approval of the President of the ICTR after the President had consulted with the judges and decided to do so in 'the interest of justice' and on the basis of 'general principles of law' (Article 27 of the ICTR Statute).

---

10 See the Statement to the Security Council by the Rwandan Representative of 8 November 1994.

In terms of structure, the ICTR was composed of three Trial Chambers and an Appeal Chamber, the Office of the Prosecutor and the Registry (Article 10 of the ICTR Statute). It was anchored in the UN administrative system, with international judges elected by the Security Council. The Registrar was appointed as an administrative officer of the UN. The UN funded the ICTR (Article 30 of the ICTR Statute). The Security Council accepted the UN Secretary-General's recommendation to locate the ICTR in a neutral geographical setting and settled on Arusha in Tanzania.[11] The ICTY Prosecutor was initially made the Prosecutor for the ICTR and he exercised the dual prosecutorial function from The Hague, the seat of the ICTY (Mose 2005: 922). Subsequent ICTY Prosecutors continued in the dual prosecutorial functions for the two Tribunals.[12] Later on, a separate prosecutor was appointed for the ICTR (Mose 2005). The President of the ICTR had to submit annual reports on the ICTR to the Security Council and the UN General Assembly (Article 32 of the ICTR Statute). The ICTR concluded its work on 31 December 2015, having indicted 93 people.[13] Of these, it prosecuted and convicted 62 people, with 14 acquittals. Ten people were referred to the national courts, three became fugitives, two died before judgment and two indictments were withdrawn before trials.

The UN established the juridical structure of the ICTR. This was done to keep the international model that it had designed and implemented with the ICTY. The ICTR was clearly mandated to administer criminal justice. In terms of the temporal jurisdiction of the ICTR, cost may have been a consideration in fixing the temporal jurisdiction of the ICTR for a limited period as opposed to the extended period requested by Rwanda. Undoubtedly, international crimes affect the international community and the entire human race, so to speak; it is therefore within the jurisdiction of the UN to take the lead in ensuring accountability for the carnage in Rwanda. However, it is the people of Rwanda who bore the brunt of the crimes and who will live with the effects of a justice intervention of whatever kind. Hence, they should have been taken seriously and their requests should have been considered. This is especially the case where their requests would not compromise the tenets of international justice. As already pointed out, Rwanda's request in this respect was not granted. Consequently, the ICTR was purely international, in terms of subject matter, selection of judges and so on, and Rwanda itself was merely an onlooker.

---

11 See Security Council Resolution 977, 22 February 1995; and Secretary General's Report of 13 February 1995 (S/1995/134).

12 Note that Richard J. Goldstone (South Africa) was appointed as Prosecutor of the ICTY by SC Res. 936 of 8 July 1994; Louise Arbour (Canada) was appointed as Prosecutor of the ICTY by SC Res. 1047 of 26 February 1996; Carla del Ponte (Switzerland) was appointed as Prosecutor for the ICTY and the ICTR by SC Res. 1259 of 11 August.

13 United Nations International Residual Mechanism for Criminal Tribunals, 'The ICTR in Brief', https://unictr.irmct.org/en/tribunal.

3. THE SCSL: INDEPENDENT HYBRID COURT

3.1. BACKGROUND TO THE ESTABLISHMENT OF THE SCSL

The SCSL was an ad hoc international criminal court. It was set up after a violent civil conflict between the government of Sierra Leone and the Revolutionary United Front (RUF). It is estimated that out of the country's population of 4.5 million, over 75,000 died (Smile, Gberieand and Hazelton 2001) and that the war left about '4,000 amputation survivors, 2,000,000 displaced internally, 500,000 refugees, and at least 5,000 children turned into brutal combatants' (Evenson 2003: 733). The war also claimed the lives of about 800 peacekeepers from the sub-region (Rashid 2000). Those who suffered the abuses were mostly civilians, and all sides to the conflict allegedly committed atrocities (Dougherty 2004).

When none of the warring factions could win the war, the parties agreed to a negotiated peaceful settlement of the war. The government agreed to a blanket amnesty and a truth and reconciliation commission to provide accountability for the war crimes in the Lomé Peace Agreement (Berewa 2001). However, hostilities broke out once more after the Lomé negotiations, with the government winning a decisive victory over the RUF for the first time. The government then denied the legality of the amnesty to the extent of its legality under international law, as provided for by the Lomé Agreement and requested assistance from the UN to establish a court to try members of the RUF. In the words of President Kabbah, the court should 'meet international standards for the trial of criminal cases, while at the same time, have a mandate to administer a blend of international and domestic Sierra Leonean Laws on Sierra Leonean soil' (Kabbah 2000).

Following the government's request for assistance, the UN as per Resolution 1315 of 2000 requested the Secretary-General to enter into negotiations with the government of Sierra Leone for the establishment of the Special Court. This resulted in an agreement between the UN and the government of Sierra Leone to establish the Special Court as an independent body outside the administrative systems of the UN and Sierra Leone (Agreement between the UN and the Government of Sierra Leone on the Establishment of the Special Court for Sierra Leone 2002). The US supported the establishment of the Special Court because it had adopted a policy against the establishment of the ICC and many observers thought that its support for the Special Court signified support for ad hoc international tribunals generally, as opposed to the ICC, a permanent international court. It has been noted that 'most support for the Court came from a small, bipartisan group of members of the US Congress, many of whom also support the ICC' (International Centre for Transitional Justice 2006: 12).

3.2. THE JURIDICAL NATURE OF THE SCSL

The Parliament of Sierra Leone anchored the agreement setting up the SCSL in the Sierra Leonean legal system by passing the Special Court Agreement (Ratification) Act 2002 (hereinafter the Special Court Act). The Special Court was composed of two Trial Chambers and one Appeals Chamber, the Office of the Prosecutor and the Registry (Article 11 of the SCSL Statute). Each Trial Chamber was composed of three judges, with one appointed by the government of Sierra Leone and two by the UN Secretary-General (Article 12(1)(a) of the SCSL Statute). The Appeal Chamber was composed of five judges, with two appointed by the government of Sierra Leone and three by the UN Secretary-General (Article 12(1)(b) of the SCSL Statute). The UN Secretary-General appointed the Prosecutor and the government of Sierra Leone appointed the Deputy Prosecutor, who had to be a Sierra Leonean (Article 15(4) of the SCSL Statute). The Registrar was appointed by the Secretary-General as a member of staff of the UN (Article 2 of the Agreement; Article 12 of the SCSL Statute). According to Article 1 of the SCSL Statute, the mandate of the Court was to:

> Prosecute persons who bear the greatest responsibility for serious violations of international humanitarian law and Sierra Leone law committed in the territory of Sierra Leone since 30 November 1996, including those leaders who, in committing such crimes, have threatened the establishment of and implementation of the peace process in Sierra Leone.

It should be noted that Article 1 states that the aim of the Court is to prosecute those bearing the greatest responsibility for the abuses that took place, as opposed to the government's request to prosecute only the RUF (Report of the Secretary-General on the establishment of a Special Court for Sierra Leone 2000). Generalising the mandate of the SCSL to cover all the warring factions gave credence to the independence, impartiality and neutrality of the SCSL, since all factions in the conflict allegedly committed breaches of international humanitarian law (Human Rights Watch 1998). Even then, there was a strong perception in Sierra Leone that the government requested the establishment of the Special Court in order to use it to get rid of its political opponents and for revenge against the RUF (Apori-Nkansah 2009). Subotic (2007) made similar findings as to how international models for conflict resolutions in the former Yugoslavia were used for other purposes. She reported that 'under specific domestic conditions, states use the very tools designed to resolve conflict for very different political purposes, including getting rid of domestic political opponents'. She further maintained that: 'When transitional justice becomes "hijacked" for local political strategies, it can foster domestic backlash, deepen political instability, and even create alternative narratives of the past that can lead to further conflicts in the future.'

With the permission of the Security Council, the Special Court could also prosecute peacekeepers and their personnel for any of the offences within its jurisdiction where the 'sending State is unwilling or unable genuinely to carry out an investigation or prosecution' (Article 1(2) and (3) of the SCSL Statute). The SCSL had no jurisdiction over persons younger than 15 at the time of commission of the crimes. It was enjoined to treat persons aged 15–18 with dignity and a sense of worth, with the overall objective of rehabilitating such persons (Article 7 of the SCSL Statute). Sierra Leone was the seat of the Special Court. Nevertheless, the UN and the government of Sierra Leone could enter into an agreement with the government of another state should it have become necessary for security reasons for the seat of the court to relocate (Article 10 of the Agreement). Prison sentences handed by the Special Court were to be served in Sierra Leone. According to Article 22, sentences could be served outside Sierra Leone in countries that had agreements with the ICTY and the ICTR on the enforcement of sentences, or any other nation the SCSL might enter into an agreement with to that effect.

The Special Court had concurrent jurisdiction with the national courts, but with primacy over them. Thus, it could request Sierra Leonean courts to defer to the Special Court at any stage in its proceedings with regard to matters within the Special Court's competency (Article 8 of the SCSL Statute). Where the Special Court had already prosecuted an offence, the national courts could not indict for the same offence. Where a matter had been tried by a national court, the Special Court could retry the same matter provided that the offence had been treated as 'an ordinary crime' or the proceedings at the national court 'were not impartial or independent, were designed to shield the accused from international criminal responsibility or the case was not diligently prosecuted' (Article 9 of the SCSL Statute).

The SCSL's model was a departure from that of the ICTY and the ICTR. This is because it was treaty-based, independent and not anchored in the administrative system of either the UN or Sierra Leone (Security Council Resolution 1315 of 2000) While the ICTY and the ICTR were established by UN Resolutions and were anchored in the UN administrative system, the SCSL was independent and the judges and the Prosecutor were enjoined not to take instructions from any outside source or government (Articles 13 and 15 of the SCSL Statute). The President of the SCSL submitted annual reports to the Secretary-General of the UN and the government of Sierra Leone (Article 25 of the SCSL Statute). The juridical structure of the SCSL appeared to make it a sovereign body that did not form part of the administrative system of any political organisation, as a mark of its independence. Anchoring the SCSL in an administrative system would not have necessarily taken away the independence of the judges of the Court. After all, courts are created as part of a state or as an organ of an organisation and are subject to the rules and administrative practices of a state or the organisation as the case may be. Nevertheless, this does not take away their independence.

Judges enjoy independence in relation to the exercise of their judicial duties as judges.

Even though the Special Court was established as an independent or sovereign entity, it was to be funded by the voluntary contributions of the UN member states and the international community. The government of Sierra Leone also had an obligation towards the Special Court to assist the Registry, the Office of the Prosecutor and the Chambers with: identifying and locating individuals; service of documents; arrest and detention; and transferring indictees to the Court (Article 17 of the Agreement). It also requires permission of the Security Council in order to prosecute peacekeepers (Article 1(2) and (3) of the SCSL Statute). The UN and the government of Sierra Leone could enter into an arrangement with States for an alternate seat for the Special Court for security reasons (Article 10 Agreement).

The Special Court was meant to be an alternative to the ICTY and the ICTR, which were situated outside the geographical jurisdictions of where the offences they were to prosecute took place (Mackay 2003; Schocken 2002). It also had jurisdiction over some crimes under Sierra Leonean law, as well as a mandate to try international offences. It was thus a hybridised domesticated international court situated in Sierra Leone. Its aim was to bring justice to Sierra Leoneans in a cost-effective way (Dougherty 2004; Knowles 2006; Stensrud 2009). The juridical structure took care of some of the concerns raised by the government of Rwanda about the ICTR, namely by locating the SCSL in Sierra Leone itself, although it invoked the alternative seat provision to relocate to The Hague for the trial of Charles Taylor.

4. INTERNATIONAL COURTS FACILITATED BY THE AU

4.1. THE EAC OF SENEGAL

4.1.1. Background to the Establishment of the EAC

The EAC was formed pursuant to an agreement between the AU and the Republic of Senegal.[14] It was inaugurated in February 2013 with the primary goal of trying Hissène Habré and his accomplices for crimes committed during his tenure as head of state of Chad from June 1982 to December 1990, when he was ousted from power.

---

14 Article 1(1) of the Agreement on the Establishment of the Extraordinary African Chambers within the Senegalese Judicial System between the Government of the Republic of Senegal and the African Union.

A Commission of Inquiry to look into the crimes committed by the Habré regime was established by Habré's successor.[15] The Commission issued a report in May 1992[16] that became the basis for the prosecution of Habré and his accomplices. The Commission found that the regime's ruthlessness and criminal acts resulted in the killing of over 40,000 people and the torture of over 200,000. The atrocities resulted in 'more than 80,000 orphans, more than 30,000 widows, [and] more than 200,000 people [were] left with no moral or material support'.[17]

In January 2000, Human Rights Watch, along with other civil society groups, filed an application before the Senegalese courts to prosecute Habré.[18] He was indicted, but the indictment was challenged on appeal for lack of jurisdiction. The appeal succeeded through the appellate courts of Senegal.[19] In April 2001, following the dismissal of the indictment, other civil society groups applied to the Committee against Torture (CAT) alleging that Habré and his regime violated the Convention against Torture and the CAT.[20]

In December 2001, some of the victims filed an application before the International Court of Justice in Belgium to extradite Habré under the Universal Jurisdiction Act.[21] Subsequently, Senegal referred the case to the AU in 2005 following international pressure. In January 2006, the Assembly of Heads of States of the AU set up an expert committee to advise on the Habré situation. On 17 May 2006, the CAT granted the application and recommended that Senegal take action against Habré by either prosecuting or extraditing him for violating the Convention.[22]

---

15 Report of the Commission of Inquiry into the Crimes and Misappropriations Committed by Ex-President Habré, His Accomplices and/or Accessories, reprinted in Neil J. Kritz (ed.), *Transitional Justice: How Emerging Democracies Reckon with Former Regimes*, pp. 51–79, available at: http://www.usip.org/sites/default/files/file/resources/collections/commissions/Chad-Report.pdf.

16 Ibid.

17 Ibid.

18 Human Rights Watch, 'Q&A: The Case of Hissène Habré before the Extraordinary African Chambers in Senegal', 26 September 2013, http://www.hrw.org/news/2012/09/11/qa-case-hiss-ne-habr-extraordinary-african-chambers-senegal.

19 *Souleymane Guengueng v. Hissène Habré*, Cour de Cassation (Cass.) (Supreme Court for Judicial Matters) crim., Arrêt No. 14 (20 March 2001) (Sen.).

20 Committee Against Torture, Decision Communication No. 181/2001, CAT/C/36/D/181/2001 19 May 2006.

21 Frédéric Foka Taffo, 'The Hissène Habré Case', 23 December 2015, available at: https://www.accord.org.za/conflict-trends/the-hissene-habre-case/. The Court ruled that, in compliance with its obligations under the Convention against Torture, Senegal must prosecute or extradite former Chadian President Habré (20 July 2012).

22 Committee against Torture, Decisions of the Committee Against Torture under Article 22 of the Convention against Torture and Other Cruel, Inhuman or Degrading Treatment or Punishment, paras. 9.6–9.12, UN Doc. CAT/C/36/D/181/2001, 19 May 2006, http://www.unhchr.ch/tbs/doc.nsf/0/aafdd8e81a424894c125718c004490f6?Opendocument.

Meanwhile, at the next sitting of the AU, the results of the AU expert report were discussed and this mandated Senegal to try the case on behalf of the continent. Senegal amended its domestic laws to this end, which led Habré to lodge a complaint before the Economic Community of West African States (ECOWAS) Court of Justice about the retroactive nature of the new Senegalese law. The Court found that there was an issue of retroactivity and held that the law violated Habré's rights.[23] The ECOWAS Court's judgment led the Senegalese government to discuss the matter involving Habré with the AU in order to reach a possible solution on how to bring Habré to accountability. In the meantime, Habré was tried in absentia in Chad and was sentenced to death in 2008 (Czajkowski 2008).

In further developments, a former minister filed an application before the African Human Rights Court against Senegal for abuse of Habré's rights, but the case was dismissed for lack of jurisdiction 'because Senegal had not made the declaration under Article 34(6) of the Protocol to the African Charter on Human and Peoples' Rights establishing the Court' (Adjovi 2013: 2). On 20 July 2012, the International Court of Justice gave a decision and advised that Senegal should prosecute Habré.[24]

Subsequently, in 2012, the AU and Senegal began negotiations for an alternate solution, which led to a signing of an agreement creating the EAC. The agreement provided for the establishment of the EAC with its operational statute in January 2012 'to implement the decision of the African Union concerning the Republic of Senegal's prosecution of international crimes committed in Chad between 7 June 1982 and 1 December 1990, in accordance with Senegal's international commitments'.[25] After lengthy deliberations, the EAC was inaugurated on 8 February 2013 and began its operations on the same date. On 2 July 2013, Habré was charged and placed in pre-trial detention. The quest to bring Habré to justice by national, regional and international actors took about three decades to create a platform to prosecute him (Adjovi 2013: 1020; Brody 2015; Cimiotta 2015: 180; Høgestøl 2016).

4.1.2. The Juridical Structure of the EAC

The EAC was created within the courts of Senegal and has an ad hoc juridical structure. It is mandated 'to prosecute and try the person or persons most responsible for crimes and serious violations of international law, customary

23 See ECOWAS Ruling, *Hissène Habré v. Republic of Senegal*, Republic of Senegal General Role No. Ecw/Ccj/App/07/08 Judgment No. ECW/CCJ/JUD/06/10, available at: http://jurisafrica.org/html/pdf_ecowa.pdf.

24 Questions relating to the Obligation to Prosecute or Extradite (*Belgium v. Senegal*), Judgment, ICJ Reports 2012, p. 422.

25 Article 1 of the Statute of the Extraordinary African Chambers.

international law and international conventions ratified by Chad, committed in the territory of Chad during the period from 7 June 1982 to 1 December 1990' (Article 1 of the EAC Statute). Primarily, the EAC was established to try Habré. Accomplices responsible for crimes under Habré's term in power could also be prosecuted (Soares 2015). The crimes that fall under the jurisdiction of the EAC are genocide, crimes against humanity, war crimes and torture (Articles 4–8 of the EAC Statute). In addition to its prosecutorial mandate, victims can appear as civil parties and claim reparation in accordance with the Statute of the EAC (Article 14).

The structure of the Court is set out in Article 2 of the Statute of the EAC, which stipulates four chambers for effectiveness and efficiency. These are: the Investigative Chamber within the Dakar Special Regional Court, which handles all pre-trial processes and procedures before the main trial; the Indictment Chamber at the Dakar Court of Appeals; the Trial Chamber at the Dakar Court of Appeals for the main trial; and the Appeals Chamber at the Dakar Court of Appeals in the event of any appeals (Article 11(1)–(5) of the EAC Statute). With the exception of the President of the Trial Chamber and the President of the Appeals Chamber, who must be non-Senegalese from another AU Member State, all the other judges are Senegalese nationals (Article 11(1)–(5) of the EAC Statute). All the judges are nominated by the Senegalese Minister of Justice and are appointed by the Chairperson of the AU Commission (Article 11(1)–(5) of the EAC Statute).

The Office of the Prosecutor comprises the Chief Prosecutor and three deputy prosecutors of Senegalese nationality nominated by the Minister of Justice and appointed by the Chairperson of the AU Commission (Article 12 of the EAC Statute). The Defence Counsel is not required to be a Senegalese national. The applicable law was set out in the EAC Statute. Where a gap existed in the Statute, Senegalese domestic laws could apply (Article 16 of the EAC Statute). The EAC Statute and in certain cases Senegalese criminal procedure governs the EAC's procedure (Article 16 and 17 of the EAC Statute). The crimes set out in the Statute cannot be subject to mediation (Article 17(2) of the EAC Statute). With regard to punishment,[26] the minimum sentence permitted under the Statute is 30 years and the maximum is life imprisonment; the death sentence was prohibited.

The EAC was the result of the efforts of many actors, including international, regional and national courts, non-governmental organisations (NGOs) and victims themselves to bring about justice. Its juridical structure was purely that of an international court of regional kind; that is, 'a kind of a new criminal tribunal, reflecting a process of regionalization of international criminal justice'

[26] See ibid, Article 24.

(Cimiotta 2015: 179). The EAC could be described as an international court with the AU as the mother and Senegal as surrogate mother carrying the EAC in the womb of the Senegalese judicial system, from which it drew its sustenance. Chad, where the offences took place, had no role to play at all to in the creation and implementation of the EAC. Was this because the government of Chad had perpetrated the abuses? The agreement to establish the EAC was between the AU and Senegal. The subject-matter jurisdiction covered international crimes, excluding crimes under the laws of Chad. The selection of judges was made by the AU and Senegal.

Habré was tried and found guilty of international crimes by the EAC (Høgestøl 2016). Earlier on, Chad had tried, convicted and sentenced Habré to death in absentia on its own for ordering the killing of 40,000 people and human rights abuses, including rape, sexual slavery and torture. Was there a need for another trial after Habré had been convicted and sentenced to death by his own country? Obviously he might have been tried for crimes under Chad's Criminal Code, which did not include international crimes or cover all the alleged international crimes perpetrated by him. In a consistent manner with the international community's prevailing standards on holding perpetrators accountable for international crimes, the EAC was clearly established to try Habré for the breaches of international law. But the question to ask is what was Chad's preference in terms of accountability and justice for the crimes committed by Habré's regime? Was it for international justice, which resulted in a life sentence for Habré? Or would Chad rather have supported having Habré extradited to face the death penalty in Chad?

4.2. THE HCSS

4.2.1. Background to the Establishment of the HCSS

In 2003, militias backed by the Sudanese government began a murderous campaign against the African tribes in the Darfur region, which left thousands of people dead and at least 1.5 million displaced from their homes. In the conflict in Darfur, it is estimated that at a certain given period during the conflict, 5,000 people died every month, 35,000 people died due to attacks and 300,000 of those who fled from the attacks died from starvation. In March 2005, the UN Security Council referred the case of Darfur to the ICC.[27] In April 2005, the UN submitted a list of 51 Sudanese suspects to the ICC, including President Omar al-Bashir. The ICC's investigations led to indictments of five persons

27 https://www.un.org/press/en/2005/sc8351.doc.htm.

all relating to abuses which have occurred in the conflict in Darfur.[28] One of the indictees was summoned before the ICC and he voluntarily appeared. The other four are still at large, but Omar al-Bashir, who is one of the indictees, has been toppled by the security forces and is currently facing trial in Sudan. The Sudanese government denies the accusations and has vowed never to surrender any citizens to The Hague. It questions the ICC's jurisdiction and has proceeded with local justice initiatives, which are widely perceived to be 'show trials' that do little to hold actual perpetrators accountable for the atrocities in Darfur. The ICC has also submitted confidential requests for summons to appear for three Darfur rebel commanders who are allegedly responsible for attacks on AU peacekeepers. In the course of the protracted conflict, South Sudan broke away from Sudan to form an independent state in 2011. Shortly after becoming independent, a civil war broke out between the government forces and a rebel group under the former vice president (Rolandsen et al. 2015).

The Intergovernmental Authority on Development (IGAD), together with the AU and the other relevant stakeholder produced the Agreement on the Resolution of the Conflict in the Republic of South Sudan (ARCSS) on 17 August 2015 (Owiso 2018). Chapter V of the ARCSS provided for the establishment of transitional justice mechanisms, among which is the HCSS. The other mechanisms are the Commission for Truth, Reconciliation and Healing (CTRH) and the Compensation and Reparation Authority (CRA). The HCSS is an independent hybrid court that does not form part of South Sudan's judicial system. The AU Commission was mandated to establish and to determine the HCSS's seat, enforcement mechanism and infrastructure, applicable jurisprudence and appointment of judges, amongst other things. In December 2017, the Council of Ministers approved the legal instrument for the establishment of the Court, including a draft statute and a draft memorandum of understanding between the AU and the South Sudan (Report of the Human Rights Council Commission on Human Rights in South Sudan 2018). The HCSS is yet to start its work, though there is international pressure on the AU to establish and operationalise it. It appears that the government of South Sudan is reluctant to push through with the HCSS agenda, so the pressure and demand for the HCSS keeps mounting.

It is curious that the warring factions agreed to prosecution as part of the transitional justice arrangements. This is a shift in position from what had happened in previous negotiated peaceful settlements of conflicts.

---

28 *The Prosecutor v. Ahmad Muhammad Harun ('Ahmad Harun') and Ali Muhammad Ali Abd-Al-Rahman ('Ali Kushayb')* ICC-02/05-01/07; *The Prosecutor v. Omar Hassan Ahmad Al Bashir* ICC-02/05-01/09; *The Prosecutor v. Bahar Idriss Abu Garda* ICC-02/05-02/09; *The Prosecutor v. Abdallah Banda Abakaer Nourain* ICC-02/05-03/09; and *The Prosecutor v. Abdel Raheem Muhammad Hussein* ICC-02/05-01/12.

Accountability by prosecution was possible when one party had been able to subdue the other and could then sit in judgment or call for judgment over the defeated party – victor's justice, as occurred at the Nuremberg and Tokyo trials after the Second World War. Usually the warring factions would insist on an amnesty, with a truth commission for restorative justice as a condition for laying down their arms, as occurred in earlier transitional justice deals in South Africa, Sierra Leone and elsewhere (van Zyl 1999). It seems that the persistent message and stance of the international community that perpetrators must be held accountable for international crimes is now clear to warring factions and warlords. War crimes tribunals in Africa suggest that it is not possible to escape accountability for certain crimes. It may also be the case that the ICC, with its universal jurisdiction over war crimes, sends a signal that no one can escape accountability for war crimes. These factors probably influenced the warring parties to settle for the HCSS.

4.2.2. The Juridical Structure of the HCSS

The HCSS has its basis in the negotiated peace agreement to end the conflict in South Sudan. The jurisdiction of the HCSS is 'to investigate and prosecute individuals bearing the responsibility for violations of international law and/or applicable South Sudanese law, committed from 15 December 2013 through [to] the end of the Transitional Period'.[29] Specifically, the HCSS is to try 'Genocide, Crimes Against Humanity, War Crimes [and] other serious crimes under international law and relevant laws of the Republic of South Sudan including gender based crimes and sexual violence'.[30] On personal jurisdiction, persons are to be held individually responsible for their alleged crimes and no person is to be excused on the basis of his/her official position.[31] The HCSS is independent of national courts and is to conduct its investigations separately. In the event of a conflict between the HCSS and the South Sudanese national courts, the former shall have primacy.[32] In terms of its structure, the HCSS is to be composed of a majority of judges from African countries other than South Sudan to form panels of the court; trial and appellate. The judges shall elect a president from among themselves.[33] Prosecutors and the defence counsel may be members of any African state except South Sudan. This is without prejudice to the right of

29 Chapter V, para. 3.1.1 of the ARCSS.
30 Ibid., Chapter V, para. 3.2.1.
31 Ibid., Chapter V, para. 3.5.5.
32 Ibid., Chapter V, para. 3.2.2.
33 Ibid., Chapter V, para. 3.3.2.

accused persons to select the defence counsel of their choice in addition to or in place of those of the HCSS.[34] The Registrar of the HCSS can be from any African state other than South Sudan.[35] Judges, prosecutors, the defence counsel and the Registrar of the HCSS shall be 'persons of high moral character, impartiality, integrity'. They should demonstrate 'expertise in criminal law and international law, including international humanitarian law and human rights law'.[36] The Chairperson of the AU Commission has the responsibility to select and appoint the judges, the prosecutors, the defence counsel and the registrar. The same selection procedure should apply to judges from other African states and those from South Sudan.[37] South Sudanese and African staff of other nationalities may be required to assist the prosecutors and the defence counsel to carry out their functions 'effectively and efficiently'.[38]

Thus, it can be observed that the HCSS is mixed as far as the composition of the judges is concerned, with a majority being from outside South Sudan. Moreover, the ARCSS strictly states that the prosecutors and defence counsels must be Africans from outside South Sudan. An accused person's right to select a defence counsel of his/her choice is limited to persons other than South Sudanese nationals.

It is important to note that, in addition to its power to hold persons individually liable for crimes, the HCSS has also been empowered to 'order the forfeiture of the property, proceeds and any assets acquired unlawfully or by criminal conduct, and their return to their rightful owner or to the state of South Sudan'.[39] 'The HCSS shall also award appropriate remedies to victims, including but not limited to reparations and compensation.'[40]

The agreement establishing the HCSS was made between the AU and South Sudan, unlike that for the EAC, which was between the AU and Senegal, leaving out Chad, the country in which the abuses occurred. The EAC was anchored in Senegal's judicial system, whereas the HCSS is supposed to be an entity in its own right. In a sense, the juridical structure of the EAC mimics that of the SCSL. Consequently, the HCSS will be able to try some offences under the laws of South Sudan, just like the SCSL could have tried specified crimes under the Sierra Leonean Criminal Code.

---

34 Ibid., Chapter V, para. 3.3.3.
35 Ibid., Chapter V, para, 3.3.4.
36 Ibid., Chapter V, para. 3.3.1.
37 Ibid., Chapter V, para. 3.3.5.
38 Ibid., Chapter V. para. 3.3.6.
39 Ibid., Chapter V, para. 3.5.2.
40 Ibid., Chapter V, para. 3.5.3.

5. INTERNATIONAL COURTS FACILITATED BY THE ICC ON A COMPLEMENTARITY BASIS

5.1. THE ICD OF UGANDA (PERMANENT STRUCTURE)

5.1.1. Background to the Establishment of the ICD

The International Crimes Division (ICD) of Uganda's High Court is a permanent court that forms part of the Ugandan judicial system. It was established in response to atrocity crimes that occurred when conflict broke out between the government of Uganda and the Lord's Resistance Army (LRA), a rebel insurgency group in Northern Uganda. For over 20 years, the Ugandan government could not quell the insurgency in which massive human rights abuses occurred, with untold suffering being inflicted upon the civilian population of Northern Uganda. In December 2003, whilst the conflict was ongoing, the Ugandan government invited the ICC to carry out an investigation and prosecute those responsible for the atrocities being committed. The ICC carried out the investigation, which resulted in the indictment of five LRA commanders/leaders in 2005. Uganda was the first country investigated by the ICC. The Ugandan government had an obligation to arrest the indictees and hand them over to the ICC. The indictees all remained at large for about 10 years until one of them, Dominic Ongwen, surrendered himself in January 2015.[41]

Meanwhile, the situation on the ground was aggravated because the LRA intensified its atrocities against defenceless civilians. Being unable to achieve its aims, the government blamed the ICC for its failure to capture the indictees and hence demanded that the ICC back away from Ugandan internal activities (Nkansah 2014). The government tried to get the ICC to withdraw the indictments as a condition for negotiation and a peaceful settlement of the conflict. The prosecutor maintained that his office would not drop the indictment. This series of events made the ICC and its affiliates furious. The government and its supporters, on the other hand, blamed the ICC for being an obstacle to the peace process and for the continuing bloodshed in Northern Uganda (Cobban 2006; Nkansah 2014).

Whilst the arrest warrants subsisted, the government entered into negotiations with the LRA in July 2006 to settle the conflict, which were known as the Juba Peace Talks. The peace negotiations culminated in the adoption of the Agreement on Accountability and Reconciliation (A&R) of June 2007, the Annexure to the A&R of February 2008 and the Final Peace Agreement (FPA), which was made up of all the negotiated agreements (although it was not

[41] See https://www.icc-cpi.int/uganda.

signed by the LRA). In these pacts, the government and the LRA agreed that accountability for the atrocities committed during the conflict should be through national mechanisms to provide justice, reconciliation, reparation and transitional justice (Clauses 2.1 and 6.1 A&R). Clause 6.1 A&R stated that: 'Formal courts provided for under the Constitution shall exercise jurisdiction over individuals who are alleged to bear particular responsibility for the most serious crimes, especially crimes amounting to international crimes, during the course of the conflict.' Clause 7 of an Annexure to the A&R signed on 29 June 2007 provided that: 'A special division of the High Court of Uganda shall be established to try individuals who are alleged to have committed serious crimes during the conflict.' This formed the basis for the establishment of the War Crimes Division (WCD) by the Ugandan Judiciary in 2008.[42] Clause 3 of the High Court (International Crimes Division) Practice Direction 2011 (Legal Notice No. 10 of 2011) subsequently renamed the WCD as the International Criminal Division (ICD).

Although Uganda asserted that the ICD was established in order to meet 'Uganda's obligation under the Rome Statute',[43] which Uganda had ratified in 2002, a strong view persists that the ICD was established in order to circumvent Uganda's obligations under the ICC. The ICC, for its part, invoked the complementarity principle under Article 17 of the Rome Statute to facilitate the establishment of the ICD in Uganda. As well as being the first case of ICC intervention, Uganda is also the first case where a specialised judicial mechanism was established to implement its obligations under the Rome Statute. In the context of the ICD, complementarity is now framed as a burden shared between Uganda and the ICC (de Vos 2016).

5.1.2. The Juridical Structure of the ICD

The ICD has jurisdiction to 'try any offence relating to genocide, crimes against humanity, war crimes, terrorism, human trafficking, piracy and any other international crime as may be provided for under the Penal Code Act, Cap 120, the Geneva Conventions Act, Cap 363, the International Criminal Court Act, No. II of 2010 or under any other penal enactment'[44] (para. 6(1) of Legal Notice No. 10 of 2011). In addition, judges of the ICD are to undertake any function required of high court or national judges under the International Criminal

---

42 See Article 133 of the Constitution on Uganda; High Court (War Crimes Division) Practice Direction of 2008.

43 See a keynote address by Hon. Justice Moses Mukiibi, Head of International Crimes Division of the High Court of Uganda at Parliamentary Conference to give effect to the Principle of Complementarity in Uganda and the Democratic Republic of the Congo held on Thursday, 17 July 2014 at Parliamentary Conference Hall.

44 Paragraph 6(1) of the High Court (International Crimes Division) Practice Direction 2011.

Court Act, No. 11 of 2010. The Act in question incorporates the ICC Statute into the Ugandan legal system.

Cases heard by the ICD are prosecuted under Article 120 of the Constitution of Uganda (para. 7 of Legal Notice No. 10 of 2011). The rules of procedure for trial and evidence are in accordance with those that pertain to trials in Uganda. The Division shall adopt a procedure in the absence of a written procedure on matters subject to section 141 of the Trial on Indictment Act, Cap 23 and section 39 of the Judicature Act, Cap 13 (para. 8 of Legal Notice No. 10 of 2011).

In terms of its structure, an ICD trial is to be composed of a minimum of three judges. An appeal is available to the Court of Appeal of Uganda and the Supreme Court as a High Court within the judicial system of Uganda. The Principal Judge, in consultation with the Chief Justice, designates the ICD's Head, Deputy Head, judges and Registrar (para. 5 of Legal Notice No. 10 of 2011). The ICD 'may sit as a panel of up to three judges as may be designated by the head of the division' (para. 4 of Legal Notice No. 10 of 2011). A seven-member Users Committee was established to serve as an advisory body to the ICD (para. 9 of Legal Notice No. 10 of 2011).

In terms of its juridical structure, the ICD forms an integral part of the Ugandan judicial system and therefore can be described as a national court with an international mandate. Uganda ratified the ICC Statute and incorporated it into its domestic legal system through an Act of Parliament. This is akin to the existing practice for the enforcement of international law generally before the upsurge of international criminal courts. It is no different from what occurs in countries that have ratified the Rome Statute, except that a special division was created for the prosecution of international crimes in Uganda, which other countries could emulate. The ICC was also directly involved and facilitated the establishment of the ICD. Uganda is thus exercising its primary responsibility under international law to prosecute international crimes by the ICD.

5.2. THE SCC

5.2.1. Background to the Development of the SCC

The Special Criminal Court (SCC) is an ad hoc international criminal court established in April 2015 within the judicial system of the Central African Republic. After becoming independent in 1960, the country suffered three decades of military dictatorship. In 1993, civilian rule was established with the UN-led democratic election of President Ange-Félix Patassé. In October 2002, former Army Chief of Staff François Bozizé launched a coup to overthrow Patassé. He succeeded in March 2003 and was elected President in 2005. During the five-month conflict, there were widespread human rights abuses, including summary executions, sexual violence, enforced disappearances and looting allegedly committed by the supporters of Patassé. In mid-2004, the judicial authorities of Central African Republic started criminal proceedings against Patassé and his military commanders for crimes committed against civilians. The highest court in the Central African Republic advised the government to refer the case to the ICC on the grounds that the national judicial system was unable to effectively investigate and prosecute crimes committed during the conflict; the government did so on 22 December. This was the first time the Prosecutor opened an investigation in which allegations of sexual crimes far outnumbered alleged killings.[45] The initial and subsequent investigations resulted in indictments.[46]

Subsequently, in 2012, violence erupted while the ICC's indictments for serious crimes were pending. The national courts lacked the capacity to prosecute the abuses. In view of the fact that the ICC would only prosecute a limited number of perpetrators, the SCC was set up by Organic Act No. 15-003 to investigate and prosecute serious human rights violations and violations of international humanitarian law committed in the Central African Republic since March 2003. This was to ensure greater accountability in view of the atrocities that had occurred in the country. Prior to this, a Special Investigation and Instruction Unit ('Cellule Spéciale d'Enquête et d'Instruction' – CSEI), tasked with investigating serious human rights violations and prosecuting the persons responsible for these crimes, had been created in April 2014. It should be noted that the UN played a key role in the establishment of the SCC. In August 2014, the UN signed a Memorandum of Understanding with the Central African Republic authorities on the SCC, which set out the composition and powers of the proposed court.

This marks the first time that a hybrid court has been established to work alongside the ICC. There are two major views on the SCC. The optimistic view is that it represents the idea that the international community should complement the efforts of national jurisdictions to fight against impunity. Hence, the SCC, a hybrid court with national and international elements, symbolises 'the promise of transnational cooperation and [may] be an integral component of an emerging global system of international justice'. The pessimistic view is that it may signify the failure of the ICC to bring about accountability in Central African Republic and prevent the persistent atrocities in the country during the period of the ICC's intervention there (Labuda 2017: 1).

---

45 http://www.globalpolicy.org/international-justice/the-international-criminal-court/icc-investigations/central-african-republic.html.

46 *The Prosecutor v. Jean-Pierre Bemba Gombo, Aimé Kilolo Musamba, Jean-Jacques Mangenda Kabongo, Fidèle Babala Wandu and Narcisse Arido* ICC-01/05-01/13. See also http://www.icc-cpi.int/en_menus/icc/situations%20and%20cases/Pages/situations%20and%20cases.aspx.

5.2.2. *The Juridical Structure of the SCC*

The SCC is established for a renewable term of five years. Its headquarters is located in Bangui in the Central African Republic, but it can be transferred to any other place within the country (Article 2 of the SCC Law).

The maximum sentence judges can hand down is restricted to life imprisonment. In terms of its structure, the SCC is made up of an Instruction Chamber, a Special Prosecution Chamber, a Trial Chamber, an Appeals Chamber, an Office of the Special Prosecutor and a Registry. The Court also has a Special Judicial Police Unit that aids in the investigation and establishment of evidence of infringements (Article 8 of the SCC Law). The SCC is presided over by a Central African magistrate. The Special Prosecutor is an international magistrate and the Deputy Special Prosecutor a national of the Central African Republic; they are supported by at least two substitutes (Article 18(1) of the SCC Law). The President of the Court is a national of the Central African Republic (Articles 11–14 of the SCC Law). The Court is composed of 25 judges, 13 of whom are Central African Republic nationals and 12 of whom are international persons. In order for a person to be eligible to be a national or international member of the SCC, he or she must have a good character, be impartial and be a person of integrity, among other qualities. It is also necessary for the person to have experience in criminal law and international law (Article 20 of the SCC Law). Tousssaint Muntazini Mukimapa was named as the Special Prosecutor in February 2017.

The subject-matter jurisdiction of the SCC touches on the competence to:

> investigate serious human rights violations and serious violations of international humanitarian law committed in the territory of the Central African Republic since 1 January 2003 as defined by the Penal Code of the Central African Republic and by virtue of the international obligations entered into by the Central African Republic in the field of international law, including the crime of genocide, crimes against humanity and war crimes, which are subjects of ongoing and future investigations (Article 3 of the SCC Law).

Where there is a jurisdictional conflict between the SCC and another national court, the former will have primacy in terms of investigating and judging crimes and related offences within the jurisdiction of the SCC (Article 3 of the SCC Law).

However, the SCC is complementary to the ICC. The ICC will focus on the prosecution of senior officials, while the SCC will investigate and prosecute other perpetrators of serious human rights violations committed since 2012. Article 37 of the SCC Law states that in the event of a jurisdictional conflict between the ICC and the SCC, the former shall have primacy.

6. TYING IT ALL TOGETHER AND CONCLUSION

As can be seen from the above discussion, the selected courts established against the backdrop of atrocity crimes that the actors – the UN, the AU, states, civil society organisations and victims – believed should be dealt with on the basis of international criminal justice. The international criminal justice platform is anchored mainly in universal norms that require certain crimes, wherever they occur, to be prosecuted and perpetrators to be punished when they are found guilty.[47] Generally the goals of international criminal justice in the context of conflict-related crimes are to: provide justice to victims and prevent vigilante justice; establish or re-establish the rule of law; deter future crimes by showing that those who have violated the law cannot do so with impunity; delegitimise those who committed crimes and diminish their potential to act as spoilers, 'incapacitating' them through trial and sentences; provide a bulwark against revisionism and the ensuing tension; avoid the demonisation of social groups and facilitate reconciliation by showing that individuals rather than entire groups bear criminal guilt; and provide a symbolic break with a violent past by exposing and condemning atrocities carried out in past eras (Nouwen 2013).

In pursuit of these goals, different international criminal courts have emerged in Africa. One type could be an organ of the UN. It could also be an independent court not forming part of the UN or the domestic criminal system, and/or it may be anchored as a division of national criminal justice systems. Other than this, there are other unique aspects of their juridical structure that characterise each type. The courts discussed in this chapter are mainly ad hoc, with only the ICD of Uganda being a permanent international criminal court. They may be located outside or within the geographical setting of where the offences within their jurisdiction took place. They may have subject-matter jurisdiction over only international crimes or both international and specified national crimes. They may be composed of only foreign judges and staff or mixed. There is therefore no one-size-fits-all juridical structure for international criminal justice in Africa. The creating actor usually informs the choice of juridical structure: the UN, the AU, the ICC and civil society organisations, as well as the countries involved themselves. Although these actors have played a critical role in

[47] See, for example, the Geneva Conventions of 1949 with their 1977 protocols; Articles 1 and 5 of the Convention on the Prevention and Punishment of the Crimes of Genocide, 1948; Article 4 of the Convention against Torture and Other Cruel, Inhuman or Degrading Treatment or Punishment, 1984; the International Convention on Civil and Political Rights, 1966; the crimes against humanity jurisprudence in Article 6(3) of the Nuremberg Charter, 1945; Article 4(h) of the Constitutive Act of the African Union; and the Ezulwini Consensus, 2005.

enforcing international criminal justice in Africa, the choice of a juridical structure should also be informed by engaging the victims.

It also emerged that these courts have concurrent jurisdiction with national criminal courts or 'in situations where states are unwilling or unable to prosecute such crimes', the ICC (Article 17 of the Rome Statute), whether expressly or impliedly, on the basis of complementarity. The exercise of concurrent jurisdiction creates dual or sometimes tripartite legal systems in respect of the same war-related offences in a given situation. Apart from the primacy mantra, there are no clear-cut criteria for determining who should be tried by the international criminal courts, the national courts or the ICC, or for that matter who should become national criminals or international criminals, and the justness of this process. There are also the legal and political consequences of concurrent jurisdiction, since the same related war crimes tried in different legal systems could lead to different legal outcomes due to the uniqueness of the respective system. For example, a national court may hand down a death penalty upon conviction, whereas international courts would not, even in relation to the same war-related offence(s). Further study is required to examine this problem.

In terms of impact, an empirical and in-depth study of the various types of courts in Africa would be required to ascertain the achievements of these courts. Nevertheless, it is possible to state what these courts represent in Africa jurisprudentially. The trials undertaken by the courts serve as a means of propagation and the building of a *mens rea* of international crimes within the consciousness of Africans, especially the political leaders. The application of international criminal law in Africa in its various forms represents a new era for the dispensation of justice, which previously did not exist or was not customary on the continent. The activities of the courts can be viewed in part as an effort to propagate the new system of justice in Africa. Propagation is a key element in any preventive strength that the court would have. African countries, through the various courts, are now integrating an awareness of international humanitarian law into their societies.

Before the existence of these courts, international humanitarian law and or international criminal justice had been more abstract than practical, especially with regard to intra-country conflicts. International humanitarian law has evolved against the backdrop of inter-state conflicts. Precedents and a practical body of knowledge with special regard to inter-country wars, like those that occurred in Rwanda, Sierra Leone, Chad, Uganda, the Central African Republic and South Sudan, are now emerging through the establishment and enforcement of these courts in Africa. In a sense, these courts are contributing to the building of jurisprudence with a unique form of justice based on African experiences with international principles.

Refining the jurisprudence of international criminal justice towards a localised sense of justice, tailor-made for unique situations, is resulting in emerging trends such as regionalisation. It has provoked the AU to take humanitarian law seriously and make it a priority, which was not the case previously. It is now trying to internalise these principles as part of its foundational duties and mandate. This represents a huge leap forward in international humanitarian law. Before these courts, the Organization of African Unity, and later the AU, had not made such an attempt to enshrine and embody these values in its core mandate. The African continent is now moving steadily towards the eradication of impunity amongst its member states, and the significance of this victory cannot be overstated. The AU is now moving forward to take personal responsibility for prosecuting these crimes. This would represent a fundamental shift in the continent's history towards a more humane appreciation of human life and freedom.

In conclusion, this chapter has provided descriptive accounts of different types of international criminal courts in Africa established against the backdrop of atrocity crimes. These courts were created out of the desire of the UN, the AU, states, civil society groups, victims and courts to ensure international justice. These courts have various juridical structures. It may be that other juridical structures may emerge in the future. However, there is the need for further research on the strengths of the types of international criminal court and the benefits for the countries involved beyond the jurisprudential gains of advancing international criminal justice.

BIBLIOGRAPHY

Adjovi, R. (2013) 'Introductory Note to the Agreement on the Establishment of the Extraordinary African Chambers within the Senegalese Judicial System between the Government of the Republic of Senegal and the African Union and the Statute of the Chambers', *International Legal Materials* 52(4): 1020–1036.

Agreement on the Resolution of the Conflict in the Republic of South Sudan, Addis Ababa, Ethiopia (17 August 2015).

Apori-Nkansah, L. (2008) 'Transitional Justice in Postconflict Contexts: The Case of Sierra Leone's Dual Accountability Mechanisms', doctoral dissertation, Walden University, Minnesota, UMI, AAT 3291475.

Apori-Nkansah, L. (2009) 'The Prosecution of War Criminals by the Special Court for Sierra Leone within the Arrangement of International Criminal Justice', *GIMPA Journal of Leadership, Management and Administration* 52(2): 22–53.

Berewa, S. (2001) 'Addressing Impunity Using Divergent Approaches: The Truth and Reconciliation Commission and the Special Court' in UNAMSIL (ed.), *Truth and Reconciliation in Sierra Leone: A Compilation of Articles on the Sierra Leone Truth and Reconciliation Commission*. Freetown: David Williams Associates, pp. 53–60.

Brody, R. (2015) 'Bringing a Dictator to Justice: The Case of Hissène Habré', *Journal of International Criminal Justice* 13(2): 209–217. https://doi.org/10.1093/jicj/mqv005.

Cimiotta, E. (2015) 'The First Steps of the Extraordinary African Chambers: A New Mixed Criminal Tribunal?', *Journal of International Criminal Justice* 13(1): 177–198.

Cobban, H. (2006) 'Think Again: International Courts', *Foreign Policy* 22–28.
Czajkowski, S. (2008) 'Chad Court Sentences Ex-dictator Habré to Death in Absentia', *Jurist*, 16 August, http://jurist.org/paperchase/2008/08/chad-court-sentences-ex-dictator-habre.php.
Damrosch, L.F., Henkin, L., Pugh, R.C., Schachter, O. and Smit, H. (2001) *International Law: Cases and Materials*, 4th edn., St Paul: West Group.
De Vos, C.M. (2016) 'A Catalyst for Justice? The International Criminal Court in Uganda, Kenya and the Democratic Republic of Congo', doctoral thesis, Leiden University.
Dougherty, B.K. (2004) 'Right-Sizing International Criminal Justice: The Hybrid Experiment at the Special Court for Sierra Leone', *International Affairs* 80(2): 311–328. doi:10.1111/j.1468-2346.2004.00385.x, http://dx.doi.org/10.1111/j.1468-2346.2004.00385.x.
Evenson, E.M. (2004) 'Truth and Justice in Sierra Leone: Coordination between Commission and Court', *Columbia Law Review* 104(3): 730–768. http://dx.doi.org/10.2307/4099329.
Hobbs, H. (2016) 'Hybrid Tribunals and Composition of the Courts: In Search of Sociological Legitimacy', *Chicago Journal of International Law* 16(2): 482–522.
Høgestøl, S.A.E. (2016) 'The Habré Judgement at the Extraordinary African Chambers: A Singular Victory in the Fight against Impunity', *Nordic Journal of Human Rights* 34(3): 147–156.
Human Rights Watch (1998) 'Sowing Terror: Atrocities against Civilians in Sierra Leone', 29 July, A103, https://www.refworld.org/docid/3ae6a84a6.html.
Knowles, P. (2006) 'The Power to Prosecute: the Special Court for Sierra Leone from a Defence Perspective', *International Criminal Law Review* 6: 387–417. http://dx.doi.org/10.1163/157181206778553860.
Labuda, P. I. (2017) 'The Special Court in the CAR: Failure or Vindication of Complementarity', *Journal of International Criminal Justice* 15(1): 175–206.
Letter from the Permanent Representative of Sierra Leone to the United Nations addressed to the President of the Security Council (Annexing Letter of President Tejan Kabbah addressed to the UN Secretary-General requesting for the assistance of the UN to prosecute the RUF, 12 June 2000), http://www.rscsl.org/Documents/Establishment/S-2000-786.pdf.
Mackay, B.M. (2003) 'A View from the Trenches: The Special Court for Sierra Leone – the First Year', *Case Western Reserve Journal of International Law* 35: 273–285.
Mose, E. (2005) 'Appraising the Role of the ICTR: Main Achievements', *Journal of International Criminal Justice* 3: 920–943.
Nkansah, L.A. (2014) 'International Criminal Court in the Trenches of Africa', *African Journal of International Criminal Justice* 1(1): 8–36.
Nouwen, S. (2013) 'The International Criminal Court: A Peacebuilder in Africa?' in D. Curtis and G.A. Dzinesa (eds), *Peacebuilding, Power, and Politics in Africa*. Johannesburg: Wits University Press.
Owiso, O. (2018) 'The Proposed Hybrid Court for South Sudan: Moving South Sudan and the African Union to Action against Impunity', *ACCORD* 18(2): 87–113.
Perriello, T. and Wierda, M. (2006), 'The Special Court for Sierra Leone under Scrutiny. Prosecutions Case Studies Series', International Centre for Transitional Justice, https://www.ictj.org/publication/special-court-sierra-leone-under-scrutiny.
Rashid, I. (2000) 'The Lome Peace negotiations. Paying the price: The Sierra Leone Peace Process', http://www.c-r.org/ourwork/accord/sierra-leone/lome-negotiations.php.

Remarks by Mr. Miguel de Serpa Soares, Under-Secretary-General for Legal Affairs and United Nations Legal Counsel United Nations Headquarters New York (2015), https://legal.un.org/ola/media/info_from_lc/mss/speeches/MSS_ABA_Day_speech-27-April-2015.pdf.

Report of the Human Rights Council Commission on Human Rights in South Sudan (2018), https://documents-dds-ny.un.org/doc/UNDOC/GEN/G19/065/05/PDF/G1906505.pdf?OpenElement.

Report of the Secretary-General on the establishment of a Special Court for Sierra Leone (2000), S/2000/9/15, https://www.refworld.org/docid/3ae6afb f4.html.

Rolandsen, O.H., Glomnes, H.M., Manoeli, S. and Nicolaisen, F. (2015) 'A Year of South Sudan's Third Civil War', *International Area Studies Review* 18(1): 87–104.

Roht-Arriaza, N. (1999) 'Institutions of International Justice', *Journal of International Affairs* 52(2): 473–491.

Schocken, C. (2002) 'The Special Court for Sierra Leone: Overview and Recommendations', *Berkeley Journal of International Law* 20(2): 436–461.

Subotic, J. (2007) 'Hijacked Justice: Domestic Use of International Norms', doctoral dissertation, University of Wisconsin.

Smile, I., Gberie, L. and Hazelton, R. (2001) *The Heart of the Matter: Sierra Leone, Diamonds and Human Security*. Ottawa: Partnership Africa Canada.

Stensrud, E.E. (2009) 'New Dilemmas in Transitional Justice: Lessons from the Mixed Courts in Sierra Leone and Cambodia', *Journal of Peace Research* 46(5): 5–15. http://dx.doi.org/10.1177/0022343308096152.

Van Zyl, P. (1999) 'Dilemmas of Transitional Justice: The Case of South Africa's Truth and Reconciliation Commission', *Journal of International Affairs* 52(2): 648–669.

CASE LAW

Hissène Habré v. Republic of Senegal, Republic of Senegal General Role No. Ecw/Ccj/App/07/08 Judgment No. ECW/CCJ/JUD/06/10.

Questions relating to the Obligation to Prosecute or Extradite *(Belgium v. Senegal)*, Judgment, ICJ Reports 2012.

Souleymane Guengueng v. Hissène Habré, Cour de Cassation (Cass.) (Supreme Court for Judicial Matters) crim., Arrêt No. 14 (20 March 2001) (Sen.).

The Prosecutor v. Abdallah Banda Abakaer Nourain ICC-02/05-03/09.

The Prosecutor v. Abdel Raheem Muhammad Hussein ICC-02/05-01/12.

The Prosecutor v. Ahmad Muhammad Harun ('Ahmad Harun') and Ali Muhammad Ali Abd-Al-Rahman ('Ali Kushayb') ICC-02/05-01/07.

The Prosecutor v. Bahar Idriss Abu Garda ICC-02/05-02/09.

The Prosecutor v. Jean-Pierre Bemba Gombo, Aimé Kilolo Musamba, Jean-Jacques Mangenda Kabongo, Fidèle Babala Wandu and Narcisse Arido ICC-01/05-01/13.

The Prosecutor v. Omar Hassan Ahmad Al Bashir ICC-02/05-01/09.

THE EXTRAORDINARY AFRICAN CHAMBERS IN THE SENEGALESE COURTS AND THE DEVELOPMENT OF INTERNATIONAL CRIMINAL LAW IN AFRICA

Juan Pablo Perez-Leon-Acevedo

1. INTRODUCTION

Between 7 June 1982 and 1 December 1990, Chad was ruled by the dictator Hissène Habré, who implemented one of the most repressive regimes in Africa in modern history. According to the findings of the Commission of Inquiry into

Crimes and Misappropriations Committed by former President Habré and his accomplices, during his tenure in power, there were around 40,000 victims of political assassinations and systematic torture.[1] Exiled to Senegal, Habré was not held accountable for his crimes for a number of years. However, the quest for justice pursued by victims and their lawyers in national and international fora, among other factors, made Senegal finally honour its international obligations to try those responsible for international crimes. This process involved both the Court of Justice of the Economic Community of West African States (hereinafter the ECOWAS Court of Justice), which found that Habré needed to be tried under 'a special ad-hoc procedure of an international character',[2] and the International Court of Justice (ICJ), which ordered Senegal to prosecute or extradite Habré without further delay.[3]

In successfully implementing and completing these judicial steps, the African Union (AU) played a pivotal role. The Extraordinary African Chambers in the Senegalese courts (EAC) were set up following an agreement between the AU and Senegal on 8 February 2013,[4] which contains the EAC Statute as an annex.[5] The EAC was given the mandate to prosecute those most responsible for international crimes, under customary international law and conventions ratified by Chad and Senegal, for crimes perpetrated in Chad from 7 June 1982 to 1 December 1990, namely during the years that Habré was in power in Chad.[6] On 30 May 2016, the EAC Trial Chamber convicted Habré of: (i) crimes against humanity, in particular rape, sexual slavery, murder, summary execution, enforced disappearance, torture and inhumane acts; (ii) torture as an autonomous crime; and (iii) war crimes, in particular murder, torture, cruel, inhumane treatment and unlawful confinement of prisoners of war.[7] This conviction was largely ratified by the EAC Appeals Chamber on 27 April 2017.[8] As confirmed on appeal, Habré's conviction marked the closure of the EAC,

1 Commission d'enquête nationale, Ministère Tchadien de la Justice, *Les crimes et détournements de l'ex-président Habré et de ses complices*, L'Harmattan, 1993.

2 Arrêt, *Hissène Habré c. Republique du Senegal*, No. ECW/CCJ/JUD/06/10, Court of Justice, ECOWAS, 18 November 2010, para. 61.

3 *Questions Relating to the Obligation to Prosecute or Extradite (Belgium v. Senegal)*, 20 July 2012, ICJ Reports (2013) 422, §122(6), paras. 119–121, 122(6).

4 Agreement between the Government of the Republic of Senegal and the African Union on the Establishment of Extraordinary African Chambers within the Senegalese Judicial System (adopted 22 August, entered into force 30 January 2013) (2013) 52 ILM 1024.

5 Statute of the Extraordinary African Chambers within the Senegalese judicial system for the prosecution of international crimes committed on the territory of the Republic of Chad during the period from 7 June 1982 to 1 December 1990.

6 EAC Agreement, art. 1.

7 Arrêt, *Le Procureur Général c. Habré*, T. Ch., EAC, 30 May 2016.

8 Arrêt, *Le Procureur Général c. Habré*, A. Ch., EAC, 27 April 2017.

except for the ongoing process of implementing the reparation award ordered by the EAC.

Against this background, this chapter seeks to identify and examine the main characteristics, innovative features and/or contributions of the law and practice of the EAC to international criminal law and international criminal justice, particularly in Africa. In order to address this research question, the present chapter has four sections.

Section 2 discusses the innovations in institutional areas introduced by the EAC. Attention is drawn to both the institutional nature of the EAC and how the EAC has pioneered the regionalisation of international criminal justice. Section 3 analyses some contributions of the EAC to substantive international criminal law, particularly the law of international crimes. Three sub-sections respectively examine crimes against humanity, war crimes and torture. Section 4 examines how the EAC can be considered an innovative institution in terms of ensuring accountability of those most responsible for mass atrocities. Attention is paid to the underlying concept of universal jurisdiction and inadmissibility of immunities at the EAC. Section 5 examines some contributions to and/or innovative features of international criminal procedure, and focuses on the accused's rights and the procedural role of victims at the EAC.

2. INNOVATIONS IN INSTITUTIONAL AREAS: THE REGIONALISATION OF INTERNATIONAL CRIMINAL JUSTICE

2.1. THE INSTITUTIONAL NATURE OF THE EAC

The legal literature has discussed the institutional nature of the EAC. Legal scholars have argued for different categorisations for the EAC, namely: the EAC as an international criminal tribunal (Schabas 2013); an internationalised, mixed or hybrid criminal tribunal (Williams 2013: 1144–1147; Carlson 2018: 355); or even a *sui generis* criminal tribunal (Cimiotta 2015: 178, 193–197). Taking into account these and other sources, it is considered here that the institutional nature of the EAC may be labelled as *sui generis* in a sense that combines two dimensions: internationalised and regional (African) aspects. Whereas this sub-section discusses the internationalised dimension of the EAC, the next sub-section examines the regional aspects.

It should be noted that both the law and practice of the EAC have labelled this institution 'international'. Thus, Article 1(4) of the EAC Agreement mentions that the EAC is '[e]ndowed with an international character'. By invoking *inter alia* the findings of the ECOWAS Court of Justice,[9] the EAC Appeals Chamber in *Habré* highlighted the international character of the EAC.[10] It considered that its international character reinforces its independence vis-à-vis both the Belgian examining magistrate who started the case against Habré and the related Belgian proceedings.[11]

Nevertheless, this characterisation of the EAC as an 'international' court is inaccurate and misplaced. As noted above, one of the main two institutional dimensions of the EAC corresponds to its character as an internationalised criminal court. Indeed, the Constitutional Council of Senegal, which was inaccurately invoked by the EAC Appeals Chamber in *Habré*, did characterise the EAC as a hybrid or internationalised criminal jurisdiction.[12] The EAC incorporates important defining elements of this kind of institution, as legal scholars have identified (Williams 2012, 249; Williams 2013: 1145–1146; Høgestøl 2016: 151–152; Cimiotta 2013: 178; Cryer et al. 2014: 181–202). First, the tribunal has to exercise a criminal judicial function (Williams 2013: 1145): pursuant to Article 1 of the EAC Statute, the EAC exercised jurisdiction over international crimes. Second, the tribunal must be temporary or transitional (ibid.: 1145): the appeals judgment and sentence in *Habré* rendered by the EAC marked the fulfilment of its mandate and its (virtual) closure. Third, the tribunal has to consist of both international and national judges (ibid.: 1145; Cimiotta 2013: 178; Høgestøl 2016: 152): the EAC combined international and national (Senegalese) judges, pursuant to Article 11 of the EAC Statute. Fourth, the EAC is (partially) financed via international financial assistance (Williams 2013: 1145; Cryer et al. 2014: 191). Article 4 of the EAC Agreement states that the mobilisation of funds has to be decided by the AU, Senegal and (international) donors. Indeed, the EAC was mainly financed by the AU, the European Union (EU) and Chad (Carlson 2018: 353). Fifth, the law applied by the EAC includes both international and domestic elements (Williams 2013: 1145; Høgestøl 2016: 152). Articles 3 and 4 of the EAC Statute granted the EAC jurisdiction over serious violations of international law, namely genocide, crimes against humanity, war crimes and torture. The EAC did not have jurisdiction over domestic crimes; however, Article 1(4) of the EAC Agreement refers to the Senegalese 'Penal Code, Senegalese Code of Criminal Procedure and other relevant laws of Senegal'. This illustrates the 'hybrid' dimension of the EAC. Sixth, a party other than the affected state, in particular the United Nations (UN) or a regional organisation, must be involved

---

9 Arrêt, *Hissène Habré c. Republique du Senegal*, No. ECW/CCJ/JUD/05/13, Court of Justice, ECOWAS, 5 November 2013, paras. 42, 47.

10 *Le Procureur Général c. Habré* (n 8), para. 367.

11 Ibid.

12 Décision, *Affaire No 1/C72015*, Conseil Constitutionnel du Sénégal, 2 March 2015, para. 24.

(Williams 2013: 1145; Cimiotta 2013: 178; Høgestøl 2016: 151; Cryer et al. 2014, 182–191): the EAC was established based on an agreement adopted by the AU and Senegal.

Therefore, the EAC is overall an internationalised criminal tribunal. However, unlike most other internationalised or hybrid criminal tribunals, the EAC has additional specific features. These are mainly: (i) the presence of less international features and instead a deference to the national level (Senegal), which seemingly places the EAC both at the limit of the group of internationalised criminal tribunals and closer to national institutions that are not hybrid criminal tribunals, but receive international assistance; and (ii) the institutional and geographical isolation of the EAC from the territorial state, namely Chad, which limited the wider transitional justice effects of the EAC in Chad and/or Senegal (Williams 2013: 1140, 1146–1147; Cimiotta 2013: 178–180; Carlson 2018: 354–358). Furthermore, the EAC has an important regional (African) dimension, which is discussed in detail in the next sub-section.

2.2. THE REGIONALISATION OF INTERNATIONAL CRIMINAL JUSTICE

Beyond international, internationalised and/or national elements, an institutional aspect of the EAC that is particularly innovative in international criminal justice is its regional dimension, namely its African dimension. Legal scholars have highlighted the potential contributions of the EAC to innovative mechanisms to implement international criminal justice in Africa and beyond. The African regional context in which the EAC was established and exercised its mandate has been identified as both a novelty in international criminal justice mechanisms and a clear example of the ongoing trends towards a gradual 'Africanisation' or 'regionalisation' of international criminal justice (Cimiotta 2015: 179, 187, 195–197; Williams 2013: 1148). Moreover, legal scholars have appropriately acknowledged that the sort of 'regional' criminal justice introduced by the establishment of the EAC may be considered to be a new alternative model for international criminal justice in Africa and elsewhere (Høgestøl 2016: 155; Cimiotta 2015: 178). In turn, the creation and overall success of the EAC could be regarded as an indicator of the AU's potential contributions and commitment to the development of international criminal justice in Africa (Williams 2013: 1148).

The regional elements of the EAC include *inter alia* the process of establishing the EAC, the law of the EAC and the practice of the EAC. Concerning the establishment of the EAC, a regional organisation, namely the AU rather than the UN, was involved in the adoption of the EAC constitutive instruments, namely the EAC Agreement and its annexed EAC Statute. This feature alone sets the EAC apart from other international and hybrid criminal courts, including those that have/had jurisdiction over atrocities committed in Africa. All the previous hybrid or internationalised criminal tribunals – such as the Special Court for Sierra Leone (SCSL), the Extraordinary Chambers in the Courts of Cambodia (ECCC) and the Special Tribunal for Lebanon – were established based on agreements adopted by the UN rather than regional organisations, together with the relevant country. In terms of international practice on ways to establish internationalised criminal tribunals, the regional participation of the AU rather than the UN in the creation of the EAC may have already given rise to trends towards the regionalisation of international criminal justice. Indeed, the most recent hybrid criminal tribunal, the Kosovo Specialist Chambers, was established in 2015 with the involvement of the EU rather than the UN.[13] Moreover, the very first regional criminal court *stricto sensu* may in fact come into existence in Africa: the Assembly of Heads of State and Government of the AU (the AU Assembly) adopted the so-called Malabo Protocol, which adds an International Criminal Law section to the prospective African Court of Justice and Human and Peoples' Rights (ACtJHPR).[14] Time will tell whether and when this regional instrument will enter into force.

The regional element is even present in the official denomination of the EAC: 'Extraordinary *African* Chambers' rather than 'Extraordinary Chadian Chambers' or 'Extraordinary Senegalese Chambers'. This was actually the first time that a regional organisation-backed agreement setting up an internationalised criminal court was signed by a state exercising universal jurisdiction (Senegal) rather than the territorial state (Chad). Aspects relating to universal jurisdiction are discussed later on.[15] What should be mentioned here is that these features suggest the intention of presenting the EAC as an institution closely linked to the AU rather than just to one African state. As early as July 2006, the AU Assembly indeed declared that it had competence over Habré and ordered Senegal to prosecute and try him on behalf of Africa.[16] The AU made this declaration despite the fact that at that time, it lacked a competent organ to exercise criminal jurisdiction over Habré. In 2009, the AU regional element underlying the EAC was also present in the case filed before the ACtJHPR by one of Habré's former ministers against Senegal, in which retroactive application of Senegalese laws to exclusively try Habré was alleged.[17] The (sub-)regional African level, namely

13 See https://www.scp-ks.org/en.

14 Protocol on Amendments to the Protocol on the Statute of the African Court of Justice and Human Rights, AU Assembly, AU doc. Assembly/AU/Dec.529(XXIII), 27 June 2014.

15 See section 3.1 below.

16 AU General Assembly, *Decision on the Hissène Habré Case and the African Union*, Assembly/AU/Dec.127 (VII), 2 July 2006, paras. 3–4.

17 Judgment, *Michelot Yogogombaye v. Republic of Senegal*, File No. 001/2008, ACtHPR, 15 December 2009.

ECOWAS, was also present when in 2010, the ECOWAS Court of Justice, in deciding on a complaint brought by Habré, found that he could not be judged by a Senegalese domestic court, but rather had to be tried by a court that was international in character.[18]

In providing a historical account of the creation of the EAC, the EAC Trial Chamber in *Habré* referred to the process of establishing the EAC, particularly the AU's intervention, including the modification of Senegalese legislation upon the request of the AU and the Committee against Torture.[19] The Trial Chamber was also mindful of: (i) the legal and political process in which the EAC and Senegal decided to create the EAC in the Senegalese courts and adopt a suitable institutional framework; and (ii) the fact that ECOWAS and the Senegalese courts, by emphasising provisions of the EAC Agreement on institutional matters, rejected motions against the creation of the EAC.[20] Indeed, in 2010, the ECOWAS Court of Justice had referred to the mandate granted by the AU to Senegal to prosecute and try Habré on behalf of Africa in a competent court with fair trial guarantees.[21]

With regard to the law of the EAC, the following norms clearly illustrate the African regional dimension/elements of the EAC. Under the EAC Agreement and the annexed EAC Statute, the purpose of the EAC Statute 'is to implement the decision of the African Union concerning the Republic of Senegal's prosecution of international crimes committed in Chad between 7 June 1982 and 1 December 1990, in accordance with Senegal's international commitments'.[22] In terms of the composition of the EAC, African regional elements are also quite clear. Article 11 of the EAC Statute provides that the judges in the EAC's Indictment, Trial and Appeals Chambers shall be nominated by the Senegalese Minister of Justice, but appointed by the Chairperson of the AU Commission. In addition, Article 11 establishes that the Presidents of each of these three Chambers shall be 'a non-Senegalese judge from another African Union Member State'. As for the Chief Prosecutor and his/her three Deputy Prosecutors, Article 12 states that they shall be nominated by the Senegalese Minister of Justice, but appointed by the Chairperson of the AU Commission. Article 15 of the EAC Statute lays down that the EAC Administrator may enter into agreements to inform the African and international public about the work of the EAC. Under Article 26 of the EAC Statute, a person who is convicted by the EAC may serve his/her prison sentence in one of the AU member states with which Senegal has signed an agreement on the enforcement of prison sentences. As for privileges and immunities of

---

18 *Hissène Habré c. Republique du Senegal* (n 2), para. 61.

19 *Le Procureur Général c. Habré* (n 7), paras. 13–14.

20 Ibid., paras. 13–30.

21 *Hissène Habré c. Republique du Senegal* (n 2), paras. 54, 58.

22 EAC Agreement, art. 1; EAC Statute, art. 1.

the EAC's Senegalese judges, prosecutors, registrars, administrator and other Senegalese personnel, the EAC Agreement and the EAC Statute establish that they shall enjoy certain privileges and immunities in accordance with the General Convention on the Privileges and Immunities of the Organisation of African Unity,[23] the predecessor of the AU.

In terms of the practice of the EAC, African regional elements were also present. For example, the EAC Trial Chamber in *Habré* highlighted the relationship between the AU legal basis underlying the EAC Agreement, the institutional framework and the competence of the EAC, and the principle of legality.[24] In turn, the EAC Appeals Chamber in the same case, invoking the findings of the Senegalese State Council, remarked that the Senegalese judges of the EAC do not pass justice on behalf of the Senegalese people, but rather do so within the framework of a hybrid or internationalised criminal tribunal whose source is the EAC Agreement adopted by the AU and Senegal, as also recalled by the ECOWAS Court of Justice.[25] When rejecting defence claims that an EAC judge had been invalidly appointed, the EAC Appeals Chamber acknowledged that the competent authority for these appointments is the AU Commission, in accordance with the EAC Agreement and the EAC Statute.[26] In turn, the establishment of the Trust Fund for Victims via Resolution of the African Union Assembly Dec. 605–620 (XXVII) in July 2016[27] also illustrates such regionalisation of justice. Despite rejecting the admissibility of an *amicus curiae* on reparations, which was filed by the NGO Redress after the deadline, the Appeals Chamber asked this NGO to submit this *amicus curiae* to the Trust Fund for Victims created by the AU.[28] The EAC Appeals Chamber in *Habré* urged the AU to proceed with a prompt and effective operationalisation of the Trust Fund for Victims.[29]

3. ENSURING ACCOUNTABILITY OF THOSE MOST RESPONSIBLE

3.1. UNIVERSAL JURISDICTION

To ensure that the most responsible individuals are held accountable, an important and innovative contribution of the EAC to the development of

---

23 EAC Agreement, art. 6(2); EAC Statute, art. 29(2).
24 *Le Procureur Général c. Habré* (n 7), paras. 31–49.
25 *Le Procureur Général c. Habré* (n 8), para. 107.
26 Ibid., paras. 124, 133 and 136.
27 Ibid., para. 892.
28 Ibid., para. 602.
29 Ibid., para. 611.

international criminal law in Africa and beyond is the exercise of universal jurisdiction for the first time among international and hybrid criminal courts. Universal jurisdiction is basically the exercise of criminal jurisdiction regardless of where the crimes were committed (territorial jurisdiction), who committed those crimes (active nationality jurisdiction) and against whom they were committed (passive nationality jurisdiction) (Cassesse 2013: 274–281). National criminal courts exercise universal jurisdiction. Western states have exercised universal jurisdiction against African citizens who were suspected of being perpetrators of international crimes (Sriram 2003: 343–347, 351–355). However, the AU has considered that such practices have abused the principle of universal jurisdiction.[30] As identified in the relevant legal literature, both this exercise of universal jurisdiction by Western countries over African nationals and the International Criminal Court's (ICC) focus on Africa have been characterised by certain African actors as alleged manifestations of neocolonialism (Sirleaf 2016: 766–768; Ssenyonjo and Nakitto 2016: 83; Jalloh and Bantekas 2017: 371; Mennecke 2017: 10). However, since the EAC is an AU-backed institution based in Africa, these claims cannot be raised in relation to its exercise of universal criminal jurisdiction over Habré.

Unlike the EAC, all the other internationalised or hybrid criminal tribunals have exercised their jurisdiction based upon traditional and more limited jurisdictional grounds. These are: (i) territorial jurisdiction, namely jurisdiction over crimes committed in the territory of the state that adopted the constitutive instrument of the respective tribunal; and to an important extent (ii) active nationality jurisdiction, namely jurisdiction over nationals of the state that adopted the constitutive instrument of the respective tribunal. There is also the factual coincidence that the overwhelming majority of victims were nationals of the state that adopted the constitutive instrument of the respective tribunal. These traditional grounds for exercising jurisdiction were also used by the International Criminal Tribunal for the former Yugoslavia (ICTY) and the International Criminal Tribunal for Rwanda (ICTR). Even the jurisdiction of the ICC is in principle subject to traditional jurisdictional links: territorial jurisdiction and active national jurisdiction.[31] However, should the UN Security Council refer a situation to the ICC, the exercise of the ICC's jurisdiction is not limited to territories or nationals of states parties to the ICC Statute. Like the EAC, the ICC may thus exercise a sort of 'universal jurisdiction' concerning cases that stem from UN Security Council referrals to the ICC (Fletcher and Ohlin 2006: 428–433). However, as legal scholars have mentioned, certain African actors and leaders have criticised *inter alia* these UN Security Council referrals,

---

[30] AU General Assembly, *Decision on the Abuse of the Principle of Universal Jurisdiction*, Assembly/AU/Dec.243(XIII)Rev.1, Doc.Assembly/AU/11(XIII), 3 July 2009.

[31] ICC Statute, art. 12(2).

i.e. referrals characterised as manifestations of neocolonialism exercised by Western powers against Africa, especially in relation to cases against senior African state leaders such as Omar al-Bashir, Muammar Gaddafi and Uhuru Kenyatta (Sirleaf 2016: 766–768; Ssenyonjo and Nakitto 2016: 83). Yet the EAC again presents the comparative advantage of not being subject to this kind of criticism or de-legitimisation attempts due to its nature as an African institution.

The need to endow the EAC with the power to exercise universal jurisdiction in Africa can be traced back to certain findings of international bodies that led to the creation of the EAC. In 2006, the Committee against Torture found that Senegal was obligated, under Articles 5(2) and 7 of the Convention against Torture, to establish universal jurisdiction over Habré, who was in Senegalese territory, or alternatively extradite him to Belgium, which had issued an extradition request.[32] As the Committee against Torture acknowledged, the purpose of Articles 5(2) and 7 is to prevent those suspected of torture from benefiting from impunity.[33] Litigation at the national level also took place. In 2005, following complaints filed by Belgians of Chadian origin and Chadians, a Belgian investigating judge had requested Senegal to extradite Habré to Belgium based on universal jurisdiction grounds, which a Senegalese court rejected (Brody 2015: 211).

By invoking the Convention against Torture and general international law on state responsibility for internationally wrongful acts, the ICJ also required Senegal to either institute national criminal proceedings against Habré on universal jurisdiction grounds or extradite him.[34] The findings of both the Committee against Torture and the ICJ used the principle of *aut dedere aut judicare*, namely the state's obligation to extradite or prosecute based *inter alia* on universal jurisdiction, laid down in the Convention against Torture and well recognised in international (criminal) law (Nowak and McArthur 2008: 313–321, 344–367). The EAC Trial Chamber in *Habré* recognised the above-mentioned failed Belgian attempt to exercise universal jurisdiction, as well as the universal jurisdiction-related findings of both the Committee against Torture and the ICJ.[35]

Overall, the EAC shows that not only national criminal courts but also internationalised criminal courts can exercise their mandate on universal jurisdiction grounds (Williams 2013: 1151). It has been suggested that international-level institutions may exercise universal jurisdiction delegated by a collective of states (e.g. the AU), at least when the territorial state (e.g. Chad) has

---

32 Decision, *Guengueng et al. v. Senegal*, Communication No. 181/2001, CAT/C/36/D/181/2001, 19 May 2006, paras. 6.3 and 10.

33 Ibid., para. 7.16.

34 *Belgium v. Senegal* (n 3), paras. 119–121 and 122(6).

35 *Le Procureur Général c. Habré* (n 7), paras. 5–12 and 21–22.

given its consent (Scharf 2001: 76; Akande 2003: 626; Williams 2013: 1152). As a mechanism to fight against impunity in Africa, the EAC can also be understood as a means to provide assistance to a state (Senegal) that is acting on the basis of universal jurisdiction (Cimiotta 2015: 191–193). The direct and active involvement of the AU in the creation and work of the EAC may indicate that the AU and African states are not (necessarily) opposed to universal jurisdiction per se, but primarily to its exercise by European or Western powers over African nationals (Williams 2013: 1153–1154; Mennecke 2017: 10–36). Although the practice of the AU (decisions and resolutions) expresses its concerns about and its opposition to the manners in which European states have exercised universal jurisdiction over African nationals, this practice of the AU seemingly evidences its overall acceptance of the applicability of the principle of universal jurisdiction in cases of international crimes.[36] In any event, whether universal jurisdiction as exercised by the EAC sets a strong precedent for future internationalised institutions in Africa and beyond is not completely clear, due to the *sui generis* nature of the EAC (Williams 2013: 1152–1153).

As highlighted by diverse actors and scholars, the importance of the trial and conviction of Habré also consists in the fact that this case constituted the first example of the exercise of universal jurisdiction in Africa and is an encouraging sign of the growing importance of universal jurisdiction in Africa and beyond (Mennecke 2017: 10, 36; Perez-Leon-Acevedo 2016). Some former heads of state have been tried and found guilty of acts that constituted serious international crimes at the domestic level in Africa and elsewhere. For example, the Ethiopian Supreme Court in 2008 sentenced former Ethiopian dictator Mengistu Haile Mariam *in absentia* to death on charges of genocide, homicide, illegal imprisonment and illegal property seizure.[37] The trial was conducted *in absentia* because Zimbabwe refused to extradite Mengistu Haile Mariam, who was in exile in Zimbabwe (Tiba 2007: 513, 517, 526). Outside Africa, the Peruvian Supreme Court in 2009 found the former Peruvian President Alberto Fujimori guilty of serious domestic offences characterised as crimes against humanity perpetrated against civilians who were allegedly members of terrorist groups.[38] Nevertheless, the trial and conviction of Habré at the EAC differs from

---

36 See Observations submitted by the African Union to the Secretary-General, *The Scope and Application of the Principle of Universal Jurisdiction*, Report of the Secretary-General, UN Doc. A/66/93, 20 June 2011; AU General Assembly, *Decision on the Abuse of the Principle of Universal Jurisdiction* (n 30); Council of the European Union, *AU-EU Expert Report on the Principle of Universal Jurisdiction*, 8672/1/09 REV 1, 16 April 2009; AU Executive Council, *Decision on the African Union Model National Law on Universal Jurisdiction over International Crimes*, Doc. EX.CL/731 (XXI)c, EX.CL/Dec.708(XXI), 9–13 July 2012.

37 Judgment, *Special Prosecutor v. Col. Mengistu Hailamariam et al.*, File No. 1/87, Ethiopian Federal High Court, 12 December 2006.

38 Judgment, *Barrios Altos, La Cantuta and Sótanos del SIN*, Transitory Criminal Chamber, Supreme Court of Peru, 7 April 2009.

the cases of Mengistu Haile Mariam and Fujimori. Whereas these earlier cases consisted in the exercise of national criminal jurisdiction based on traditional jurisdictional links, such as territorial and active nationality grounds, the exercise of universal jurisdiction was a distinctive feature of the prosecution, trial and conviction of Habré at the EAC.

3.2. INADMISSIBILITY OF IMMUNITIES

In general, there are two main categories of immunities in international law. Functional immunities concern the conduct of state agents acting in their official capacity, protect the public nature of the act of the state agent in his/her official capacity, and continue after the termination of the functions of the state agent (Cassese 2013: 318–319). In turn, personal immunities protect an individual who exercises a specific function abroad and covers both official and private acts, but only lasts while he/she holds the relevant position (Cassese 2013: 318–319).

The fact that the crimes under the jurisdiction of the EAC were committed by Habré during his time as the head of state of Chad did not preclude the exercise of jurisdiction by the EAC. The irrelevance of official capacity is explicitly set out in Article 3 of the EAC Statute, which establishes that: 'The official position of an accused, whether as Head of State or Government, or as a high-ranking government official, shall not relieve him or her of criminal responsibility under this Statute, nor shall it, in and of itself, constitute a ground for reduction of sentence.' This provision reflects norms found in the instruments of previous international and hybrid criminal tribunals, particularly the Statutes of the ICTY,[39] the ICTR,[40] the ICC[41] and the SCSL.[42] Hence, Article 3 of the EAC Statute is consistent with international criminal justice standards. It indeed reaffirms the inadmissibility of immunities at international and hybrid criminal courts established in Africa and/or with jurisdiction over mass atrocities perpetrated in Africa.

However, Article 3 paradoxically stands in sharp contrast to another criminal justice initiative of the AU, namely the Malabo Protocol, which introduces the International Criminal Law section of the prospective ACtJHPR. Article 46A *bis* of this instrument reads as follows: 'No charges shall be commenced or continued before the Court against any serving AU Head of State or Government, or anybody acting or entitled to act in such capacity, or other senior state officials based on their functions, during their tenure of office.' As determined by legal scholars, under international law, this

39 ICTY Statute, art. 7(2).
40 ICTR Statute, art. 6(2).
41 ICC Statute, art. 27.
42 SCSL Statute, art. 6(4).

provision is inconsistent with the general inapplicability of these immunities at international courts and thus makes this project of African regional criminal justice controversial (du Plessis 2014; Tladi 2015: 3–17; Ssenyonjo and Nakitto 2016: 100).

With regard to the specific matter of inadmissible immunities under analysis, the contribution of the EAC to the development of international criminal law in Africa not only concerns the consistency of Article 3 of the EAC with the well-established international principle of the irrelevance of official capacity, but also corresponds to the *sui generis* circumstances and context in which the trial and conviction of Habré took place, particularly in a comparative perspective.

Habré marked the first trial both conducted by national courts and with the presence of regional elements in which the accused and later convicted person was a former head of state of another country. There had certainly been other cases involving former or even sitting heads of states before international and hybrid criminal courts (Perez-Leon-Acevedo 2016). For example, for atrocities committed in Africa, the ICTR found former Rwandan Prime Minister Jean Kambanda guilty of genocide, conspiracy to commit genocide, direct and public incitement to commit genocide, complicity in genocide, and crimes against humanity (murder and extermination), to which he had pleaded guilty.[43] The SCSL convicted former Liberian President Charles Taylor of international crimes committed in the Sierra Leonean armed conflict. Taylor was still the President of Liberia at the time of the criminal proceedings, but the SCSL rejected any kind of immunity.[44] In 2006, Taylor was surrendered to the SCSL by Nigeria, where he was in exile, upon the request of Ellen Johnson Sirleaf, who was then the newly elected President of Liberia. Taylor was found guilty of the war crimes of acts of terrorism and violence to life, health and physical or mental well-being of persons (particularly, murder, outrages upon personal dignity, cruel treatment and pillage).[45] Taylor was also convicted of conscripting or enlisting children under the age of 15 into armed forces or groups, or using them to participate actively in hostilities.[46] In addition, he was found guilty of the crimes against humanity of murder, rape, sexual slavery and any other form of sexual violence, other inhumane acts and enslavement.[47]

However, the case against Habré at the EAC has specific attributes compared to the above-mentioned earlier cases that also concerned mass atrocities in Africa (Perez-Leon-Acevedo 2016). Unlike the conviction of Habré, the earlier

---

43 Judgment and Sentence, *Prosecutor v. Kambanda*, ICTR 97-23-S, T. Ch., ICTR, 4 September 1998.

44 Decision on Immunity from Jurisdiction, *Prosecutor v. Taylor*, SCSL-2003-01-I, A. Ch., SCSL, 31 May 2004.

45 Judgment, *Prosecutor v. Taylor*, SCSL-03-01-T, T. Ch. II, SCSL, 18 May 2012; Judgment, *Prosecutor v. Taylor*, SCSL-03-01-T, A, SCSL, A. Ch., ICTR, 26 September 2013.

46 See ibid.

47 See ibid.

conviction of Kambanda was rendered by an international criminal tribunal, namely the ICTR, set up by the UN Security Council. As for the conviction of Taylor, the SCSL is a hybrid criminal court, but unlike the EAC, it is not part of a national judiciary because its institutional framework is largely that of an autonomous international organisation. An additional specific feature surrounding the EAC is that the EAC, unlike other international and hybrid criminal courts, only exercised jurisdiction over one individual – Habré – whose status as a former head of state was irrelevant at the EAC.

4. THE EAC'S CONTRIBUTIONS TO THE LAW OF INTERNATIONAL CRIMES

4.1. CRIMES AGAINST HUMANITY

Crimes against humanity are regulated under Article 6 of the EAC Statute. In terms of the chapeaux or contextual elements of crimes against humanity, Article 6 is consistent with definitions contained in instruments of previously established international and hybrid criminal tribunals, including the Statutes of the ICTY (Article 5), the ICTR (Article 4), the SCSL (Article 2) and the ICC (Article 7). Thus, Article 6 of the EAC Statute states: 'For the purpose of this Statute, "crime against humanity" means any of the following acts when committed as part of a widespread or systematic attack directed against any civilian population.'

Citing international case law, particularly ICTY jurisprudence, the EAC Trial Chamber in *Habré inter alia* made the following points about the contextual legal elements of crimes against humanity. First, 'attacks' do not necessarily involve the use of armed force.[48] Second, a 'widespread' attack corresponds to a large-scale attack, which can be carried out via the cumulative effect of individual attacks or the singular effect of an attack of extraordinary magnitude.[49] Third, a 'systematic' attack corresponds to the organised character of the acts of violence, namely the intentional and regular repetition of similar criminal actions.[50] Fourth, the attack, rather than the individual actions of the accused, needs to be widespread or systematic.[51] Fifth, 'population' does not mean that the whole population of the geographical entity under attack is targeted, and the presence of some individuals who are not civilians does not deprive the 'civilian population' of its 'civilian' nature.[52] Finally, the accused

48 *Le Procureur Général c. Habré* (n 7), paras. 1356–1357.
49 Ibid., para. 1359.
50 Ibid., para. 1360.
51 Ibid., para. 1361.
52 Ibid., para. 1373.

knew that there was an attack against a civilian population and the conduct was part of the aforementioned attack.[53]

When it comes to the list of underlying criminal conducts, Article 6 of the EAC Statute has in certain aspects gone beyond the norms of the statutes of other international and hybrid criminal courts. Unlike the ICTY and ICTR Statutes, Article 6 includes 'apartheid' (Article 6(e)) and enforced disappearance (Article 6(f)), and not only includes rape but also incorporates a comprehensive list of sexual crimes (Article 6(a)), namely '[r]ape, sexual slavery, enforced prostitution, enforced sterilisation, or any other form of sexual violence of comparable gravity'. This list is even more comprehensive than that under Article 2 of the SCSL Statute because the latter does not explicitly mention enforced sterilisation. In these respects, Article 6 of the EAC reflects the detailed regulation in Article 7 of the ICC Statute.

The regulation of sexual crimes (and not only rape) contained in Article 6 contributes to consolidating, both in Africa and beyond, the trend of comprehensively regulating these heinous actions, which have been particularly recurrent and pandemic in Africa. This regulation was adapted in order to prosecute and try the widespread and systematic commission of sexual violence during the regime of Habré. Indeed, Habré was the first former head of state of any country to be convicted of personally raping someone. In cases against former heads of states at the national and international levels, the defendants are generally normally accused and/or convicted of planning, ordering or knowingly/recklessly neglecting the commission of systematic and/or widespread human rights violations, including sexual and gender violence offences, perpetrated by their subordinates. The cases against Radovan Karadžić at the ICTY and Kambanda at the ICTR illustrate this.[54] At the ICC, Trial Chamber III found Jean-Pierre Bemba Gombo, former Vice-President of the Democratic Republic of the Congo, guilty in his capacity as military commander (i.e. command responsibility) as he knowingly failed to meet his duties of prevention and sanction, or submission of the matter to the competent authorities, concerning *inter alia* war crimes and crimes against humanity of rape committed by his subordinates.[55] Nevertheless, the ICC Appeals Chamber in a close majority decision (three to two) overruled all convictions of Bemba because the majority found significant errors in the Trial Chamber's decision.[56]

---

53 Ibid., paras. 1363–1365.

54 Judgment, *Prosecutor v. Karadžić*, IT-95-5/18, T. Ch., ICTY, 24 March 2016; *Kambanda* (n 43).

55 Judgment pursuant to Article 74 of the Statute, *Prosecutor v. Bemba*, ICC-01/05-01/08-3399, T. Ch. III, ICC, 21 June 2016.

56 Judgment on the appeal of Mr Jean-Pierre Bemba Gombo against Trial Chamber III's 'Judgment Pursuant to Article 74 of the Statute', *Prosecutor v. Bemba*, ICC-01/05-01/08-3636-Red, A. Ch., ICC, 8 June 2018.

Thus, unlike in *Habré*, it is not common for the most senior defendants to be convicted of having personally committed sexual and gender crimes. However, the conviction of Habré for the direct commission of rape was the only one of the EAC Trial Chamber's findings on Habré's criminal liability that was overturned by the EAC Appeals Chamber, due to issues related to witness credibility (Carlson 2018: 363–364). In any event, the EAC invoked international case law, particularly ICTY jurisprudence, in identifying and discussing the constitutive elements of sexual slavery and rape as underlying conducts of crimes against humanity.[57] Thus, the EAC was both consistent with international jurisprudence on sexual offences and contributed to the reaffirmation thereof in Africa.

The other underlying forms of criminal conduct under Article 6 of the EAC Statute largely correspond to lists of underlying offences contained in the statutes of other international and hybrid criminal courts. Thus, besides sexual crimes and apartheid, Article 6 criminalises the following as crimes against humanity: murder, extermination, deportation, enslavement, summary executions, torture and inhumane acts. The case law of the EAC examined the material and subjective legal elements of these crimes against humanity in detail. Importantly, the EAC relied on the robust jurisprudence of international and hybrid criminal tribunals, particularly ICTY case law, when interpreting and applying the legal elements of crimes against humanity under Article 6 of the EAC Statute.[58]

Despite its overall normative consistency, Article 6 of the EAC Statute presents two normative gaps. First, unlike the statutes of other international and hybrid criminal courts, Article 6 contains no explicit reference to the crime against humanity of persecution on political, racial, ethnic, etc. grounds. Nevertheless, Article 6(g) to some extent compensates for this deficit by covering: 'inhumane acts ... on political, racial, national, ethnic, cultural, religious or gender grounds'. Second, the EAC does not contain some of the contents of Article 7(2)(a) of the ICC Statute. In particular: '"Attack directed against any civilian population" means a course of conduct involving the multiple commission of acts referred to in paragraph 1 against any civilian population, pursuant to or in furtherance of a State or organisational policy to commit such attack.' In fact, however, this provision is only present in the ICC Statute; the Statutes of the ICTY, the ICTR and the SCSL do not include a similar norm. This may explain why the EAC Trial Chamber in *Habré* invoked ICTY jurisprudence to establish that the existence of a state policy or plan for the perpetration of crimes is not a legal element of crimes against humanity.[59] Nevertheless, the EAC Trial Chamber importantly

---

57 See *Le Procureur Général c. Habré* (n 7), paras. 1482–1512.

58 Ibid., paras. 1355–1374.

59 Ibid., paras. 1358 and 1386 (invoking Judgment, *Prosecutor v. Kunarac*, IT-96-23 and IT-96-23/1-A, A. Ch., ICTY, 12 June 2002, para. 98).

pointed out that the existence of a state policy or plan may be useful to prove the perpetration of crimes against humanity.[60]

4.2. WAR CRIMES

As for war crimes, Article 7 of the EAC Statute explicitly recognises two categories. First, Article 7(1) incorporates grave breaches of the 1949 Geneva Conventions (applicable in international armed conflicts), namely criminal acts such as murder, torture or inhuman treatment, extensive destruction of property, unlawful deportation or transfer, and attacks against civilians or property protected under these Conventions. Second, Article 7(2) regulates serious violations of both Article 3 common to the 1949 Geneva Conventions and the Second Additional Protocol to the 1949 Geneva Conventions (applicable in non-international armed conflicts), including acts such as violence to life, torture, terrorism, rape, enforced prostitution, pillage and execution without due process.

In encompassing war crimes committed in both international and non-international armed conflicts, the EAC Statute follows the ICC Statute. Indeed, the EAC Statute is more complete than the instruments of other international and hybrid criminal courts. For example, the Statutes of the ICTR and the SCSL only included war crimes committed during non-international armed conflicts. In turn, although the ICTY Statute included grave breaches of the Geneva Conventions and violations of the laws or customs of wars, it contained no explicit reference to common Article 3 or the Second Additional Protocol. These differences in normative provisions no doubt correspond to the specific contexts of armed conflict addressed by each of the above-mentioned international and hybrid criminal courts, namely whether they were national and/or international armed conflicts. However, this does not negate the fact that the EAC Statute provides one of the most comprehensive regulations in terms of war crimes among the instruments of international and hybrid criminal courts. This feature is particularly relevant in applying substantive international criminal law in Africa, where there has in recent decades been both a number of different types of armed conflicts and a wide variety of war crimes.

In any event, the EAC Statute is certainly not as comprehensive as the ICC Statute, whose catalogue of war crimes is the longest of the international treaties that deal with international crimes or statutes of international and hybrid criminal tribunals. Compared to the EAC Statute, the main gap in the EAC Statute is the absence of norms that explicitly criminalise serious violations of the laws and customs in international and non-international armed conflicts.

60 Ibid., para. 1358.

However, these comparisons should take into account specific contexts. The ICC Statute was drafted in such a detailed manner in order that the ICC could exercise jurisdiction over a number of war crimes committed in diverse contexts of (future) armed conflicts. In turn, the EAC Statute was drafted with the particular context of and war crimes committed during the dictatorial regime of Habré in mind.

Similar to the situation with crimes against humanity, the EAC in *Habré* paid close attention to the jurisprudence of international and hybrid criminal tribunals, particularly the ICTY case law. By invoking this jurisprudence, the EAC identified and discussed four contextual legal elements of war crimes,[61] which were examined as follows. First, the act needs to be committed within the context of an armed conflict.[62] An armed conflict consists in the use of force between states or protracted hostilities between governmental authorities and armed organised groups or between armed groups within a state, and international humanitarian law recognises both international and internal armed conflicts.[63] Second, the act needs to be linked to an armed conflict.[64] War crimes, unlike domestic offences, are determined by the context of armed conflict in which they are perpetrated.[65] Although a cause–effect link between the armed conflict and the commission of the crime is not required, the existence of the armed conflict must substantially influence the capability and the decision of the perpetrator to commit the crime, as well as the manner of commission.[66] It is not required that war crimes take place in parallel to the hostilities or as part of the hostilities, but a close space–temporal link between the crimes attributed to the perpetrator and the hostilities is necessary.[67] Third, it is necessary that the accused knew of the characteristics of the war crimes.[68] Concerning the subjective element (*mens rea*), sufficient knowledge of the factual existence of an armed conflict is required.[69] Fourth, there is an element related to the status of the victims: in the context of an international armed conflict, the victims need to be protected persons under the Geneva Conventions, namely civilians, prisoners of war and combatants who can no longer fight because of injuries, sickness or shipwreck.[70] As for internal armed conflicts, victims of war crimes are persons who do not directly participate in the hostilities, a factor that has to be examined

61 See ibid., paras. 1622–1649.
62 Ibid., paras. 1623–1637.
63 Ibid., para. 1623.
64 Ibid., paras. 1623–1624.
65 Ibid., paras. 1638–1642.
66 *Kunarac* (n 59), para. 58. Cited by *Le Procureur Général c. Habré* (n 7), para. 1639.
67 *Kunarac* (n 59), para. 57. Cited by *Le Procureur Général c. Habré* (n 7), para. 1640.
68 *Le Procureur Général c. Habré* (n 7), para. 1643.
69 Ibid., para. 1644.
70 Ibid., para. 1645.

on a case-by-case basis and in light of the personal circumstances of the victim when the events took place.[71] It is required that the accused must have known the factual circumstances concerning the status of the victims.[72]

4.3. TORTURE

Besides crimes against humanity and war crimes, the EAC Statute includes torture as a discrete or autonomous crime. In other words, acts of torture do not need to be committed in a widespread or systematic manner (crimes against humanity) or as part of and in connection with an armed conflict (war crimes). Single acts of torture when committed by or with the acquiescence of state actors may constitute autonomous international crimes (Cassese 2013: 132–135). As international practice[73] and domestic practice[74] acknowledge, the prohibition of torture constitutes an *ius cogens* norm.

The EAC Statute drafters used the definition of torture contained in Article 1 of the UN Convention against Torture and Other Cruel, Inhuman or Degrading Treatment or Punishment. Thus, Article 8 of the EAC establishes that:

> For the purpose of this Statute, the term 'torture' shall encompass any act by which severe pain or suffering, whether physical or mental, is intentionally inflicted on a person for such purposes as obtaining from him or a third person information or a confession, punishing him for an act he or a third person has committed or is suspected of having committed, or intimidating or coercing him or a third person, or for any reason based on discrimination of any kind, when such pain or suffering is inflicted by or at the instigation of or with the consent or acquiescence of a public official or other person acting in an official capacity.

The inclusion of torture as a discrete offence in the EAC Statute certainly reflected the widespread use of torture during Habré's regime. On a comparative analysis, the fact that torture is not only an underlying criminal conduct of crimes against humanity and war crimes but also an autonomous crime arguably constitutes one of the most important contributions of the law of the EAC to the catalogue of crimes under the jurisdiction of future international, hybrid and/or regional criminal courts to be established in Africa and elsewhere.

---

71 Ibid., paras. 1647–1648.

72 Ibid., para. 1649.

73 Judgment, *Prosecutor v. Furundzija*, IT-95-17/1-T, T. Ch., ICTY. 10 December 1998, para. 144; Judgment, *Al-Adsani v. United Kingdom*, Application no. 35763/97, ECtHR, 21 November 2001, paras. 60–61.

74 Judgment, *R. v. Bow Street Metropolitan Stipendiary Magistrate and Others, ex parte Pinochet Ugarte (No. 3)*, House of Lords, 24 March 1999.

In fact, the Statutes of the ICTY, the ICTR, the SCSL and the ICC do not criminalise torture as an offence, but only as an underlying criminal act or a sub-category of crimes against humanity and war crimes. Moreover, the Statute of the prospective ACtJHPR-International Criminal Law section only recognises torture as part of the catalogue of underlying criminal conduct constitutive of crimes against humanity or war crimes rather than as an independent international crime.[75] Furthermore, the criminalisation of torture as an independent offence may be replicated or further developed in African criminal systems. This would complement the ongoing national implementation of ICC jurisdiction crimes in Africa (Bekou 2017: 273–288).

By invoking international jurisprudence, particularly ICTY case law,[76] the EAC stated that the legal elements of torture under customary international law are as follows:[77] first, there is an action or omission that inflicts severe physical or mental pain or suffering; second, this action or omission needs to be intentional; and, third, this action or omission aims at obtaining information or a confession, punishing, intimidating or coercing the victim or a third person, or discriminating, on any ground, against the victim or a third person. In addition, the EAC Trial Chamber discussed the legal element of the presence or acquiescence of a state agent.[78] Based on international case law,[79] the EAC Trial Chamber correctly pointed out that: (i) unlike the UN Convention against Torture, customary international law requires no presence or acquiescence of a state agent as a legal element of torture; (ii) the UN Convention against Torture is limited to actions that are related to or involve state actors; and (iii) the UN Convention against Torture does not fully reflect the definition of torture in general, namely the fact that under customary international law, torture is not confined to acts committed by or with the acquiescence of state agents.[80]

Nevertheless, the EAC Trial Chamber decided that Article 8 of the EAC Statute explicitly requires the involvement of a state agent as a legal element of torture as an independent crime.[81] The EAC Trial Chamber did not discuss this. As the Chamber correctly pointed out, the requirement of the involvement of state actors as part of the legal definition of torture did not have any impact in practice because the instances of torture considered in *Habré* were committed by state agents.[82] However, from a normative perspective, the EAC Trial Chamber should have been more accurate. In the relevant section of the judgment on

---

75 Articles 28(A)(1), 28(C) and 28(D).
76 *Kunarac* (n 59), para. 142.
77 *Le Procureur Général c. Habré* (n 7), para. 1545.
78 Ibid., paras. 1546–1549.
79 *Kunarac* (n 59), paras. 146–148.
80 *Le Procureur Général c. Habré* (n 7), para. 1547.
81 Ibid., para. 1548.
82 Ibid., para. 1549.

torture as a crime against humanity/war crime and torture as an autonomous crime, the EAC should have added that whereas the former requires no involvement or acquiescence of a state agent, the latter does.

5. THE EAC'S CONTRIBUTIONS TO INTERNATIONAL CRIMINAL PROCEDURE

5.1. RIGHTS OF THE ACCUSED

International criminal trials have to fully respect the rights of the accused in order to guarantee *inter alia* the legality, legitimacy and legacy of the respective institutions (McDermott 2016: 22–28; Luban 2010). Overall, the law and practice of the EAC have paid close attention to international criminal justice standards on the rights of the accused. Thus, similar experiences could help to develop (international) criminal procedure in Africa with full respect for the rights of the accused. Prospective or future international, regional or hybrid criminal tribunals which may be established in Africa could benefit from these lessons. This may also provide some guidance to African countries when reforming their respective national criminal procedural laws and practices to guarantee the rights of the accused. The respect for the rights of the accused at international criminal tribunals, which scholars have extensively examined (Schabas 2016: 1016–1051), is crucial for the delivery of procedural fairness or justice by judicial institutions such as the EAC in Africa and elsewhere (Vasiliev 2015: 361–379).

In the EAC Statute, there are several provisions that are *mutatis mutandis* adaptations of norms of the statutes of previous international and hybrid criminal tribunals. Article 21 (Rights of the Accused) is the EAC Statute's most important provision on defendant rights. Article 21 lists a catalogue of defence rights that is similar to the relevant provisions of the ICTY, the ICTR, the SCSL and the ICC Statutes.[83] Likewise, Article 46A of the Statute of the prospective ACtJHPR-International Criminal Law section contains similar norms on the rights of the accused.

Article 21(1)–(3) of the EAC Statute provides for: (i) the principle of equal treatment; (ii) fair and public hearings subject to protective measures for witnesses and victims; and (iii) the presumption of innocence until proven guilty.[84] The EAC Trial Chamber in *Habré* established that the aforementioned presumption of innocence determines that the Prosecutor must shoulder the burden of proof of the elements of crimes, modes of criminal liability and

83 ICTY Statute, art. 21; ICTR Statute, art. 20; SCSL Statute, art. 17; ICC Statute, art. 67.
84 EAC Statute, art. 21(1)–(3).

facts that are necessary in order for the Chamber to find the accused guilty beyond reasonable doubt.[85] The Chamber also added that the accused should be found innocent if the evidence shows a reasonable explanation that rules out his/her guilt.[86] In turn, the EAC Appeals Chamber noted that public hearings are a corollary of the rights of the accused, as provided for in Article 21, and thus claims arguing that this publicity may have negatively impacted certain testimonies must be rejected.[87]

In addition, Article 21(4) of the EAC Statute contains the following minimum guarantees:

a) To be informed promptly, and in detail, in a language which he or she fully understands, of the nature and content of the charge levelled against him or her;
b) To have adequate time and facilities for the preparation of his or her defence and to communicate freely with counsel of his or her own choosing;
c) To be tried without undue delay;
d) To be present at his or her trial, and to conduct the defence in person or with legal assistance of his or her choosing; and if he or she does not have legal assistance, to be informed of this right, and to have legal assistance assigned without charge whenever the interests of justice so require, if the accused is unable to pay;
e) To examine, or have examined, the witnesses against him or her and to obtain the attendance and examination of witnesses on his or her behalf under the same conditions as witnesses against him or her;
f) To have, without cost, the assistance of an interpreter if he or she cannot understand the language used in the Extraordinary African Chambers;
g) Not to be compelled to testify against him/herself or to confess guilt.

In the practice of the EAC, the following examples illustrate how these minimum guarantees have been applied. First, the EAC Trial Chamber in *Habré* explicitly stated that it did not infer any conclusion from the accused person's silence during the trial because Article 21(4)(g) of the EAC Statute provides that the accused cannot be requested to testify against himself/herself or confess guilt.[88]

Second, the EAC Appeals Chamber in *Habré* found that the provision of a summary of the trial judgment rather than the whole judgment during the

85 *Le Procureur Général c. Habré* (n 7), paras. 185–186.
86 Ibid., para. 186.
87 *Le Procureur Général c. Habré* (n 8), para. 337.
88 *Le Procureur Général c. Habré* (n 7), para 202.

time limit to file appeals does not necessarily breach the accused person's rights under Article 21 (particularly Article 21(4)(a) and (b)).[89] This is provided that the aforementioned summary establishes, in a sufficiently clear manner, the judicial reasoning and motivations concerning *inter alia* the factual conclusions on the crimes committed, the criminal liability of the convicted person and the imposed sentence.[90] The Chamber reached this finding by invoking *inter alia* the jurisprudence of the European Court of Human Rights and international criminal law sources.[91] In turn, the EAC Appeals Chamber found that the judicial public reading of the summary of the trial judgment, rather than the judicial reading of the whole judgment, was not inconsistent with Senegalese law and legal sources of other international and hybrid criminal tribunals.[92]

Third, concerning the alleged incomplete identification of the witnesses and civil parties in *Habré*, the EAC Appeals Chamber found that the identity of the persons heard was determined during the preparatory stage.[93] The EAC Trial Chamber checked and verified whether there was a correlation between the evidence concerning the identities of the persons appearing before the Chamber and their identity to be found in the documents and facts submitted to the Chamber.[94] In discussing this issue, the EAC Appeals Chamber paid attention to the case law of international and hybrid criminal tribunals, and particularly the jurisprudence of the ECCC.[95]

Fourth, although Habré was legally represented and his defendant rights were exercised via court-appointed legal counsellors, there were several problems that made his defence challenging (Carlson 2018: 359). These were his lawyers' lack of specialised knowledge of or experience in international criminal law and procedure, the reduced amount of time allocated to review extensive dossiers and the uncooperative attitude of Habré himself (Carlson 2018: 359).

Similar to the statutes of other international and hybrid criminal tribunals,[96] the EAC contains additional normative provisions that also constitute and/or are closely related to the rights of the accused. First, Article 19 provides for the prohibition of double jeopardy or *ne bis in idem*. This protects: (i) anyone already tried by the EAC from a second trial at the EAC with respect to conduct that constituted the basis of crimes for which the person was already convicted or

89 *Le Procureur Général c. Habré* (n 8), paras. 287–289 and 291.
90 Ibid.
91 Ibid., paras. 280–290.
92 Ibid., paras. 219–229.
93 Ibid., para. 244.
94 Ibid.
95 Ibid., paras. 239–241.
96 E.g. ICC Statute, arts 20, 22–24.

acquitted by the EAC; (ii) anyone from being tried by another court for crimes under the EAC's jurisdiction for which that person was already convicted or acquitted by the EAC; and (iii) anyone who was already tried by another court for conduct proscribed under the EAC-jurisdiction crimes from being tried at the EAC with respect to the same conduct, unless the proceedings at the other court sought to shield that person from justice or these proceedings lacked independence or impartiality. In addition, Article 22 states that: 'Hearings shall be held in public.' Article 25 recognises that final decisions may be appealed before the EAC Appeals Chamber by the Prosecutor or persons convicted by the EAC Trial Chamber due to: (i) a procedural error; (ii) an error on a legal question invalidating the decision; or (iii) a factual error that caused a miscarriage of justice. In *Habré*, the convicted person exercised his right to appeal on these three grounds. Finally, Articles 33 and 34 of the EAC Statute respectively recognise the adoption of all reasonable measures to guarantee access to the trial for all parties and the obligation of Senegal to ensure, within its territory, the protection of all parties.

5.2. THE PROCEDURAL ROLE OF VICTIMS

The procedural role of victims of mass atrocities before international and hybrid criminal tribunals may have one or more of these main dimensions: (i) they may be witnesses; (ii) they may be victim participants or civil parties; or (iii) they may claim and benefit from reparations against the convicted (Heikkilä 2004; de Brouwer 2005: 227–314, 383–424; Perez-Leon-Acevedo 2014). In turn, these dimensions correspond to the victims' general rights to protection, participation and/or reparations (McGonigle-Leyh 2011: 93–131; Ochoa 2013: 37–146; Perez-Leon-Acevedo 2014: 35–47).

Overall, the law and practice of the EAC have arguably contributed to and been consistent with the trends towards an enhanced role for victims in international criminal proceedings concerning serious crimes committed in Africa and beyond. The role of victims as civil parties in criminal proceedings certainly reflects the civil law tradition (Hoegen and Brienen 2000: 27, 129, 320) where victims are parties to criminal proceedings (Damaška 1986: 200, 212–213). Civil parties are present in those African countries that belong to the civil law tradition, including Senegal and Chad. Unlike the ICTY, the ICTR and the SCSL, the role of victims at the EAC is not merely confined to being mere witnesses. Besides the closed Special Panels for Serious Crimes in East Timor and the ECCC, the EAC is the only court among the international and hybrid criminal tribunals in which victims can be civil parties in order to both participate in criminal proceedings and claim reparations. Thus, the role of the victims at the EAC is stronger than at the ICC and the Special Tribunal for Lebanon because at the latter tribunals, victims can be participants in order to voice their views and concerns rather than parties.[97] At the ICC, victims can claim and receive reparations, and thus victims as reparation claimants and beneficiaries may be considered to be parties. However, this 'party' status is confined to post-conviction reparations proceedings at the ICC. Conversely, victims as civil parties are proper parties to both pre-conviction and post-conviction proceedings at the EAC. Indeed, victims and their lawyers in their search for justice played a crucial role in the establishment of the EAC and the trial and conviction of Habré (Sperfeldt 2017: 1243–1251).

Article 14 of the EAC Statute provides for general principles on victim participation as civil parties. These include that: (i) civil parties may be constituted during the investigation via a written request to the Registrar submitted by a victim or his/her rightful claimants; (ii) victims may elect to form groups and decide to be represented by a common legal representative; and (iii) financial assistance can be provided if a group of victims lacks the means to pay a joint representative. Article 25 of the EAC Statute explicitly recognises the right of civil parties to appeal final decisions with regard solely to their civil interests.

As the trial of Habré shows, victims of the crimes for which Habré was convicted arguably exercised the two main goals or objectives of the civil party participation, namely: (i) participation in criminal proceedings against those responsible for crimes within the jurisdiction of the EAC by supporting the prosecution, but without becoming auxiliary prosecutors; and (ii) application for reparations, compensation included (Hoegen and Brienen 2000: 27). In areas concerning civil party participation and related goals, both the lawyers of the civil parties and the EAC have invoked a number of relevant international sources to interpret and apply norms on civil parties contained in the EAC Statute or even to fill some normative gaps. For example, the EAC Statute contains no definition of 'victims'. Therefore, the EAC Appeals Chamber considered the law and practice of the ICC and the ECCC in order to find *inter alia* that: (i) 'victims' are those who suffered injury or harm as a result of the commission of crimes under the jurisdiction of the EAC; (ii) there exist two main categories of victims, namely direct and indirect victims; (iii) indirect victims need to prove the harm inflicted on them through admissible evidence of their relationship with direct victims; and (iv) the group of indirect victims is not confined only to relatives, since the existence of 'harm' is what determines the admissibility of indirect victims.[98]

The EAC Statute contains important provisions on reparations, which are the grounds for the role of victims as reparation claimants and beneficiaries (parties) at the EAC. Article 27 (Reparations) lays down *inter alia* that: (i) the EAC reparation award shall include restitution, compensation and

---

97 See ICC Statute, art. 68(3); Special Tribunal for Lebanon (STL) Statute, art. 17.

98 *Le Procureur Général c. Habré* (n 8), paras. 583–585.

rehabilitation;[99] (ii) the EAC may before making a reparation award invite observations from *inter alia* victims;[100] and (iii) Article 27 provisions cannot be interpreted as prejudicing victims' rights under national or international law.[101] In addition, Article 27(2) states that the EAC may order that the reparation award be made through a trust fund for victims. Besides the ICC, the EAC is the only body among the international and hybrid criminal tribunals that has a trust fund for victims. Article 28(1) establishes that: (i) the aforementioned Trust shall be established to benefit both victims of crimes under the EAC's jurisdiction and the rightful claimants of such victims; and (ii) the Trust shall be financed through voluntary contributions from foreign governments, international institutions, NGOs and other entities that wish to support victims. Also, under Article 28(2), reparations may be individually or collectively awarded to victims even if they did not participate in the EAC proceedings.

In terms of the practice of the EAC, it ordered Habré to pay individual compensatory awards to 7,396 civil parties. Rape/sexual slavery victims, massacre victims and indirect victims were granted 20, 35 and 10 million West African francs (CFA) per person respectively (approximately US$36,000, 63,000 and 18,000).[102] Thus, the total compensation that Habré was ordered to pay was CFA 82.29 billion (approximately US$147.5 million) for 7,396 civil parties. These amounts are (much) higher than the compensatory figures ordered by other international tribunals in cases of serious human rights violations or international crimes.[103] In addition, the EAC has established that victims who could not participate as civil parties in the proceedings against Habré can still claim and potentially receive compensatory awards via proceedings at the Trust Fund for Victims. This is important because victims may, due to a number of factors, be unable or unwilling to participate as civil parties in international criminal proceedings. In any event, it is unfeasible for Habré to pay the high sums ordered since he lacks the necessary financial resources. His confiscated goods and assets are insufficient to cover all the compensatory awards. Indeed, most convicted persons at international and hybrid criminal tribunals are judicially indigent. This constitutes an important challenge to the implementation of reparation awards ordered by international and hybrid criminal tribunals. These judicial institutions cannot order states to grant compensation or provide other forms of reparation. A shortcoming of the reparation award in

99 EAC Statute, art. 27(1).
100 Ibid., art. 27(3).
101 Ibid., art. 27(4).
102 Reparations Order, *Le Procureur Général c. Habré*, T. Ch., EAC, 29 July 2016, para. 58.
103 E.g., Inter-American Court of Human Rights, Judgment (Reparations), *Plan de Sanchez Massacre v. Guatemala*, Series C No 116, 19 November 2004, para 88.

Habré is that the EAC rejected collective reparation measures consisting in the establishment of centres for practical training of victims' children, development projects, the teaching of Chadian history relevant to the case against *Habré* in Chadian schools, a commemoration day and monuments in memory of victims.[104] The absence of details and, in particular, the need for Chad's involvement in implementing these reparations and Chad's negative attitude to these projects meant that the EAC rejected these requests from the lawyers of the civil parties.

In any event, the EAC Appeals Chamber invited states to cooperate with the Trust Fund for Victims.[105] Furthermore, the Chamber encouraged the EAC Trust Fund to seek collaboration not only from Chad, but also from other actors, such as associations assisting victims, interested organisations, civil party organisations, interested states and experts, in order to effectively implement the compensation ordered by the EAC and also potentially collective and moral reparations requested by victims.[106] Whether the implementation of reparations for victims of crimes committed by Habré may have transformative effects is yet to be seen (Sperfeldt 2017: 1251–1254). In January 2018, the AU, in the Resolution that introduced the EAC Trust Fund for Victims Statute, importantly referred not only to the assets of the convicted but also to other resources to finance the Trust Fund, namely voluntary contributions of AU member states, foreign governments, international institutions, NGOs and other entities willing to support the victims.[107] In realising the procedural role of victims as reparation claimants and beneficiaries at international and hybrid criminal courts, the EAC Trust Fund for Victims may be highly informative for future similar institutions in Africa, for example, the Trust Fund for Victims of the International Criminal Law section of the prospective ACtJHPR.

6. CONCLUSION

Despite the short existence and limitations of the EAC, its (potential) contributions to the development of international criminal law in Africa and beyond may be identified in four main areas. These areas are, broadly speaking: (i) innovations in the institutional framework of international criminal justice bodies; (ii) mechanisms to ensure the criminal accountability of the most responsible for mass atrocities; (iii) substantive criminal law, in particular the law of international crimes; and (iv) international criminal procedure aspects, especially the rights of the accused and the role of victims.

---

104 *Le Procureur Général c. Habré* (n 102), para. 69.

105 *Le Procureur Général c. Habré* (n 7), p. 226.

106 Ibid., paras. 612–615, p. 226.

107 African Union, Statute of the Trust Fund for Victims of Hissène Habré's Crimes, EX.CL/1040(XXXI) Annex, Article 15(1).

With regard to institutional innovations, the EAC itself constitutes an interesting and even *sui generis* option to design and establish criminal courts at the international level in Africa and elsewhere. Arguably, the EAC, to an important extent and in an efficient manner, merges features of internationalised or hybrid criminal tribunals with innovative regional criminal justice elements that directly involved and concerned the AU. This model endeavours to combine the best of both worlds: a hybrid criminal court, supported by a regional organisation. This model may *mutatis mutandis* be replicated both elsewhere in Africa and in other regions.

As for ways to ensure the accountability of those individuals who are the most responsible for international crimes in Africa, the EAC is the first of any hybrid, internationalised or even international criminal tribunal (other than *mutatis mutandis* the ICC) to exercise its jurisdiction on universal jurisdiction grounds. In addition, the inadmissibility of immunities at the EAC is consistent with international standards.

In terms of substantive criminal law, particularly the legal elements of crimes against humanity, war crimes and torture, the law and practice of the EAC have overall been consistent with international criminal justice standards, especially relevant normative instruments and jurisprudence. The EAC in *Habré* appropriately relied on these sources, as adapted to the normative framework of the EAC and applied to the specific facts and circumstances. The consideration of torture as an autonomous international crime at the EAC may be followed by other international and hybrid criminal courts.

Concerning international criminal procedure, the EAC law and practice overall followed international standards on the rights of the accused to guarantee impartial, independent, effective and fair proceedings for the defendant Habré, despite some practical challenges. As for the victims' procedural role, the law and practice of the EAC are consistent with international criminal justice trends of allowing victims to properly participate in the proceedings, even as civil parties, and claim reparations. The incorporation of a Trust Fund for Victims should also be followed by similar courts.

Therefore, the law and practice of the EAC have important and innovative institutional, procedural and substantive features that arguably contribute to the development of international criminal law in Africa and beyond. Subject to adaptations, these aspects should be taken into account by similar ongoing and/or future African criminal justice initiatives, such as the International Criminal Law section of the prospective ACtJHPR. The same may be said *mutatis mutandis* about similar regional and/or international(ised) criminal justice mechanisms in Africa and elsewhere that may come into existence in the future. African national jurisdictions may also take note of some of the important features of the law and practice of the EAC, especially in terms of substantive criminal law and to some extent procedural criminal law.

BIBLIOGRAPHY

Akande, D. (2003) 'The Jurisdiction of the International Criminal Court over Nationals of Non-parties: Legal Basis and Limits', *Journal of International Criminal Justice* 1(3): 618–650.

Bekou, O. (2017) 'National Implementation of the ICC Statute to Prosecute International Crimes in Africa' in C. Jalloh and I. Bantekas (eds), *The International Criminal Court and Africa*. Oxford: Oxford University Press, pp. 272–289.

Brody, R. (2015) 'Bringing a Dictator to Justice: The Case of Hissène Habré', *Journal of International Criminal Justice* 13(2): 209–217.

Carlson, K. (2018) 'Trying Hissène Habré "on Behalf of Africa": Remaking Hybrid International Criminal Justice at the *Chambers Africaines Extraordinaires*' in J. Nicholson (ed.), *Strengthening the Validity of International Criminal Tribunals*. Leiden: Brill, pp. 342–365.

Cassese, A. (2013) *International Criminal Law*, 3rd edn. Oxford: Oxford University Press.

Cimiotta, E. (2015) 'The First Steps of the Extraordinary African Chambers', *Journal of International Criminal Justice* 13(1): 177–197.

Cryer, R., Friman, H., Robinson, D. and Wilmshurst, E. (2014) *An Introduction to International Criminal Law and Procedure*, 3rd edn. Cambridge: Cambridge University Press.

Damaška, M. (1986) *The Faces of Justice and State Authority*. New Haven: Yale University Press.

De Brouwer, A. (2005) *Supranational Criminal Prosecution of Sexual Violence: The ICC and the Practice of the ICTY and the ICTR*. Antwerp: Intersentia.

Du Plessis, M. (2014) *Shambolic, Shameful and Symbolic: Implications of the African Union's Immunity for African Leaders*. Pretoria: Institute for Security Studies.

Fletcher, G. and Ohlin, J. (2006) 'The ICC – Two Courts in One?', *Journal of International Criminal Justice* 4(3): 428–433.

Heikkilä, M. (2004) *International Criminal Tribunals and Victims of Crime*. Åbo: Åbo Akademi University Press.

Hoegen, E. and Brienen, M. (2000) *Victims of Crime in 22 European Criminal justice Systems*. Nijmegen: Wolf Legal Publishers.

Høgestøl, S. (2016) 'The *Habré* Judgment at the Extraordinary African Chambers', *Nordic Journal of Human Rights* 34(3): 147–156.

Jalloh, C. and Bantekas, I. (2017) 'Conclusion' in C. Jalloh and I. Bantekas (eds), *The International Criminal Court and Africa*. Oxford: Oxford University Press, pp. 371–377.

Luban, D. (2010) 'Jurisdiction, Legality, and the Legitimacy of International Criminal Law' in S. Besson and J. Tasioulas (eds), *The Philosophy of International Law*. Oxford: Oxford University Press, pp. 569–588.

McDermott, Y. (2016) *Fairness in International Criminal Trials*. Oxford: Oxford University Press.

McGonigle-Leyh, B. (2011) *Procedural Justice? Victim Participation in International Criminal Proceedings*. Antwerp: Intersentia.

Mennecke, M. (2017) 'The African Union and Universal Jurisdiction' in C. Jalloh and I. Bantekas (eds), *The International Criminal Court and Africa*. Oxford: Oxford University Press, pp. 10–38.

Nowak, M. and McArthur, E. (2008) *The United Nations Convention against Torture: A Commentary*. Oxford: Oxford University Press.

Ochoa, J. (2013) *The Rights of Victims in Criminal Justice Proceedings for Serious Human Rights Violations*. Leiden: Martinus Nijhoff Publishers.

Perez-Leon-Acevedo, J. (2014) *Victims' Status at International and Hybrid Criminal Courts: Victims' Status as Witnesses, Victim Participants/Civil Parties and Reparations Claimants*. Åbo: Åbo Akademi University Press.

Perez-Leon-Acevedo, J. (2016) 'The Conviction of Hissène Habré by the Extraordinary African Chambers in the Senegalese Courts: Bringing Justice in Cases of Serious Human Rights Violations in Africa', *AfricLaw Blog*, 30 June, https://africlaw.com/2016/06/30/the-conviction-of-hissene-habre-by-the-extraordinary-chambers-in-the-senegalese-courts-bringing-justice-in-cases-of-serious-human-rights-violations-in-africa.

Scharf, M. (2011) 'The ICC's Jurisdiction over the Nationals of Non-party States: A Critique of the U.S. Position', *Law and Contemporary Problems* 64: 67–118.

Schabas, W. (2013) 'Senegal's Chambres africaines extraordinaires to judge Habré', *PhD Studies in Human Rights Blog*, 5 February, http://humanrightsdoctorate.blogspot.com/2013/02/senegals-chambres-africaines.html.

Schabas, W. (2016) *The International Criminal Court: A Commentary on the Rome Statute*, 2nd edn. Oxford: Oxford University Press.

Sirleaf, M. (2016) 'Regionalism, Regime Complexes, and the Crisis in International Criminal Justice', *Columbia Journal of Transnational Law* 54(3): 699–788.

Sperfeldt, C. (2017) 'The Trial against Hissène Habré: Networked Justice and Reparations at the Extraordinary African Chambers', *International Journal of Human Rights* 21(9): 1243–1260.

Sriram, C. (2003) 'Revolutions in Accountability: New Approaches to Past Abuses', *American University International Law Review* 19(2): 301–429.

Ssenyonjo, M. and Nakitto, S. (2016) 'The African Court of Justice and Human and Peoples' Rights "International Criminal Law Section": Promoting Impunity for African Union Heads of State and Senior State Officials?', *International Criminal Law Review* 16(1): 71–102.

Tiba, F. (2007) 'The Mengistu Genocide Trial in Ethiopia', *Journal of International Criminal Justice* 5: 513–528.

Tladi, D. (2015) 'The Immunity Provisions in the AU Amendment Protocol: Separating the (Doctrinal) Wheat from the (Normative) Chaff', *Journal of International Criminal Justice* 13(1): 3–17.

Vasiliev, S. (2015) 'Procedural Fairness in the International Criminal Court' in A. Sarvarian, F. Fontanelli, R. Baker and V. Tzevelekos (eds), *Procedural Fairness in International Courts and Tribunals*. London: British Institute for International and Comparative Law, pp. 361–379.

Williams, S. (2012) *Hybrid and Internationalised Criminal Tribunals: Selected Jurisdictional Issues*. Oxford: Hart Publishing.

Williams, S. (2013) 'The Extraordinary African Chambers in the Senegalese Court: An African Solution to an African Problem?', *Journal of International Criminal Justice* 11(5): 1139–1160.

CASE LAW

CONSEIL CONSTITUTIONNEL DU SÉNÉGAL

Décision, *Affaire No 1/C72015*, Conseil Constitutionnel du Sénégal, 2 March 2015.

ECOWAS

Arrêt, *Hissène Habré c. Republique du Senegal*, No. ECW/CCJ/JUD/06/10, Court of Justice, ECOWAS, 18 November 2010.
Arrêt, *Hissène Habré c. Republique du Senegal*, No. ECW/CCJ/JUD/05/13, Court of Justice, ECOWAS, 5 November 2013.

EAC

Arrêt, *Le Procureur Général c. Habré*, T. Ch., EAC, 30 May 2016.
Reparations Order, *Le Procureur Général c. Habré*, T. Ch., EAC, 29 July 2016.
Arrêt, *Le Procureur Général c. Habré*, A. Ch., EAC, 27 April 2017.

ICJ

Questions Relating to the Obligation to Prosecute or Extradite (Belgium v. Senegal), 20 July 2012, ICJ Reports (2013) 422.

INTERNATIONAL AND HYBRID CRIMINAL COURTS AND TRIBUNALS

Judgment pursuant to Article 74 of the Statute, *Prosecutor v. Bemba*, ICC-01/05-01/08-3399, T. Ch. III, ICC, 21 June 2016.
Judgment on the appeal of Mr Jean-Pierre Bemba Gombo against Trial Chamber III's 'Judgment pursuant to Article 74 of the Statute', *Prosecutor v. Bemba*, ICC-01/05-01/08-3636-Red, A. Ch., ICC, 8 June 2018.
Judgment, *Prosecutor v. Furundzija*, IT-95-17/1-T, T. Ch., ICTY, 10 December 1998.
Judgment and Sentence, *Prosecutor v. Kambanda*, ICTR 97-23-S, T. Ch., ICTR, 4 September 1998.
Judgment, *Prosecutor v. Karadžić*, IT-95-5/18, T. Ch., ICTY, 24 March 2016.
Judgment, *Prosecutor v. Kunarac*, IT-96-23 and IT-96-23/1-A, A. Ch., ICTY, 12 June 2002.
Decision on Immunity from Jurisdiction, *Prosecutor v. Taylor*, SCSL-2003-01-I, A. Ch., SCSL, 31 May 2004.
Judgment, *Prosecutor v. Taylor*, SCSL-03-01-T, T. Ch. II, SCSL, 18 May 2012.
Judgment, *Prosecutor v. Taylor*, SCSL-03-01-T, A, SCSL, A. Ch., ICTR, 26 September 2013.

HUMAN RIGHTS COURTS AND BODIES

Decision, *Guengueng et al. v. Senegal*, Communication No. 181/2001, CAT/C/36/D/181/2001, 19 May 2006.

Inter-American Court of Human Rights, Judgment (Reparations), *Plan de Sanchez Massacre v. Guatemala*, Series C No. 116, 19 November 2004.

Judgment, *Al-Adsani v. United Kingdom*, Application no. 35763/97, ECtHR, 21 November 2001.

NATIONAL COURTS

Judgment, *Barrios Altos, La Cantuta and Sótanos del SIN*, Transitory Criminal Chamber, Supreme Court of Peru, 7 April 2009.

Judgment, *Michelot Yogogombaye v. Republic of Senegal*, File No. 001/2008, ACtHPR, 15 December 2009.

Judgment, *R. v. Bow Street Metropolitan Stipendiary Magistrate and Others, ex parte Pinochet Ugarte (No. 3)*, House of Lords, 24 March 1999.

Judgment, *Special Prosecutor v. Col. Mengistu Hailamariam et al.*, File No. 1/87, Ethiopian Federal High Court, 12 December 2006.

THE USE OF INTERNATIONAL CRIMINAL LAW IN AFRICAN COUNTRIES

Ellah T.M. Siang'andu*

1. INTRODUCTION

It has been argued that 'no continent has paid more dearly than Africa for the absence of legitimate institutions of law and accountability, resulting in a culture of impunity' (Mochochoko 2005: 249). On the contrary, this chapter illustrates the application of international criminal law in Africa prior and after the adoption of the Rome Statute of the International Criminal Court (ICC).

* I would like to thank Professor Jeremy Sarkin for the valuable comments made on the earlier draft which have helped to improve the chapter.

The ICC represents the idea that individuals who violate fundamental human rights must be held responsible. The body of laws that enables individuals to be prosecuted for such offences is called international criminal law (ICL), which provides a legal framework for the investigations, arrest, prosecution and punishment of such individuals nationally or internationally. It is crucial to investigate and assess the use of ICL as well as the incorporation of the Rome Statute crimes into national legal systems in Africa because the continent plays a vital role in ICL and justice generally. This has been made clear by the situations and cases before the ICC, the majority of which are based in Africa. The creation of a permanent ICC by a multilateral treaty was indeed a breakthrough, as it provides a forum for ensuring persons suspected of committing international crimes are held accountable. Focusing on selected countries, the chapter traces instances when national courts of African states have either attempted to investigate and prosecute international crimes or have successfully investigated, charged and prosecuted individuals for offences within the ICC's jurisdiction. This is done by first examining the notion of jurisdiction of states as sovereign entities in the context of prosecuting international crimes. It then considers the principle of complementarity under the Rome Statute framework. Thereafter, a synopsis of how African states have implemented ICL is provided and, finally, examples of how states have incorporated the Rome Statute are considered. The contention is that more needs to be done than merely the incorporation and training of a few state representatives or governments officials in order to comply with the international obligations. Addressing the culture of impunity demands that sensitisation occurs from a grassroots level and ensures that ordinary people appreciate the need to make sure every person suspected of committing international crimes is held accountable before the national courts.

2. THE JURISDICTION OF STATES AS SOVEREIGN ENTITIES IN INTERNATIONAL LAW

In order to address the culture of impunity for international crimes and ensure that individuals who perpetrate international crimes are held accountable, states must implement relevant laws in place to facilitate such prosecutions. States as sovereign entities have two types of jurisdiction: prescriptive (also referred to as legislative) jurisdiction and enforcement jurisdiction. The former refers to the right or power of states to make rules, while the latter denotes the right of states to enforce the legal rules adopted in their national legal systems. The basis for states' prescriptive jurisdiction is the *SS Lotus* case, where the Permanent Court of International Justice established the fundamental rule of international law that the state's jurisdiction within its own territory is complete and absolute. With reference to international crimes, this means that states have the authority to adopt laws, including incorporating the Rome Statute offences into their national legal systems and applying the rules to individuals whenever necessary.

African states have the capacity to employ their prescriptive jurisdiction to treat offences under the Rome Statute as crimes within their national legal systems. This is done through various means, including the adoption of primary or secondary legislation, judicial action or by means of an executive decree, as will be illustrated in this chapter. Before considering how national courts on the African continent have used ICL prior to and after the adoption of the Rome Statute, it is vital to address the key terms and to define their meaning within the context of this chapter. These concepts are the notions of crime, international crime and individual criminal responsibility.

A crime or offence is a legal wrong that is prohibited by law. It may be a prohibited act or conduct, an omission or a state of affairs that contravenes the law. A prosecution normally follows the violation of legal rules. If convicted, the accused is subjected to punishment as a consequence. Usually, national legal systems clearly stipulate offences that are regarded as crimes within their national legal systems. For the purposes of this chapter, a 'crime' is synonymous with 'international crime': it refers to the offences within the ICC's jurisdiction, that is, genocide, war crimes, crimes against humanity and crimes of aggression. These offences are defined in Articles 6, 7, 8 and 8 *bis* of the Rome Statute, as well as the ICC's *Elements of Crimes* 2002 and 2010 documents that were adopted by the Assembly of States Parties pursuant to Article 9(1) of the Rome Statute. The definitions clearly stipulate the circumstances under which individual criminal responsibility can be established. Similarly, the offences within the jurisdiction of the ICC are also prohibited under customary international law and the Geneva Conventions of 1949.

With reference to the concept of an international crime, one of the fundamental characteristics of an international crime is that its commission gives rise to individual criminal responsibility under international law as well as under national law (O'Keefe 2017: 47). This implies that states must prohibit the core international crimes such that where any person suspected of commission of these offences must be held accountable before the national courts. As addressed above, individual criminal responsibility can be established in ICL on the basis of customary international law (CIL), domestic law or treaty law (international law). The focus of this section is individual criminal responsibility on the basis of treaty law, as well as national legislation. Individual criminal responsibility for international crimes under the Rome Statute involves establishing liability on the basis of the Statute.

Under treaty law, by virtue of any state having ratified the Rome Statute, states parties are obliged to ensure that the Statute is implemented into their national legal system on the basis of the principle of *pacta sunt servanda.*

This principle is further enshrined in Article 26 of the Vienna Convention on the Law of Treaties (VCLT, 1969), which reaffirms the notion that every treaty that is in force is deemed binding on the parties and must be implemented in good faith. Thus, it is imperative for states parties to enact national legislation in order to integrate the Rome Statute crimes into their domestic systems. States cannot invoke provisions of their internal rules as a justification for a failure to implement a treaty (Article 27 VCLT).

While the Rome Statute does not specifically provide a positive obligation on states to incorporate its provisions into domestic systems, states parties to the Rome Statute have an obligation under treaty law as well as international customary law to ensure that individuals responsible for horrendous atrocities within the ICC's jurisdiction, are prosecuted in national courts. The implementation of the Rome Statute crimes in domestic legal systems as well as taking active measures to prosecute the perpetrators is the only way in which African states can avoid being subjected to the scrutiny and ultimately the jurisdiction of the ICC by way of intervention in situations that occur within their territories. It is important to examine national legal systems and ascertain the measures available to ensure that individuals who violate ICL do not escape accountability with impunity. This is not only because states have primary responsibility for prosecuting those suspected of committing international crimes, but also in order to encourage a culture of respect for human rights, deterrence, preventing a recurrence of the offences and upholding the rule of law (Kleffner 2008: 26; Nouwen 2013: 38).

So far, out of the 33 African states parties to the Rome Statute, only half have either passed legislation or have draft bills pending incorporation of the Rome Statute into their national legal systems.[1] States parties have a primary responsibility for ensuring that individuals suspected of committing international crimes are held accountable in accordance with the Statute (para. 6 of the Preamble and Articles 5 and 17(1)(a)). Therefore, ideally, individuals suspected of having committed the most serious offences ought to be prosecuted before national courts and only as a last resort before the ICC in line with Article 25 of the Statute. It is imperative for states parties to the Statute to ensure that measures are introduced into their national systems to ensure that suspected persons are held accountable. The doctrine of complementarity and its implications are considered further in the next section.

1 Benin, Burkina Faso, Cape Verde, the Central African Republic, Comoros, Côte d'Ivoire, Democratic Republic of the Congo, Guinea, Kenya, Lesotho, Mali, Mauritius, Niger, the Republic of the Congo, Senegal, South Africa and Uganda.

3. THE PRINCIPLE OF COMPLEMENTARITY

Africa faces a wide range of challenges including poor leadership, armed conflicts since the Second World War, lack of adherence to the rule of law, high levels of corruption, human rights violations, exploitation of natural resources, cheap labour and the highest levels of violence compared to the rest of the world (Meyersfeld 2012: 148). In order to give effect to its complementarity obligations under the Rome Statute, states parties must incorporate the Rome Statute crimes into their domestic laws. The ICC operates on the basis of the principle of complementarity (para. 10 of the Preamble and Article 1 of the Rome Statute). This implies that national courts have a responsibility to ensure that individuals suspected of having committed the most serious atrocities are held accountable in national courts. States are therefore obliged to prosecute perpetrators of Rome Statute offences in their domestic courts. The principle of complementarity is further manifested in Article 17 of the Rome Statute, which deals with issues relating to the admissibility of cases before the ICC. The principle of complementarity means that the ICC can only exercise jurisdiction where the territorial state is not currently investigating or prosecuting the case or where it is unwilling or unable to do so. National criminal courts thus enjoy primacy over the ICC, as reaffirmed by the Appeals Chamber in the *Prosecutor v. Katanga and Ngudjolo.*[2]

Therefore, states parties are expected to ensure that the Rome Statute offences are incorporated into their national jurisdictions in order to make it possible for suspects to be prosecuted. The idea underlying the principle of complementarity is that the ICC can only exercise its jurisdiction if no state that has jurisdiction initiates a criminal prosecution. This can only be possible if states take the necessary measures to integrate the Rome Statute offences into their national jurisdictions and to ensure that the perpetrators of such offences do not escape without accountability. The consequences of not dealing with international crimes are that the ICC can intervene to prosecute individuals suspected of committing the most serious offences. According to the principle of complementarity, the national legal system takes primacy over the prosecution in the ICC. States parties are obliged to incorporate the Rome Statute in order to ensure that their national courts take an upper hand in the prosecution of any alleged perpetrators of international crimes. The analysis relating to the question of incorporation of the Rome Statute is based on ensuring states parties put appropriate measures in place to allow for the prosecution of such crimes to be conducted in national courts.

---

2 ICC-01/04-01/07-1497, Appeals Chamber. Judgment on the Appeal of Germain Katanga against the Oral Decision of Trial Chamber II of 12 June 2009 on the Admissibility of the Case, 25 September 2009, paragraph 85.

Apart from adopting the relevant legislation implementing the Rome Statute, clear procedures must also be put in place to allow for such prosecutions. States must endeavour to have the necessary infrastructure to enable the national courts to cooperate with the ICC in line with the ICC's standards and practices. This implies that combating international crimes requires states parties to do more than just incorporate the Rome Statute; it requires capacity building and the sensitisation of the public and the criminal justice system as a whole on the importance of prosecuting international crimes. The next section provides an overview of the use of ICL in African countries generally.

The use of ICL with reference to the Rome Statute offences is appraised by examining the progress made in seeking to ensure individuals suspected of committing offences within the jurisdiction of the Rome Statute are held accountable. On this basis, the national criminal laws of selected states – in particular, Uganda, Kenya and South Africa – are considered. The laws of the states are scrutinised in order to assess the extent to which they constitute the domestication of the Rome Statute crimes. In addition, the progress of national courts in seeking to establish individual accountability for international criminal offences is considered.

4. OVERVIEW: AFRICA AND THE USE OF INTERNATIONAL CRIMINAL LAW

Historically, the national courts of African states have mostly been either unable or unwilling to investigate and prosecute individuals suspected of committing Rome Statute offences (Weldesellasie 2017: 267). African national courts have not been at the forefront in terms of prosecuting international crimes, because such offences always tend to be highly political, sensitive and, due to their nature, liability would extend to high-profile individuals serving in government positions. More needs to be done to transform the national legal systems in African states. Despite the most serious offences having been committed on the continent, there are limited examples of instances when ICL has been applied for the purposes of establishing individual accountability for international crimes.

One notable example is that of the Dergue trials conducted in Ethiopia after the creation of the Special Prosecutor's Office (SPO) in August 1992 (Proclamation No. 22/1992). The Dergue was the military junta that governed Ethiopia from 1974 to 1987 (Jallow and Bensouda 2008: 28).

Ethiopia's response to the violence perpetrated during the Dergue regime was to initiate criminal proceedings against suspects of the offences committed. The main objectives of creating the SPO was to investigate and prosecute atrocities and to establish a historical record of what had occurred. The initial assertion provides that 'it is in the interest of just historical obligation to record for posterity the brutal offences, the embezzlement of property perpetrated against the people of Ethiopia and to educate the people and make them aware of these offences in order to prevent the recurrence of such a system of government' (Proclamation No. 22/1992 Preamble).

Menguistu and his co-accused were charged with 211 counts of genocide and crimes against humanity, and were tried by the Ethiopia Federal High Court on the basis of a national criminal law provision in Article 281 of the 1957 Ethiopian Penal Code. Though trials were conducted *in absentia*, 55 individuals were prosecuted over a period of 12 years, and 25 were found guilty. On 11 January 2007, the sentence was issued, marking the first time on the continent of Africa that representatives of a regime were investigated and prosecuted before a national court (Jallow and Bensouda 2008: 28).

Article 281 of the 1957 Ethiopian Penal Code refers to genocide as a crime against humanity. It further provides wider protection than that afforded under the Convention on the Prevention and Punishment of the Crime of Genocide 1948 (hereinafter the Genocide Convention). Article 2 of the Genocide Convention defines genocide as undertaking certain conducts 'with intent to destroy, in whole or in part, a national, ethnical, racial or religious group'. The elimination of political groups, population transfer or dispersion are excluded from protection under the Convention. Hence, Article 281 goes beyond the scope of the protection provided by the Genocide Convention. The provision considers genocide and crimes against humanity to be the same offences. In fact, genocide is described as a crime against humanity. Therefore, prohibited forms of conduct such as the elimination of political groups, population transfer or dispersion that would not normally amount to genocide are incorporated into Article 281, consequently making the scope of protection of human rights in Ethiopia wider. The Ethiopian national courts were able to successfully prosecute the international crimes due to the existence of political will by the Ethiopian government to hold accountable those who were responsible for the atrocities. However, the fact that the trials were conducted *in absentia* raises a number of concerns about their credibility, particularly with reference to protection of the rights of the accused during the trial.

Apart from the Ethiopian example, ICL was applied in Africa prior to the adoption of the Rome Statute in Rwanda. Prosecutions were undertaken in the Rwandan national courts and *gacaca* courts following the genocide in 1994. The majority of the Rwandan genocide suspects were tried in Rwanda. Twenty-six years after the genocide, Rwandan courts have continued to prosecute suspects for genocide-related cases. More recently, trials have been conducted in the High Court Specialised Chamber for International Crimes and the Supreme Court for Rwanda. On 21 November 2018, genocide convict Charles Bandora appealed against his 30-year sentence for genocide before the Supreme Court in Kigali, Rwanda.[3] The High Court Specialised Chamber found him guilty of genocide in May 2015, following his extradition from Norway in 2013. This decision is significant because it illustrates the application of ICL by a national court in relation to offences that were committed before the creation and entry into force of the Rome Statute. This is a classic example of national courts effectively implementing ICL in a nation that is not a state party to the Rome Statute. It highlights the importance of putting an end to the culture of impunity for international crimes by ensuring that individuals are held accountable for any alleged offences.

The continent has also witnessed the creation of special tribunals. These include the International Criminal Tribunal for Rwanda (ICTR), which played a fundamental role in the development of ICL generally. For instance, the ICTR played a vital role in contributing to the development of the jurisprudence of international criminal justice on the subject of rape as an international crime for the first time in history of international justice, as illustrated in the decision of *Prosecutor v. Jean Pau Akayesu.*[4] This illustrates Africa's active contribution of international criminal justice.

Recently the African Union (AU) and Senegal have undertaken an active role in ensuring the prosecution of Hissène Habré, the former President of Chad from 1982 to 1990 at a national level and on the basis of universal jurisdiction. This is despite that fact that Senegal only proceeded to prosecute Habré after the ruling of the ICJ in the case *Belgium v. Senegal*,[5] in which the court considered questions relating to Senegal's obligations to prosecute or extradite. The decision made it clear that Senegal was obliged to either prosecute or extradite Habré. This decision is a triumph for Africa as Senegal and the AU proceeded to sign an agreement on 22 August 2012 establishing the Extraordinary African Chambers as part of the courts of Senegal (Fall 2014: 117). This issue is considered in depth elsewhere in this volume;[6] however, in the context of this chapter, the exercise of universal jurisdiction for the first time by an African state is a great achievement for the African continent. It is a step towards addressing the culture of impunity that has confronted the continent for decades. It also provides an example for African states to emulate and ensure former leaders that violate fundamental human rights are held accountable within their national courts. It further illustrates African potential and capacity to prosecute international crimes.

Sierra Leone also carried out prosecutions for international crimes involving murder on the basis of domestic law. The trials involved 88 individuals who

3 *The New Times*, 22 November 2018.
4 *Prosecutor v. Jean Pau Akayesu*, Case No. ICTR 96-4-1, Judgment of 2 September 1998.
5 *Belgium v. Senegal*, ICJ, Judgment of 20 July 2012.
6 See 'The Application of Universal Jurisdiction in Africa' by O'Brien Kaaba.

had allegedly committed such offences during the armed conflict. Also in Sierra Leone, individuals have been tried for international crimes relating to the use of child soldiers during periods of armed conflict before the Special Court of Sierra Leone (SCSL), which was established pursuant to Security Council Resolution 1315 of 14 August 2000. The SCSL has been instrumental in the development of ICL, particularly by clarifying that the act of recruiting child soldiers amounts to a war crime and is contrary to international humanitarian law. This was established in the Court's first decision in *Prosecutor v. Sam Hinga Norman.*[7] Subsequently, away from the SCSL, the prohibition on the recruitment of child soldiers has been reaffirmed in the ICC context in Article 8(2)(b)(xxvi) and (c)(vii) of the Rome Statute and the decision in *Prosecutor v. Thomas Lubanga Dyilo.*[8]

5. INCORPORATION OF THE ROME STATUTE CRIMES BY SELECTED AFRICAN COUNTRIES

Following the adoption of the Rome Statute, some states have proceeded to adopt measures intended to implement it into their national legal systems. This section considers the use of ICL in Uganda, Kenya and South Africa, following the incorporation of the Rome Statute into domestic law. As addressed above, the application of the principle of complementarity in practice implies that states must take responsibility for prosecuting individuals suspected of having committed Rome Statute offences. Complementarity implies that there is need for states to ensure individuals who commit the most serious offences are prosecuted. In the absence of prosecutions in national courts, the ICC can intervene to prosecute the most serious perpetrators, implying that there is a danger of less serious perpetrators escaping with impunity, mainly if states parties do not take up their responsibility to prosecute or if they fail to cooperate with the ICC. The ICC is unable to prosecute all suspects of international crimes and nor was the intention for it to do so. Hence, national legal systems of states parties to the Rome Statute need to do more to address past human rights violations and to ensure they are not repeated. An evaluation of how these states have proceeded to integrate the Rome Statute into their domestic systems follows.

---

7 *Prosecutor v. Sam Hinga Norman*, Decision on Preliminary Motion Based on Lack of Jurisdiction (Child Recruitment), Case No. SCSL-2004-14-AR72(E), Special Court for Sierra Leone, 31 May 2004, available at: https://www.refworld.org/cases,SCSL,49abc0a22.html.

8 *Situation in the Democratic Republic of the Congo, in the case of the Prosecutor v. Thomas Lubanga Dyilo*, ICC-01/04-01/06, International Criminal Court (ICC), 14 March 2012, available at: https://www.refworld.org/cases,ICC,4f69a2db2.html.

5.1. SOUTH AFRICA

South Africa became the first state to fully implement the Rome Statute in Africa on 18 July 2002, just after the entry into force of the Rome Statute (Kemp 2014: 66) The Rome Statute was incorporated into South African law by the Implementation of the Rome Statute of the International Criminal Court Act 27 of 2002 (hereinafter the ICC Act 2002). The Act integrates the crime of genocide, war crimes and crimes against humanity directly into South African law as defined by the Rome Statue. The incorporation of the Rome Statute implies that South African Court can now exercise jurisdiction over the ICC crimes in line with the complementarity principle. Prior to the ICC Act 2002, South Africa had no municipal law on the subject of war crimes or crimes against humanity, and no domestic prosecutions of international crimes had taken place in South Africa (du Plessis 2012: 25). Ten years after the adoption of the ICC Act 2002, South Africa proceeded to implement the Geneva Conventions of 1949 by adopting the Geneva Conventions Act, 2012 into its national legal system. Like the Rome Statute, the Geneva Conventions deals with the international crimes within the ICC's jurisdiction. Therefore, South Africa now has adequate systems and personnel for the prosecution of international crimes.

South Africa has had an opportunity to apply international law and ICL in its jurisdiction in a number of cases relating to its duty to arrest a sitting head of state subject to ICC arrest warrants for war crimes, crimes against humanity and genocide in *Southern African Litigation Centre v. Minister of Justice and Constitutional Development and Others*.[9] The case involved al-Bashir's visit to South Africa. The issue was contentious because of South Africa's obligation at national level, with reference to section 4(1) of the ICC Act 2002, and at international level, in accordance with Article 27 of the Rome Statute. Both provisions provide that no person, regardless of his/her position, would be exempted from criminal responsibility. Max du Plessis argues that the ICC Act 2002 is an indication of South Africa's 'support of the International Criminal Court system, and shows that the country is responding to the world public's demand for a stand on genocide, crimes against humanity, and war crimes', but notes that the Act's eventual 'success lies not in the strength of its internal provisions, but on the external will of the Government to use the Act to full effect against international criminals' (du Plessis 2012: 24). This proposition suggests that the application of ICL in Africa depends on the political will of the government of the day. However, this chapter argues that more needs to be done in terms of the sensitisation of the people on the importance of fundamental human rights and the need to ensure that perpetrators of crimes under the

9 *Southern African Litigation Centre v. Minister of Justice and Constitutional Development and Others* [2015] Case No. 27740/2015.

Rome Statute are held accountable. The course on ICL must be incorporated into all higher learning institutions. Students must be exposed to Africa's role in ICL generally and especially the need for states to undertake their role to prosecute suspects of international crime.

Similarly, in *Southern Africa Litigation Centre and Others v. National Director of Public Prosecutions and Others*,[10] also known as the *Zimbabwe Torture Docket case*, allegations of torture as a crime against humanity were made against Zimbabwean officials. The Supreme Court of South Africa seized the opportunity to consider the duties of South Africa in the context of its obligations under the Rome Statute (Kemp 2014: 67). The decision illustrates the capacity of African national courts to handle international crimes. The decision marks the first time that a national court in Africa engaged in the direct interpretation and application of the Rome Statute and the appropriate implementing legislation.

However, holding perpetrators of international crimes to account must never depend on the government of the day. Conducting trials of international crimes in national courts can contribute towards ensuring deterrence of similar offences on the African continent and beyond, as well as installing values of respect for individual accountability, the rule of law and human rights. International criminal law must be taught to all key players within the criminal justice system of every state. So far these values have not been realised on the continent, as evident by the number of crimes that are committed and as seen in the trials conducted.

5.2. UGANDA

This section illustrates how ICL has been employed in Uganda as a state party to the Rome Statute. It demonstrates how Uganda has incorporated the offences that fall within the ICC's jurisdiction into its national laws and how its national courts have used these laws to ensure perpetrators of past human rights violations are held accountable. Applying the principle of complementarity to the situation in Uganda implies that it is obliged to prosecute any suspect of international crimes. Ideally, trials must be conducted in Ugandan national courts and, as a last resort, before the ICC.

Uganda ratified the Rome Statute in June 2002. However, it was only incorporated into Ugandan law by the International Crimes Act No. 11 of 2010 (hereinafter the ICC Act 2010) and entered into force on 25 June 2010. The courts in Uganda now have jurisdiction over the core crimes since 2002,

10 *Southern African Litigation Centre and Another v. National Director of Public Prosecutions and Others* (77150/09) [2012] ZAGPPHC 61; 2012 (10) BCLR 1089 (GNP); [2012] 3 All SA 198 (GNP) (8 May 2012).

and given that most atrocities that have occurred in Uganda were committed between 1986 to 2002, the ICC Act 2010 cannot be used to prosecute crimes committed in that period. This implies that a different Act or measure would need to be implemented to ensure that individuals responsible for past atrocities are held to account.

The ICC Act 2010 therefore implements Uganda's assumed obligations to criminalise offences within the Rome Statute in Uganda.[11] Apart from incorporating the core crimes, the Act also stipulates punishments for the crimes. The ICC Act 2010 empowers Uganda with the capacity to investigate and prosecute perpetrators of international crimes in cooperation with the ICC where necessary. The High Court of Uganda is vested with the responsibility to try, convict and sentence individuals who have committed genocide, war crimes and crimes against humanity (Article 2(g) of the ICC Act 2010). Thus, Uganda has a sufficient legal framework that allows for the prosecution of international crimes perpetrators in national courts. Article 18 of the ICC Act 2010 provides that courts also have jurisdiction over offences committed elsewhere if the alleged perpetrator: (a) is a citizen or permanent resident of Uganda; (b) is employed by Uganda in a civilian or military capacity; (c) has committed an offence against a citizen or permanent resident of Uganda (the principle of passive personality); or (d) is present in Uganda following the commission of the offence. Ugandan courts can thus exercise territorial, passive nationality or universal jurisdiction under the ICC Act 2010. This is progressive as Ugandan courts enjoy a broad jurisdiction to prosecute international crimes compared to the ICC whose jurisdiction can only be triggered under strict circumstances. This includes a referral to the court by either the Security Council, a self-referral by a state party to the Rome Statute or the initiation of the investigation based on the prosecutor's discretion (Article 13 of the Rome Statute).

The offence of genocide is addressed in Article 7 of the ICC Act 2010. Accordingly, the Ugandan courts have territorial and universal jurisdiction over any person suspected of the offence of genocide. Article 7 of the ICC Act 2010 refers to Article 6 of the Rome Statute for the definition of genocide. Genocide is defined as acts directed towards members of the group when committed with an intent to destroy, in whole or in part, a national, ethnical, racial or religious group.

Examples of such acts include killing, causing serious bodily or mental harm directed towards members of the group, deliberately inflicting on the group conditions of life calculated to bring about its physical destruction in whole or in part imposing measures intended to prevent births within the group, or forcibly transferring children of the group to another group.[12] The definition of genocide

[11] Article 2 ICC Act 2010.

[12] Article 7 ICC Act 2010.

provided in the Statute is exactly the same as that in Article II of the Genocide Convention, which has been criticised for being too narrow. The definition has come to be accepted as constituting customary international law.

Genocide can be established by proving the commission of any of the five acts addressed above, and the mental element of intent to destroy in whole or in part either a national, ethnic, racial or religious group. It is this special specific intent that distinguishes the offence of genocide from other offences, such as war crimes or crimes against humanity. In the absence of specific intent, an accused cannot be convicted of genocide, but only of crimes against humanity. The punishment for genocide or conspiring to commit the offence is imprisonment for life or a lesser term. The ICC Act 2010 provides the same penalty for all these three offences. The implication is that the three offences are regarded as being equal in terms of seriousness. The definition of genocide adopted under the ICC Act 2010 is yet to be interpreted and applied by the Ugandan courts. It remains to be seen how the courts will interpret the various elements that constitute genocide.

Crimes against humanity are considered in Article 8 of the ICC Act 2010. Like genocide, the ICC Act 2010 adopts the same definition as that provided under Article 7 of the Rome Statute. Article 7 begins with a chapeau or exploratory paragraph stating that 'for the purposes of this statute, "crime against humanity" means any of the following acts when committed as part of a widespread or systematic attack directed against any civilian population, with knowledge of the attack'. As in the case for genocide, there is a threshold that needs to be met in order for the offence to constitute crimes against humanity. It is necessary to prove that the offence committed was widespread or systematic. Unlike the offence of genocide, which requires specific intent to be established, for crimes against humanity, it is only necessary to establish that the perpetrator was aware that his or her actions were part of widespread or systematic attacks. In the absence of knowledge, it is not possible to secure a conviction for crimes against humanity. Instead, the accused can be convicted for war crimes. Any person convicted of this offence would be sentenced to imprisonment for life or a lesser term (Article 8 of the ICC Act 2010).

Article 9 of the ICC Act 2010 provides for criminal liability for any person convicted of having committed war crimes on the territory of Uganda or elsewhere since the time the Act came into force (i.e. June 2010). For the purposes of this provision, a war crime is defined as any conduct listed in Article 8(2) of the Rome Statute, which is similar to the list of grave breaches under the Geneva Conventions Act. The ICC Act 2010 uses the definition of war crimes in Article 8(2)(a) of the Rome Statute, which is the same as that provided under the Geneva Conventions. Like the Rome Statute definition, the ICC Act 2010 covers war crimes committed during international armed conflicts (IAC) and non-international armed conflicts (NIAC). Article 9(4) of the ICC Act further acknowledges that nothing in this provision alters the effect of section 2 of the Geneva Conventions Act, which makes grave breaches of the Geneva Conventions an offence under Ugandan law. This implies that prior to the adoption of the ICC Act 2010, war crimes had already been incorporated into the Ugandan legal system.

The ICC Act 2010 acknowledges general principles of criminal law, such as the notion that criminal proceedings cannot be initiated where the accused has already been acquitted or convicted (Article 19). This is the principle of *ne bis in idem* and is in line with Article 20 of the Rome Statute. Other principles included in the Act include the principle of individual criminal responsibility[13] and the exclusion of jurisdiction over persons under the age of 18.[14] In addition, the accused person may rely on any defence available under the laws of Uganda or international law, regardless of whether it is justificatory or excusatory in nature.

This further illustrates the comprehensive Ugandan legal structure that provides for international crimes, an indication that the Ugandan legal system has the relevant laws to actively prosecute international crimes in the national courts. The punishment for war crimes under the Act is imprisonment for life or a lesser term. A lesser term of imprisonment can be imposed for grave breaches that do not involve wilful killing of persons protected under the Geneva Conventions Act, which permits a term of imprisonment no longer than 14 years. War crimes have been regarded as an offence in Uganda since 1964 and yet no person has ever been held accountable under the ICC Act 2010. Nobody was held liable for the violence during the tenure in power of Idi Amin and more recently the violence of the LRA. This is despite Uganda having a functional effective legal framework and personnel that have the capacity to facilitate the prosecution of such offences. Perhaps the vital question is why Uganda has persistently failed to prosecute perpetrators of international crimes despite having adequate laws in place. The crimes under the Rome Statute are also criminalised under the Geneva Conventions of 12 August 1949, which are discussed below.

5.2.1. The Geneva Conventions Act 1964

Uganda ratified the Geneva Conventions of 12 August 1949 and incorporated them into domestic law via the Geneva Conventions Act.[15] The Act has been in force since 16 October 1964. The key issues considered by the Act include grave breaches of the Conventions, notice of prosecution, matters relating to legal representation, appeals, reduction of sentences, custody of protected persons and interpretation. Of relevance to this chapter are the types of

---

13 In line with Article 25 of the Rome Statute.

14 In accordance with Article 26 of the Rome Statute.

15 Chapter 363 of the Laws of Uganda.

conduct prohibited under the Act, Uganda's obligations that arise by virtue of having ratified and incorporated the Geneva Convention and the implication thereof.

According to section 2 of the Geneva Conventions Act, persons suspected of committing international crimes referred to as grave breaches in the Geneva Conventions can be investigated, arrested and prosecuted by the Ugandan courts, regardless of their nationality. Section 2 of the Geneva Conventions Act confers universal jurisdiction on Ugandan courts to prosecute grave breaches of the Geneva Conventions, regardless of where they are committed. Persons who commit grave breaches that involve the wilful killing of protected persons would be liable to life imprisonment upon conviction (section 2(1)(e) of the Geneva Conventions Act). For any other grave breaches, the penalty is imprisonment for a term not exceeding 14 years (section 2(1)(f) of the Geneva Conventions Act). In the Supreme Court decision on amnesty in the case of *Uganda v. Thomas Kwoyelo*,[16] it was held that Uganda as a state party to the Geneva Conventions is obliged to investigate, arrest and prosecute perpetrators as long as they are guaranteed a fair trial in the courts of law. However, grave breaches as established under section 2 of the Geneva Conventions Act can only be prosecuted if committed in an IAC and not in a NIAC. Offences that are committed during a NIAC can be prosecuted on the basis of Article 3 common to the Geneva Conventions. Thus, section 3(1) of the Geneva Conventions Act establishes an obligation for states, and particularly Uganda, to prosecute those suspected of having committed grave breaches which are international crimes in both IAC and NIAC. Thus, Uganda has adequate laws to allow for the prosecution of such individuals.

5.2.2. *The International Crimes Division of the High Court*

The International Crimes Division (ICD) of the High Court of Uganda, formerly known as the Special War Crimes Division, was established by a principal judge, Justice James Ogoola, pursuant to the then Article 141 of the Constitution of the Republic of Uganda 1995[17] (the Constitution) for the purpose of prosecuting international crimes. It was remodelled in May 2011, when the Chief Justice proceeded to issue the ICD Practice Directions. It is the only court authorised to adjudicate international crimes in Uganda. It was created in order to comply with the ICC's complementarity regime, and its creation is a sign that Uganda is taking measures to prosecute the atrocities committed within its territory

16 Constitutional Appeal No. 1 of 2012 [2015] UGSC 5 (8 April 2015) paragraphs 25–30.

17 The 1995 Constitution has since been amended a number of times, however, the amendments are incorporated in the Constitution (Amendment) Act 2005 and the Constitution (Amendment) (No. 2) Act 2005. Note that the 1995 Constitution still remains in force.

in line with the Preamble and Article 17 of the Rome Statute. The ICD has jurisdiction over international crimes, particularly war crimes, crimes against humanity, genocide, terrorism, human trafficking, piracy, drug trafficking and other transnational crimes (section 6 of the ICD Practice Directions). It also has jurisdiction over any other international crimes stipulated in other relevant national legislation.[18] It is thus vested with broad jurisdiction to handle a wide range of offences.

The ICD is composed of three High Court judges and a unit in the Department of Public Prosecutions (DPP), with a mandate to investigate and prosecute international crimes. It is located in Kololo in Kampala, the capital city of Uganda. However, the trial of the former LRA commander Thomas Kwoyelo, also known as Latoni, was conducted in Gulu in Northern Uganda, where the atrocities were committed.[19] The case of Thomas Kwoyelo has come before various domestic courts prior to proceeding to the ICD. The pertinent issues raised at various stages are summarised below.

5.2.3. First Instance Before the ICD

The first international crimes trial before the ICD is *Uganda v. Thomas Kwoyelo alias Latoni*[20] Former LRA commander Thomas Kwoyelo was apprehended by the Uganda Peoples' Defence Forces (UPDF) in March 2009 in Garamba National Park in the Democratic Republic of the Congo (DRC). He was later returned to Uganda, where he was held in custody for nearly two years prior to his indictment. While in detention in the Upper Prison, Luzira, on 12 January 2010 he made a pronouncement before an officer in charge of the prison that he was giving up his rebellion and would seek amnesty. The declaration was submitted to the Amnesty Commission under the Amnesty Act 2000. Section 3 of the Amnesty Act confers discretion on the DPP to certify whether a detained applicant qualifies for amnesty and subsequent release. However, the DPP never responded to the application, instead focusing on the criminal charges against Kwoyelo that were before the Chief Magistrate's Court in Kampala. Kwoyelo was charged with war crimes pursuant to Article 147 of the Fourth Geneva Convention and other alternative charges under the Penal Code Act. He was subsequently referred to the ICD for trial.

On the first day of the trial, a constitutional reference challenging the charges was filed on the following basis. First, the question was whether the failure by

---

18 Chapter 120 of the Penal Code Act, the Geneva Conventions Act, the ICC Act or any penal law. Other applicable laws include the Constitution of the Republic of Uganda 1995 (as amended), Chapter 23 of the Trial on Indictment Act, Chapter 6 of the Evidence Act, the Judicature (High Court) (ICD) Rules 2016 and the High Court (ICD) Practice Directions.

19 The case is still ongoing, but it has since been adjourned amidst the COVID-19 pandemic.

20 HCD-00-ICC Case No. 02/2010 2011 Uganda Amended Indictment 1–25, 2011.

the DPP and the Amnesty Commission to grant Kwoyelo a certificate of amnesty constituted discrimination, contrary to Article 21 of the Constitution, which guarantees equal protection under the law. The contention was that other more senior LRA commanders such as Kenneth Banya and Sam Kolo, who were apprehended in similar circumstances to the respondent, had been granted certificates of amnesty. Second, the question was whether Kwoyelo's indictment under Article 147 of the Geneva Conventions Act for alleged crimes committed between 1993 and 2005 was contrary to Ugandan Law.[21] On this basis, the respondent argued that the crimes for which he had been indicted permitted him to qualify for amnesty under the Amnesty Act 2000.

5.2.4. Second Instance Before the Constitutional Court

The matter went on appeal to the Supreme Court of Uganda, where the issue of the constitutionality of the Amnesty Act 2000 was raised. For that reason, the Constitutional Court had to make a determination with regard to the following: first, whether the failure by the DPP and the Amnesty Commission to process Kwoyelo's application for a certificate of amnesty, even though such certificates had previously been given to other persons in comparable situations, was discriminatory; second, whether this constituted an infringement of, and was contrary to, Articles 1, 2, 20(2), 21(1) and (3), of the 1995 Constitution of Uganda; third, whether prosecuting Kwoyelo under Article 147 of the Fourth Geneva Conventions Act[22] for crimes purportedly committed in Uganda between 1993 and 2005 was inconsistent with, and in violation of, Articles 1, 2, 8(a) and 287 of the 1995 Constitution, and Objectives 1 and XXVIII(b) of the National Objectives and Directive Principles of State Policy contained in the 1995 Constitution; and, lastly, whether the apparent detention of Kwoyelo in the isolated home of an unidentified official of the Chieftaincy of Military Intelligence (CMI) was in breach of, and inconsistent with, Articles 1, 2, 4(b), 23(3), 24 and 44(a) of the 1995 Constitution.

The Constitutional Court ruled that the Amnesty Act did not remove the DPP's right to conduct prosecutions independently. The DPP was thus at liberty to prosecute anyone who had not been granted amnesty, had declined to give up rebellion or was suspected of having committed grave violations.[23] Most importantly, the Court contended that the Ugandan national legal system did not provide for a blanket amnesty with no possibility of prosecution. In addition,

---

21 The Constitution of Uganda and the National Objectives and Directive Principles of State Policy.

22 Chapter 363 of the Laws of Uganda.

23 *Thomas Kwoyelo v. Uganda*, Constitutional Court of Uganda, Constitutional Petition No. 036/11, Judgment of 22 September 2011.

the Court observed that while Uganda had observed treaty law, there were no clear international standards and practices forbidding states from granting of amnesties. However, the recent proliferation of institutions created for the purposes of prosecuting perpetrators of international crimes – in particular, the establishment of the ICC, which seeks to address the problem of impunity and to serve a deterrent purpose for would-be offenders of such atrocities – indicated that suspects must always be held accountable. Notwithstanding these facts, the Constitutional Court held that the applicant had attained a legal right to be granted amnesty under the Amnesty Act, and that the Amnesty Commission and the DPP had failed to accord him equal treatment under the Act. This conduct was thus contrary to Article 21(1) and (2) of the Constitution. The Constitutional Court's action in upholding Kwoyelo's reference formed the basis for the Attorney General's appeal of the decision to the Supreme Court.

5.2.5. Appeal Before the Supreme Court

The new Supreme Court decision found that the Amnesty Act was limited to persons having committed political acts such as treason, or those aiding treason or other offences; it did not extend to those suspected of having committed the international crimes. This decision overturned the findings of the Constitutional Court and permitted the ICD to carry out its mandate to prosecute the accused. In making its determination, the Supreme Court had to consider three issues: whether the Amnesty Act conflicted with the Constitution of Uganda on the basis that it undermined the prosecutorial powers of the DPP; whether the Amnesty Act was inconsistent with the Constitution of Uganda, as well as with Uganda's obligations under international law, on the basis that it sought to grant a blanket amnesty for all offences, including those under the Geneva Conventions; and, finally, whether the respondent was discriminated against in a manner contrary to the Constitution.

The Supreme Court concluded that the Amnesty Act does not grant amnesty for all offences, nor does it contravene Uganda's international obligations. The Supreme Court's decision means that the Amnesty Act does not in any way bar the DPP from exercising his/her powers to initiate criminal proceedings against the accused. The discretion as to whether or not to prosecute is thus vested solely in the DPP. Reference was made to Article 120 of the Constitution, which establishes the office of the DPP, and it was clarified that the provision not only empowers the DPP to institute criminal proceedings against any person, but also provides that he/she is not subject to the direction, control or authority of any other person. It also clarified that the provisions of the Amnesty Act cannot override clear provisions of the Constitution, which is the supreme law in accordance with Article 2 of the Constitution. The Supreme Court further dismissed Kwoyelo's contention that failure to grant him amnesty amounted to discrimination because more senior LRA commanders had been granted amnesty, on the basis that there was no evidence about the nature of the offences for which they were granted amnesty. The indictment was deemed not to be discriminatory pursuant to Article 120 of the Constitution and section 3(2) of the Amnesty Act, as amended.

The Supreme Court decision is fundamental in clarifying a number of issues with regard to the prosecution of international crimes in Uganda. First, the decision explains that the Amnesty Act does not offer a blanket amnesty to all persons responsible for the commission of international crimes. This implies that the prosecution of Kwoyelo constitutes a positive precedent in the fight against immunity in Uganda. The expectation is that more individuals will be tried for serious human rights violations before the ICD. The case further reaffirms the power of the DPP under the Constitution.

5.2.6. *The Second Instance International Crimes Division*

The charges in *Uganda v. Thomas Kwoyelo alias Latoni*[24] were confirmed on 30 August 2018 by Judge Susan Okalany, who concluded, on the basis of evidence presented by the prosecution, that there were substantial grounds to believe that Kwoyelo was responsible for the charges brought against him in the indictment. On that basis, the accused was referred for trial before the ICD. The indictment against the accused contained 93 counts of charges based on CIL, and domestic charges in the alternative that would be relied upon following the failure to secure a conviction on the basis of the first charge under customary international law. The customary international law charges included the crimes against humanity of murder, enslavement, rape, torture, imprisonment and other inhumane forms of conduct that constitutes violations of Article 3 common to the Geneva Conventions and the Penal Code Act.

Prosecuting the accused on the basis of CIL was the only possible way to secure individual responsibility for the alleged offences. This is because the ICC Act 2010 is subject to temporal jurisdiction, which is restrictive as it would not allow for atrocities committed prior to 2010 to be tried. An indictment under CIL thus permits for the prosecution of offences allegedly committed between 1992 and 2005. The ICC is not retrospective in effect and can only be applied to offences committed after the ICC Act's entry into force. However, what is important is not the basis of the charge, but the fact that international crimes were prosecuted in national courts. The confirmation charges decision establishes that CIL is applicable to the Ugandan legal system as it does not contravene the Constitution, nor does the Constitution prohibit its application.

---

24 *Uganda v. Thomas Kwoyelo alias Latoni*, HCT – WCD-Criminal Case No. 0002 of 2010 (Arising from Criminal Case No. BUG RD. Court Case 09/2010.

Consequently, all charges under the amended indictment were confirmed and the accused went to trial. The trial began on 24 September 2018 in the ICD of the High Court sitting in Gulu. To date the trial of the former LRA commander Thomas Kwoyelo still continues.[25] Individual accountability for the offences committed between 1992 and 2005, in the Abera Village, the Parubanga Parish, Pabbo Sub country and Kilak county, which are now part of the Amuru District is yet to be established.

The year 2019 marked 11 years since the creation of the ICD of the High Court of Uganda, yet at this stage it was still trying to find its feet. Despite the Court being established for the purpose of prosecuting international crimes committed on the territory of Uganda over the last 30 years of the armed conflict, its ability to secure justice for the victims is yet to be tested by the case of Kwoyelo. This is because the verdict is yet to be pronounced.[26] So far, the ICD has only convicted six people on charges of terrorism and murder since its creation (Athumani 2018). In order for trials to be relevant, it is necessary for them to be expedited so that they can effectively contribute towards being a deterrent measure for would-be offenders and to achieve other objectives such as establishing the rule of law and a culture of respect for human rights among the people of Uganda.

5.3. KENYA

Kenya signed the Rome Statute on 11 August 1999 and proceeded to ratify it on 15 March 2005. Following the announcement of Kenya's presidential election results on 27 December 2007, both planned and spontaneous violence erupted in many parts of the country, which lasted for a period of two months. During this time, horrendous atrocities were committed, including the killings of about 1,330 people, numerous incidents of rape, the forcible displacement of 350,000 people and the injury of 3,600 people.[27] According to the Report of the Commission of Inquiry Post-Election Violence, the atrocities amounted to widespread and systematic attacks against the population and that the politicians and business leaders allegedly contributed towards the commission of the atrocities. Based on the occurrences in Kenya, the ICC Prosecutor initiated investigations *proprio motu* in March 2010. The allegations were that between

---

25 Kwoyelo, Thomas (ICD-002/2010) see Avocats San Frontieres https://www.asf.be/blog/trialobservation/kwoyelo-thomas-icd-002-2010/.

26 The case was initially adjourned to 24 March 2020, but due to the COVID-19 pandemic and strict measures introduced in Uganda to combat it, it is not clear when the trial is likely to resume.

27 Report of the Commission of Inquiry Post-Election Violence: October: 2008, the ICC OTP Press Conference: 2009.

2007 and 2008, crimes against humanity were committed during the post-election violence in Kenya. In its investigations, the ICC focused on six Kenyan provinces, namely Nairobi, North Rift Valley, Central Rift Valley, South Rift Valley, Nyanza and Western Province. An independent Commission of Inquiry (the Waki Commission), named after its President, Justice Philip Waki, was established for the purpose of determining the root causes of the post-election violence. Among the root causes of the violence was Kenya's deep-rooted culture of impunity.[28] The Commission recommended the following: the establishment of a hybrid special tribunal for Kenya with a mandate to prosecute offences committed during the post-election violence, or alternatively identifying the perpetrators of the atrocities and referring them to the ICC for the purpose of conducting further investigations and possibly trials.[29]

However, the special tribunal for Kenya was never established, as Parliament rejected the bill that was intended to establish the court. After Kenya's inaction and reluctance to hold suspected individuals accountable for the atrocities committed, on 26 November 2009 the Prosecutor, for the first time in the history of the ICC, invoked Articles 13C and 15 and sought authorisation from the Pre-Trial Chamber to initiate an investigation in Kenya.[30] The Pre-Trial Chamber II of the ICC approved the Prosecutor's request to open an investigation *proprio motu* into the situation on 31 March 2010, following its determination in accordance with Article 15(4) of the Rome Statute. It thus held that there was a reasonable basis to proceed with the investigation of apparent crimes against humanity in the territory of Kenya from 1 June 2005 to 26 November 2009.[31]

As a result, the Pre-Trial Chamber II confirmed charges and sent the following individuals to trial: William Samoei Ruto (a former Kenyan Minister of Higher Education, Science and Technology), Joshua Arap Sang (head of operations at Kass FM in Nairobi, Kenya),[32] Francis Kirimi Muthaura (former head of the civil service, secretary to the Cabinet of Kenya and Member of Parliament) and Uhuru Muigai Kenyatta (at the time, Deputy Prime Minister and former Minister of Finance).[33] A wide range of individuals were indicted, a combination of the

---

28 Ibid, 22–36.

29 Ibid, 8, 22–36, 472–475.

30 Request for Authorisation of an Investigation Pursuant to Article 15, No. ICC-01/09-3, 26 November 2009.

31 Decision Pursuant to Article 15 of the Rome Statute on the Authorization of an Investigation into the Situation in Kenya 2010.

32 *Case of the Prosecutor v. William Samoei Ruto, Henry Kiprono Kosgey and Joshua Arap Sang*, Decision on the Confirmation of Charges Pursuant to Article 61(7)(a) and (b) of the Rome Statute, No. ICC-01/09-01/11 (2012).

33 *Case of the Prosecutor v. Francis Kirimi Muthaura, Uhuru Muigai Kenyatta and Mohammed Hussein Ali*, Decision on the Confirmation of Charges Pursuant to Article 61(7)(a) and (b) of the Rome Statute, No. ICC-01/09-02/11 (2012).

most serious as well as middle-ranging level individuals in terms of seniority in the political hierarchy. Ideally, it is expected that the national courts should take active measures to prosecute the less serious suspects.

In addition, the duly elected President and Deputy President, Uhuru Kenyatta and William Ruto respectively, were deemed suspects in the investigations in accordance with the Kenyan Supreme Court's decision in *Raila Odinga and Two Others v. Independent Electoral and Boundaries Commission and Three Others*.[34]

Nonetheless, trials at the ICC were terminated following evidence of witness interference in the form of bribes and threats by the Kenyan authorities and the absence of cooperation with the ICC. The Court terminated the proceedings on the basis that there was insufficient evidence to prosecute in the case, as per decisions in *William Samoei Ruto, Joshua Arap Sang* and *Uhuru Muigai Kenyatta*.[35] Since the failed ICC trials, Kenya has attempted to incorporate the Rome statute crimes into its own national legal system. Article 2(6) of the Kenyan Constitution provides that: 'Any treaty or convention ratified by Kenya shall form part of the law of Kenya under this Constitution.' The Constitution in effect transforms the Kenyan legal system into a monist legal system. This implies that an international treaty will become enforceable in Kenya once it is ratified.

Kenya has since adopted the International Crimes Act No. 16 of 2008 (ICA 2008) which incorporates the Rome Statute into Kenyan national law. It entered into force on 1 January 2009. Under the Act, the High Court of Kenya has jurisdiction to prosecute genocide, war crimes and crimes against humanity (Article 37 of the ICA 2008). The definition and elements of these offences are consistent with the provisions of the Rome Statute (Article 5(4) of the ICA 2008). It also enables Kenya to cooperate with the ICC as it undertakes its mandate of prosecuting international offences. Like the Ugandan Act, any person who commits genocide, crimes against humanity or war crimes within Kenya or elsewhere can be held liable for international crimes (Article 6 of the ICA 2008). The provision further establishes criminal liability for a secondary perpetrator who conspires, attempts to commit the offence or counsels the perpetrator of the principal offence in the commission of the above-mentioned offences,

---

34 *Raila Odinga and Two Others v. Independent Electoral and Boundaries Commission and Three Others*, Petitions 5, 4, and 3 of 2013 [2013] eKLR (Supreme Court of Kenya judgment, 30 March 2013).

35 *Prosecutor v. William Samoei Ruto and Joshua Arap Sang*, ICC-01/09-01/11 (19 August 2015), Decision on Prosecution Request for Admission of Prior Recorded Testimony; *Prosecutor v. Uhuru Muigai Kenyatta*, ICC-01/09-02/11 OA 5 (19 August 2015); Judgment on the Prosecutor's Appeal against Trial Chamber V(B)'s Decision on Prosecution's Application for a Finding of Non-compliance under Article 87(7) of the Statute; and *Prosecutor v. William Samoei Ruto and Joshua Arap Sang*, ICC-01/09-01/11 (5 April 2016), Decision on Defence Applications for Judgments of Acquittal.

and at the time of commission of the offence is within Kenya or elsewhere (Article 6(2) of the ICA 2008). A person found guilty and convicted may be liable to imprisonment for life or for a lesser term.

The definitions of the offences of war crimes, genocide and to a large extent crimes against humanity, all have the same definitions as those provided under the Rome Statute. However, with reference to crimes against humanity, the definition goes beyond that provided under the Rome Statute by incorporating definitions of crimes against humanity under conventional international law or CIL that are not addressed in the Rome Statute. The definition allows for the retroactive application of international criminal law, as it extends to include even those offences that are not yet crimes against humanity under CIL (Article 6(4) of the ICA 2008).

Article 7 of the ICA 2008 incorporates the fundamental principles of criminal law addressed under the Rome Statute into Kenyan law, such as the principles of *ne bis in idem* (Article 20 of the Rome Statute), *nullum crimen sine lege* (Article 22), the concept of individual criminal responsibility (Article 25) and the exclusion of jurisdiction for persons under the age of 18 (Article 26). The Act further addresses issues in relation to commander responsibility and superiors (Article 28 of the Rome Statute) and other key issues such as mistakes of fact or law, superior orders and prescription of law (Article 32). In addition, the Act allows the application of the provisions of Kenyan law and the principles of criminal law pertinent to the offence under Kenyan law. As in Uganda, any person charged with an offence may rely on any justification, excuse or defence available under Kenyan law or under international law (Article 7(2) of the ICA). Despite the existence of a sound legal framework, no one has been held accountable for international crimes in Kenya, not even in relation to the post-election violence of 2007 and 2008. Currently, there are no matters before the Kenyan national courts relating to international crimes.

The High Court of Kenya has the jurisdiction to try any person for international crimes (Article 8(2) of the ICA 2008) on the following grounds: (i) if the act or omission is committed in Kenya; (ii) if it was committed by a Kenyan citizen or a person employed by the Kenyan government; (iii) if the suspect is a citizen of a state that was engaged in an armed conflict against Kenya or Kenya's allies; or (iv) if the victim of the alleged offence was a Kenyan citizen. There are thus a number of grounds on which the Court can exercise jurisdiction over international crimes, including the most common modes, territorial jurisdiction, passive personality jurisdiction and universal jurisdiction, as acknowledged in Article 6 of the ICA 2008. Prosecution of international crimes can only proceed in Kenya if the suspect is present in Kenya. Recently, there have been proposals to establish an International Crimes Division (ICD) of the High Court of Kenya. This follows an announcement to establish the ICD which was made by the Chief Justice of the Kenya Judiciary in April 2013 (Kaberia 2013). It will have jurisdiction over the Rome Statute offences, that is, genocide, crimes against humanity and war crimes, as well as transnational crimes such as organised crime, piracy, terrorism, wildlife crimes, cybercrime, human trafficking, money laundering and counterfeiting.[36] In order to ensure that perpetrators of international crimes are tried in domestic courts, it is vital for Kenya to have the necessary measures in place. However, seven years since the proposition was made, the ICD has not been established in Kenya.

Despite having the adequate laws in place such as the ICA 2008, Kenya has failed to prosecute international crimes in its national courts. Asaala (2016: 31) describes Kenya's experience in trying to prosecute crimes against humanity in national courts as having resulted in several challenges, including 'the jurisdictional question, inadequate investigations by police, inadequate competencies and human, technical resources, lack of legitimacy and local ownership, lack of political will and the influence of international politics informed by the ICC-related cases'. She argues that the attempts to prosecute the key perpetrators of the atrocities in Kenya led to the national prosecution being what she refers to as 'deeply compromised.' Like Uganda, the ICA 2008 cannot apply retrospectively as it would be contrary to the fundamental principles of legality *nullum crimen, nulla poena sine lege*.[37] However, this seems to be simply an excuse – if the political will was there to pursue the perpetrators of the post-election violence in Kenya, means to hold them accountable would have been devised. This is because states as sovereign entities have the capacity to pass laws as appropriate and recourse can also be made to ICL, as illustrated in the case of *Kwoyelo*.[38] This includes passing relevant laws for the purposes of holding post-election violence perpetrators to account. The only problem is that usually individuals in leadership positions are involved in the actual commission of these offences. This provides another reason why it is necessary to inculcate the values of respect for human rights, the rule of law, and individual accountability among the people of Kenya and beyond.

6. CONCLUSION

This chapter has considered the use of ICL in Africa prior to the adoption of the Rome Statute and subsequently. It has demonstrated how certain African states have applied ICL within their national legal systems. It further considers the incorporation of the Rome Statute in three different states. It indicates that the states under consideration – South Africa, Uganda and Kenya – do indeed have the relevant legislation to allow for the prosecution of international crimes.

---

36 Kaberia, Judie, 'Mutunga sets up an International Crimes Division', available at https://www.capitalfm.co.ke/news/2013/04/mutunga-sets-up-an-international-crimes-division.

37 See also Article 22 of the Rome Statute.

38 See above.

However, there is a need to go beyond the mere incorporation of the Rome Statute and to inculcate the advantages of ensuring individual responsibility for international crimes. Despite having the relevant legal framework required to ensure the prosecution of international crimes, the national courts have yet to secure a conviction for these offences. This chapter has revealed that the prosecution of international crimes is normally hindered by a lack of political will to prosecute, international crimes forming part of state crimes, ignorance on the importance of respecting the rule of law and respect for human rights. In order to avoid the intervention of the ICC in African states, more needs to be done to arraign individuals for the most serious offences of international concern. There is a need for African states as well as other key players in the criminal justice systems to enhance the dissemination of ICL in education generally. International criminal law must be made mandatory and offered as part of training for students of law, politics, magistrates, judges, the police and other security and defence services. This chapter has argued that it is essential to inculcate values that encourage respect of human rights in order to deal with the deep-rooted culture of impunity and to ensure that perpetrators of such offences are held accountable in national courts.

BIBLIOGRAPHY

Asaala, E.O (2016) 'Prosecuting Crimes Related to the 2007 Post-Election Violence in Kenyan Courts: Issues and Challenges' in H.J. Van der Merwe and G. Kemp (eds), *International Criminal Justice in Africa: Issues, Challenges and Prospects*. Nairobi: Strathmore University Press, pp. 27–46.

Athumani, H. (2018) 'Uganda's International Crimes Division Struggling', https://www.voanews.com/a/uganda-s-international-crimes-division-struggles-10-years-after-creation/4396361.html.

Bekou, O. (2017) 'National Implementation of the ICC Statute to Prosecute International Crimes in Africa', in C.C. Jalloh and I. Bantekas (eds), *The International Criminal Court and Africa*. Oxford: Oxford University Press, pp. 272–288.

Carey, H.F. and Mitchell, S.M. (2013) *Trials and Tribulations of International Prosecution*. Lanham, MD: Lexington Books.

Commission of Inquiry on Human Rights in Eritrea, Thirty-Second Session, Agenda Item 4, Human Rights Situations that Require the Council's Attention's, UN Doc. A/HRC/32/CRP.1 (8 June 2016).

Du Plessis, M. (2007) 'South Africa's Implementation of the ICC Statute', *Journal of International Criminal Justice* 5: 460–479.

Fall, M. (2014) 'The Extraordinary African Chambers: the Case of *Hissène Habré*' in G. Werle et al. (eds), *Africa and the International Criminal Court, International Criminal Justice Series Volume 1*. The Hague: Springer/Asser Press.

Horovitz, S. (2009) 'Sierra Leone: Interaction between International and National Responses to the Mass Atrocities', *3 DOMAC*, December 2009, at p. 26, https://en.ru.is/media/domac/DOMAC3-SH-corr.pdf.

Human Rights Committee (2018) 'Sudan Concluding observations', CCPR/C/SDN/CO/5.
Human Rights Watch (2012) 'Justice for Serious Crimes before National Courts: Uganda's International Crimes Division', http://www.hrw.org/sites/default/files/reports/uganda 0112ForUpload_0.pdf.
Jalloh, C.C. and Bantekas, I. (eds) (2017) *The International Criminal Court and Africa*. Oxford: Oxford University Press.
Jallow, H. and Bensouda, F. (2008) 'International Criminal Law in an African Context' in M. du Plessis (ed.), *African Guide to International Criminal Justice*. Pretoria: Institute for Security Studies, pp. 15–53.
Kaberia, J. (2013) 'Mutunga sets up an International Crimes Division', https://www.capitalfm.co.ke/news/2013/04/mutunga-sets-up-an-international-crimes-division.
Kebreab, I.W. (2017) 'The Development of Criminal Law and Criminal Justice in Africa from Pre-Colonial Rule to the Present Day', in C.C. Jalloh and I. Bantekas (eds), *The International Criminal Court and Africa*. Oxford: Oxford University Press, pp. 247–271.
Kemp, G. (2012) 'Implementing at National Level the Amendments to the Rome Statute of the International Criminal Court with Respect to the Crime of Aggression: A South African Perspective' in K. Ambos and O.A. Maunganidze (eds), *Power and Prosecution Challenges and Opportunities for International Criminal Justice in Sub-Saharan Africa*. Göttingen: Universitätsverlag Göttingen, pp. 39–56.
Kemp, G. (2014) 'The Implementation of the Rome Statute' in G. Werle et al. (eds), *Africa and the International Criminal Court, International Criminal Justice Series Volume 1*. The Hague: Springer/Asser Press, pp. 61–78.
Kihika, K.S and Regue, M. (2015) 'Pursuing Accountability for Serious Crimes in Uganda's Courts' International Centre of Transitional Justice', *Briefing*, https://www.ictj.org/publication/pursuing-accountability-serious-crimes-uganda.
Kleffner, J.K. (2008) *Complementarity in the Rome Statute and National Criminal Jurisdictions*. Oxford: Oxford University Press.
McNamara, K. (2013) 'Seeking Justice in Ugandan Courts Amnesty and the Case of Thomas Kwoyelo', *Washington University Global Studies Law Review* 12: 653–671.
Meyersfeld, B. (2012) 'Implementing the Rome Statute in Africa: Potential and problems of the prosecution of gender crimes in Africa in accordance with the Rome Statute's Perspective', in K. Ambos and O.A. Maunganidze (eds), *Power and Prosecution: Challenges and Opportunities for International Criminal Justice in Sub-Saharan Africa*. Göttingen: Universitätsverlag Göttingen, pp. 145–178.
Mochochoko, P. (2005) 'Africa and the International Criminal Court' in E. Ankumah and E. Kwakwa (eds), *African perspectives on International Criminal Justice, Ghana*. Accra, Maastricht, Pretoria: Africa Legal Aid.
Moreno-Ocampo, L. (2009) 'Press Conference by the Prosecutor of the International Criminal Court', https://www.icc-cpi.int/NR/rdonlyres/21A59DA2-F207-4A69-96D9-E445311BBB5C/281314/OTPNotesfortheMediaBackgrounderonly26112009FINALEN.pdf.
Nouwen, S.M.N. (2013) *Complementarity in the Line of Fire: The Catalysing Effects of the International Criminal Court in Uganda and Sudan*. Cambridge: Cambridge University Press.
O'Keefe, R. (2017) *International Criminal Law*. Oxford: Oxford University Press.

Quinn, J. (2013) 'Comparing Formal and Informal Mechanisms of Acknowledgment in Uganda', in H.F. Carey and S.M. Mitchell (eds), *Trials and Tribulations of International Prosecution*. Lanham, MD/UK: Lexington Books, pp. 239–254.

Report of the Commission of Inquiry into Post-Election Violence (2008) https://www.theelephant.info/documents/the-waki-report-commission-of-inquiry-into-post-election-violence/.

Rwamapera, K. (2018) 'Bandora Appeals 30-Year Jail Term for Genocide', https://www.newtimes.co.rw/rwanda/bandora-appeals-30-year-jail-term-genocide.

Tillier, J. (2013) 'The ICC Prosecutor and Positive Complementarity: Strengthening the Rule of Law?', *International Criminal Law Review* 13(3): 507–591.

United States Institute of Peace (1994) 'Ethiopia: Report of the Office of the Special Prosecutor: The Special Prosecution Process of War Criminals and Human Rights Violators in Ethiopia', https://www.usip.org/sites/default/files/Ethiopia-SPODossier-2.pdf.

Van der Merwe, H.J. (2016) 'Assessing the Role of Indirect Enforcement in the "Project" of International Criminal Justice: Some Lessons from South Africa' in H.J. van der Merwe and G. Kemp (eds), *International Criminal Justice in Africa: Issues, Challenges and Prospects*. Nairobi: Strathmore University Press, pp. 115–136.

Werle, G., Fernandez, L. and Vormbaum, M. (eds) (2014) *Africa and the International Criminal Court, International Criminal Justice Series Volume 1*. The Hague: Springer/Asser Press.

Weldesellasie, K.I. (2017) 'The Development of Criminal Law and Criminal Justice in Africa from Pre-colonial Rule to the Present Day' in C.C. Jalloh and I. Bantekas (eds), *The International Criminal Court and Africa*. Oxford: Oxford University Press, pp. 247–271.

CASE LAW

Belgium v. Senegal, ICJ, Judgment of 20 July 2012 (Questions Relating to the Obligation to Prosecute or Extradite), ICJ Reports 2012.

Case of the Prosecutor v. Francis Kirimi Muthaura, Uhuru Muigai Kenyatta and Mohammed Hussein Ali, Decision on the Confirmation of Charges Pursuant to Article 61(7)(a) and (b) of the Rome Statute, No. ICC-01/09-02/11 (2012).

Case of the Prosecutor v. William Samoei Ruto, Henry Kiprono Kosgey and Joshua Arap Sang, Decision on the Confirmation of Charges Pursuant to Article 61(7)(a) and (b) of the Rome Statute, No. ICC-01/09-01/11 (2012).

Decision on the Withdrawal of Charges against Mr Kenyatta, No. ICC-01/09-02/11 (13 March 2015).

Decision Pursuant to Article 15 of the Rome Statute on the Authorization of an Investigation into the Situation in the Republic of Kenya, No. ICC-01/09 (31 March 2010).

National Commissioner of the South African Police Service and Another v. Southern African Human Rights Litigation Centre and Another, Supreme Court of Appeal of South Africa, Judgment of 27 November 2013, Case No. 485/2012.

National Commissioner of the South African Police Service v. Southern African Human Rights Litigation Centre and Another 2014 (12) BCLR 1428 (CC).

Prosecutor v. Jean Pau Akayesu, Case No. ICTR 96-4-1, Judgment of 2 September 1998.
Prosecutor v. Katanga and Ngudjolo, ICC-01/04-01/07-1497, Appeals Chamber, Judgment on the Appeal of Mr Germain Katanga against the Oral Decision of Trial Chamber II of 12 June 2009 on the Admissibility of the Case, 25 September 2009.
Prosecutor v. Sam Hinga Norman, Decision on Preliminary Motion Based on Lack of Jurisdiction (Child Recruitment), Case No. SCSL-2004-14-AR72(E), Special Court for Sierra Leone, 31 May 2004.
Prosecutor v. Uhuru Muigai Kenyatta, Case No. ICC-01/09-02/11. OA 5, Judgment on the Prosecutor's Appeal against Trial Chamber V(B)'s Decision on Prosecution's Application for a Finding of Non-compliance under Article 87(7) of the Statute (19 August 2015).
Prosecutor v. William Samoei Ruto and Joshua Arap Sang, Case No. ICC-01/09-01/11, Decision on Prosecution Request for Admission of Prior Recorded Testimony (19 August 2015).
Prosecutor v. William Samoei Ruto and Joshua Arap Sang, ICC-01/09-01/11, Decision on Defence Applications for Judgments of Acquittal (5 April 2016).
Raila Odinga and Two Others v. Independent Electoral and Boundaries Commission and Three Others, Petitions 5, 4, and 3 of 2013, [2013] eKLR (Supreme Court of Kenya, Judgment of 30 March 2013).
Situation in the Democratic Republic of the Congo, in the case of the Prosecutor v. Thomas Lubanga Dyilo, No. ICC-01/04-01/06 (14 March 2012).
Southern African Litigation Centre v. Minister of Justice and Constitutional Development and Others [2015] Case No. 27740/2015.
Southern Africa Litigation Centre and Others v. National Director of Public Prosecutions and Others [2012] ZAGPPHC 61 (8 May 2012).
The Case of the Prosecutor v. Francis Kirimi Muthaura, Uhuru Muigai Kenyatta and Mohammed Hussein Ali, Decision on the Confirmation of Charges Pursuant to Article 61(7)(a) and (b) of the Rome Statute, No. ICC-01/09-02/11 (23 January 2012).
The Case of the Prosecutor v. William Samoei Ruto, Henry Kiprono Kosgey and Joshua Arap Sang, Decision on the Confirmation of Charges Pursuant to Article 61(7)(a) and (b) of the Rome Statute, No. ICC-01/09-01/11 (23 January 2012).
The Special Prosecution Process of War Criminals and Human Rights Violators in Ethiopia, Office of the Special Prosecutor, Transitional Government of Ethiopia (February 1994) 2.
Thomas Kwoyelo v. Uganda, Constitutional Court of Uganda, Constitutional Petition No. 036/11, Judgment of 22 September 2011.
Thomas Kwoyelo alias Latoni v. Uganda, Case No. 36/2011, Constitutional Court 2011 Uganda 1–3.
Uganda v. Thomas Kwoyelo alias Latoni, HCD-00-ICC, Case No. 02/2010, 2011 Uganda Amended Indictment 1–25 2011.
Uganda v. Thomas Kwoyelo alias Latoni, HCT – WCD-Criminal Case No. 0002 of 2010 (Arising from Criminal Case No. BUG RD. Court Case 09/2010.
Uganda v. Thomas Kwoyelo, Supreme Court of Uganda, Constitutional Appeal No. 1 of 2012.
Uganda v. Thomas Kwoyelo (Constitutional Appeal No. 1 of 2012) [2015] UGSC 5 (8 April 2015).

THE NUREMBERG PRINCIPLES IN THE CONTEXT OF AFRICA

The Theory and Practice of Individual and Corporate Criminal Responsibility

Evelyne Owiye Asaala

1. INTRODUCTION

The Nuremberg principle of individual criminal responsibility has played a foundational role in international criminal law. Post-Second World War treaties on criminal liability have all embodied this principle. Based on this principle, the post-Second World War trials began a trend where individuals have been held accountable through prosecution for violating established norms of international law. The prosecution of individuals responsible for international crimes has also been conducted in domestic courts of the country in which the crimes occurred, in international tribunals or in the domestic courts of other countries through the exercise of universal jurisdiction. Thus, international criminal law has historically been premised on the principle of individual criminal responsibility.

The practice in post-conflict states of Africa has also adopted the principle of individual criminal liability, albeit with different theoretical approaches. The ad hoc tribunals in Rwanda and the hybrid court of Sierra Leone have particularly pursued individual criminal liability for crimes committed in the respective state. There have also been several efforts to enforce the principle of individual criminal responsibility for international crimes in the national courts of some post-conflict states. These have been faced with numerous challenges alongside a few successful instances. Traditional African approaches to justice in some post-conflict states have also embraced individual accountability for past crimes, even though some practices also have elements of collective responsibility. It is the Protocol on Amendments to the Protocol on the Statute of the African Court of Justice and Human Rights (hereinafter the Malabo Protocol)[1] that has sought to expand the principle of criminal liability for international crimes to expressly provide for corporate criminal liability for international crimes. The Malabo Protocol is the first international treaty to expressly incorporate the doctrine of corporate criminal liability. This is a significant step towards narrowing down the gap of impunity for international and transnational crimes committed by corporations. This chapter argues that although the principle of individual criminal responsibility is essential in fighting impunity in Africa, expanding it to include corporate criminal liability significantly seals the impunity gap for international crimes committed on the African continent. The study undertaken in this chapter is convinced by the argument that most of the conflicts in Africa are resource-based and that these are fuelled by multinational corporations (MNCs) that commit heinous crimes in the process of extracting and exporting the resources, often with impunity.[2] The addition of corporate criminal responsibility to traditional individual criminal responsibility is therefore contextually relevant for Africa. The essence of this chapter is thus to trace the theory and practice of individual criminal responsibility and corporate criminal responsibility in international law and, in particular, to bring out its relevance in Africa.

1 STC/Legal/Min/7(I) Rev.1 (adopted in Malabo in July 2014).

2 'Final Report of the Panel of Experts on the Illegal Exploitation of Natural Resources and Other Forms of Wealth of the Democratic Republic of the Congo' (16 October 2002) UN Doc. S/2002/1146; 'Final Report of the Monitoring Mechanism on Angola Sanctions' (21 December 200) UN Doc. S/2000/1225; 'Report of the Panel of Experts Appointed Pursuant to Security Council Resolution 1306 (2000), Paragraph 19, in Relation to Sierra Leone' (20 December 2000) UN Doc. S/2000/1195.

2. THE THEORY AND PRACTICE OF THE PRINCIPLE OF INDIVIDUAL CRIMINAL RESPONSIBILITY

The theory of individual criminal responsibility has developed over the years through the practice of both national and international criminal tribunals. Personal liability for international crimes has existed since the United Nations (UN) General Assembly affirmed the Nuremberg Principles. The chief prosecutor at Nuremberg emphasised the importance of individual criminal responsibility for international crimes thus: 'While this law is first applied against German aggressors, the law, if it is so to serve a useful purpose, must condemn aggression by any other nations, including those which sit here now in judgment. We are able to do away with domestic tyranny and violence and aggression by those in power against the rights of their own people only when we make all men answerable to the law' (Jackson 1947: 154).

The International Military Tribunal of Nuremberg maintained that international crimes 'are committed by men, not by abstract entities, and only by punishing individuals who commit such crimes can the provisions of international law be enforced'.[3] In this regard, the German and Japanese industrialists who supported the Nazi regime were all subjected to individual prosecution without any reference to the doctrine of corporate criminal liability of their respective companies.[4] The underlying reason at the time was noble. The purpose of this approach was to gravitate away from state responsibility, which had previously been the norm. At the time, the move was designed to increase accountability by holding individual government officials accountable instead of allowing them to hide behind the organisation of the state.

Gerhard Werle and Florian Jessberger have described the Nuremberg Charter provisions on the different modes of individual responsibility for international crimes as 'rudimentary and fragmentary' (Werle and Jessberger 2014: 194). This is because the Charter lacks clear provisions on individual criminal participation. For example, Article 6(a) criminalises 'participation in a common plan or conspiracy' to accomplish any of the acts amounting to aggression.

---

3 *Trial of the Major War Criminals before the International Military Tribunal*, Nuremberg, Vol. I, 1947, p. 223, www.loc.gov/rr/frd/Military_Law/pdf/NT_Vol-I.pdf.

4 *Trial of Bruno Tesch and Two Others* (*The Zyklon B Case*), 1–8 March 1946, *Law Reports of the Trials of War Criminals*, vol. I; *Trial of Friedrich Flick and Five Others*, 20 April–22 December 1947, *Law Reports of the Trials of War Criminals*, vol. IX; *Trial of Alfried Felix Alwyn Krupp von Bohlen und Halbach and Eleven Others*, US Military Tribunal, Nuremberg, 17 November 1947–30 June 1948, *Law Reports of Trials of War Criminal*, vol. X; *I.G. Farben Trial*, Case No. 57, US Military Tribunal, Nuremberg, 14 August 1947–29 July 1948, *Law Reports of War Criminals*, vol. X. For further discussion on these cases see Chella (2012: 200–201).

Article 6(c) also criminalises acts by 'leaders, organisers, instigators and accomplices participating in the formulation or execution of a common plan or conspiracy to commit any of the foregoing crimes are responsible for all acts performed by any persons in execution of such plan'. Under the Nuremberg Charter, it appears as though anyone could be prosecuted for crimes against peace, regardless of their mode of participation. This does not clearly bring out the different modes of individual participation in international crime; nonetheless, it laid the foundations for further development of the concept.

These rudimentary and vague provisions were later refined by the practice of subsequent international criminal tribunals. Not only did the latter recognise the principle of individual criminal liability, but they also developed it with more clarity. The statutes establishing the International Criminal Tribunal for the former Yugoslavia (ICTY), the International Criminal Tribunal for Rwanda (ICTR), the Special Court for Sierra Leone (SCSL) and the Special Tribunal for Lebanon (STL) expressly provide for jurisdiction of these tribunals over natural persons.[5] The statutes also make a clear distinction between 'committing', 'planning', 'ordering', 'instigating' and 'aiding and abetting', and the respective requirement of *actus reus* and *mens rea*.[6] The ICTY has developed the concept further by introducing an additional mode of participation – 'the doctrine of joint criminal enterprise'.[7] Unlike the ICTY, the Rome Statute did not adopt the doctrine of joint criminal enterprise.

Like its predecessors, the Rome Statute of the International Criminal Court (hereinafter the Rome Statute) limits its jurisdiction to natural persons (Article 25(1)). Under the Rome Statute, a person who commits international crimes shall be 'individually responsible and liable for punishment' (Article 25). This is regardless of whether the crime was committed individually, jointly with others or through another person, notwithstanding the fact that the other person is criminally responsible (Article 25(3)).

Article 25(3) of the Rome Statute sets out with clarity the following modes of individual criminal responsibility: individual perpetration, joint perpetration, perpetration through another person, perpetration by ordering, soliciting or inducing, aiding, abetting or providing means for the commission of the crime, or perpetration in any other way that contributes to the commission or attempted commission of the crime. Any of these modes leads to individual criminal liability for international crimes specified under the Rome Statute, once the requisite elements have been proven. Werle and Jessberger have summarised these into a four-tier system of modes of perpetration under the

5 Article 7 of the ICTY Statute; art. 6 of the ICTR Statute; art. 6 of the SCSL Statute; and art. 3 of the STL Statute.

6 Ibid.

7 *Tadic*, ICTY (AC), judgment of 15 July 1999, para. 185.

Rome Statute: commission; inducement; assistance; and contribution to a group crime (Werle and Jessberger 2014: 197).

Like the statutes of the ad hoc tribunals, the Rome Statute does not distinguish between the degree of responsibility attached to each of the modes of participation (Werle and Jessberger 2014: 196). Article 25(3) of the Rome Statute fails to completely distinguish between actual perpetration and simple accessorial role. All these ad hoc tribunals plus the Rome Statutes adopt 'a unified perpetrator model' (ibid.: 196). As Werle and Jessberger (ibid: 196) note, these differentiations 'in terminology and the placement into separate categories would not have any practical effect if it were not taken into account in sentencing matters'. It is therefore during sentencing that the varying degree of responsibility is factored in.

3. THE THEORY AND PRACTICE OF INDIVIDUAL CRIMINAL RESPONSIBILITY IN AFRICA

The notion of individual criminal responsibility is not new to Africa. There exist two levels at which this doctrine can be conceptualised: the traditional African conception and the African Union (AU) conception. Traditional African approaches have played a key role in the fight against impunity in most post-conflict African societies. Despite their perceived flaws, traditional approaches to justice have been taken in seeking accountability for historic crimes in post-conflict African states. In Rwanda, for example, the *gacaca*[8] courts were formalised and eventually contributed to justice in the post-genocide period. Similarly, Uganda has experimented with *mato oput*[9] in its transitional justice period.

Traditional approaches to justice in post-conflict African states are all indicative of a practice that embraces the principle of individual criminal responsibility. *Gacaca* and *mato oput* all concern the responsibility of the individual for acts that are treated as crimes. While the accountability measures in all these approaches may not entail criminal prosecution, the underlying factor is that each individual should account for his/her actions in one way or

8 According to Lahiri (2009: 325), *gacaca* literally translates as 'grass' or 'lawn', since those involved in dispute resolutions would ordinarily sit on the grass or lawn. This is an ancient method of dispute resolution in Rwanda. It involved respected members of the community known as 'inyangamugayo' – one who detests disgrace – serving as judges in a process of resolving civil matters.

9 According to Hovil and Quinn (2005), *mato oput* entails the drinking of bitter root as a form of reconciliation ritual. It is a cleansing ceremony carried out traditionally by the Acholi of Northern Uganda and was only used when a member of one clan killed a member of another.

another. Unlike *gacaca*, which were formalised courts, *mato oput* involves a process that is usually undertaken when misfortunes have befallen the offending clan, thus leading to social pressure on the perpetrator or his/her family to seek reconciliation (Bako 2009). Within the *mato oput* process, punishment is first carried out by the spirits occasioning misfortune. It is the spiritual world that punishes offenders, thus compelling them to initiate a *mato oput* process as a way of cleansing themselves. This is because the Acholi people believe in the notion of the 'living dead', a belief that influences the manner in which disputes are resolved and reconciliation is achieved (ibid.). At this stage, it may seem as though punishment within the *mato oput* is a collective affair. Nevertheless, it should be noted that the *mato oput* process occurs in four distinct stages: the separation of clans of the perpetrator and victim; mediation; compensation; and finally the *mato oput* reconciliation ceremony (Gordon 2009; Rose 2008: 362). It is the final stage that clearly brings out the notion of individual criminal liability. The reconciliation ceremony marks the final step of the process and it seeks to seal the reconciliation. This step is presided over by the local chief (*rwot moo*) and involves the communities of the two families for the purposes of reconciliation. It entails the following elaborate steps:

> First, the offending party beats a stick to broadly symbolize *mato oput*'s restorative purpose and then runs away to signify acceptance of guilt for the murder. Second, the parties cut in half a sheep and a goat and exchange opposite sides. The offending clan supplies the sheep, which represents the *cen*, or misfortune, haunting the clan of the offender, while the injured clan supplies the goat, which symbolizes unity and a willingness to forgive and reconcile. Third, the clans eat *boo mukwok*, spoiled *boo*, or local greens, which signifies that tension between the clans persisted long enough for food to spoil, and also symbolizes the clans' readiness to reconcile after this long period of time. Fourth, a representative from each party drinks *oput*, bitter root, from a calabash. The root represents the bitterness between the clans, and drinking it symbolizes washing away the bitterness between them. Fifth, both parties cook and eat the *acwiny*, liver, of the sheep and the goat to show that their blood has been mixed and united and to symbolically wash away the bitterness within the blood of the human liver. One of the last rituals involves consuming *odeyo*, the remains of a saucepan, which is thought to free the parties to eat together again. The ceremony is not complete until the parties have eaten all of the food prepared for the day; finishing the food means that no bitterness remains between the two clans. (Rose 2008: 363–364)

The *mato oput* process symbolises individual criminal responsibility in two ways. First, the punishment of the accused person is exhibited through humiliation. It can be argued that making an accused go through the process and publicly acknowledge his/her wrongs is in itself punitive. Second, the sharing of the bitter roots symbolises reconciliation between the perpetrator and the victim, as well as the two communities, and their unwillingness to repeat the offence and experience the bitterness caused by the offence in the future. The modern sense of punishment of the perpetrator may seem to be greatly downgraded in this process.

Although there are African traditional practices that embrace collective punishment for selected heinous crimes,[10] the procedural approaches recently embraced by post-conflict states in Africa signify total disregard for collective punishment and the embrace of the Nuremberg principle of individual responsibility.

At the AU level, the African Charter on Human and Peoples' Rights is categorical that '[p]unishment is personal and can be imposed only on the offender' (Article 7(2)). In fact, the Malabo Protocol establishing the International Criminal Law Section of the African Court of Justice and Human Rights (hereinafter, the International Criminal Law Section of the African Court) adopts the principle of individual criminal responsibility. Article 46B of the Malabo Protocol further provides that '[a] person who commits an offence under this Statute shall be held individually responsible for the crime'. This implies that a person who individually commits any of the crimes specified under the Malabo Protocol will personally be held criminally responsible upon satisfying the requisite *mens rea* and *actus reus* of the respective offence. This signals a general acceptance of the principle of individual responsibility within the AU's own conceptions of justice.

Using Werle and Jessberger's theoretical categorisation of modes of individual participation under the International Criminal Court (ICC), the AU has adopted a two-tier system of modes of participation: commission and assistance. The Malabo Protocol does not expressly mention participation through a group of people. However, this section argues that this can be broadly construed within the meaning of assistance.

3.1. COMMISSION

Like the Rome Statute, commission of a crime under the Malabo Protocol is in three forms: by an individual, jointly with another person and through another person. Under Article 28N of the Malabo Protocol, a person commits an offence under the Protocol if he/she participates 'as a principal, co-principal, agent or accomplice in any of the offences'. Common to all these forms of commission is the aspect of 'control over the commission of the offence' (Werle and Jessberger 2014: 198).

---

10 In some Kenyan communities, the offence of murder is still punished by banishing an entire family of the perpetrator by burning their homesteads, since they are deemed to be outcasts.

The first aspect of participation – commission by the principal – holds the individual who actually fulfils the requisite *mens rea* and *actus reus* for any of the crimes specified under the Malabo Protocol responsible. In this regard, the principal offender will be the actual perpetrator of the crime and shall personally be held responsible for the crime in question. Since the Protocol does not expressly include commission through omission, it is doubtful whether the International Criminal Law Section of the African Court will adopt a broad interpretation of this notion to include omission. The ICTR has previously held that the notion of commission is not limited to direct and physical perpetration.[11] The International Criminal Law Section of the African Court should thus adopt this approach, as this is the standard practice in criminal prosecution.

The second aspect – commission by a co-principal – occurs when two or more persons form a common intention to commit a crime and they actually go ahead and commit the crime in conjunction or jointly with one another. Where this is the case, each of the persons taking part in the commission of the crime will be held individually responsible as a co-perpetrator. Notably, like other modes of perpetration, the notion of control is central to the definition of joint commission (Werle and Jessberger 2014: 206). This implies that 'each co-perpetrator could frustrate the joint commission of the crime by not carrying out his or her task' (ibid.).

The notion of co-principal under the Malabo Protocol is similar to that of 'joint commission' under Article 25(3) of the Rome Statute. However, it is not yet known whether the International Criminal Law Section of the African Court will follow the narrow construction of 'joint commission' as requiring a 'common plan' and 'essential contribution' like the ICC or whether it will adopt the ICTY's joint criminal enterprise, which instead entails a 'plurality of persons', a 'common plan, design or purpose' and 'any kind of assistance'.[12]

Finally, commission through an agent occurs when a person (D) engages another person (A) to commit the crime. In such a case, D will be held individually responsible for the crime. This is similar to the ICC's notion of commission through another person under Article 25(3)(a) of the Rome Statute. Under this mode of responsibility, the 'perpetrator-by-means exercises control over the will of those who physically perform the material elements of the crime' (Werle and Jessberger 2014: 208). This would naturally include those in control of hierarchies of power (ibid.: 209). These are those individuals whose commands to commit a crime would automatically be executed by their subordinates. Although the Malabo Protocol does not provide for the aspect of ordering or inducing as a mode of responsibility, these two would thus naturally fall under this mode of perpetration.

---

11 *Gacumbitsi*, ICTR (AC), Judgment of 7 July 2006, para. 60; *Munyakazi* (AC), Judgment of 28 September 2011, para. 135.

12 For more on these aspects, see Werle and Jessberger (2014: 200–207).

The Malabo Protocol further subjects the application of the principle of individual criminal liability to the immunity clause as follows: 'No charges shall be commenced or continued before the Court against any serving AU Head of State or Government, or anybody acting or entitled to act in such capacity, or other senior state officials based on their functions, during their tenure of office' (Article 46A *bis*).

This position is problematic for several reasons. First, the provision above assumes that the Protocol is the primary international treaty on criminal law. What happens to African states that are likely to become parties to this Protocol and are also parties to the Rome Statute, which abjures any form of immunity for individual participation in international crimes? How does one reconcile a state's obligations under the different treaties?

Second, the Malabo Protocol does not clearly distinguish between immunity *ratione personae* and immunity *ratione materiae*, and is unclear on the nature of its immunity *ratione materiae*. Nevertheless, Garth Abraham (2015: 14) makes a convincing case that, despite its vagueness, the provision bestows personal immunity. The wording 'during their tenure of office' implies personal immunities, since this type of immunity attaches to the office and exists only during one's tenure in office (Akande 2004; Koller 2004). Yet the inclusion of 'other senior state officials based on their function' could naturally imply functional immunity. It could be argued that the qualification on functional immunity is applicable only to senior state officers and not to all those officials listed earlier.

Another possible interpretation is that this provision applies to both types of immunities for all the listed state officials. However, this in itself is problematic. First, the provision can be taken as providing absolute personal immunity to a wide range of 'other senior state officers'. Given the nature of personal immunities, this implies that no senior AU state official can be prosecuted for international crimes until such time as the official relinquishes power. Regarding immunities *ratione materiae*, the Protocol envisages a possibility of future prosecution after the officers involved leave office.

While the recognition of these immunities is well anchored in customary international law, their incorporation into the Malabo Protocol raises a few policy arguments about the wisdom of such a rule of international law and its likely impacts on the development of the principle of individual criminal responsibility. For example, though it envisages the possibility of future prosecution after an officer leaves office, the Protocol does not seem to foresee the very real possibility that state officers who engage in the commission of international crimes may fail to relinquish power for fear of prosecution. Should such officers be left to continue with the atrocities until their time in office is over? What if they never leave office? It is also not clear who is included under the phrase 'other senior state officials'. How does one reconcile these immunities with the duty to hold individuals who commit international crimes accountable? In view of all these concerns, one needs no further analysis to foresee the confusion that is likely to hamper the AU in combating impunity through the principle of individual criminal responsibility.

As such, the Protocol has rightly raised eyebrows, with certain scholars calling it a rubber stamp for impunity (Abraham 2015: 15). According to Garth Abraham (ibid.: 14), for example, this amendment 'represents a major setback in the advance of international criminal justice; in fact, it can only be construed to be in the interest of those African leaders fearful of an end to a culture of impunity'. What is more, Chacha Murungu (2011: 1077), referring to the context of leaving office, observes that 'immunity of state officials is no longer a valid defence for the commission of international crimes'. The sum effect of such a provision not only denies justice to victims but is also detrimental to the fight against impunity (Kariri 2014), signalling retrogression in the war against impunity for international crimes in Africa. Evidently, the need to recognise the immunity of heads of state and government and other state officials must have been a major driver in expanding the mandate of the African Court of Justice and Human and Peoples' Rights. It can also be argued that African states' reluctance to ratify the Malabo Protocol[13] suggests that its adoption may have been mere political posturing rather than an expression of genuine intention.

3.2. ASSISTING

A person can be held individually criminally responsible for international crimes under the Malabo Protocol if he/she offers assistance to the principal perpetrators of the crime. However, this form of assistance must be substantial in the sense that 'the crime would have been substantially less likely without the assistance' (Werle and Jessberger 2014: 216–217). The Malabo Protocol provides for two instances where this is possible: first, where the person '[a]ids or abets the commission of any of the offences'; and, second, where the person '[i]s an accessory before or after the fact or … participates in a collaboration or conspiracy to commit any of the offences' (Article 28N(ii) and (iii) of the Malabo Protocol).

Often, the terms 'aiding' and 'abetting' are used in conjunction with each other without a clear distinction between them. Basically, this is the giving of any 'direct and substantial assistance' or encouraging (Friman, Robinson and Wilmshurst 2010: 375) principal offenders either before or after the commission

13 At the time of writing, the Malabo Protocol had 11 signatories, with no ratifications. The AU itself has expressed 'concern at the slow pace of ratification of the Protocol' (see AU Assembly, Assembly/AU/Dec.672(XXX), para. 3(iii)).

of a crime. Knowledge of the crime intended is key. The aider or abettor should be aware that his/her conduct is assisting a certain crime (ibid.: 376).

An individual is likely to be an accessory before the fact if he/she associates himself/herself with the actual perpetrators of an offence in circumstances which give rise to a presumption that there was a common intention to commit the crime. This may also include aiding and abetting. Thus, any kind of association suffices to hold an individual criminally liable. In practice, the notion of an accessory before and after the fact is likely to overlap with assistance as either an aider or abettor. In this sense, any form of assistance offered by an accessory before the fact to either an individual perpetrator or a group, so long as it is substantial to the commission of the crime, can lead to his/her individual criminal liability. Arguably, the Rome Statute provision for assisting the commission of a crime by a group would parallel the Malabo Protocol's provision for accessory before the fact. An accessory after the fact assists an offender in evading punishment or by destroying incriminating materials. The Protocol also uses the term 'conspiracy' in the context of either an accessory before or after the fact. This would refer to the traditional common law offence, which is 'an agreement to commit an offence, and does not require that any further action is taken in pursuance of that agreement' (Friman, Robinson and Wilmshurst 2010: 368).

4. A CRITIQUE OF AFRICAN STATE PRACTICES WITH INDIVIDUAL CRIMINAL RESPONSIBILITY FOR INTERNATIONAL CRIMES

Uganda, the Democratic Republic of the Congo (DRC) and Senegal (via the Extraordinary African Chambers) are the only regional states with practices that demonstrate visible effort in enforcing individual criminal responsibility for international crimes and in a manner that resembles the Nuremberg practice and the practice of the ad hoc tribunals and the ICC.

Uganda established an International Crimes Division (ICD) of the High Court in 2008.[14] It was anticipated that the ICD would improve national efforts to ensure individual criminal responsibility for international crimes, particularly with regard to cases related to the Lord's Resistance Army (LRA). Once it was fully operationalised, the ICD's first trial was against Thomas Kwoyelo, a former LRA commander arrested in the DRC in 2008. Kwoyelo was arraigned in court in September 2010, but his trial began only in July 2011 after several delays. These delays, according to Sharon Nakandha (2016), were due to the numerous challenges the ICD faced as a result of its budgetary constraints. Chief among

[14] This was designated in 2011 through Legal Notice No. 10 of 2011, High Court (International Crimes Division) Practice Directions 2011, clause 3.

these was the lack of key internal structures such as a victims and witnesses unit and an outreach unit. This is what, for example, compelled the Court to postpone Kwoyelo's trial by months. Although the government offered the use of its media to reach out to affected communities, it was important for the Court to reach out physically to Northern Uganda, which may not have been possible due to constrained resources. Another serious challenge bedevilling Uganda's ICD was the lack of adequate human resources. Appeals from the ICD are send to the ordinary appeal courts, which handle numerous other civil and criminal matters; however, the human resources of these courts have not been bolstered (Acirokop 2013). It is feared that this is likely to lead to adjournments of many cases due to a lack of forum, as has been the situation with ordinary cases (ibid.). Moreover, in a constitutional petition in November 2011, Kwoyelo challenged his prosecution on the basis of Uganda's Amnesty Act; not only was the amnesty law declared constitutional, but the Constitutional Court also ordered the ICD to cease Kwoyelo's trial.[15]

As regards the DRC, following its ratification of the Rome Statute in 2002, the Military Penal Code was passed in the same year. This formed the basis upon which the military tribunals prosecuted individuals for past crimes. These tribunals were initially the only tribunals prosecuting international crimes. However, the International Centre for Transitional Justice (ICTJ) has found that some of the provisions of the Military Penal Code fall short of international standards – for example, its mode of responsibility falls short of the command responsibility under Article 28 of the Rome Statute. Other shortcomings not directly related to the principle of individual criminal responsibility include its definitions of war crimes and crimes against humanity, which fall short of the Rome Statute definitions, its omission of penalties for war crimes, and its inclusion of the death penalty (ICTJ 2015). In order to remedy this situation, judges have referred directly to Rome Statute provisions since the DRC is a monist state. In April 2013, Parliament passed the Law on the Organization, Functioning and Jurisdiction of the Courts (LOCJ), granting civilian courts (and particularly the courts of appeals) jurisdiction over the prosecution of individuals for core international crimes.[16]

A study conducted by the ICTJ (2015) found that 'between January 2009 and December 2014, judicial authorities in the DRC had opened 39 cases related to events that had occurred between 2002 and 2014 in eastern DRC

---

15 *Thomas Kwoyelo Alias Latoni v. Uganda*, Constitutional Petition No. 036/11 (Arising out of HCT-00-ICD-Case No. 2/10), Ruling of the Court of 22 September 2011 (Constitutional Court of Uganda), para. 625.

16 Projet de loi modifiant et complétant la loi organique No 13/011-B of April 11, 2013 portant organisation, fonctionnement, et compétences des juridictions de l'ordre judiciaire en matière de répression des crimes de génocide, des crimes contre l'humanité et des crimes de guerres, April 2014.

(Ituri, North Kivu, and South Kivu)'. This is a very small number relative to the mass atrocities that were committed during the period under investigation. Political pressure where special interests are at stake, coupled with a lack of political will (especially from the neighbouring Rwandan government) in relation to proceedings against foreign armed groups, have been cited as the major challenges contributing to the low levels of investigation. In addition, due to limited access to areas where serious crimes have been committed, the DRC's judicial system relies on information from external partners, such as the United Nations Organization Stabilization Mission in the Democratic Republic of the Congo (MONUSCO), UN agencies and non-governmental organisations (NGOs). As a result, 'whenever crimes occur outside of the realm of an international partner's area of intervention, little or no information is gathered and no investigations or prosecutions are initiated'. Given these challenges, it is impossible to argue that the DRC's judicial system provides an effective national system to hold individuals to account for international crimes.

In the third instance, the Extraordinary African Chambers (EAC) in Senegal was established as an internationalised court under the auspices of the AU to prosecute international crimes committed in Chad between 7 June 1982 and 1 December 1990.[17] This period corresponds to the time in power of the then President Hissène Habré. On 30 May 2016, the EAC convicted Habré for war crimes, crimes against humanity and torture.[18]

This conviction is significant for a number of reasons. First, the history preceding Habré's conviction was so riddled with uncertainties that one would have expected a different verdict from the Senegalese courts. In January 2000, Senegal began criminal proceedings against Hissène Habré, who was in exile there, for crimes against humanity and torture. Senegal's Appeal Court held that it had no jurisdiction to prosecute Habré for the alleged crimes, since Senegal had not enacted legislation implementing the Convention against Torture and Other Cruel, Inhuman or Degrading Treatment and Punishment of 1984 (hereinafter the UN Convention against Torture) and because Habré was a non-Senegalese and the alleged crimes had been committed outside of Senegal.[19] Senegal's highest court, the Cour de Cassation, later upheld this decision.[20]

---

17 Statut des Chambres africaines extraordinaires au sein des juridictions sénégalaises pour la poursuite des crimes internationaux commis au Tchad durant la période du 7 juin 1982 au 1er décembre 1990.

18 *Ministère Public v. Hissene Habré*, Judgment of 30 May 2016, Chambre Africaine Extraiordinaire d'Assises, http://www.chambresafricaines.org/pdf/Jugement_complet.pdf. For further reading on the judgment, see Høgestøl (2016). However, Habré is appealing his conviction; see *BBC News* (2015).

19 *Questions Relating to the Obligation to Prosecute or Extradite (Belgium v. Senegal) Judgment*, [2012] ICJ Reports 422, para. 76 (referring to Court of Appeal (Dakar), *Chambre d'accusation, Public Prosecutor's Office and François Diouf v. Hissène Habré*, Judgment No. 135, 4 July 2000).

20 Ibid. (also referring to Court of Cassation, première chambre statuant en matière pénale, *Souleymane Guengueng et al. v. Hissène Habré*, Judgment No. 14, 20 March 2001).

Belgium sought the extradition of Habré to Belgium to stand trial for his alleged crimes. Senegal's rejection of the extradition was applauded by the AU, which called upon Senegal to ensure his prosecution.[21] The AU mandated 'the republic of Senegal to prosecute and ensure that Hissen Habré is tried, on behalf of Africa, by a competent Senegalese court with guarantees for fair trial'.[22] This was never done. Hence, in February 2009, Belgium instituted proceedings against Senegal before the ICJ, claiming that Senegal was in breach of its international treaty and customary law obligations. The ICJ duly found Senegal to be in breach of its international conventional obligations to expedite investigations and the subsequent prosecution of Habré.[23] The Court argued that Article 27 of the Vienna Convention on the Law of Treaties (VCLT), which reflects customary international law, could not allow Senegal to rely on its domestic law in order to defeat its international law obligations.[24]

In July 2015, Habré's trial recommenced before a Senegalese court and led to his conviction, which gives renewed hope that an African court can convict a former head of state for international crimes. Arguably, since the establishment of the Court under the auspices of the AU involved other African states, the conviction confirms that, despite numerous challenges, African states have resolved to enforce individual criminal responsibility for international crimes.

5. THE MALABO PROTOCOL AND CORPORATE CRIMINAL LIABILITY

The Malabo Protocol also extends criminal liability for international crimes to corporations. However, the Malabo Protocol is not the originator of corporate criminal liability for international crimes. Although the Nuremberg Charter failed to expressly provide for corporate criminal liability, Articles 9 and 10 of the Charter allowed for groups or organisations to be declared criminal in nature.[25] In this regard, mere membership of a criminal organisation was

---

21 AU Assembly, 'Decision on the Hissène Habré Case and the African Union', Assembly/AU/Dec.127 (VII), Doc. Assembly/AU/3 (VII), 7th Ordinary Session, 1–2 July 2006.

22 Ibid., para. 5(iii).

23 *Supra* note 19, para. 70.

24 Ibid, para. 113.

25 Article 9 states: 'At the trial of any individual member of any group or organization the Tribunal may declare (in connection with any act of which the individual may be convicted) that the group or organization of which the individual was a member was a criminal organization.' Article 10 states: 'In cases where a group or organization is declared criminal by the Tribunal, the competent national authority of any Signatory shall have the right to bring individuals to trial for membership therein before national, military or occupation courts. In any such case the criminal nature of the group or organization is considered proved and shall not be questioned.'

regarded as criminal, irrespective of whether an individual's participation in the organisation was voluntary or not. Individuals who had no knowledge of the criminal purposes or acts of the organisation were excluded from criminal liability unless they were personally implicated in the commission of acts. The notion of 'criminal organisation' was understood through the aspects of 'criminal conspiracy or complicity', 'knowledge' and 'personal liability'.[26] Thus, scholars argue that these laid the foundations for the doctrine of corporate complicity in international crimes (Engle 2006: 291; Chella 2012: 201).

It is also noteworthy that the Allied Control Council (governing occupied Germany at that time) – even before the trials – imposed several sanctions on legal persons for violations of international law.[27] The sanctions covered under this law included the dissolution of legal personality and the seizure of the assets of the corporation for reparations.[28]

Article 46C of the Malabo Protocol is the first provision to expressly provide for this mode of criminal responsibility in an international forum:

1. For the purpose of this Statute, the Court shall have jurisdiction over legal persons, with the exception of States.
2. Corporate intention to commit an offence may be established by proof that it was the policy of the corporation to do the act, which constituted the offence.
3. A policy may be attributed to a corporation where it provides the most reasonable explanation of the conduct of that corporation.
4. Corporate knowledge of the commission of an offence may be established by proof that the actual or constructive knowledge of the relevant information was possessed within the corporation.
5. Knowledge may be possessed within a corporation even though the relevant information is divided between corporate personnel.
6. The criminal responsibility of legal persons shall not exclude the criminal responsibility of natural persons who are perpetrators or accomplices in the same crimes.

This provision clarifies the *mens rea* element necessary to establish corporate liability. In order to prove corporate liability, the criminal elements of *actus reus* and *mens rea* must both be attributed to the corporation. Traditionally, the law has shied away from apportioning criminal liability to inanimate entities. This is

---

26 *Trial of the Major War Criminals before the International Military Tribunal*, Nuremberg (1947) 262, 268, 273, https://www.loc.gov/rr/frd/Military_Law/pdf/NT_Vol-I.pdf; see van der Wilt 2007: 93–95.

27 This was done in accordance with Control Council Law No. 10.

28 Control Council Law No. 10, Punishment of Persons Guilty of War Crimes, Crimes Against Peace and Against Humanity 306 (20 December 1945); see also *Flomo v. Firestone Nat'l. Rubber Co.*, 643 F.3d 1013, 1017 (7th Cir. 2011).

mainly due to the difficulty inherent in apportioning the mental element of the guilty mind to corporations, given their inanimate nature (Williams 1961: 856).

5.1. *ACTUS REUS* AND *MENS REA* FOR CORPORATE CRIMINAL LIABILITY

In order to prove *actus reus* of a corporation, it is necessary to prove the specific elements of the crime in question. It must be proven that the acts or omissions of the corporation constituted the elements of the relevant crime.

Under the Malabo Protocol, the *mens rea* element comprises two aspects: the corporate intention to commit the crime and the corporate knowledge of the offence in question. The 'intention' part is proved once it is established that a policy of the corporation required the commission of the act that constitutes the offence. By analogy with the ICC's interpretation of a policy, such a policy need not be express, but can also be inferred from a series of events.[29] This implies that under the Malabo Protocol, the existence of a policy could also be construed from implied acts or omissions permitted by the corporation. Corporate knowledge, on the other hand, will be deemed to be proven if it is established that the actual or constructive knowledge of the relevant information of the commission of the offence was possessed within the corporation. Again, such knowledge may either be actual or constructive (Chesterman 2000: 321). It is irrelevant whether such information was divided between corporate personnel.

Thus, the Malabo Protocol adopts an entirely different approach to establishing *mens rea* to corporations. Rather than following the traditional method applied by national courts, in which the state of mind of the leaders or heads of a corporation is regarded to show the *mens rea* of the corporation,[30] the Malabo Protocol finds a direct way of attributing *mens rea* to the corporation itself as an entity. Corporate criminal liability under the Malabo Protocol is not derived from the criminal liability of natural persons within the corporation, but is purely organisation-based (Kyriakakis 2016: 4). The concept of vicarious liability does not arise as the Malabo Protocol does not adopt the derivative approach, but directly imputes criminal liability to the corporate entity.

However, it is questionable whether this corporate criminal liability can be extended to individual criminal liability with respect to the personnel of the

29 *Prosecutor v. Germain Katanga*, Judgment, ICC-01/04-01/07 (Judgment pursuant to Article 24 of the Statute), 7 March 2014, para. 1109; *Prosecutor v. Blaskic*, IT-95-14-T, Trial Chamber of the ICTY, (2000) 81 para. 203; Badar 2004.

30 *HL Bolton (Engineering) Co Ltd v. TJ Graham & Sons Ltd.* [1957] 1 QB 159, 172 (CA); *Lennard's Carrying Co Ltd v. Asiatic Petroleum Co Ltd.* (1915) AC 705, 713; Pinto and Evans 2008: 39, cited in Nwafor 2013, 83.

corporation. The Malabo Protocol bestows jurisdiction over both natural and legal persons. This implies that individuals who commit such crimes will be held liable. It can thus be questioned whether a corporation that has been found guilty of the listed crimes can pass on this criminal liability to its personnel, who may otherwise not have been held accountable. As cited above, 'the criminal responsibility of legal persons shall not exclude the criminal responsibility of natural persons who are perpetrators or accomplices in the same crimes'. The significance of this provision is twofold. First, it acknowledges that corporate criminal liability does not shield the individuals involved from criminal liability. Thus, corporate criminal liability may also involve the prosecution of natural persons within that same corporation. The second significant aspect of Article 46B(6) is whether (and if so how) this corporate liability translates into individual criminal liability. Once the existence of corporate liability has been proven, natural persons who are the actual perpetrators or accomplices to the offences will also be held criminally liable. Borrowing from national practice, this will not involve all the employees of the corporation, but the policy makers of these entities (Chesterman 2000). Yet this may not always be the case. The Malabo Protocol opens itself up to actual perpetrators of, and accomplices to, corporate crimes. With respect to individual responsibility in relation to corporate liability, the prosecution has to go further and prove that the natural persons were either the actual perpetrators or accomplices in the same crimes. Persons accused of international crimes are required to meet a very high threshold in order to be held criminally liable, in the sense that they must be those bearing the highest criminal responsibility. The Malabo Protocol is likely to be interpreted as lowering these standards with respect to persons held criminally liable as a result of corporate criminal liability. This is so because, in the context of corporate criminal liability, the natural persons held criminally liable will be either the actual perpetrators or accomplices, in which case not all of them will necessarily bear the highest responsibility for international crimes.

However, it is not clear whether the prosecution of the natural persons will happen subsequent to or simultaneously with that of the legal person. The Malabo Protocol is not clear on this. Although this is a matter of prosecutorial discretion, it is submitted that the prosecution of the natural persons should always follow that of the corporate entity. It makes logical sense that once a corporate entity has been found criminally liable, then the actual perpetrators and accomplices should be held to account for their actions. It will be absurd for actual perpetrators of or accomplices to corporate crimes to be declared guilty, but for corporate criminal liability to be found to be non-existent. Any other way of looking at this is likely to lead to a duplication of resources.

It is also possible that the actual acts of the respective crimes may be committed by independent organs or groups of persons working in concert with the organisation. It is possible that such independent organs or groups are neither agents of the corporation nor its personnel. Does this therefore imply that the actual perpetrators of these crimes should be brought to book under the concept of corporate criminal responsibility? It remains to be seen how the International Criminal Law Section of the African Court will interpret these controversial issues. Of significance is the fact that persons who engage in corporate or collective criminal activity will still be held individually responsible.

Therefore, the Malabo Protocol makes a significant contribution by clarifying how to prove corporate criminal liability as well as individual criminal liability for the actual perpetrators or accomplices of the corporate acts. Unlike the ICC and ad hoc tribunals, the prosecution of international crimes in Africa is likely to put more emphasis on corporate criminal liability of both a national and transnational character. This has much contextual relevance, given that the majority of intra-state conflicts in Africa – e.g. in Angola, the DRC, Liberia and Sierra Leone – are resource-based. Often, MNCs have been accused of perpetrating these heinous crimes in the process of extracting and exporting the resources.[31] For example, it has been documented that most of these resources are under the control of rebel groups that commit gross human rights violations.[32] The complex nature of most MNCs poses a great challenge to national prosecutions in countries falling victim to their violations. In most instances, the countries in question are either complicit in the crimes or lack the local institutional capacity to prosecute these entities due to the immense powers exercised by the MNCs. Corporate criminal jurisdiction over these organisations would be a big and pioneering achievement for the African region. In addition, this regional achievement is likely to catalyse concerted national efforts towards pursuing corporate criminal liability for international crimes. African states should therefore adopt or re-align their national legislation to provide for corporate criminal liability for international crimes at the national level.

However, some dissenting voices may argue that corporate criminal liability is not necessarily a good thing for Africa, given its potential practical implications. For instance, such liability might result in indirect adverse consequences for innocent shareholders, loss of employment and negative economic effects. It is the author's position that Africa must sanitise corporate investments in the region. It must dictate the conditions under which foreign corporations may operate there. Corporations must comply with the local

31 'Final Report of the Panel of Experts on the Illegal Exploitation of Natural Resources and Other Forms of Wealth of the Democratic Republic of the Congo' (16 October 2002) UN Doc. S/2002/1146; 'Final Report of the Monitoring Mechanism on Angola Sanctions' (21 December 200) UN Doc. S/2000/1225; 'Report of the Panel of Experts Appointed Pursuant to Security Council Resolution 1306 (2000), Paragraph 19, in Relation to Sierra Leone' (20 December 2000) UN Doc. S/2000/1195.

32 Ibid.

laws of the countries in which they operate. African states cannot tolerate the facilitation or commission of international crimes by corporations for mere economic gain. It is important to uphold the Malabo Protocol approach that whosoever wants to invest in Africa must abide by certain human rights standards.

5.2. THE DEFECTS OF CORPORATE CRIMINAL LIABILITY IN THE MALABO PROTOCOL

The Malabo Protocol's provisions on corporate criminal liability are not above criticism. First, unlike individual criminal responsibility, the Malabo Protocol does not prescribe the punishment applicable to corporate entities found criminally liable for any international or transnational crimes, or for the natural persons who either acted as the actual perpetrators or accomplices of the same. It is important to distinguish this latter category from the other general perpetrators of the listed international crimes because the other category of offenders has to meet a very high threshold to be held criminally liable. They must be those bearing the highest criminal responsibility. As previously mentioned, concerning the natural persons to be held criminally liable in the context of corporate criminal liability, it will be either the actual perpetrators or accomplices. In both these instances, not all of them will necessarily carry the highest responsibility for international crimes. Thus, the Protocol must prescribe the punishments and penalties to be levied against corporate entities found to be criminally liable, as well as against the categories of offenders to whom the corporate entity passes its liability.

Second, the Malabo Protocol offers a one-size-fits-all, uniform application of corporate criminal liability to all Malabo Protocol crimes, whether international or transnational in nature. While this may pose no challenge with respect to international crimes – which embody an in-built threshold requirement to prove the crimes – it is likely to raise challenges with respect to transnational crimes.

Unlike international crimes, transnational crimes do not have criteria that can be applied to determine whether the gravity threshold has been met. Gravity is an essential factor for any court that is required to analyse the admissibility of a case. Within the Rome Statute, the notion of gravity is embedded in the contextual definitions of crimes. For example, to prove genocide, one must prove not just the listed acts but also that the listed acts were intended to 'destroy, in whole or in part, a national, ethnical, racial or religious group, as such'. Similarly, crimes against humanity require the prosecution not just to prove the listed acts, but also that the acts were committed 'as part of a widespread or systematic attack directed against any civilian population, with knowledge of the attack'. Again, to prove war crimes, the prosecution must prove that the listed acts were 'committed as part of a plan or policy or as part of a large-scale commission of such crimes'. Arguably, this is the test that is most likely to be followed by the International Criminal Law Section of the African Court insofar as the Rome Statute crimes are concerned. In this regard, the admissibility question for corporate crimes will be determined with certainty and within a clear context of the gravity question. Only when the required gravity of the listed crimes is fulfilled will the corporate character of the legal person be held to account for its involvement. However, this certainty of gravity standards in determining the admissibility of cases is missing in the case of transnational crimes.

How should the International Criminal Law Section of the African Court determine which transnational cases involving legal persons to take on board and which not? Using the crime of terrorism or piracy as examples, should the International Criminal Law Section of the African Court prosecute all terrorism or piracy cases referred to it? Would this therefore imply that whatever the level of involvement of legal persons in any of these cases, the International Criminal Law Section of the African Court will hold all the corporations criminally liable? Alternatively, what gravity test should the International Criminal Law Section of the African Court employ in deciding which cases to take or not to take? While it is true that a corporation can commit crimes at different thresholds of seriousness, it is important for a supranational criminal court to focus on cases where corporations bear the highest criminal responsibility. The Malabo Protocol must address itself to this reality in order to avoid opening up the International Criminal Law Section of the African Court to all manner of cases with a transnational character involving corporate criminal liability for any kind of involvement at whatever level. A failure to do so means that the International Criminal Law Section of the African Court is likely to be overwhelmed with cases, thus running the risk that it may become ineffective.

In addition, the clause on corporate criminal responsibility applies to all corporations and only excludes states. While this is an advantage inasmuch as it subjects both private and public corporations to criminal accountability for international as well as transnational crimes, it poses a challenge to the International Criminal Law Section of the African Court, especially when it comes to investigating international crimes perpetrated by state-owned corporations or corporations in which the state holds shares. There is a risk that, to some extent, the International Criminal Law Section of the African Court may be perceived to be investigating the state. This may not auger well with some African states. Although the acts of these corporations do not translate to official acts of a state, the probability of state reluctance to cooperate with such investigations should be expected. This is likely to undermine the effectiveness of prosecuting corporate crimes. Moreover – judging by the regional prosecution of international crimes – while it is easy to prosecute persons out of power, it is almost impossible for states to effectively cooperate in prosecutions of persons in high office.

Another possible cooperation-related concern involves non-member states of the Malabo Protocol. The African Court will exercise its criminal jurisdiction where a member state to the Malabo Protocol is '[t]he State on the territory of which the conduct in question occurred' or where '[e]xtraterritorial acts by non-nationals … threaten a vital interest of that State' (Article 46E *bis* of the Malabo Protocol). Given the nature of transnational crimes, it is possible that a corporation found guilty by the International Criminal law Section of the African Court may be registered in a state that is not party to the Malabo Protocol. This presents a challenging area for enforcing court orders and decisions, particularly where the relevant state is a beneficiary of the acts of the guilty corporation. Nonetheless, the International Criminal Law Section of the African Court should adopt relevant guidelines on how to proceed in such circumstances in order to address this anomaly.

6. CONCLUSION

This chapter set out to discuss the Nuremberg principle of individual criminal responsibility in the context of Africa. It has argued that the theory and practice of individual criminal liability in Africa exists at two levels: the traditional African conception and the AU's conception. Although there are instances in which some traditional African practices portray a contrary view, the predominant approach in post-conflict African states and the AU's practices embrace the principle of individual criminal liability. The practice at the AU has even gone further and has expanded the principle of criminal liability for international crimes to expressly provide for corporate criminal liability for international crimes. Thus, the overall conclusion of this chapter is that although the principle of individual criminal liability is essential for accountability in international criminal law, it does not sufficiently address the impunity concerns on the African continent, thus prompting the AU to further incorporate the doctrine of corporate criminal liability.

BIBLIOGRAPHY

Abraham, G. (2015) 'Africa's Evolving Continental Court Structures: At the Crossroads?' South African Institute of International Affairs' South African Institute of International Affairs Occasional Paper No. 209.

Acirokop, P. (2013) 'Accountability for Mass Atrocities: The LRA Conflict in Uganda', LLD thesis, University of Pretoria, https://repository.up.ac.za/bitstream/handle/2263/23898/06chapter6.pdf?sequence=7.

Akande, D. (2004) 'International Law Immunities and the International Criminal Court', *American Journal of International Law* 98: 407–433.

Badar, M.E. (2004) 'From the Nuremberg Charter to the Rome Statute: Defining the Elements of Crimes against Humanity', *San Diego International Law Journal* 5: 73–144.

Bako, P. (2009) 'Does Traditional Conflict Resolution Lead to Justice? The *Mato Oput* in Northern Uganda', *Pretoria Student Law Review* 3: 100–108.

BBC News (2015) 'Chad's Hissen Habré Removed from Senegal Court', 20 July, www.bbc.com/news/world-africa-33592142.

Chambres africaines extraordinaires (2016) 'Communiqué de presse: Démarrage des audiences du procès en appel', http://www.chambresafricaines.org/index.php/le-coin-des-medias/communiqu%C3%A9-de-presse/649-communiqu%C3%A9-de-presse-d%C3%A9marrage-des-audiences-du-proc%C3%A8s-en-appel.html.

Chella, J. (2012) 'The Complicity of Multinational Corporations in International Crimes: An Examination of Principles', PhD thesis, Bond University.

Chesterman, S. (2000) 'An Altogether Different Order: Defining the Elements of Erimes against Humanity', *Duke Journal of Comparative & International Law* 10: 307–344.

Control Council Law No. 10, Punishment of Persons Guilty of War Crimes, Crimes Against Peace and Against Humanity 306 (20 December 1945).

Engle, E. (2006) 'Extraterritorial Corporate Criminal Liability: A Remedy for Human Rights Violations?', *St. John's Journal of Legal Commentary* 20(2): 287–337.

Friman, C.H., Robinson, D. and Wilmshurst, E. (2010) *An Introduction to International Criminal Law and Procedure*, 2nd edn. Cambridge: Cambridge University Press.

Gordon, G.S. (2009) 'Complementarity and Alternative Justice', *Oregon Law Review* 88(3): 621–702.

Høgestøl, S.A.E. (2016) 'The Habré Judgment at the Extraordinary African Chambers: A Singular Victory in the Fight against Impunity', *Nordic Journal of Human Rights* 34(3): 147–156.

Hovil, L. and Quinn, J.I. (2005) 'Peace First, Justice Later: Traditional Justice in Northern Uganda', Refugee Law Project Working Paper No. 17, http://www.refugeelawproject.org/files/working_papers/RLP.WP17.pdf.

ICTJ (2015) 'The Accountability Landscape in Eastern DRC: Analysis of the National Legislative and Judicial Response to International Crimes (2009–2014)', July, https://www.ictj.org/sites/default/files/ICTJ-Briefing-DRC-Prosecutions-2015_1.pdf.

Jackson, R. (1947) 'Second Day, Wednesday, 11/21/1945, Part 04' in *Trial of the Major War Criminals before the International Military Tribunal*. Volume II. Proceedings: 11/14/1945-11/30/1945, 98-102. Nuremberg: IMT.

Kariri, J.N. (2014) 'Can the New African Court Truly Deliver Justice for Serious Crimes?', *ISS Today*, https://issafrica.org/iss-today/can-the-new-african-court-truly-deliver-justice-for-serious-crimes.

Koller, D.S. (2004) 'Immunities of Foreign Ministers: Paragraph 61 of the *Yerodia* Judgment as it Pertains to the Security Council and the International Criminal Court', *American University International Law Review* 20(7): 7–42.

Kyriakakis, J. (2016) 'Corporate Criminal Liability at the African Criminal Court', Briefing Paper – ACRI Meeting, Arusha.

Lahiri, K. (2009) 'Rwanda's Gacaca Courts: A Possible Model for Local Justice in International Crime', *International Criminal Law Review* 9: 321–332.

Legal Notice No. 10 of 2011, The High Court (International Crimes Division) Practice Directions 2011, clause 3.

Murungu, C. (2011) 'Towards a Criminal Chamber in the African Court of Justice and Human Rights', *Journal of International Criminal Justice* 1067–1088.
Nakandha, S. (2016) 'The Kwoyelo Case at the ICD: The Realities of Complementarity in Practice', 5 May, https://www.ijmonitor.org/2016/05/the-kwoyelo-case-at-the-icd-the-realities-of-complementarity-in-practice.
Nwafor, A.O. (2013) 'Corporate criminal responsibility: A comparative analysis', *Journal of African law* 57(1): 81–107.
Pinto, Q.C. and Evans, M. (2008) *Corporate Criminal Liability*, 2nd edn. London: Sweet & Maxwell.
Rose, C. (2008) 'Looking beyond Amnesty and Traditional Justice and Reconciliation Mechanisms in Northern Uganda: A Proposal for Truth-Telling and Reparations', *Boston College Third World Law Journal* 28(2): 345–400.
Trial of the Major War Criminals before the International Military Tribunal, Nuremberg (1947) vol. I, www.loc.gov/rr/frd/Military_Law/pdf/NT_Vol-I.pdf.
Werle, G. and Jessberger, F. (2014) *Principles of International Law*, 3rd edn. Oxford: Oxford University Press.
Van der Wilt, H. (2007) 'Joint Criminal Enterprise: Possibilities and Limitations', *Journal of International Criminal Justice* 5: 91–108.
Williams, G. (1961) *Criminal Law: The General Part*. London: Steven & Sons.

CASE LAW

Flomo v. Firestone Nat'l. Rubber Co., 643 F.3d 1013, 1017 (7th Cir. 2011).
Gacumbitsi, ICTR (AC), Judgment of 7 July 2006.
HL Bolton (Engineering) Co. Ltd. v. TJ Graham & Sons Ltd. [1957] 1 QB 159 (CA).
I G Farben Trial, Case No. 57, US Military Tribunal, Nuremberg, 14 August 1947–29 July 1948, *Law Reports of War Criminals*, vol. X.
Lennard's Carrying Co. Ltd. v. Asiatic Petroleum Co. Ltd. (1915) AC 705.
Ministère Public v. Hissene Habré, Judgment of 30 May 2016, Chambre Africaine Extraiordinaired'Assises (Extraodinary African Chambers), http://www.chambresafricaines.org/pdf/Jugement_complet.pdf.
Munyakazi (AC), Judgment of 28 September 2011.
Prosecutor v. Germain Katanga, Judgment, ICC-01/04-01/07, (Judgment pursuant to article 74 of the Statute) 7 March 2014.
Prosecutor v. Blaskic IT-95-14-T, Trial Chamber of the ICTY, 3 March 2000, https://www.refworld.org/cases,ICTY,4146f1b24.html.
Public Prosecutor's Office and François Diouf v. Hissène Habré, Court of Appeal (Dakar), Judgment No. 135, 4 July 2000.
Questions Relating to the Obligation to Prosecute or Extradite (Belgium v. Senegal) Judgment, [2012] ICJ Reports 422.
Souleymane Guengueng et al. v. Hissène Habré, Judgment No. 14, 20 March 2001.
Tadic, ICTY (AC), Judgment of 15 July 1999.
Thomas Kwoyelo Alias Latoni v. Uganda, Constitutional Petition No. 036/11 (Arising out of HCT-00-ICD-Case No. 2/10), Ruling of the Court of 22 September 2011 (Constitutional Court of Uganda).

Trial of Alfried Felix Alwyn Krupp von Bohlen und Halbach and Eleven Others, US Military Tribunal, Nuremberg, 17 November 1947–30 June 1948, *Law Reports of Trials of War Criminal*, vol. X.
Trial of Bruno Tesch and Two Others (*Zyklon B Case*), 1–8 March 1946, *Law Reports of the Trials of War Criminals*, vol. I.
Trial of Friedrich Flick and Five Others, 20 April–22 December 1947, *Law Reports of the Trials of War Criminals*, vol. IX.

THE APPLICATION OF UNIVERSAL JURISDICTION IN AFRICA

O'Brien Kaaba

1. INTRODUCTION

The existence of universal jurisdiction is a subject of controversy and debate, and its application in Africa has sometimes caused a stir, sparking allegations that the doctrine is unfairly used to target African leaders. Some scholars doubt its legitimacy and argue that it lacks a basis in state practice and is not supported by cogent authorities. This chapter explores the application of universal jurisdiction within Africa. It attempts to demonstrate that the doctrine of universal jurisdiction is founded in customary international law and is evident in state practice, and also manifests itself several other legal authorities. The focus of the chapter is the African continent. It begins with an overview of what constitutes universal jurisdiction. This is important in order to understand what constitutes universal jurisdiction in international law. The next section draws on recognisable authorities to demonstrate that universal jurisdiction is an established doctrine in international law. This is followed by another section discussing the application of universal jurisdiction in Africa. The third section of the chapter is divided into two parts: the first part discusses universal jurisdiction at the African Union (AU) level, while the second looks at universal jurisdiction at the national level. At the AU level, the discussion seeks to draw on the regional normative mechanisms to establish the recognition of universal jurisdiction by African states. At the national level, it seeks to demonstrate that universal jurisdiction is either recognised or has actually been enforced by some African states. Finally, a conclusion is drawn.

2. UNIVERSAL JURISDICTION: AN OVERVIEW

The existence of universal jurisdiction is not universally acknowledged. Matthew Garrod (2018: 129), for example, argues that universal jurisdiction is merely a hollow concept that is not backed by state practice and that its assertion is based on misconceived views of duties arising from treaty obligations to extradite or prosecute. Accordingly, this would mean the doctrine does not exist and what is considered as universal jurisdiction is nothing more than a mistaken view of the correct position of the law. Therefore, universal jurisdiction does not exist. Similarly, Reydams (2010: 26) argues that universal jurisdiction is 'an unhelpful misnomer', a post-Cold War invention perpetuated by non-governmental organisations, human rights activists, lawyers, over-zealous judges, academics and the mass media. In Reydams' view (ibid.: 27), universal jurisdiction is a contradiction and cannot exist because limitations on a state's jurisdiction are a condition *sine qua non* for the existence of the global multi-state system. This view seems to be supported by Kontorovich (2004: 184), who, despite acknowledging the existence of universal jurisdiction, has argued that the exercise of universal jurisdiction may create conflict and hostility between states, as it can be seen as an encroachment on the sovereignty of other countries.

Although there is often conceptual confusion in the literature between universal jurisdiction and the treaty obligations to extradite or prosecute, it does not follow that universal jurisdiction does not exist. The existence of universal jurisdiction has been asserted by courts and scholars.[1] Kontorovich (2010: 8), for example, in a study spanning 10 years from 1998 to 2007, found that universal jurisdiction was still being used as a basis for trying pirates. Kontorovich found that the application of universal jurisdiction increased significantly from about 2008 due to the Somali pirate surge. In the African context, the AU-EU Ad Hoc Expert Group tasked with studying the application of universal jurisdiction in Europe and Africa concluded that: 'African States welcomed the principle of universal jurisdiction and are committed to addressing impunity.'

What then is universal jurisdiction? The AU-EU Technical Ad Hoc Expert Group (2009: para. 8) has defined it as follows:

> Universal criminal jurisdiction is the assertion by one state of its jurisdiction over crimes allegedly committed in the territory of another state by nationals of another

---

1 For example, *Attorney General of the Government of Israel v. Eichmann* (1962) 36 ILR; *R v. Bow Street Metropolitan Stipendiary Magistrate ex parte Pinochet Urgarte (No. 3)* [2000] 1 AC 147. See de Than and Shorts 2003; Broomhall 2003: 105–127.

> state where the crime alleged poses no direct threat to vital interests of the state asserting jurisdiction.[2]

In order to understand universal jurisdiction, it is important to appreciate that under customary international law, each sovereign state has the power to prosecute individuals according to its domestic criminal law for crimes committed within its territory or connected to its territory (de Than and Shorts 2003: 35; Jalloh 2019: 227). This is as a result of the inherent power of states to criminalise conduct they consider harmful to individuals or other vital interests within their territories (Jalloh 2019: 227). Invariably, this means that a state may not exercise its power in relation to the territory of another state. This principle was succinctly stated in the *Lotus* case:

> A state may not exercise its power in any form in the territory of another state. In this sense jurisdiction is certainly territorial, it cannot be exercised by a state outside its territory except by virtue of a permissive rule derived from international custom or a convention.[3]

However, there are at least five exceptions to this restriction in international law, permitting states to exercise jurisdiction even in relation to crimes occurring in foreign territories (Palestinian Centre for Human Rights 2010: 15; Pretorius 2013: 20). These exceptions are the territoriality, protective, passive personality, nationality and universal jurisdiction principles (Broomhall 2003: 20). The territoriality principle recognises the right of each state to punish or prosecute crimes occurring within its territory; the protective principle safeguards a country's fundamental interests by imposing criminal liability on foreign nationals who commit acts abroad which injure the concerned state's fundamental interests; the passive personality principle applies where neither the crime nor the defendant is within the boundaries of the concerned state, but the state asserts jurisdiction because the actual or possible victims are its nationals; and the nationality principle allows each state to determine how to impose criminal liability on its nationals even for conduct occurring outside the national territory (de Than and Short 2003: 35–46; O'Keefe 2015: 9–20). For these four bases of jurisdiction, the state asserting jurisdiction has to show a direct link or nexus between the state and the alleged crime.

Unlike the other four bases of jurisdiction, universal jurisdiction is anchored in customary international law and is founded on the belief that certain crimes are so heinous that they offend the collective conscience of the international community and humanity (Colangelo 2005: 10). Universal jurisdiction is

2 See Jalloh 2010: 6.
3 *France v. Turkey* (1927) PCLJ Series A. No. 10.

therefore founded on the nature of the crime and collective human revulsion against that crime. As such, it can be said that universal jurisdiction is based on the appalling nature of certain crimes and not on any clear nexus between the state and the crime, as crimes which are subject to universal jurisdiction are considered so serious that they are considered the concern of every state. As stated by the International Court of Justice:

> By their very nature [some matters] are the concern of all states. In view of the importance of the rights involved, all states can be held to have a legal interest, in their protection, they are obligations *erga omnes*.[4]

Universal jurisdiction is usually said to have been applied first to the crime of piracy, as a pirate was considered to be *hostis humani generis*, or enemy of the human race (Palestinian Centre for Human Rights 2010: 16; Pretorius 2013: 22). Its roots go back to the sixteenth century. Usually the crime of piracy took place outside the territorial sovereignty of any state, while the crew of pirate ships usually represented several nationalities (Arajarvi 2011: 10). The victims also generally came from various states. These circumstances made it difficult for any state to claim jurisdiction based on any traditional principles of criminal jurisdiction, such as territory or nationality. Therefore, the universal jurisdiction to prosecute and try pirates emerged out of the need to enable the prosecution of those who committed the crime of piracy on the high seas when they were captured (ibid.: 10).

Today, apart from piracy, it is widely accepted that customary international law allows the exercise of universal jurisdiction in relation to the international crimes of genocide, crimes against humanity, war crimes, and torture (AU-EU Technical Ad Hoc Expert Group 2009: 9; Simbeye 2004: 41; O'Keefe 2015: 23). The extension of universal jurisdiction to these crimes evolved gradually. Unlike piracy, which was founded on the necessity of prosecuting pirates who committed crimes on the high seas over which no state had jurisdiction, the other crimes were included under universal jurisdiction on the rationale that all serious international crimes ought to be punished. Therefore, any state that had custody of the perpetrators of the concerned crimes should exercise jurisdiction (Arajarvi 2011: 8).

Langer has argued that universal jurisdiction imposes two kinds of obligations on states. Under the first obligation, states may exercise universal jurisdiction in order to prevent and punish serious international crimes occurring anywhere in the world. The second kind of obligation is the duty imposed on states to ensure that no state becomes a safe haven or place of refuge for persons who have committed serious international crimes (Langer 2015b: 2). It should also

[4] *Barcelona Traction* case [1970] ICJR 3, para. 3.

be mentioned that universal jurisdiction has been asserted in two versions. The first version, which is the most widespread, asserts universal jurisdiction in narrow circumstances, that is, where the accused is in custody of the asserting state (Padmanabhan 2010: 3). Thus, in order to exercise its jurisdiction, the state needs to have the accused in its territory. Under the second version, which is relatively rare, a state may prosecute persons accused of serious international crimes regardless of where the person is (ibid.: 4). The presence of the accused in the forum state is not a prerequisite for exercising jurisdiction.

The principle of universal jurisdiction has been affirmed in a few cases. One of the most well known is the case of *Attorney General of the Government of Israel v. Eichmann*.[5] The case involved the trial of Adolf Eichmann, who was the head of the Jewish office of the German Gestapo and was in charge of 'the Final Solution', the policy that led to the extermination of around 4 million Jews in Europe. He was captured in Argentina and prosecuted in Israel. In justifying its jurisdiction, the Israeli court in part held that:

> The abhorrent crimes defined in the law are not crimes under Israel law alone. These crimes, which struck at the whole of mankind and shocked the conscience of nations, are grave offences against the law of nations itself (*delicta juris gentium*). Therefore, so far from international law negating or limiting the jurisdiction of countries with respect to such crimes, international law is, in the absence of an International Court, in need of the judicial and legislative organs of every country to give effect to its criminal interdictions and to bring the criminals to trial. The jurisdiction to try crimes under international law is universal.[6]

The court further ruled that its right to punish the accused derived from many sources, which includes a universal source that vests the right to prosecute and punish crimes of the nature the accused was charged with within the family of nations and within specific national laws.[7]

More recently, universal jurisdiction was asserted in the *Pinochet* case,[8] where Lord Millet stated:

> In my opinion this systematic use of torture on a large scale and as instrument of state policy had joined piracy, war crimes and crimes against peace as an international crime of universal jurisdiction well before 1984. I consider that it had done so by 1973. For my own part therefore I would hold that the courts of this country already possessed extra territorial jurisdiction in respect to torture on the scale of charges in the present case and did not require the authority of the statute to exercise it …

5 *Attorney General of the Government of Israel v. Eichmann*, above n 1.
6 Ibid., para. 12.
7 Ibid., para. 30.
8 *R v. Bow Street Metropolitan Stipendiary Magistrate ex parte Pinochet Ugarte (No. 3)*, above n 1.

The *Pinochet* case also demonstrates the confusion that can arise between the concept of universal jurisdiction and treaty obligations to extradite or prosecute. Lord Browne-Wilkinson, for example, seemed to wrongly assume that the UN Convention against Torture gave rise to universal jurisdiction, arguing in part that 'the Torture Convention was agreed not in order to create an international crime which had not previously existed but to provide an international system under which the international criminal, the torturer, could find no safe haven'.

Closely related to the concept of universal jurisdiction is the concept of *aut dedere, aut judicare* ('either extradite or prosecute'), which arises from treaty undertakings. Several treaties proscribing serious international crimes define a crime and obligate states parties to prosecute suspects or extradite them to another state willing to prosecute them (Broomhall 2003: 106). It has actually been argued that the obligation to extradite or prosecute is inextricably linked to universal jurisdiction because the obligation is quasi-universal or conditionally universal, that is, it is based on what is allowed in the enabling international instrument (Alston and Goodman 2013: 1140).

In the case of *Belgium v. Senegal*,[9] the International Court of Justice stated that the obligation to extradite or prosecute has a preventive and deterrent character. This is because by equipping themselves with the necessary legal tools to prosecute this type of offence, the states parties ensure that their legal systems will operate to prevent such crimes and commit themselves to coordinating their efforts to eliminate the risk of impunity.

The International Court of Justice further held that such treaty obligations require a concerned state to submit a case to the competent authorities for the purposes of prosecution.[10] However, the obligation to submit the case to the competent authorities does not necessarily have to result in institution of proceedings. Proceedings should only be instituted in light of the available evidence.[11] Where a state has received a request for extradition from another member state, the state where the suspect is in custody or resident relieves itself of the obligation to prosecute by acceding to the request.[12] However, the Court indicated that extradition should be seen as an option given to the state under an applicable treaty, whereas prosecution is an international obligation under the Convention against Torture 1984, the violation of which is a wrongful act engaging the responsibility of the state.[13] The most significant crimes in treaties incorporating the principle of *aut dedere, aut judicare* include torture under the

9 *Questions Relating to the Obligations to Prosecute or Extradite (Belgium v. Senegal) General List No. 144* Judgment of 20 July 2012.
10 Ibid., para. 94.
11 Ibid., para. 95.
12 Ibid.
13 Ibid.

Convention against Torture 1984, grave breaches of the Geneva Conventions of 1949 and Additional Protocol 1 of 1977, enforced disappearance under the Convention against Enforced Disappearance 2006 and attacks against UN personnel under the Convention on Crimes against UN Personnel of 1994 (AU-EU Technical Ad Hoc Expert Group 2009: 9).

3. THE APPLICATION OF UNIVERSAL JURISDICTION IN AFRICA

This section examines the application of the doctrine of universal jurisdiction in Africa. The section is divided into two sub-sections: the first looks at the application of the doctrine at the AU level across the continent, while the second looks at how the doctrine is applied at the national or domestic level within Africa.

3.1. UNIVERSAL JURISDICTION AT THE AU LEVEL

Formal intergovernmental relations between African states date back to the establishment of the Organisation of African Unity (OAU) on 25 May 1963. The OAU was founded on a very frail normative framework in relation to human rights. The OAU Charter did not make the slightest reference to the protection of the fundamental rights. Its purpose was simply to foster the following: unity and solidarity of African states; the coordination of cooperation activities; the defence of state sovereignty; territorial integrity and independence; the eradication of all forms of colonialism; and international cooperation (Article II(1) of the OAU Charter 1963).

In the pursuit of these purposes, the OAU Charter enjoined member states to observe, *inter alia*, the principles of sovereign equality, territorial integrity and non-interference in the internal affairs of other states (Article III of the OAU Charter 1963). These principles had the unfortunate effect of coalescing into a norm of indifference as to how a government treated its nationals within its territory. The OAU itself could not interfere or be seen to meddle in the domestic affairs of member states. This approach was well articulated by President Sekou Touré of Guinea, the then OAU Chairperson, when he stated that the OAU was not a tribunal that could sit in judgment on any member states. Non-interference in the internal affairs of member states was so firmly asserted by the OAU that it was adopted as a continental norm to guide the relations and conduct among all African states.[14] Under these circumstances, it is hardly surprising

[14] Border Disputes among African States Resolution AHG/Res.16 (1) Adopted at the First Ordinary Session of the Assembly of Heads of States and Government, July 1964.

that there was no mention of the doctrine of universal jurisdiction in the OAU normative framework and not a single case of the application of the doctrine by any member state during the time that the OAU was in existence.

The OAU transformed itself into the AU in 2000 following the formal adoption of the AU Constitutive Act on 11 July 2000 in Lomé, Togo and its formal launch on 9 July 2004 in Durban, South Africa. Unlike the OAU Charter, which lacked human rights norms underpinning it, the AU Constitutive Act included among its objectives the promotion and protection of human and peoples' rights (Article 3(h) of the Constitutive Act 2000). Although the AU Constitutive Act adopted the OAU practice of non-interference (Article 4(g) of the Constitutive Act 2000), it tempered it with a new principle entitling the AU to intervene in a member state in respect of grave circumstances, that is, war crimes, genocide and crimes against humanity (Article 4(h)). This development is significant as it demonstrates an official AU policy shift in seeing certain international crimes not solely as domestic matters, but rather as grave concerns that go beyond national frontiers.

Although Article 4(h) does not directly deal with the issue of universal jurisdiction, its implementation opens up the possibility of the use of the universal jurisdiction doctrine. This was recognised by the AU-EU Technical Ad Hoc Expert Group, which recommended complementing Article 4(h) with measures aimed at preventing and punishing crimes against humanity (AU-EU Technical Ad Hoc Expert Group 2009: para. 46). To this end, it was recommended that the AU should develop a model law for the implementation of these measures.

The AU acted on this recommendation with the AU Executive Council's adoption of the African Model National Law on Universal Jurisdiction over International Crimes in July 2012. The adoption of the Model Law, although laudable, was not entirely altruistic, but was instead a reaction to perceptions by African leaders that they were being unfairly targeted by the European application of universal jurisdiction and the International Criminal Court (ICC) indictments (Dube 2015: 451).

The Model Law signifies the understanding of the doctrine of universal jurisdiction by African states, its contents and limits. It is significant as it provides a flexible template for the development of universal jurisdiction legislation by member states and potentially allows for harmonised content of universal jurisdiction laws across the African continent (Dube 2015: 457). It is intended for individual states to adopt and implement according to their national laws and specific contexts.

The preamble to the Model Law recognises that certain crimes are of the utmost serious concern to the AU and its member states and should therefore not go unpunished. It recalls the significance of Article 4(h) of the Constitutive Act, which empowers the AU to intervene in member states in respect of grave circumstances (relating to genocide, war crimes and crimes against humanity) and places primary responsibility for the prosecution of international crimes with member states.

The Model Law's reach over crimes subject to universal jurisdiction is somewhat more extensive than what is generally considered to be part of customary international law. The 'international crimes' (Article 1) to which universal jurisdiction applies are genocide, crimes against humanity, war crimes, piracy, trafficking in drugs and terrorism. Although some of these crimes, such as trafficking in drugs and terrorism, are well-known international or transnational crimes, they have not hitherto been subject to universal jurisdiction.

In order for a state to exercise jurisdiction under the Model Law, the accused must be present within its territory. However, it should be noted that although presence is stated as a requirement for prosecution, the provision is silent on whether or not investigations without the accused are allowed. However, since presence is only explicitly required for prosecutions, it should be assumed that the presence of an accused is not a bar to investigations. This was the approach taken by the South African Constitutional Court in *National Commissioner of the South African Police Service v. Southern African Human Rights Litigation Centre and Others*,[15] although the decision was largely based on the interpretation of relevant South African law.

Article 4(b) of the Model Law innovatively requires that a court shall cede priority to the court of a state in which the crime is committed. The rationale for this is that the territorial state is the one most affected by the crime and therefore must have priority in terms of prosecuting the offence. However, in the event of inaction by the territorial state or its unwillingness and inability to prosecute, any other state may prosecute.

It must be noted that the Model Law uses the words 'is willing and able to prosecute' (Article 4(b)). The use of the conjunctive 'and', as opposed to the disjunctive 'or', suggests that the items being linked must be present together. This entails that before another state can assume the power to prosecute, it must show that the two elements have not been satisfied – that is, it must show that the territorial state is both unwilling and unable to prosecute. According to Dube (2015), this is a more stringent approach than is found under the Rome Statute of the ICC and may have the effect of defeating the goal of ending impunity. Article 17 of the Rome Statute uses the word 'or' as opposed to 'and', thereby simply requiring one element to be present. The Article, which is the main provision on complementarity between the ICC and member states in the Rome Statute, provides that the Court shall consider the case to be admissible in circumstances where 'it is being investigated or prosecuted by a state which has

15 *National Commissioner of the South African Police Service v. Southern African Human Rights Litigation Centre and Others* [2014] ZACC 30.

jurisdiction over it, unless the state is unwilling or unable genuinely to carry out the investigation or prosecution'.

Article 16 of the Model Law makes the jurisdiction of courts over international crimes subject to 'any national or international law immunities'. The provision consequently ensures the effectiveness of the immunity of heads of state and government. This approach is a significant departure from the approach under the Rome Statute, where it is expressly stated that official capacity shall not bar the court from exercising its jurisdiction (Article 27). Considering that heads of state and other senior government officials are the most likely to bear the greatest responsibility for the perpetration of these crimes, the approach by the Model Law seems to leave wide scope for official impunity. However, as argued below, this is a kind of immunity that attaches to the office of the leader and only protects the concerned leader as long as he/she remains in office. Once the leader vacates office, he/she no longer enjoys immunity from criminal prosecution.

Another major development with regard to the doctrine of universal jurisdiction in Africa relates to the adoption of the Protocol Amendment to the Protocol on the Statute of the African Court of Justice and Human Rights in June 2014. The Statute of the Court, which is annexed to the 2014 Protocol, expands the scope of the African Court of Justice and Human Rights (hereinafter the African Court) by establishing within it an international criminal law section (Article 3 of the 2014 Protocol; Articles 16 and 17(3) of the Statute of the African Court). This vests the African Court with jurisdiction to hear all cases relating to international crimes. Just as the Model Law has been criticised for not being born out of altruism, the criminal jurisdiction of the African Court is also seen as being driven by a desire to stave off the perceived targeting of African leaders by the ICC. This is often justified on the basis that between 2009 and 2014, the Court Protocol was the subject of a series of politically charged rhetoric by African leaders to quicken the broadening of the African Court's mandate to include criminal jurisdiction as an alternative to the ICC (Clarke et al. 2019: 2). It is for this reason that some scholars consider it 'a rebel court against the ICC' (ibid.: 2). Regardless of the circumstances leading to the assigning of criminal jurisdiction to the African Court, the fact remains that the Court is now equipped with criminal jurisdiction.

The list of crimes over which the African Court has jurisdiction is extensive, but includes genocide, crimes against humanity and war crimes, piracy, terrorism, trafficking in persons and drug trafficking (Article 28A of the Statute of the African Court 2014). However, the Statute does not directly vest the African Court with universal jurisdiction. Instead, it establishes the traditional bases of jurisdiction, that is, the territoriality, nationality, passive personality and protective jurisdiction principles (Article 46E(2)). Although universal jurisdiction is not expressly provided for in the Statute, it has been argued that it has a potential role to play at the African Court (Ventura and Bleeker 2016: 6).

The argument about the relevance of universal jurisdiction in the criminal mandate of the African Court is anchored in Article 46H(1), which states that the jurisdiction of the African Court 'shall be complementary to that of National Courts'. This entails that the African Court can only admit the matter if a state with jurisdiction over the concerned international crime is unwilling or unable to investigate or prosecute the offence itself. Article 46H(2) specifically uses the phrase 'a state which has jurisdiction'. According to Ventura and Bleeker (2016: 6), this means any state, and not just member states with jurisdiction. The importance of this is that where a state has vested its courts with universal jurisdiction and is willing and able to prosecute, based on the complementarity principle, the African Court would be prevented from admitting or hearing such a case.

However, on the other hand, the effectiveness of the African Court in curbing impunity, particularly with regard to African leaders, is in doubt as the Statute equips serving leaders with immunity. Article 46A *bis* states that no charges shall be brought or continued before the African head of state or government or anyone acting in that capacity. The immunity extends to 'other senior state officials based on their functions and during their tenure of office'. Considering that these leaders are those most likely to bear the greatest responsibility for international crimes because they control the levers of power, the provision significantly weakens the possibility of holding African leaders accountable. Clarke et al. (2019: 36) have noted that there is irony in this development. This is because African leaders equipped the African Court with criminal jurisdiction in order to avoid being targeted by the ICC. However, by clothing themselves with immunity and therefore placing themselves beyond the reach of the African Court, it means that only the ICC, among the international tribunals, has power to try them. Therefore, rather than shielding them, the immunity clause has left them more exposed to the ICC (ibid.: 36).

It should also be noted that Article 46A *bis* only protects African leaders while in office; once they leave office, they no longer enjoy immunity from prosecution by the African Court. This is because immunity is a procedural rather than a substantial rule which is concerned with *if* and *when* a person falls under the jurisdiction of a particular court (Clarke et al. 2019: 34). In the current context, this would mean that the African leaders entitled to immunity before the African Court will be beyond the reach of the Court while they are still in office. However, this does not mean that they have been exonerated from criminal liability; they still bear criminal responsibility for their actions and can be prosecuted once they leave office (ibid.: 34). Nevertheless, this may have the unintended consequence of incentivising African leaders to prolong their stay in office indefinitely.

Outside of the Model Law and the framework of the African Court, perhaps the best illustration of the potential use of the doctrine of universal jurisdiction in ending impunity for grave human rights violations is demonstrated by the case of Hissène Habré.[16] Considering that this case is the subject of Chapter 3 in this volume, it will not be analysed in detail here.

Hissène Habré was President of Chad from 1982 to 1990. His regime was accused of gross human rights violations, which included the systematic use of torture, murder and enforced disappearances. It is estimated that more than 40,000 people were killed and 20,000 were tortured under the Habré regime (Reed Brody 2017: 7). After protracted efforts to bring Habré to justice, the AU and Senegal (the country giving Habré safe haven at that time) signed an agreement to try Habré on 22 August 2012 (see Agreement between the Government of the Republic of Senegal and the African Union on the Extraordinary African Chambers within the Senegalese Judicial System 2012).

The Extraordinary African Chambers (EAC) was established within the Senegalese judicial system to prosecute international crimes committed in the territory of the Republic of Chad between 7 June 1982 and 1 December 1990 (Article 2). Most significantly, the Statute of the EAC vested it with jurisdiction over 'person(s) most responsible for crimes and serious violations of international law and conventions ratified by Chad' (Article 3(1)). Høgestøl argues that vesting the EAC with jurisdiction over crimes not committed in Senegal effectively grounds the jurisdiction of the EAC in the doctrine of universal jurisdiction, as the EAC is not located within Chad, but outside of it, rendering its jurisdictional basis not on the territoriality principle, but on the basis of universalism (Høgestøl 2016: 153).

Habré was eventually convicted in May 2016 and his conviction was sustained on appeal in 2017, making him the first former head of state to be convicted of serious international crimes in the 'municipal' courts of another state. The involvement of the AU in bringing Habré to justice in a sense means that the *Habré* case was tried under the international criminal mechanism set up by the AU to implement universal jurisdiction.

3.2. THE APPLICATION OF UNIVERSAL JURISDICTION AT THE NATIONAL LEVEL

By 2012, 37 out of 54 African states had legislation allowing for universal jurisdiction over one or more serious international crimes (Ventura and Bleeker 2015). There are generally two approaches by which African states legislate for or implement universal jurisdiction at the national level. The first approach is based on legislating for universal jurisdiction premised on customary international law. Countries that apply this approach include

16 *Prosecutor v. Habré, 'Judgment' Chambre Africaine extraordinaire D'Assise* (30 May 2016).

Cameroon, the Democratic Republic of the Congo, Ethiopia and South Africa (AU-EU Technical Ad Hoc Expert Group 2009: 15).

The second approach has been the infusion of provisions relating to universal jurisdiction in legislation implementing the Rome Statute of the International Criminal Court at the domestic level. There are at least 34 African states parties to the Rome Statute and about half of these have either drafted or passed legislation implementing it (Pretorius 2013: 66). Countries that have taken this approach include Uganda, Kenya, Mauritius, Senegal, Burkina Faso, Comoros and the Central Africa Republic (ibid.: 66).

To illustrate how legislation implementing the Rome Statute incorporates universal jurisdiction, South Africa, Uganda and Kenya are used as examples. In the case of South Africa, it was the first African state to sign the Rome Statute. In order to implement its obligations under the Rome Statute, it enacted the Implementation of the Rome Statute of the International Criminal Court Act 27 of 2002 (hereinafter the Rome Statute Act).

Section 4(3)(c) of the Rome Statute Act vests South African courts with jurisdiction where any person commits a crime outside of South African territory, but is present in the South African territory after committing the crime. Thus, the only prerequisite for a South African court to exercise its jurisdiction is the presence of the accused in South Africa. It does not matter where the crime was committed, who the victims were or what major interests were offended. In *National Commissioner of the South African Human Rights Litigation Centre and Another*,[17] the South African Constitutional Court held that the presence of an accused in South Africa is not a prerequisite for the law enforcement agencies to be able to investigate alleged international crimes. Thus, although trial cannot take place until an accused is before the court, this does not act as a bar to the successful investigation of the alleged crime or crimes.

In the case of *Minister of Justice and Constitutional Development and Others v. Southern Africa Litigation Center and Others*,[18] the South African Supreme Court of Appeal confirmed that in implementing its obligations under the Rome Statute by passing legislation implementing the Statute, the country did so on the basis that all forms of immunity, including head of state immunity, would not constitute a bar to the prosecution of international crimes in South Africa.[19] The case related to the arrest of the Sudanese President Omar al-Bashir, who was in South Africa for an international meeting while he was the subject of an arrest warrant issued by the ICC.

---

17 *National Commissioner of the South African Human Rights Litigation Centre and Another*, above n 15.

18 *Minister of Justice and Constitutional Development and Others v. Southern Africa Litigation Center and Others* [2016] ZASCA 17.

19 Ibid., para. 103.

Similarly, section 8(c) of Kenya's International Crimes Act 2008 vests Kenyan courts with jurisdiction over international crimes if the accused is present in Kenya. Therefore, where the offence was committed and who the victims were is immaterial. As in the South African case, it can be assumed that while adjudication would require the victim to be present, investigations can be carried out in the absence of the accused. Further, in 2008, Kenya signed a Memorandum of Understanding (MOU) with the US to prosecute captured pirates in its territory. Similar MOUs were subsequently signed with the UK, the European Union and other foreign states (Gathii 2010: 101). In order to effectively carry out this mandate, Kenya passed the Merchant Shipping Act 2009. However, Kenya's assertion of universal jurisdiction over piracy pre-dates both the 2008 and 2009 Acts. For example, in 2006, the US handed over to the Kenyan authorities 10 Somali pirates it had captured on the high seas in January 2006. The pirates were charged with hijacking a ship on the high seas, threatening its crew and demanding a ransom. They were convicted and sentenced to seven years' imprisonment.[20] Internally, the case rested in part on a generous interpretation of the territorial jurisdiction of the Kenyan courts (ibid.: 108).

In the case of Uganda, the relevant statute is the International Criminal Court Act 2010. Universal jurisdiction is provided for under section 18(d), in similar words to those in the Kenyan statute. The section vests Ugandan courts with jurisdiction where a person commits an international crime outside of the territory of Uganda, but is present in Uganda after committing the crime. In addition, in 2008, Uganda established a war crimes division of the High Court with jurisdiction to try the offences of genocide, war crimes, crimes against humanity, terrorism, piracy and human trafficking (Pretorius 2013: 66).

The inclusion of universal jurisdiction in domestic laws implementing the Rome Statute obligations gives African states an appropriate additional and potentially significant mechanism for redressing impunity. However, it should be noted that outside the context of the prosecution of Somali pirates in the Kenyan courts and the conviction of Habré in Senegal, there does not seem to have been any single case successfully completed in the domestic courts of any African state that has applied or relied on the mechanism or doctrine of universal jurisdiction. In addition, there are at least three major limitations found in most of the legislation implementing universal jurisdiction in African states. First, many states require that the accused should be present in the territory in order for the courts to be seized with the case. In the absence of

20 See *R v. Hassan M. Ahmed and Nine Others* (2006) Criminal Case No. 434.

the accused, the courts cannot proceed against the accused. Second, in some countries (for example, Botswana and Nigeria), universal jurisdiction is limited to certain superior courts; lower courts cannot exercise that power. Third and finally, in many countries (for example, Botswana, Eswatini, Kenya, Lesotho, Namibia, Nigeria, the Seychelles, Sierra Leone, Tanzania and Zimbabwe), proceedings can only be commenced by the Attorney General (AU-EU Technical Ad Hoc Expert Group 2009: para. 18). Since the Attorney General is usually a senior government official, usually an *ex officio* cabinet minister and chief legal advisor to the government, decisions to prosecute are more likely to be influenced by political considerations than by the merits of the case.

The paucity of universal jurisdiction prosecutions in Africa suggests that making crimes subject to universal jurisdictions does not in any way guarantee that states will use that jurisdiction. As asserted by Kontorovic (2010: 10): 'The endorsement by nations of universal jurisdiction as an international legal norm seems almost entirely unrelated to their willingness to put it into practice.' However, this should not be taken as tolerance for impunity. There could be several reasons that may inhibit states from easily invoking this doctrine, ranging from logistical challenges of collecting evidence of crimes committed in a far-away place and locating witnesses to the costs involved of successfully mounting the whole prosecution. For many countries with limited resources and faltering domestic criminal justice systems, prosecuting international crimes under the doctrine of universal jurisdiction may entail assuming a significantly heavy burden.

A question may be raised about the continuing relevance of universal jurisdiction in Africa, considering that the majority of African states (33 out of 54) are members of the ICC. Langer (2015b) has provided three convincing reasons for the continuing relevance of universal jurisdiction in Africa. The first argument is that universal jurisdiction still has functional legitimacy in the sense that in many cases, it is the only mechanism available to prosecute perpetrators of core international crimes. This is in view of the fact that pursuant to Article 12 of the Rome Statute, the ICC only has jurisdiction to try crimes occurring in the territories of member states. This means that about 22 African states that are not members of the ICC are ordinarily not within the reach of the mandate of the ICC (Langer 2015b: 16).

The second argument in favour of the continuing existence of universal jurisdiction is that the ICC has limited resources and capacity, and therefore can only prosecute a small number of global crimes. As such, there will a continuing role for states to play in bringing international criminals to justice. The third and final reason for maintaining universal jurisdiction in Africa is that it has received wide support from a large number of states, international human rights organisations and other global actors (Langer 2015b: 20).

4. CONCLUSION

This chapter has discussed the application of universal jurisdiction in Africa. Although the doctrine of universal jurisdiction is controversial, it has been embraced by African states. This has been shown through the adoption of the Model Law that each AU member state could enact, taking into account its specific context. In developing the Model Law, the African states have included crimes such as drugs and human trafficking and terrorism, which are traditionally not considered subject to the exercise of universal jurisdiction under customary international law. Therefore, the scope of crimes over which universal jurisdiction can be exercised in Africa is far broader than those ordinarily recognised under customary international law. Another notable way in which universal jurisdiction may play a role is through the African Court, which has been vested with the jurisdiction to try international crimes. By including the practice of complementarity in the Statute of the African Court, it means that any state that has jurisdiction has to be considered before the African Court can exercise jurisdiction. However, this mandate of the African Court is not yet active as the 2014 Protocol has not yet come into force.

At the national level, most of the legislation implementing universal jurisdiction was inspired by states' membership of the ICC. Although ICC membership does not require the inclusion of universal jurisdiction in implementing domestic legislation, many African states have provisions on universal jurisdiction. However, these statutes require the accused to be present in the territory of the forum state in order for the courts to exercise jurisdiction. Despite these efforts at crystallising the application of universal jurisdiction in Africa, there is no successful case involving the application of universal jurisdiction that has been concluded in the domestic courts of any African state, except that of Hissène Habré at the hands of the EAC in Senegal and case of Somali pirates in Kenya.

BIBLIOGRAPHY

Alson, P. and Goodman, R. (2013) *International Human Rights*. Oxford: Oxford University Press.

Arajarvi, N. (2011) 'Looking Back from Nowhere: Is There a Future for Universal Jurisdiction over International Crimes?', *Tilburg Law Review* 16: 5–20.

AU-EU Technical Ad Hoc Expert Group on the Principle of Universal Jurisdiction Report, Brussels (2009) 8672/1/09 Rev1.

Brody, R. (2017) *Victims Bring A Dictator to Justice: The Case of Hissene Habre*. Berlin: Bread of the World.

Broomhall, B. (2003) *International Justice and the International Criminal Court: Between Sovereignty and the Rule of Law*. Oxford: Oxford University Press.

Clarke, K.M., Jalloh, C.C. and Nmehielle, V.O. (2019) 'Origins and Issues of the African Court of Justice and Human and Peoples; Rights' in C.C. Jalloh, K.M. Clarke and V.O. Nmehielle (eds), *The African Court of Justice and Human and Peoples' Rights in Context: Development and Challenges*. Cambridge: Cambridge University Press, pp. 1–54.

Colangelo, A.J. (2005) 'The Legal Limits of Universal Jurisdiction', *Virginia Journal of International Law* 47: 10–58.

De Than, C. and Shorts, E. (2003) *International Criminal Law and Human Rights*. London: Sweet & Maxwell.

Dube, A. (2015) 'The AU Model Law on Universal Jurisdiction: An African Response to Western Prosecutions Based on the Universality Principle', *Potchefstroom Electronic Law Journal* 18: 450–487.

Garrod, M. (2018) 'Unravelling the Confused Relationship between Treaty Obligations to Extradite or Prosecute and Universal Jurisdiction in Light of the Habré Case', *Harvard International Law Journal* 59: 125–1196.

Gathii, J.T. (2010) 'Jurisdiction to Prosecute Non-national Pirates Captured by Third States under Kenyan and International Law', *Loyola International and Comparative Law Review* XX: 101–140.

Høgestøl, S.A.E. (2016) 'The Habré Judgment at the Extraordinary African Chambers: A Singular Victory in the Fight against Impunity', *Nordic Journal of Human Rights* 34(3): 147–156.

Jalloh, C.C. (2010) 'Universal Jurisdiction, Universal Prescription? A Preliminary Assessment of the African Union Perspective on Universal Jurisdiction', *Criminal Law Forum* 21: 1–65.

Jalloh, C.C. (2019) 'A Classification of the Crimes in the Malabo Protocol' in C. Jalloh, K.M. Clarke and V.O. Nmehielle (eds), *The African Court of Justice and Human and Peoples' Rights in Context: Development and Challenges*. Cambridge: Cambridge University Press, pp. 225–256.

Kontorovich, E. (2004) 'The Piracy Analogy: Modern Universal Jurisdiction's Hallow Foundations', *Harvard International law Journal* 45: 184–199.

Kontorovich, E. (2010) 'An Empirical Examination of the Universal Jurisdiction for Piracy', Northwestern University Public Law and Legal Theory Series No. 09–25.

Langer, M. (2015a) 'The Archipelago and the Wheel: The Universal Jurisdiction and the International Criminal Court Regimes' in M. Minow, C. True-Frost and A. Whiting (eds), *The Global Prosecutor: Constraints and Promise*. Michigan: University of Michigan Press, pp. 1–54.

Langer, M. (2015b) 'Universal Jurisdiction is Not Disappearing', *Journal of International Criminal Justice* 13: 2–15.

O'Keefe, R. (2015) *International Criminal Law*. Oxford: Oxford University Press.

Padmanabhan, A. (2010) 'Origin, Development and Evolution of the Principle of Universal Jurisdiction: A Study of its Application in National Courts and Practical Obstacles Facing its Implementation'. Available at SSRN: https://ssrn.com/abstract=1629437 or http://dx.doi.org/10.2139/ssrn.1629437.

Palestinian Centre for Human Rights (2010) *The Principle and Practice of Universal Jurisdiction*. Palestine: PCHR Ltd.

Pretorius, J.P. (2013) 'Does Universal Jurisdiction in Southern African Legislation Implementing the Rome Statute Provide Some Solution to Impunity in the African Context?', LLM Thesis, University of Pretoria.
Reydams, L. (2010) 'The Rise and Fall of Universal Jurisdiction' in W. Schabas and N. Bernas (eds), *Handbook of International Criminal Law*. London: Routledge, pp. 337–373.
Simbeye, Y. (2004) *Immunity and International Criminal Law*. London: Routledge.
Ventura, M.J. and Bleeker, A.J. (2015) 'AU Protocol on Amendment to the Protocol on the Statute of the African Court of Justice and Human Rights', paper delivered to the Africa Legal Aid Symposium on Universalizing the Rome Statute of the International Criminal Court, Johannesburg, South Africa, 18–19 May.
Ventura, M.J. and Bleeker, A.J. (2016) 'Universal Jurisdiction, African Perceptions of the International Criminal Court and the New AU Protocol on Amendments to the Protocol on the Statute of the African Court of Justice and Human Rights' in E.A. Ankumah (ed.), *The International Criminal Court and Africa: One Decade on*. Cambridge: Intersentia, pp. 441–460.

CASE LAW

Attorney General of the Government of Israel v. Eichmann (1962) 36 ILR.
Barcelona Traction case [1970] ICJR 3.
France v. Turkey (1927) PCLJ Series A. No. 10.
Minister of Justice and Constitutional Development and Others v. Southern African Litigation Centre and Others [2016] ZASCA 17.
National Commissioner of the South African Police Service v. Southern African Human Rights Litigation Centre and Another [2014] ZACC 30.
Prosecutor v. Habré, 'Judgment' Chambre Africaine extraordinaire D'Assise (30 May 2016).
R v. Bow Street Metropolitan Stipendiary Magistrate ex parte Pinochet Urgarte (No. 3) [2000] 1 AC 147.
R v. Hassan M. Ahmed and Nine Others (2006) Criminal Case No. 434.
Questions Relating to the Obligation to Prosecute or Extradite (Belgium v. Senegal), General List No. 144, Judgment of 20 July 2012.

AFRICAN VICTIMS OF MASS ATROCITIES BEFORE DOMESTIC JURISDICTIONS AND THE INTERNATIONAL CRIMINAL COURT

Bargaining for Justice

Felix Mukwiza Ndahinda

1. INTRODUCTION

On 8 June 2018, the Appeals Chamber of the International Criminal Court (ICC) rendered an acquittal verdict in favour of Jean-Pierre Bemba Gombo, the founding leader of the Movement for the Liberation of Congo (MLC), an armed movement turned political party in the Democratic Republic of the Congo (DRC). Bemba had been previously convicted on 21 March 2016 by a Trial Chamber for his command responsibility for crimes allegedly committed by a contingent of his subordinates deployed in the Central African Republic (CAR) at the request of the then sitting President Ange-Felix Patassé to fend off an armed insurgency. He was found guilty on counts of murder and rape as both crimes against humanity and war crimes. He was also found guilty of pillaging as a war crime, and was sentenced, three months later, to 18 years' imprisonment.[1] The Appeals Chamber acquitted him on the grounds that the Trial Chamber had erred in establishing his command responsibility through a failure to take 'all necessary and reasonable measures in response to MLC crimes in the CAR'.[2] The Appeals Chamber concluded that Bemba could not be held liable because 'one of the elements of command responsibility under article 28(a) of the Statute was not properly established'.[3] Just as Bemba's earlier conviction was widely celebrated by victim rights advocates as a 'historic step forward for victims', particularly victims of sexual violence (Clark 2016),[4] his acquittal was, predictably, denounced as an 'affront' to victims, particularly to the 5,229 victims who participated in ICC proceedings instituted by the prosecution against him.[5]

The ICC verdict in the Bemba case concluded a long chapter of criminal judicial proceedings instituted in the domestic courts of the CAR against Bemba and other actors involved in the conflict. Proceedings in the CAR against former President Patassé and others, including Bemba, for crimes committed during the 2002/2003 period of protracted conflict in the country were initiated in 2003. However, political manoeuvring and local sensitivities involved in prosecuting high-profile political actors still enjoying some level of popular backing in a polarised context resulted in a discontinuation of domestic proceedings followed by a referral of the CAR situation to the ICC by the new administration led by François Bozizé (Carayannis 2015: 258–262). The proceedings against Bemba epitomise the challenges faced by domestic and international tribunals in delivering justice to victims of mass atrocities, the

---

1 *The Prosecutor v. Jean-Pierre Bemba Gombo*, Judgment pursuant to Article 74 of the Statute, ICC-01/05-01/08-3343, 21 March 2016, para. 752; Decision on Sentence pursuant to Article 76 of the Statute, ICC-01/05-01/08-3399, 21 June 2016, para. 97.

2 *The Prosecutor v. Jean-Pierre Bemba Gombo*, Judgment on the appeal of Mr Jean-Pierre Bemba Gombo against Trial Chamber III's 'Judgment pursuant to Article 74 of the Statute', ICC-01/05-01/08-3636-Red, 8 June 2018, para. 194.

3 Ibid.

4 Amnesty International, 'International Criminal Court: Bemba Verdict a Historic Step Forward for Victims of Sexual Violence', 21 March 2016, https://www.amnesty.org/en/latest/news/2016/03/international-criminal-court-bemba-verdict-a-historic-step-forward-for-victims-of-sexual-violence.

5 FIDH (International Federation for Human Rights), 'Acquittal of Jean Pierre Bemba on Appeal: An Affront to Thousands of Victims', 8 June 2018, https://www.fidh.org/en/region/Africa/central-african-republic/acquittal-of-jean-pierre-bemba-on-appeal-an-affront-to-thousands-of.

ambiguous interactions between these forums of justice, and the hurdles faced by victims in navigating paths towards justice and reparations.

The present inquiry seeks to discursively examine the contours of victims' rights and agency in African societies involved in conflicts that have attracted legal responses from domestic courts and the ICC. The establishment of the ICC was widely celebrated as a great achievement in fighting impunity for atrocious crimes and an unprecedented milestone in the global acknowledgement and vindication of victims' rights (Doria, Gasser and Bassiouni 2009: 895; Stahn 2015: 1133 ff). After decades of asserting the principle of international criminal responsibility for the most atrocious crimes through the development of a criminal branch of international law, the establishment of the ICC took the extra step of creating a space for victims within the workings of the institutions (Fischer 2003: 187–192; Markus 2010: 79–91). Rather than being mere potential witnesses, victims were, in principle, afforded the opportunity to actively participate in criminal proceedings. From subjects in a judicial process focused on protecting the interests of society at large, the ICC system turned them into actors in their own right.

Accommodation of victims' rights within the Statute creating the ICC was a culmination of a long, global campaign – initiated in developed countries from the Global North – for recognition of victim rights within the criminal justice system (Karmen 2015: 40–57). In essence, these campaigns, which generated a progressive recognition of victims' rights within the criminal justice process, represented a global rediscovery and re-activation, beyond the currently dominant punitive paradigms, of the reparative and restorative functions of justice known to many traditional African societies. In the more than 15 years since the entry into force of the Statute establishing the ICC, narratives on victims' rights to participate in criminal proceedings and receive reparations are frequently involved in justifying the Court's involvement in African and other conflict settings.

The promise of victims' rights in the ICC system has limitations inherent to the limited ability of any international criminal tribunal to deliver justice to thousands, if not millions, of victimised individuals within contexts where such tribunals are called upon to deliver justice. International crimes characteristically imply mass victimisation. Yet the experiences of international or hybrid tribunals such as the Nuremberg Tribunal, the International Criminal Tribunal for the former Yugoslavia, the International Criminal Tribunal for Rwanda, the Special Court for Sierra Leone and the Extraordinary Chambers within the Courts of Cambodia, among others, show that these institutions can only handle a fairly limited number of cases. Such limitations are also reflected in the still relatively limited number of situations and cases processed at different stages before the ICC since the entry in force of the Statute creating the Court. These inherent limitations of international justice imply that justice can be best served if it complements work done at domestic levels.

Much has been written about victims' rights, participation and reparations before the ICC (Funk 2010; Bonacker and Safferling 2013; Fletcher 2015; Tibori-Szabó and Hirst 2017; Moffett 2017). Other studies have examined domestic transitional justice dynamics in various contexts, including within countries subject to proceedings before the ICC (Shaw, Waldorf and Hazan 2010; Anders and Zenker 2015). Drawing insights from four contrasting domestic contexts of ICC interventions – namely the CAR, the DRC, Uganda and Côte d'Ivoire – the present analysis seeks to understand how victims' rights and needs are catered for in these contexts. The inquiry will in particular seek to better understand victims' agency, their ability to meaningfully participate in available domestic and international processes, and whether and how their voice is carried and interests served in these different platforms. It builds on existing research, data and case law from the ICC and relevant domestic courts.

2. VICTIMHOOD AND MASS ATROCITIES

The literature in the fields of criminology and victimology has captured the complex meanings, manifestations and implications of victimisation. Karmen defines victimisation as 'an asymmetrical interpersonal relationship that is abusive, painful, destructive, parasitical, and unfair' (2015: 2). In his call for a free victim agency, the criminologist and victimologist van Dijk captured the disempowering attribute attached to the notion of victimhood in Western languages, tracing the concept back to the Christian account of the Passion of Christ, the sacrificial lamb (2009: 3). The author contends that based on this loaded background, 'conventional representations of victimhood' carry the image of 'passive suffering and helplessness' (ibid.: 12). This and several other studies have elaborated on the multiple manifestations, consequences and reactions to victimisation by the victim, the wrongdoer and wider society. In order to better capture the complex manifestations of victimhood, it is important to revisit certain key findings in studies on individual and collective victimisation.

First, studies on the impact of crime show that individuals may directly or indirectly be negatively affected by the criminal offence or by societal responses to such offences (Mawby and Walklate 1994: 32–33). Harm inflicted on a person primarily affects the individual considered to be the direct victim. However, the victim's next of kin may also be indirectly affected because of their intimate affinity with the primary victim. Moreover, members of the wider community may also experience the reverberations of an offence, for instance, in terms of changing their behaviour and attitudes out of fear of being victimised themselves (ibid.: 33). Societal responses to the harm suffered by victims may also give rise to further victimisation or what is known as secondary victimisation. For instance, studies have shown that victims or witnesses involved in the criminal justice process 'frequently feel let down by that process through not being kept informed of what was happening in their case, being treated unsympathetically by the professionals working in the criminal justice process, or not being believed when they are giving their evidence' (Walklate 2007: 74).

Second, the existing literature shows that individuals are affected differently by the harm inflicted upon them (Hoyle 2012: 404; Wolhuter, Olley and Denham 2009). Various factors – such as the type of crime, the personality or personal circumstances of the victim or the offender, whether the harmful behaviour occurs only once or is repeated and the suitability of societal responses to victimisation – either mitigate or exacerbate the impact of victimisation. Accordingly, it is documented that 'the impact of crime is greater for more serious crimes' (Wolhuter, Olley and Denham 2009: 44). Based on these considerations, studies caution against treating victims as a homogeneous whole with the same reactions to and needs after being victimised. Depending on these contextualised realities surrounding victimisation, some victims may demonstrate relative resilience (Dutton and Greene 2010; Walklate 2011) and hence require tailored responses to their unfortunate experience.

Third, harmful behaviour may be inflicted upon individuals, a group of individuals or a collective entity, such as an ethnic, religious, racial or national community. The legal concept of genocide defined as targeting individuals because of their belonging to a defined group. The same goes for the notion of ethnic cleansing. Understanding the dynamics of collective victimisation is therefore even more challenging: in addition to capturing individual dimensions of victimhood, examinations of the effects of mass atrocities, particularly those committed within protracted conflicts, require special attention to be paid to the effects of the harm inflicted on a certain group or on individuals because of their connection to the group. Bar-Tal (2000, 2003, and 2007) and Noor et al. (2012), among others, have elaborated on the cycle of violence and suffering associated with competing claims of victimhood by different communities involved in protracted conflicts. In such contexts, it is contended that victimhood 'can be experienced through one's direct exposure to an out-group's acts of victimization … or indirectly through witnessing fellow in-group members suffer at the hands of the out-group' (Noor et al. 2012: 532). In contexts where competitive claims of victimhood prevail, society's responses to victimisation in such domains as justice and memorialisation are instrumentally shaped by the tensions underlying such claims. Once expectations for redress, particularly from vulnerable victims, go unmet, those victims run the risk of becoming even more vulnerable and subjected to secondary victimisation (Wemmers and de Brouwer 2011: 290–294; Hobbs 2014: 11). Subsequent sections in the present analysis will examine how victims' agency is deployed in contexts where parallel domestic and international processes seek to redress the harm done to victims of mass atrocities.

3. THE DEVELOPING LEGAL FRAMEWORK ON VICTIMS' RIGHTS

3.1. INTERNATIONAL RECOGNITION OF VICTIMS' RIGHTS

Accommodation of victims' rights within criminal justice processes and reparation for the harm suffered by victims of crimes have been major concerns in several domestic legal systems for decades, particularly since the United Nations adopted the 1985 Declaration of Basic Principles of Justice for Victims of Crime and Abuse of Power. This defines victims as 'persons who, individually or collectively, have suffered harm, including physical or mental injury, emotional suffering, economic loss or substantial impairment of their fundamental rights, through acts or omissions that are in violation of criminal laws operative within Member States, including those laws proscribing criminal abuse of power' (para. 1). It recognises four sets of victims' rights, namely: (i) access to justice and fair treatment; (ii) restitution; (iii) compensation; and (iv) assistance (paras. 4–17).

The reference to violations of domestic criminal laws in the above definition was later replaced by 'gross violations of international human rights law, or serious violations of international humanitarian law' in para. 8 of the 2005 UN Basic Principles and Guidelines on the Right to a Remedy and Reparation for Victims of Gross Violations of International Human Rights Law and Serious Violations of International Humanitarian Law. These Guidelines reiterate the obligation of states to abide by human rights and humanitarian law norms as a means of preventing or minimising risks of victimisation (paras. 1–3). Once victimisation occurs, states are reminded of their duty to treat victims with humanity and respect (para. 10) and to uphold victims' substantive and procedural rights, which cover: (i) equal and effective access to justice; (ii) adequate, effective and prompt reparation for harm suffered; and (iii) access to relevant information concerning violations and reparation mechanisms (para. 11). In the particular case of reparation for the harm suffered, victims are entitled to 'full and effective reparation' in the form of 'restitution, compensation, rehabilitation, satisfaction and guarantees of non-repetition' (para. 18).

By offering victims the ability to participate in proceedings and seek reparations, the Rome Statue of the ICC[6] represented a logical outcome of the preceding developments in international human rights, and humanitarian law whose central preoccupation concerned the treatment of individuals rather than states (Gasser 2009: 1111; Van den Wyngaert 2011). Substantively, the Statute puts victims' interests at the centre of prosecutorial

6 Rome Statute of the International Criminal Court, UN Doc. A/CONF.183/9, 17 July 1998.

decisions to initiate investigations and prosecutions (Articles 15 and 53). Once proceedings are instituted, Article 68(3) mandates the ICC to allow victims whose interests are affected to present their views and concerns 'at stages of the proceedings determined to be appropriate by the Court and in a manner which is not prejudicial to or inconsistent with the rights of the accused and a fair and impartial trial'. The provision specifies that such views and concerns 'may be presented by the legal representatives of the victims where the Court considers it appropriate', under modalities to be determined in the Court's Rules of Procedure and Evidence (RPE).[7] Article 75 announces the framework for reparations for victims, which explicitly covers restitution, compensation and rehabilitation. The Court is empowered to determine 'the scope and extent' of the harm to the victim, directly order the convicted person to make specific reparation to the victim and/or order that the award for reparations be made by a trust fund for victims (TFV), the establishment of which is provided for under Article 79 (for more on these provisions, see Wemmers 2009; Markus 2010: 79–91; McCarthy 2015; Vasiliev 2015). The Rome Statute neither elaborates on the definition of who qualifies as a victim nor expands on victims' entitlement to protection, participation and reparation. These details are covered in the RPE (Rules 85–99) and form part of the growing jurisprudence of the Court.

3.2. EVOLVING VICTIMS' RIGHTS WITHIN DOMESTIC LEGAL PROCESSES IN AFRICA

Legal systems across the world are increasingly influenced by the developing international norms on victims' rights. An examination of the relevant domestic legal and institutional frameworks in Uganda, the DRC, the CAR and Côte d'Ivoire shows different levels of accommodation of the rights and needs of victims of mass atrocities. By ratifying the Rome Statute, these countries undertook to abide by their treaty obligations, including by accommodating victims' rights and needs. However, each has followed a unique trajectory in dealing with victims' rights issues within its domestic legal system.

In Uganda, since the signing of the Juba Peace Agreement on Accountability and Reconciliation between the Government of the Republic of Uganda and the Lord's Resistance Army (LRA) on 29 June 2007, victims' rights have taken centre stage in protracted debates over the desirability of domestic transitional justice processes. In a reflection of the legal pluralism that characterises many

---

7 ICC, Rules of Procedure and Evidence, ICC-ASP/1/3 and Corr.1), Part II.A, 3–10 September 2002.

African countries, the Agreement contemplated a plurality of 'legal arrangements' (para. 2.1) aimed at ensuring accountability and reconciliation. It provides for victims' rights under the proposed proceedings, including the right to legal representation (paras. 3.7 and 3.8) and reparation (para. 6.4), participation (para. 8.2) and access to information (para. 8.3). A key step in the enforcement of the Agreement was the creation of an International Crimes Division (ICD) of the High Court of Uganda in 2008, which is tasked with trying serious international crimes codified under Ugandan law.[8] Such existing laws were further complemented by the enactment of the ICC Act in 2010, which aimed at giving effect to the Rome Statute within the domestic legal system.[9] A more comprehensive national transitional justice policy was debated for several years, with a first draft circulated in 2013,[10] before it was finally adopted by the Ugandan government in June 2019.[11] The policy is presented as a 'holistic intervention to achieving lasting peace' by addressing 'justice, accountability and reconciliation needs of post-conflict Uganda'. Given its untested nature, it remains to be seen whether the new policy will trigger new dynamics that reinforce reparative justice for victims.

The Congolese legal system gives the status of *parties civiles* (civil parties) to individuals and even collective entities harmed through criminal conduct in cases brought before domestic military and ordinary courts. The distinction between ordinary and military courts in this context is important because until 2013 – when a new law empowered appeals courts to prosecute cases of genocide, war crimes and crimes against humanity[12] – international crimes were mainly prosecuted by military tribunals. Having been granted the right to participate as *parties civiles*, victims of ordinary or serious (international) crimes can participate in proceedings during the trial and seek reparations (Mbokani 2016: 347). Mbokani points out that Congolese law does not provide legal guarantees that victims can initiate criminal proceedings, receive information or protection, or express views/concerns in the pre-trial phase of proceedings (ibid.: 352–355). Despite progressive reforms undertaken to enable prosecutions of international crimes in domestic courts, Congolese law, compared to emerging

8 http://judiciary.go.ug/data/smenu/18/International%20Crimes%20Division.html; Kasande Sarah Kihika and Meritxell Regué, 'Pursuing Accountability for Serious Crimes in Uganda's Courts: Reflections on the Thomas Kwoyelo Case', January 2015, https://www.ictj.org/sites/default/files/ICTJ-Briefing-Uganda-Kwoyelo-2015.pdf.

9 International Criminal Court Act, Act No. 11/2010 (2010).

10 According to Avocats sans Frontières (ASF), 'Reparations at the Core of Transitional Justice in Uganda', https://www.asf.be/blog/2017/01/25/reparations-at-the-core-of-transitional-justice-in-uganda, an eighth draft of the policy was debated in 2015.

11 Government of Uganda, Justice, Law & Order Sector, *The National Transitional Justice Policy: An Overview*, June 2019.

12 See Article 91 of Loi organique n°13/011-B du 11 avril 2013 portant organisation, fonctionnement et compétences des juridictions de l'ordre judiciaire, JORDC N° Special, 1 April 2013.

international norms, still harbours shortcomings in such areas as victims' rights to participate in pre-trial proceedings, to legal representation, particularly legal aid, to protection, and to call and/or question witnesses during trial proceedings (ibid.: 364).

Moreover, in a country that has witnessed mass victimisation for more than two decades, with victims estimated to be in the hundreds of thousands, if not millions (Ndahinda 2016: 167–171), where large-scale sexual violence crimes have been and are still committed, and where rampant corruption is institutionalised, gaps remain in terms of legal codification, legal practice and enforcement of legal decisions.[13] Demands for recognition and justice for many thousands of individuals victimised over decades, including a projected establishment of credible legal mechanisms of accountability in the form of a special tribunal for the DRC, have remained trapped in the prevailing climate of violence, insecurity and political uncertainties in the country's governance. Attempts to establish other victim-centric transitional justice processes, including a functional Truth and Reconciliation Commission (TRC), have remained unsuccessful. A TRC established in 2003 with an ambitious mandate covering events dating back to the country's independence closed in 2007 with the presentation of a report to Parliament, without achieving its main goal of 'establishing truth and promoting peace, justice reparation, forgiveness and reconciliation'.[14] Instead, it recommended the creation of a second TRC which did not materialise (Naughton 2014: 47). The work of domestic courts and the ICC's intervention in the DRC are still considered to be insufficient in providing remedies to all victims in view of persistent calls for a more robust and comprehensive transitional justice process in the country (ICTJ 2017: 17).

In the neighbouring CAR, after years of instability, violence and failed attempts to institute domestic proceedings against high-ranking officials, the country recently achieved what the DRC has failed to do so far in establishing its Special Criminal Court (Cour Pénale Speciale (CPS)). The Law Establishing the Cour Pénale Speciale (hereinafter the CPS Law), adopted in June 2015,[15] entrusts the Court with the mission to 'try serious violations of human rights law and serious violations of international humanitarian law committed on the territory of the Central African Republic since 1 January 2003, as defined by the Central African Republic Penal Code, and under the international obligations entered into by the Central African Republic in the field of international law,

13 MONUSCO and OHCHR, *Progress and Obstacles in the Fight against Impunity for Sexual Violence in the Democratic Republic of the Congo*, April 2014.

14 Loi N° 04/018 du 30 Juillet 2004 portant organisation, attributions et fonctionnement de la Commission Vérité et Réconciliation, JORDC, Special Issue, 1 August 2004.

15 Loi N° 15.003 Portant Création, Organisation et Fonctionnement de la Cour Pénale Spéciale, Journal Officiel de la République Centrafricaine, Special Edition, 5 June 2015.

in particular the crime of genocide, crimes against humanity and war crimes'.[16] The CPS Law and its RPE bear strong imprints from the ICC's own founding documents, despite the institutional differences between the two courts, particularly the fact that, unlike the ICC, the CPS fits within an existing judiciary largely influenced by the French legal system.[17] The influence of the ICC is not surprising given the fact that the Court has been involved in the CAR twice, under the ongoing CAR I and CAR II Situations – the former focuses on crimes committed in the country during the 2002/2003 conflict while the latter covers crimes committed since 2012 – both initiated prior to the creation of the CPS. The CPS Law puts the interests of victims at the centre of the institution's mission by guaranteeing victims (and witnesses) entitlement to protection (Article 3 of the CPS Law; Articles 151–156 RPE) and legal representation (Article 64 of the CPS Law).

The CPS's investigations are informed by a mapping report of human rights violations covering 'descriptions of 620 incidents which occurred within the territory of the Central African Republic between January 2003 and December 2015' (MINUSCA et al. 2017: 14). Interestingly, the temporal mandate of the Court and the period covered in the mapping exercise formally exclude a crucial period of Bemba's MLC intervention in the CAR, which took place between the end of October 2002 and mid-March 2003. Paradoxically, the single CAR case against Bemba before the ICC so far was built on a large number of alleged criminal acts that took place between October and December 2002.[18] How CPS prosecutions and the wider transitional justice framework in the CAR – including a Truth, Justice, Reparations and Reconciliation Commission – will remain coherent and serve the interests of all categories of victims of the protracted conflict in the CAR remains to be seen, given the fact that these processes are still in the edification phase and therefore remain untested.

Elsewhere, since 1995, but mostly in 1999, Côte d'Ivoire has witnessed successive socio-political and identity-related crises that have claimed numerous civilian victims. The violent toppling of President Laurent Gbagbo following an electoral crisis in 2010–2011, succeeded by his political rival Alassane Ouattara, was accompanied by a quest for justice and redress by victims and victims' rights advocates. The opening of an investigation by the ICC on post-electoral violence and other crimes committed in the country since 2002 resulted in an indictment and the surrender of President Gbagbo and his ally, youth leader Charles Blé Goudé, to the ICC, where they were tried but acquitted on 15 January 2019 due

---

16 Article 3 of the CPS Law.

17 Loi N° 18.010 du 2 Juillet 2018, *Portant Règlement de Procédure et de Preuve devant la Cour Pénale Spéciale de la République Centrafricaine*, JORCA/ES N°5, 1 August 2018.

18 ICC-01/05-01/08-3343, pp. 217–276.

to a failure by the prosecution to present sufficient evidence tying them to the investigated crimes.[19] Domestically, multiple transitional justice processes have been activated in attempts to address the legacy of the socio-political crises that culminated in the 2010–2011 post-electoral violence.

A Dialogue, Truth and Reconciliation Commission (Commission Dialogue, Vérité et Réconciliation (CDVR) was instituted with a very ambitious mandate of establishing a record of tragic events that took place in the country, identifying the actors involved, listening to and providing a platform for recognition of the victims, recommending processes aimed at assuaging their suffering and trauma, and contributing to national reconciliation (CDVR 2014: 19). The CDVR collected testimonies from 72,483 victims, perpetrators and witnesses about violations of human rights that spanned a 21-year period from 1990 to 2011, and of these testimonies, 81 cases were selected for public hearings that took place in September 2014 (ibid.: 67–69, 83). The CDVR formulated recommendations for the state on how to design a programme of reparations for the harm suffered by victims (which will be discussed in section 4.3). Parallel to the work of the CDVR and the ICC's involvement in Côte d'Ivoire, the country's judicial institutions initiated criminal investigations and prosecutions within months of the end of the electoral violence in 2011. A Special Inquiry and Investigation Unit was established and its investigations led to 1,038 individuals being charged with violent crimes, economic crimes or crimes against state security within four years of the electoral violence (ICTJ 2016: 15).

Victims' rights are, in principle, accommodated in law: they are entitled to trigger the initiation of proceedings through complaints, benefit from legal assistance to enable them to participate in proceedings as civil parties, and seek reparations, even if limited resources are available to ensure that these rights are effectively implemented (ICTJ 2016: 23–26). Most cases that have been investigated have not yet reached the trial phase, and in spite of adopting a number of transitional justice initiatives, Côte d'Ivoire authorities have been denounced for being one-sided (targeting Gbagbo supporters) and putting politics before the interests of victims in their implementation of transitional justice processes (HRW 2016; ICTJ 2016). Even more contentious was the decision announced by President Ouattara on 6 August 2018 to grant an amnesty to 800 individuals, including Simone Gbagbo (the wife of former President Gbagbo), within a context where judicial proceedings remain subject to the fragile and unstable political climate that is characteristic of the post-electoral violence era.[20]

---

19 ICC, 'ICC Trial Chamber I Acquits Laurent Gbagbo and Charles Blé Goudé from All Charges', press release, ICC-CPI-20190115-PR1427, 15 January 2019, https://www.icc-cpi.int/Pages/item.aspx?name=pr1427.

20 HRW, 'Côte d'Ivoire: No Amnesty for Serious Crimes of 2010–11 Crisis', press release, 7 August 2018, https://www.hrw.org/news/2018/08/07/cote-divoire-no-amnesty-serious-crimes-2010-11-crisis.

The above overview has highlighted international developments and domestic dynamics on victims' rights in Uganda, the DRC, the CAR and Côte d'Ivoire. The following sections will focus on key themes related to victims' rights – participation, representation and reparation – in order to better grasp the content of the legal norms, their application and the interactions between the various actors and processes involved.

4. VICTIM PARTICIPATION, REPRESENTATION AND REPARATIONS

4.1. VICTIM PARTICIPATION IN DOMESTIC AND INTERNATIONAL LEGAL PROCESSES

Since domestic processes are increasingly influenced by international norms and practice on victims' rights, it is crucial to first take a look at victim participation before the ICC, before zooming in on selected domestic contexts. Victim participation has proven to be an important yet thorny issue in the ICC's practice as the Court still struggles to strike the right balance between its cultivated profile as an institution established to vindicate victims and accountability for crimes framed as committed against humankind. The decisions rendered by different chambers reflect these tensions (Vasiliev 2015). The ability for victims whose interests are affected to 'present their views and concerns' in proceedings before the ICC was formally recognised by the inclusion of Article 68(3) in the Rome Statute. While Article 68 relates to instituted proceedings against an accused, Article 15(3) allows victims to participate even earlier in the process when the Prosecutor takes the initiative to start preliminary investigations after receiving information from various sources – including victims – about the commission of crimes within the Court's jurisdiction. Where the Prosecutor decides to proceed, Article 15(3) instructs him/her to 'submit to the Pre-Trial Chamber a request for authorization of an investigation, together with any supporting material collected'. Since victims play a crucial role in supplying the Prosecutor with information leading to that decision (Baumgartner 2008: 413), the provision allows them to 'make representations to the Pre-Trial Chamber'. In the event of a challenge to the jurisdiction of the Court or the admissibility of a case, Article 19(3) enables victims to 'submit observations to the Court'.

Accommodation of victims' interests at various stages of proceedings before the ICC does not turn this essentially penal institution into some kind of restorative justice platform where the interests of the victim and the restoration of the societal balance shaken by the deviant behaviour are central to the justice process (Foley 2014: 14–15; Van Ness and Strong 2015).[21] As reflected by most provisions of the Statute, the dominant features of a criminal trial in liberal societies, centred on due process guarantees for a fair and impartial trial, remain the central focus of the ICC's mission (see also Zappala 2010). Accordingly, Article 68(3) specifies that victim participation is possible as long it is not 'prejudicial to or inconsistent with the rights of the accused and a fair and impartial trial'.

In interpreting relevant provisions of the statute and the RPE, the ICC's Pre-Trial, Trial and Appeals Chambers have determined that victims may qualify for participation at the pre-trial (particularly during the confirmation of charges), trial and/or reparations phases of proceedings (see Baumgartner 2008 and Vasiliev 2015 for a detailed analysis of the case law). While participation in proceedings is open to individual victims, as demonstrated by, among many others, the ICC's initial decision on victim participation in the *Lubanga* case,[22] a quest for efficiency in dealing with victims' applications shows the Court's increasing preference for collective rather than individual participation – through common representation – of victims in proceedings (Vasiliev 2015: 1153).

The first decision on victim participation handed down by Pre-Trial Chamber I on 17 January 2006 in the DRC Situation granted six victims the right to participate in proceedings at the investigation stage.[23] Subsequently, reports show that for the period between 2008 and 2017, the Court received 22,846 applications for participation in proceedings as victims.[24] In the first prosecution case against Thomas Lubanga Dyilo, leader of the dominant Hema Union des Patriotes Congolais (UPC) armed group in the Ituri region/province, 129 victims were allowed to participate in proceedings that saw him sentenced to 14 years' imprisonment.[25] More victims – a total of 151 individuals – were authorised to participate in proceedings before the

21 For an emphasis on the restorative function of the court, see Assembly of States Parties, Report of the Court on the implementation in 2013 of the revised strategy in relation to victims, 11 October 2013, ICC-ASP/12/41, para. 28.

22 Ibid.

23 Decision on the applications for participation in the proceedings of VPRS1, VPRS2, VPRS3, VPRS4, VPRS5, and VPRS6, ICC-Ol/04-lOl-tEN-Corr.

24 Assembly of States Parties, *Report on Activities and Programme Performance of the International Criminal Court for the Year 2017*, 1 August 2018, ICC-ASP/17/2, p. 75; Assembly of States Parties, *Report on Activities and Programme Performance of the International Criminal Court for the Year 2012*, ICC-ASP/12/9, 4 June 2013, p. 65.

25 *The Prosecutor v. Thomas Lubanga Dyilo*, Judgment pursuant to Article 74 of the Statute, 12 March 2012, ICC-01/04-01/06, paras. 15–21. Nine victims later saw their status withdrawn subsequently on the basis of evidence that disqualified them (paras. 484–502).

Appeals Chamber, where Lubanga's conviction was reaffirmed,[26] and a larger number (425 out of 473 applications) were awarded reparations.[27] In the ICC's case against Germain Katanga – leader of the Force de Résistance Patriotique en Ituri (FRPI) – 366 applicants were authorised to participate as victims, a status subsequently withdrawn for two applicants, and two of the remaining 364 victims appeared as witnesses in the trial.[28] Katanga was convicted of murder, attack against a civilian population, destruction of property and pillaging, and was sentenced to 12 years' imprisonment.[29] In the reparations phase, the Court determined that '297 of the 341 Applicants [had] shown to the standard of proof of a balance of probabilities that they [were] victims of the crimes of which Mr Katanga was convicted'.[30] In the *Ntaganda* case concluded on 8 July 2019 with a conviction on several counts on crimes against humanity and war crimes, 2,129 victims were granted the right to participate in the trial.[31]

In recent cases, the level of victim participation is even more impressive. As stated above, 5,229 victims participated in proceedings against Bemba.[32] The reversal of his early conviction by the Appeals Chamber on 8 June 2018 meant that no reparations could be claimed against him by the victims, whose involvement in proceedings was motivated by hopes for a favourable outcome in terms of recognition, retribution and, indeed, reparation. In the Uganda situation, the Pre-Trial Chamber II granted 41 victims the right to participate in proceedings against Joseph Kony and Vincent Otti, who were still at large, while as of March 2020, 4,065 victims had been granted the right to participate in proceedings in the Dominic Ongwen trial, which was in deliberations

26 *The Prosecutor v. Thomas Lubanga Dyilo*, Decision on the participation of victims in the appeals against Trial Chamber I's conviction and sentencing decisions, ICC-01/04-01/06 A 4, A 5, A 6, 13 December 2012, paras. 2–3; *The Prosecutor v. Thomas Lubanga Dyilo*, Judgment on the appeal of Mr Thomas Lubanga Dyilo against his conviction, ICC-01/04-01/06 A 5, 1 December 2014, Annex 3, para. 15.

27 *The Prosecutor v. Thomas Lubanga Dyilo*, Corrected version of the 'Decision Setting the Size of the Reparations Award for Which Thomas Lubanga Dyilo is Liable', ICC-01/04-01/06-3379-Red-Corr-tENG, 21 December 2017, paras. 190–191.

28 *The Prosecutor v. Germain Katanga*, Judgment pursuant to Article 74 of the Statute, ICC-01/04-01/07, 7 March 2014, para. 36.

29 Ibid., paras. 658–659; Decision on Sentence pursuant to Article 76 of the Statute, ICC-01/04-01/07-3484, 23 May 2014, paras. 146–147.

30 *The Prosecutor v. Germain Katanga*, Order for Reparations pursuant to Article 75 of the Statute, ICC-01/04-01/07-3728, 24 March 2017, p. 118.

31 *The Prosecutor v. Bosco Ntaganda*, Third decision on victims' participation in trial proceedings, ICC-01/04-02/06, 2 July 2015, paras. 2–5; *The Prosecutor v. Bosco Ntaganda*, Thirteenth Periodic Report on Victims in the Case and Their General Situation, ICC-01/04-02/06-2353 06-06-2019 1/9 NM T, 6 June 2019, *The Prosecutor v. Bosco Ntaganda*, ICC-01/04-02/06, ICC-PIDS-CIS-DRC-02-014/19_Eng, updated July 2019.

32 *The Prosecutor v. Jean-Pierre Bemba Gombo*, supra note 1, para. 18.

at the time of writing.[33] In the Côte d'Ivoire situation, based on data from January 2016, 727 individuals were admitted to participate in proceedings in the joint case against former President Laurent Gbagbo and Charles Blé Goudé.[34] Elsewhere, in the Kenyan situation, 725 and 628 victims participated in proceedings in the Kenyatta and Ruto/Sang cases, respectively, before the two cases were closed due to a lack of evidence.[35] Victims have also applied and, where applicable, been admitted to participate in proceedings in other African Situations before the ICC, such as those in Darfur/Sudan, Mali and Libya.[36]

In domestic proceedings, Thomas Kwoyelo, an LRA colonel, was the first suspect to have been tried by the ICD of the High Court of Uganda for numerous counts of war crimes and crimes against humanity. In proceedings initiated against him in 2009, a pre-trial ruling informed, among others, by the ICD's RPE,[37] which were inspired by the ICC's RPE, granted victims the right to participate at all stages of proceedings. In November 2018, the ICD made a ruling on applications from 98 victims to participate in the trial.[38] These were grouped into three categories, namely: victims admitted to participate (A), victims whose applications were rejected for not meeting the criteria (B) and victims who could reapply by producing further documentation (C).[39] Only 30 victims were admitted to participate.[40] With still limited court

33 *The Prosecutor v. Joseph Kony and Vincent Otti*, Case Information Sheet, ICC-02/04-01/15, ICC-PIDS-CIS-UGA-02-013/18_Eng, updated June 2018; *The Prosecutor v. Dominic Ongwen*, Case Information Sheet, ICC-PIDS-CIS-UGA-02-018/20_Eng, updated March 2020.

34 *The Prosecutor v. Laurent Gbagbo and Charles Blé Goudé*, Case Information Sheet, ICC-02/11-01/15, ICC-PIDS-CIS-CI-04-03/16_Eng, updated January 2016.

35 *The Prosecutor v. Uhuru Muigai Kenyatta*, Case Information Sheet, ICC-01/09-02/11, ICC-PIDS-CIS-KEN-02-014/15_Eng, updated 13 March 2015; *The Prosecutor v. William Samoei Ruto and Joshua Arap Sang*, Case Information Sheet, ICC-01/09-01/11, ICC-PIDS-CIS-KEN-01-012/14_Eng, updated April 2016.

36 See *The Situation in Georgia*, Report on the Victims' Representations Received Pursuant to Article 15(3) of the Rome Statute, with Public Annex A and Confidential Annex B, ICC-01/15, 4 December 2015, referring to the court receiving representations for 6,335 victims by December 2015.

37 Statutory Instruments 2016 No. 40, The Judicature (High Court) (International Crimes Division) Rules, 2016 – Arrangement of Rules, in Statutory Instruments Supplement to the Uganda Gazette No. 42, Volume CIX, dated 15 June 2016, REDRESS, *Ugandan International Crimes Division (ICD) Rules 2016: Analysis on Victim Participation Framework*, August 2016, https://redress.org/wp-content/uploads/2017/12/1608REDRESS_ICD-Rules-Analysis.pdf.

38 Lawyers Without Borders (Avocats Sans Frontières (-ASF)), 'A Trial for History: Thomas Kwoyelo in Uganda', https://www.asf.be/blog/2018/09/20/thomas-kwoyelo-in-uganda-a-trial-for-history.

39 Lino Owor Ogora, 'Ugandan Court Rules on Victims' Participation and Bail as Thomas Kwoyelo Denies All 93 Charges Leveled against Him', https://www.ijmonitor.org/2018/11/ugandan-court-rules-on-victims-participation-and-bail-as-thomas-kwoyelo-denies-all-93-charges-leveled-against-him.

40 Patricia Bako, 'Victim Fatigue in the Case of Thomas Kwoyelo', https://justicehub.org/article/victim-fatigue-in-the-case-of-thomas-kwoyelo.

rulings on the subject matter, many aspects of victims' rights to, *inter alia*, participation, protection and information guaranteed under the RPE remain untested.

In the DRC context, until 2016, prosecutions of international crimes were essentially conducted by military courts, with one notable exception being a 17 December 2011 case known as the *Kimbanguistes* case, where Kumba Ado and seven others were found guilty of genocide and were all sentenced to life imprisonment by a Kinshasa civilian court (ASF 2013: 10).[41] In this and other cases before military courts, victims and victims' rights advocates played an instrumental role in driving the prosecutions of international crimes in a context where state authority, including within the judicial branch, was lacking. In these cases, victims were able to participate as civil parties in proceedings and seek reparations (ASF 2013; ICTJ 2015; Mbokani 2016). An ICTJ study of 39 cases of serious crimes tried by military tribunals in the eastern Congolese provinces of South Kivu, North Kivu and Ituri between 2009 and 2014 shows different levels of victim participation depending on the nature of the case and the context surrounding the institution of proceedings: for instance, in the *Bweremana-Minova* case, 1,016 victims participated in proceedings against 39 governmental soldiers accused of crimes against civilians, including numerous rapes, 723 victims participated in the case against Lieutenant Colonel Bedi Mobuli and 91 participated in the *Fizi/Baraka* case (ICTJ 2015: 31, 41–67).

In Côte d'Ivoire, domestic proceedings pertaining to the 2010–2011 post-election violence allow victims to trigger proceedings through a complaint and participate as civil parties. However, analyses of the applicable laws have highlighted shortcomings regarding witness protection and legal assistance, to the extent that victim participation in proceedings is mostly enabled by assistance from civil society organisations (ICTJ 2016: 25–27). Domestic prosecutions include the highly contentious and mediatised trial of former first lady Simone Gbagbo, together with 78 co-defendants. She was convicted and sentenced to 20 years' imprisonment for undermining state security, after Côte d'Ivoire refused to surrender her to the ICC (Heller 2016, 637). Ms Gbagbo, together with 60 other convicted co-defendants (18 others were acquitted), were ordered to pay 965 billion CFA francs (or around $1.591 billion at the time) in damages to the Ivorian state, which was represented in the trial as the victim of the offences.[42] Paradoxically, Ms Gbagbo was subsequently acquitted of crimes against humanity in March 2017 after a trial criticised for procedural irregularity

41 Tribunal de Grande Instance de Kinshasa/Kalamu, *Affaire Mputu Muteba et Consorts (Kimbanguistes case)*, RP 11.154/11.155/11.156, 17 December 2011.

42 Haby Niakate, 'Côte d'Ivoire: Simone Gbagbo, la prison, l'amnistie ou la CPI', *Jeune Afrique*, 19 March 2015, https://www.jeuneafrique.com/227815/politique/c-te-d-ivoire-simone-gbagbo-la-prison-l-amnistie-ou-la-cpi.

and even partially boycotted by both the defence and representatives of more than 250 civil parties.[43]

Finally, the laws creating the CPS in the CAR, specifically the RPE, provide that victims may participate in all stages of proceedings (Article 6), including by initiating proceedings through a petition before the Special Prosecutor (Article 63). A Victims and Witnesses Support and Protection Unit was established within the Registry (Articles 46–47). The common form of participation envisaged in the law is for victims to apply for a status as civil parties (Article 40 of the CPS Law; Article 75–76 RPE). The RPE provide that once the CPS has reached a verdict in criminal proceedings against an accused, the Court shall rule on reparations requests by civil parties, to be paid by the accused or, in the event of indigence, through the Court's victim and witness support service (Article 129). Since the Court is still in the investigations phase and no trials have started yet, the implementation of progressive victims' rights incorporated into the CPS system remains to be seen.

4.2. VICTIM REPRESENTATION IN TRANSITIONAL JUSTICE PROCESSES: WHO SPEAKS FOR THE VICTIMS?

In several African contexts that have experienced mass atrocities, the quest for justice for victims involves numerous domestic and international actors. Individual victims, victims' organisations, and domestic and international human rights advocacy groups – often lumped together as 'civil society' – coalesce in complex networks involved in assisting victims to recover, seek justice and claim reparations. Contextual realities in Uganda, the DRC, the CAR and Côte d'Ivoire offer powerful illustrations of how justice for victims of mass atrocities is hard to achieve within characteristically toxic political climates that prevail during and after conflicts. Where governmental institutions fail to take the first step in assisting and empowering victims in their recovery process as they seek justice and redress – which tends to be the rule rather than an exception – local and global non-governmental organisations (NGOs) step in to fill the gap.

Unlike in contexts such as Argentina or Rwanda, where strong victims' associations (namely the Mothers of the Plaza de Mayo and IBUKA, respectively) played a central role in mobilisation for victims' assistance,

---

[43] Cyril Bensimon, 'Jugée pour « crimes contre l'humanité », Simone Gbagbo plaide non coupable', *Le Monde*, 1 June 2016, https://www.lemonde.fr/afrique/article/2016/06/01/simone-gbagbo-a-nouveau-devant-les-juges_4929961_3212.html; Claire Rainfroy, 'Côte d'Ivoire: Simone Gbagbo acquittée de crime contre l'Humanité et de crime de guerre', *Jeune Afrique*, 29 March 2017, https://www.jeuneafrique.com/422338/societe/cote-divoire-simone-gbagbo-acquittee-de-crimes-contre-lhumanite-de-crimes-de-guerre.

justice and redress, there seem to be no such strongly coordinated victims' agencies at the domestic level in the DRC. Instead, international NGOs or Intergovernmental Organisations (IGO) acting directly or in partnership with smaller local peace-building NGOs play a central role in providing advocacy and assistance to victims in pursuit of redress. Lawyers Without Borders, the American Bar Association and the United Nations Joint Human Rights Office have played a key role in victim mobilisation for justice within domestic proceedings (ICTJ 2015: 25). Neighbouring Uganda has a more vibrant and globally connected civil society – including organisations such as the Kitgum Concerned Women's Association (KICWA), the Justice and Reconciliation Project, Ker Kwaro Acholi (KKA), the Acholi Religious Leaders' Peace Initiative, and the African Youth Initiative Network – working in peace-building, including in the justice sector (Omach 2016). However, even here, international organisations such as Lawyers Without Borders and the International Center for Transitional Justice (ICTJ) play a central role in shaping domestic narratives and processes on justice and reparations for victims.[44]

A constellation of civil society organisations is equally active in advocating for justice and reparations in Côte d'Ivoire. As in the other contexts above, the struggle for the vindication of victims' rights is led by global bodies and local civil society organisations rather than the victims themselves. Global NGOs such as the France-based International Federation for Human Rights (FIDH) and the ICTJ, working with local organisations such as LIDHO (Ligue ivoirienne des droits de l'Homme), MIDH (Mouvement ivoirien des droits humains), AFJCI (Association des Femmes juristes de Côte d'Ivoire) and OFACI (Organisation des femmes actives de Côte d'Ivoire) play a central role in pushing the government to live up to its promises of justice and reparations and, in most cases, in supporting victims to navigate ongoing criminal proceedings (ICTJ 2016: 25). FIDH is also, arguably, the international organisation most involved in advocacy for justice in the CAR context. The organisation has been extensively documenting atrocities committed in the country since the crises of the early 2000s and has since worked with local collaborators such as LCDH (Ligue centrafricaine des droits de l'Homme) and OCDH (Observatoire centrafricain des droits de l'Homme) and other international organisations, including REDRESS, in advocating for justice and victims' rights in proceedings before the ICC and in triggering domestic processes, including the creation of the CPS (FIDH 2017).[45]

---

44 See: https://www.asf.be/action/field-offices/asf-in-uganda and https://www.ictj.org/our-work/regions-and-countries/uganda.

45 REDRESS, LCDH, OCDH, FIDH, 'Intégrer les droits des victimes dans les procédures de la Cour pénale spéciale en République centrafricaine', September 2017, https://redress.org/wp-content/uploads/2017/12/CAR_Paper_Rules_FINAL_FRENCH.pdf.

As in the domestic contexts examined above, victim participation in proceedings before the ICC is mediated by several actors, to the extent that one can easily get lost among the multiple acronyms or, more importantly, the roles played by the various actors involved. Legal representation of victims before the court is foreseen in the Rome Statute under Article 68, which provides for victims' rights. Details on legal representation before the Court are worked out in, among others, Rules 90–93 RPE. According to Rule 90, victims are free to choose a legal representative. Laconically formulated in the first paragraph, the principle is complemented by the second paragraph, which provides for the common representation of victims to ensure efficiency in proceedings. Since all situations and cases before the Court pertain to contexts of large-scale victimisation, as would be expected from the very nature of the crimes within the Court's jurisdiction, common legal representation of victims has been the norm rather than the exception (Hébert-Dolbec 2015: 47; Garbett 2017: 209). Collective legal representation is, in a way, a pragmatic articulation of victims' agency before the court. It can hardly be expected to accommodate the complex manifestations of victimhood or faithfully convey the expectedly multiple – and at times dissonant – voices, needs and desires of individual and collective victims whose experiences can only be fully captured in their singularity.

In practical terms, collective legal representation is best illustrated by proceedings in the *Bemba* case, where the 5,229 victims admitted to participate were divided into five groups 'depending on the location of the harm allegedly suffered, as well as the victims' status' and initially represented by only two teams of legal representatives.[46] During the trial, the legal representatives of victims were allowed to call two witnesses – compared to 40 witnesses called by the prosecution and 34 by the defence – and three victims were allowed to orally present their views and concerns.[47] Following the death of one of the two legal representatives, the victims represented by him were reassigned to the other counsel, whose team ended up representing all 5,229 victims.[48] Beyond information provided in the standard forms required for victim participation, it is unrealistic in cases like this to expect a single team composed of only five to six people (Tibori-Szabó et al. 2017: 441) to interact and empathically represent the individuality of victims who suffered harm before the ICC. Filtering the

46 *The Prosecutor v. Jean-Pierre Bemba Gombo*, supra note 1, para. 23; Decision on common legal representation of victims for the purpose of trial, ICC-01/05-01/08-1005, 10 November 2010.

47 *The Prosecutor v. Jean-Pierre Bemba Gombo*, supra note 1, para. 17.

48 *The Prosecutor v. Jean-Pierre Bemba Gombo*, Order on the legal representation of victims previously represented by Me Assingambi Zarambaud, ICC-01/05-01/08-2964, 7 February 2014.

voices of numerous victims through collective representation limits their ability to effectively participate in proceedings and truly share their views and concerns (Kendall and Nouwen 2014: 250; Dovi 2017: 264; Garbett 2017). In essence, this articulation of victims' agency in court proceedings can be seen as both direct and indirect: it is direct in the sense that victims are formally represented by counsel, which advocates for their rights and interests, but it is indirect in the sense that victims' ability to voice their 'views and concerns' by directly accessing the Court, participating in proceedings or even conferring with their appointed representatives is very limited, particularly in cases such as *Bemba, Ntaganda* or *Ongwen*, which recorded quite high levels of victim participation. The victims' agency represented in court proceedings, in the words of Kendall and Nouwen, 'transcends all actual victims and corresponds to no individual victims in their particularity' (2014: 241).

Institutionally, the Registry of the Court, particularly its Victims and Witnesses Unit, plays a central, representational role as the main interlocutor of the victims in accessing and getting involved in court proceedings. The Registry's role in assisting victims with legal representation covers both providing advice on suitable legal representatives and bearing the costs of such representation where victims wishing to participate in proceedings are unable to do so financially. A Victims Participation and Reparations Section was established within the Registry. The Regulations of the Court further mandate the Registry to establish an autonomous Office of Public Counsel for the Victims (OPCV) tasked with providing 'support and assistance to the legal representative for victims and to victims'.

In practical terms, the OPCV and the ICC's Public Information and Outreach Section initiate contact with victims 'for the purpose of informing them of their right to participate in the proceedings' (Tibori-Szabó et al. 2017: 437). The OPCV makes further arrangements for the legal representation of victims and advises the relevant ICC Chambers 'on the grouping of victims for the purposes of legal representation, and selects or recommends common legal representatives', who may be drawn from the ranks of counsel within the OPCV (Hirst 2017: 114). The OPCV also represents victims in court proceedings: for instance, all the 2,129 victims participating in the *Ntaganda* trial were represented by the Office, while in the *Ongwe*n case, 1,501 victims were represented by the OPCV, 2,564 by lawyers selected by the victims, and representation of the remaining four was to still be clarified as of March 2020. Legal aid for participating victims is managed by another unit of the Registry, namely the Counsel Support Section (ibid.: 114). In contexts subject to ICC proceedings, various forms of agency and intermediaries are active in advocating for the rights of victims, including supporting them in filling in and filing applications for participation as victims before the ICC (Pena 2017: 84 ff).

4.3. REPARATIONS AND ASSISTANCE TO VICTIMS

Reparations for victims of harmful conduct that violates societal norms are generally considered to be a central justification for punishment in most criminal justice systems. It is argued that '[m]any victims want punishment to restore their losses and to vindicate their sense of grievance' (Tonry 2011: 95). In proceedings before the ICC, the Court 'may make an order directly against a convicted person specifying appropriate reparations to, or in respect of, victims, including restitution, compensation and rehabilitation' (Article 75(2) of the Rome Statute). The same provision states that the Court may also order that the award for reparations be made through the TFV. In its first order on principles guiding reparations in the *Lubanga* case,[49] the Court, building on numerous submissions by a plethora of victims' rights advocates admitted to intervene on the subject matter,[50] displayed an awareness of the challenges and sensitivities involved in delivering justice, and indeed reparations, to large and diverse communities of victims. Trial Chamber I determined that the purpose of reparations was to:

> relieve the suffering caused by these offences; afford justice to the victims by alleviating the consequences of the wrongful acts; deter future violations; and contribute to the effective reintegration of former child soldiers ... assist in promoting reconciliation between the convicted person, the victims of the crimes and the affected communities.[51]

The beneficiaries of reparations are direct and indirect victims. While the former category covers individuals who suffered a personal harm, the latter category requires some clarification as to the boundaries of indirect harm that still make a person qualify as a victim. The Appeals Chamber determined that indirect victims include: '(i) the family members of direct victims, (ii) anyone who attempted to prevent the commission of one or more of the crimes under consideration, (iii) individuals who suffered harm when helping or intervening on behalf of direct victims, and (iv) other persons who suffered personal harm as a result of these offences'.[52] The harm to be repaired 'does

---

49 *The Prosecutor v. Thomas Lubanga Dyilo*, Decision establishing the principles and procedures to be applied to reparations, ICC-01/04-01/06-2904, 7 August 2012; Judgment on the appeals against the 'Decision establishing the principles and procedures to be applied to reparations' of 7 August 2012 with AMENDED order for reparations (Annex A) and public annexes 1 and 2, ICC-01/04-01/06-3129 and ICC-01/04-01/06-3129-AnxA, 3 March 2015.

50 On submissions from the OPCV, the feedback of the registry and numerous submissions by NGOs and other bodies, see ICC-01/04-01/06-2904, paras. 20–181.

51 Ibid., para. 179.

52 ICC-01/04-01/06-3129-AnxA, para. 6.

not necessarily need to have been direct, but it must have been personal to the victim',[53] while reparations are 'intrinsically linked to the individual whose criminal liability is established in a conviction and whose culpability for the criminal acts is determined in a sentence'.[54] Individual or collective reparations may be awarded: the former 'should be awarded in a way that avoids creating tensions and divisions within the relevant communities', while the latter 'should address the harm the victims suffered on an individual and collective basis'.[55]

Under the principles and procedures on reparation adopted in the *Lubanga* case, reparations may take the form of restitution, compensation and/or rehabilitation. Restitution is interpreted broadly to encompass a return of the victim to 'his or her family, home and previous employment; providing continuing education; and returning lost or stolen property'.[56] Compensation is interpreted by the Appeals Chamber as 'a form of economic relief that is aimed at addressing, in a proportionate and appropriate manner, the harm that has been inflicted'.[57] It may be adopted as the form of reparations where: 'i) the economic harm is sufficiently quantifiable; ii) an award of this kind would be appropriate and proportionate ... and iii) in view of the availability of funds, this result is feasible'.[58] The harm to be compensated could be physical harm, moral and non-material damage, material damage, lost opportunities, costs of legal or other relevant experts, medical services, or psychological and social assistance.[59] According to the Court, rehabilitation should cover the 'provision of medical services and healthcare, psychological, psychiatric and social assistance to support those suffering from grief and trauma; and any relevant legal and social services'.[60] A TFV established in September 2002 by the Assembly of States Parties was entrusted with a dual mandate of: (i) implementing Court-ordered reparations; and (ii) providing physical and psychosocial rehabilitation or material support to victims of crimes that fall within the jurisdiction of the Court.[61]

In four separate cases – the *Lubanga* and *Katanga* cases in the DRC Situation, the *Bemba* case in the CAR Situation and the *Al Mahdi* case in Mali Situation – the ICC has had an opportunity to interpret the relevant provisions of founding texts on what reparations to victims of crimes within its jurisdiction should entail. Trial Chamber II issued the first ICC ruling on a convict's liability for

53 Ibid., para.10.
54 Ibid., para. 20.
55 Ibid., para. 33.
56 Ibid., para. 224.
57 ICC-01/04-01/06-3129-AnxA, para. 40.
58 Ibid., para. 37.
59 Ibid., para. 40.
60 Ibid., para. 42.
61 On the trust fund, see: https://www.trustfundforvictims.org/en/what-we-do/reparation-orders.

reparations in the *Katanga* case by awarding both individual and collective reparations to the 297 recognised victims of crimes committed by Katanga.[62] The Court evaluated the total monetary value of the extent of the harm suffered by the 297 victims at $3,752,620, determined that, while indigent, Katanga was nonetheless liable for $1,000,000 in reparations, fixed the admittedly symbolic amount of individual reparations (compensation) for each recognised victim at $250 and in addition awarded collective reparations 'designed to benefit each victim, in the form of support for housing, support for an income-generating activity, support for education and psychological support'.[63] The TFV undertook to front or 'complement' the reparations awarded to victims until Katanga's liability could be triggered, should he become solvent in the future.[64]

In the *Lubanga* case, following the 2012 ruling determining reparations guidelines, victims had to wait until 15 December 2017 for an order specifying Lubanga's liability for reparations.[65] The Court decided to award collective reparations to '425 of the 473 potentially eligible victims in the sample [who had] shown on a balance of probabilities that they are direct or indirect victims of the crimes of which Mr Lubanga was convicted'.[66] Nonetheless, it considered the 425 victims as 'only a sample of potentially eligible victims', who were estimated to be in the hundreds or possibly thousands, who 'suffered harm as a consequence of the crimes of which Mr Lubanga was convicted'.[67] It decided to:

> [Set] the reparations award for which Mr Lubanga is liable at a total of USD 10,000,000, which consists of his liability in respect of the 425 victims in the sample, amounting to USD 3,400,000, and his liability in respect of any other victims who may be identified, amounting to USD 6,600,000.[68]

Since Lubanga was found to be indigent, the Court instructed the TFV to explore whether and how it could implement the reparations award, subject to the availability of funds, and to 'contact the Government of the DRC with a view to establishing how it may contribute to the reparations process'.[69]

In the *Al Mahdi* case, the defendant, who pleaded guilty and expressed remorse and empathy towards his victims, was convicted of attacking protected

62 *The Prosecutor v. Germain Katanga*, supra note 30.

63 Ibid. This means that the total amount for individual reparations is $74,250, while the remaining $925,750 were set for collective reparations.

64 See 'Trust Fund for Victims Decides to Provide $1 Million for the Reparations Awarded to Victims in the *Katanga* Case, Welcomes Earmarked Donations of €200,000 from the Netherlands', https://www.icc-cpi.int/Pages/item.aspx?name=pr1305.

65 *The Prosecutor v. Thomas Lubanga Dyilo*, supra note 27.

66 Ibid., p. 111.

67 Ibid.

68 Ibid.

69 Ibid., p. 112.

objects and was sentenced to nine years' imprisonment.[70] The ICC determined that since all the sites but one damaged through the actions of the defendant were UNESCO World Heritage sites, the victims of his actions included 'direct victims of the crimes, namely the faithful and inhabitants of Timbuktu, but also people throughout Mali and the international community'.[71] As the Court only received applications for reparations from the community of Timbuktu, it acknowledged 'the suffering endured by the Malian community and the international community as a whole as a result of the destruction of the Protected Buildings',[72] but decided to only award '(i) individual reparations for those whose livelihoods exclusively depended upon the Protected Buildings and (ii) collective reparations for the community of Timbuktu as a whole'.[73] As only nine victims participated in the trial proceedings, although 139 victims applied for individual reparations, the Court took note of the fact that 'the number of applications received in the … case pales in comparison to the number of persons who were in fact harmed' in a city in which approximately 70,000 people lived around the time of the attack.[74] It determined that Al Mahdi was liable to pay €2,700,000 in individual, collective and symbolic reparations to the community of Timbuktu.[75] Unlike in the *Katanga* case, the Court did not specify the precise amount of individual reparations to be paid. The award for individual reparations did not only target the 139 victims who participated in proceedings, because, as the Court reasoned, owing to the prevailing insecurity in the Timbuktu area, the names of all the victims meeting its parameters for individual reparations were not known.[76] It ruled that contrary to the TFV's general position consisting of prioritising collective awards, the awarded individual reparations should be prioritised 'because of the particular extent to which they were harmed by Mr Al Mahdi's conduct'.[77] An implementation plan drafted by the TFV and backed by the Court had already identified other victims who would qualify for individual reparations.[78]

The final case in which the Court discussed reparations was the *Bemba* case, considered above. Under the applicable norms and principles, Bemba's acquittal meant that no reparations could be claimed against him by the

---

70 *The Prosecutor v. Ahmad Al Faqi Al Mahdi*, Judgment and Sentence, ICC-01/12-01/15-171, 27 September 2016, paras. 103, 104 and p. 49.

71 Ibid., para. 80.

72 *The Prosecutor v. Ahmad Al Faqi Al Mahdi*, Reparations Order, CC-01/12-01/15-236, 17 August 2017, para. 53.

73 Ibid., para.83.

74 Ibid., para. 141.

75 Ibid., para. 134.

76 Ibid., para. 141.

77 Ibid., para. 140.

78 *The Prosecutor v. Ahmad Al Faqi Al Mahdi*, Public redacted version of 'Decision on Trust Fund for Victims' Draft Implementation Plan for Reparations', ICC-01/12-01/15-273-Red, 12 July 2018.

5,229 victims who participated in his trial before the ICC. As Trial Chamber III noted, proceedings on reparations in the *Bemba* case had been going on for two years and numerous actors – including the usual participants in ICC proceedings, experts and a long list of organisations advocating for victims' rights – had produced a considerable body of work and submissions on reparations that could not be of great use in the case following the acquittal.[79] In their final submissions to the Chamber after the verdict, legal representatives of the victims stated that in reaction to the acquittal verdict, victims unanimously expressed 'their deep disappointment and loss of confidence in justice in general, and towards the Court, in particular'.[80] The Trial Chamber backed the decision taken by the TFV in the wake of Bemba's acquittal to 'accelerate the launch of a programme under its assistance mandate for the benefit of victims and their families in the situation of the Central African Republic'.[81] Since the *Bemba* case had thus far the largest number of victims participating in proceedings before the Court and was the only case in the CAR, it is easy to understand the huge disappointment of victims who suffered through nearly two decades of bloody conflicts and political instability.

From the above discussion, it is clear that reparations go hand in hand with the second mandate of the TFV, namely assistance to victims. Over the last decade, the TFV has initiated numerous assistance projects in Situation countries, specifically in Uganda, the DRC and more recently Côte d'Ivoire (TFV 2016; ICC 2017: 57). Unlike reparations, which can only be ordered by the Court, the assistance mandate provides the TFV with more flexibility to intervene within victimised communities. In partnership with local actors, the TFV has engaged in activities that benefit not only victims but also wider communities in areas affected by conflicts and crimes investigated by the ICC (Pena 2017: 88–90). Existing reports show that as of 30 September 2017, 101,970 victims from Uganda, the DRC and Côte d'Ivoire had benefited directly from TFV projects related to its assistance mandate, while indirect victims who benefited from such projects numbered 260,626 (ICC 2017: 57).

The principles and procedures to be applied to reparations in the *Lubanga* case highlighted the link between proceedings before the ICC and dynamics at the national level. The Court ruled that its reparations awards should not 'interfere with the responsibility of States to award reparations to victims under other treaties or national law'.[82] The concept of reparative complementarity

---

79 *The Prosecutor v. Jean-Pierre Bemba Gombo*, Final decision on the reparations proceedings, ICC-01/05-01/08-3653, 3 August 2018, paras. 8–10.

80 *The Prosecutor v. Jean-Pierre Bemba Gombo*, Appeals Chamber's Judgment dated 8 June 2018 on the reparations proceedings, ICC-01/05-01/08, 12 July 2018, para. 21.

81 Ibid., paras. 11–15. On the TFV statement, see Communication from the Chair of the Board of Directors of the TFV to the President of the Assembly of States Parties, 13 June 2018.

82 Ibid., para. 50.

is used to convey this idea that reparations by the ICC should to some extent go hand in hand with domestic reparative processes (Moffett 2017: 1214). Interestingly, the principle of complementarity supposes that national courts have primary responsibility for prosecuting and punishing crimes that fall within the jurisdiction of the ICC, and the latter will only intervene when the former are unable or unwilling to do so.[83] Once the ICC assumes jurisdiction, it is rather optimistic to expect national authorities in that particular context to effectively and complementarily address the issue of reparations for victims participating in proceedings before the ICC unless the circumstances that prevailed when the Court intervened have changed dramatically.

In African countries ravaged by protracted conflicts that span decades, repairing the harm caused to thousands (or millions) of victims remains an impossible task. The attention of reparations advocates therefore tends to focus on the most vulnerable victims, like victims of sexual violence, victims bearing the physical and psychological scars of atrocities or victims rendered economically fragile with limited scope for resilience. In the Uganda and CAR respectively, victims involved in proceedings in the *Kwoyelo* case and potentially future cases before the ICD, and victims closely following the initial investigative steps of the CAR's CPS still have to wait for potential reparations that may be awarded in proceedings before these criminal justice institutions. Moreover, broader transitional justice processes involving reparations for thousands of victims of protracted conflicts in these two countries have been contemplated, but are still subject to renegotiation within contentious domestic socio-political spaces.

The DRC and Côte d'Ivoire, on the other hand, have witnessed some, albeit still limited, court-ordered or government-sponsored reparations decisions for victims of atrocities. In the DRC context, evolving international norms and national legislation enabling victims to participate in proceedings as civil parties have allowed domestic courts to award reparations to the victims involved in proceedings (civil parties). Reparations rulings by courts in the DRC follow certain patterns. First, there is a lack of consistency in the figure of reparations awarded to victims by various (military) courts across the country. For instance, 128 civil parties were awarded $300,000 in the *Bokala* case,[84] 13 civil parties were awarded $500,000 in the *Kahwa Panga* case[85] and three civil parties were awarded $165,000 in the *Bongi* case[86] (Inganya 2014: 82).[87]

---

83 Articles 17 and 18 of the Rome Statute.

84 Tribunal Militaire de Garnison (TMG) – Mbandaka, *Affaire dite BOKALA*, RP 101/006, 20 June 2006.

85 TMG Bunia, *Affaire KAHWA Panga*, RP 039/2006, 2 August 2006.

86 Cour Militaire (CM) – Orientale, *Affaire Bongi*, RPA 003/07, 28 July 2008.

87 The *Tribunal Militaire de Garnison* are lower military courts found wherever important military units are deployed, while the *Cours Militaires* are competent to try, among others, highly ranked military officers.

Within the Congolese socio-economic context, these amounts may fail to repair the damage suffered by victims, but they are non-negligible and, if paid, could make a difference in the lives of the beneficiaries. Second, since most of the accused were members of regular armed forces, Congolese (military) courts have regularly pronounced reparations not only against the accused but also against their employer, the Congolese state (Inganya 2014: 82; Mbokani 2016: 377). This is significant, since most convicts are insolvent and unable to actually pay the reparations, whereas, with some goodwill, the Congolese state, however dysfunctional it might be, might be able to do so. Finally, the limited investment by the Congolese state in the judiciary and the limited political commitment to implementing judicial decisions have resulted in the non-payment of reparations awards pronounced against the state.[88] In fact, proceedings against suspects of international crimes in the DRC have been criticised for overreliance by judicial institutions involved in the process on non-governmental partnerships – UN agencies and various donors – to support their activities, rendering their independence questionable. The fact that the state remains unable to execute decisions on reparations may result in secondary victimisation for civil parties whose promised reparations do not materialise. Moreover, beyond reparations awarded within criminal proceedings against a limited number of offenders tried so far, the absence of comprehensive transitional justice mechanisms in the country for crimes committed over nearly three decades of violent conflicts imply that the overwhelming majority of victims have no realistic prospects of redress.

Like the DRC, the legal system of Côte d'Ivoire allows victims to participate in criminal proceedings as civil parties and claim reparations. However, because prosecutions conducted by Ivorian courts have so far focused on crimes against the state and Simone Gbagbo was acquitted in her second trial for crimes against humanity, victims of the 2010–2011 post-election violence and other harmful acts committed since 1990 are still waiting for court-ordered reparations.[89] In addition to these reparations, in the wake of the activities of the CDVR recommending, among other things, the adoption by the government of a reparations programme for individuals or entities harmed during the crises in the country from 1990 to 2011, the government of Côte d'Ivoire established a National Commission for the Reconciliation and Compensation for Victims (CONARIV) in 2015, (CDVR 2014: 107–110; ICTJ 2016: 27). Capitalising on

---

88 HRW, 'États généraux de la justice en République démocratique du Congo: Recommandations sur la lutte contre l'impunité pour les graves crimes internationaux', 27 April 2015, https://www.hrw.org/fr/news/2015/04/27/etats-generaux-de-la-justice-en-republique-democratique-du-congo.

89 Drissa Traoré, Yacouba Doumbia and Jim Wormington, 'Les victimes oubliées de la Côte d'Ivoire', *Jeune Afrique*, 23 February 2018, https://www.jeuneafrique.com/535346/societe/les-victimes-oubliees-de-la-cote-divoire.

the work of the CDVR, the CONARIV, which operated until early July 2017, identified 316,954 victims of atrocities committed from 1990 to 2011.[90] Even before the establishment of CONARIV, a reparations fund was announced in 2014 and endowed with around $16 million for payment in reparations, initially channelled through an inter-ministerial National Social Cohesion Programme. The reparations programme initially handled 4,500 cases of deceased (3,500) and injured (1,000) victims seeking reparations. Families or surviving relatives of the deceased received roughly $1650, while injured persons were offered coverage for medical treatment.[91]

5. CONCLUSION: BETWEEN GLOBAL AND DOMESTIC PROCESSES, HOPES AND DISAPPOINTMENTS

The exercise of domestic, international and even universal criminal jurisdiction is predicated on the necessity to punish perpetrators of crimes that are considered to have been committed against humankind and to use punishment as a pedagogical tool to prevent such crimes. Such punishment has generally been conceived as serving the interests of victims, many of whom seek retribution for wrongs committed against them (Cryer 2010: 25). Retribution, through punishment, is in itself construed as a form of recognition of victims' suffering, a form of redress (Cryer 2010). Taking a cue from developments in international law – particularly ICC law – several domestic contexts where mass atrocities have been committed are increasingly involved in processes of revisiting their existing legal norms and practices in order to better accommodate victims' demands for justice.

The special recognition offered to victims of crimes under the ICC system represents the most unequivocal acknowledgement of their pain and suffering as a result of horrendous crimes, such as those falling under the Court's jurisdiction. In the founding documents and the growing practice of the Court, victims are offered a space to voice their suffering, seek recognition and claim redress for the wrongs done to them. Judging from the reluctance of many modern criminal justice systems to adopt truly restorative justice models to deal with crime, whereby the rights of offenders and those of victims are given the same consideration, the accommodation of victims across the various

[90] 'Côte d'Ivoire: fin de mandat de la Commission nationale pour la réconciliation', *Jeune Afrique*, 4 July 2017, https://www.jeuneafrique.com/453885/politique/cote-divoire-fin-de-mandat-de-commission-nationale-reconciliation.

[91] 'Côte d'Ivoire: quels montants pour l'indemnisation des victimes de la crise postélectorale?', *Jeune Afrique*, 19 October 2015, https://www.jeuneafrique.com/272817/societe/cote-divoire-quels-montants-pour-lindemnisation-des-victimes-de-la-crise-postelectorale.

stages of proceedings before the ICC is certainly a very positive development in societal attempts to properly address crime and its consequences. Since the ICC assumes jurisdiction where the national authorities, mostly in the territorial state in which the crimes are committed, are unable or unwilling to act, victims generally place high hopes in proceedings before the Court. It is therefore not surprising to note that despite the distance that separates The Hague from the dominantly African contexts where ICC-investigated crimes were committed, thousands of victims have taken steps to participate in proceedings, seeking recognition and/or reparation. Yet the distance between the Court and the victims, their large number and the bureaucratic machinery of international justice, which only allows the ICC to process a limited number of cases at a time, signal that only a very small number of victims are able to directly participate in proceedings at The Hague. Most victims are collectively represented by teams with rather limited personnel, making it quite impossible for each victim to be properly represented. Furthermore, while thousands of victims have been involved in ICC proceedings, pushes for domestic proceedings are an acknowledgement of the limits of an institution such as the ICC to provide justice to the large numbers of victims harmed in the countries in question. Even then, in many African countries ravaged by conflicts, the majority of victims of large-scale atrocities face almost impossible odds of securing justice and redress for the harm inflicted on them. Despite an increasing empathy towards victims and a growing recognition of their rights, a combination of factors – including the limited institutional capacity of resource-constrained societies ravaged by conflict to handle the magnitude of atrocities and the often-limited political will to navigate the contentious terrain of accountability for violations committed by different sides – limits victims' chances of securing justice.

In contexts such as Uganda, the DRC, the CAR and Côte d'Ivoire, where the ICC has opened investigations, victims who have suffered numerous violations have, in principle, the possibility of participating and seeking reparations in more than one forum of justice. While the existence of multiple legal avenues for justice and reparations keeps victims' hopes alive, victims and their advocates face steep hurdles in trying to translate rights into enforceable decisions. First, formal commitments to justice by most post-conflict societies are rarely followed by concreate policies that look at violations by all actors involved in the conflict. Instead, domestic and international prosecutions remain selective and therefore likely to accommodate a limited number of victims, in cases where they are enabled to participate at all. Whether that selectivity conforms to the 'victors' justice' critique or is linked to the limited capacity of the institutions involved to handle the magnitude of the task at hand, selective prosecutions and reparations may provide solace to a few victims and yet may be a source of resentment for those victims left out of the process. This is particularly true in many rural African societies, whose characteristically communitarian features shape members' perceptions about the dynamics of conflict and redress.

Second, the growing recognition of victims' rights in international and domestic processes and the existence of networks of solidarity and advocacy for victims are empowering dynamics for victims. However, among the lessons to be learned from the *Bemba* case is the fact that actors invested in advocacy for and empowerment of victims may, at times, end up raising unmanageable expectations that, once unmet, might result in cases of revictimisation. The challenge of raised expectations is linked to the question of victim agency after mass atrocities. The mobilisation of multiple domestic and global actors in solidarity with victims is in general rarely coordinated. The actors involved in advocacy for victims claim that role with contrasted, often limited, levels of vetting and/or accountability. Genuine victim empowerment supposes reinforcing their autonomous agency to enable them to navigate the processes of seeking redress. It is doubtful whether the current practices of collective representation of hundreds or thousands of victims before the ICC or the uncoordinated and ad hoc mobilisation of victims in domestic trials always contribute to such empowerment. Overreliance on donor-led initiatives for justice and reparations by various actors, including governmental bodies, does not suggest the long-term resilience of the beneficiary societies.

Finally, the limited dialogue or even competition between domestic and international legal processes, as illustrated in the Simone Gbagbo and other cases discussed above (Heller 2016: Clark 2018), exemplify the limits of victim-centric narratives used to justify these actions. Navigating multiple, often unfamiliar terrains of justice exposes victims to the burden of relieving their traumatic experiences without any assurances of securing the expected outcomes in terms of accountability and reparations. But beyond these challenges, the emergent shift in international and domestic laws from narrow constructions of criminal accountability to more restorative responses to crime opens up spaces for victims to assert their claims for reparative justice. Real improvements in the legal situation of victims, particularly in domestic settings, require normative and institutional reforms that can only be sustained if and when post-conflict societies become more socio-politically stable.

BIBLIOGRAPHY

Anders, G. and Zenker, O. (2015) *Transition and Justice Negotiating the Terms of New Beginnings in Africa*. Oxford: Wiley Blackwell.

Avocats Sans Frontières (ASF) (2013) *Recueil de Jurisprudence Congolaise en Matière de Crimes Internationaux*. Brussels: ASF.

Bar-Tal, D. (2000) 'From Intractable Conflict through Conflict Resolution to Reconciliation: Psychological Analysis', *Political Psychology* 21: 351–365.

Bar-Tal, D. (2003) 'Collective Memory of Physical Violence: Its Contribution to the Culture of Violence' in E. Cairns and M.D. Roe (eds), *The Role of Memory in Ethnic Conflict*. Basingstoke: Palgrave Macmillan, pp. 77–93.

Bar-Tal, D. (2007) 'Sociopsychological Foundations of Intractable Conflicts', *American Behavioral Scientist* 50: 1430–1453.

Baumgartner, E. (2008) 'Aspects of Victim Participation in the Proceedings of the International Criminal Court', *International Review of the Red Cross* 90(870): 409–440.

Bonacker, T. and Safferling, C. (eds) (2013), *Victims of International Crimes: An Interdisciplinary Discourse*. The Hague: T.M.C Asser/Springer.

Carayannis, T. (2015) 'CAR's Southern Identity: Congo, CAR, and International Justice' in T. Carayannis and L. Lombard (eds), *Making Sense of the Central African Republic*. London: Zed Books, pp. 244–266.

CDVR (2014) *Rapport Final*, République de Côte d'Ivoire, December.

Clark, J.N. (2016) 'The First Rape Conviction at the ICC: An Analysis of the Bemba Judgment', *Journal of International Criminal* Justice, 14(3): 667–687.

Clark, P. (2018) *Distant Justice: The Impact of the International Criminal Court on African Politics*. Cambridge: Cambridge University Press.

Cryer, R. et al. (2010) *An Introduction to International Criminal Law and Procedure*, 2nd edn. Cambridge: Cambridge University Press.

De Casadevante Romani, C.F. (2012) *International Law of Victims*. New York: Springer.

Doria, J., Gasser, H.-P. and Bassiouni, C.M. (eds) (2009) *The Legal Regime of the International Criminal Court Essays in Honour of Professor Igor Blishchenko*. Boston: Martinus Nijhoff.

Dovi, S. (2017) 'Representation in Context: Constructing Victims' Claims in the International Criminal Court', *Representation* 53(3–4): 263–275.

Druliolle, V. and Brett, R. (2018) 'Introduction: Understanding the Construction of Victimhood and the Evolving Role of Victims in Transitional Justice and Peacebuilding' in V. Druliolle and R. Brett (eds), *The Politics of Victimhood in Post-conflict Societies: Comparative and Analytical Perspectives*. Cham: Palgrave Macmillan, pp. 1–22.

Dutton, M.A. and Greene, R. (2010) 'Resilience and Crime Victimization', *Journal of Traumatic Stress* 23(2): 215–222.

FIDH (2017) '"Tout ce que j'attends, c'est la réparation": Les vues de victimes de violences sexuelles en matière de réparations dans l'affaire Bemba devant la Cour pénale internationale', Report, November.

Fischer, P.G. (2003) 'The Victims' Trust Fund of the International Criminal Court – Formation of a Functional Reparations Scheme Comment', *Emory International Law Review* 17: 187–240.

Fletcher, L.E. (2015) 'Refracted Justice: The Imagined Victim and the International Criminal Court' in C. de Vos, S. Kendall and C. Stahn (eds), *Contested Justice: The Politics and Practice of International Criminal Court Interventions*. Cambridge: Cambridge University Press, pp. 302–325.

Foley, T. (2014) *Developing Restorative Justice Jurisprudence: Rethinking Responses to Criminal Wrongdoing*. Farnham: Ashgate.

Garbett, C. (2017) 'The International Criminal Court and Restorative Justice: Victims, Participation and the Processes of Justice', *Restorative Justice* 5(2): 198–220.

Gasser, H.-P. (2009) 'The Changing Relationship between International Criminal Law, Human Rights Law and Humanitarian Law' in J. Doria, H.-P. Gasser and M.C. Bassiouni (eds),

The Legal Regime of the International Criminal Court Essays in Honour of Professor Igor Blishchenko. Leiden: Brill, pp. 1111–1117.

Hébert-Dolbec. M.-L. (2015) 'Towards Bureaucratization: An Analysis of Common Legal Representation Practices before the International Criminal Court', *Revue québécoise de droit international*, Special Edition: 35–61.

Heller, K.J. (2016) 'Radical Complementarity', *Journal of International Criminal Justice* 14: 637–665.

Hirst, M. (2017) 'Legal Representation of Participating Victims' in K. Tibori-Szabó and M. Hirst (eds), *Victim Participation in International Criminal Justice: Practitioners' Guide*. The Hague: T.M.C. Asser Press/Springer.

Hobbs, H. (2014) 'Victim Participation in International Criminal Proceedings: Problems and Potential Solutions in Implementing an Effective and Vital Component of Justice', *Texas International Law Journal* 49(1): 1–33.

Hoyle, C. (2012) 'Victims, the Criminal Process, and Restorative Justice', in M. Maguire, R. Morgan and R. Reiner (eds), *The Oxford Handbook of Criminology*, 5th edn. Oxford: Oxford University Press, pp. 398–425.

Human Rights Watch (HRW) (2016) '"Justice Re-establishes Balance": Delivering Credible Accountability for Serious Abuses in Côte d'Ivoire', March.

ICC (2017) *Situation in the Republic of Burundi, Public Redacted Version of 'Decision Pursuant to Article 15 of the Rome Statute on the Authorization of an Investigation into the Situation in the Republic of Burundi*, ICC-01/17-X-9-US-Exp, 25 October, ICC-01/17-X, 9 November.

ICC (2017) 'Third Court's Report on the Development of Performance Indicators for the International Criminal Court', 15 November.

ICC/OPCV (2010) 'Representing Victims before the International Criminal Court: A Manual for Legal Representatives', https://www.icc-cpi.int/iccdocs/opcv/OPCV Manual-4-Eng.pdf.

ICC/Registry (2018) *Situation in the Islamic Republic of Afghanistan: Final Consolidated Registry Report on Victims' Representations Pursuant to the Pre-Trial Chamber's Order ICC-02/17-6 of 9 November 2017*, ICC-02/17 1/6, 20 February.

ICTJ (2015) 'The Accountability Landscape in Eastern DRC Analysis of the National Legislative and Judicial Response to International Crimes (2009–2014)', July.

ICTJ (2016) 'Disappointed Hope: Judicial Handling of Post-election Violence in Cote d'Ivoire', April.

ICTJ (2017) 'Victims Fighting Impunity: Transitional Justice in the African Great Lakes Region, Great Lakes Region', March.

Inganya, M.E. (2014) 'La réparation des crimes internationaux en droit congolais: Analyse des pratiques indemnitaires des juridictions militaires au regard du Statut de Rome de la Cour pénale internationale', ASF, December.

Karmen, A. (2015) *Crime Victims: An Introduction to Victimology*, 9th edn. Boston, MA: Cengage Publishers.

Kelly, M.J. (2013) 'The Status of Victims under the Rome Statute of the International Criminal Court' in T. Bonacker and C. Safferling (eds), *Victims of International Crimes: An Interdisciplinary Discourse*. The Hague: T.M.C Asser/Springer, pp. 47–66.

Kendall, S. and Nouwen, S. (2014) 'Representational Practices at the International Criminal Court: The Gap between Juridified and Abstract Victimhood', *Law & Contemporary Problems* 76: 235–262.

Markus Funk, T. (2010) *Victims' Rights and Advocacy at the International Criminal Court*. Oxford: Oxford University Press.

Mawby, R.I. and Walklate, S. (1994) *Critical Victimology: International Perspectives*. London: Sage Publications.

Mbokani, J.B. (2016) *La jurisprudence congolaise en matière de crimes de droit international: Une analyse des décisions des juridictions militaires congolaises en application du Statut de Rome*. New York: Open Society Foundations.

McCarthy, C. (2015) 'The Rome Statute's Regime of Victim Redress: Challenges and Prospects' in C. Stahn (ed.), *The Law and Practice of the International Criminal Court*. Oxford: Oxford University Press, pp. 1203–1221.

MINUSCA et al., (2017) 'Report of the Mapping Project documenting serious violations of international human rights law and international humanitarian law committed within the territory of Central African Republic between January 2003 and December 2015', May.

Moffett, L. (2017) 'Reparations for Victims at the International Criminal Court: A New Way Forward?', *International Journal of Human Rights* 21(9): 1204–1222.

Naughton, E. (2014) 'Democratic Republic of the Congo: Case Study' in International Centre for Transitional Justice (ICTJ), *Challenging the Conventional: Can Truth Commissions Strengthen Peace Processes*? ICTJ Report, pp. 47–55.

Ndahinda, F.M. (2016) 'Collective Victimization and Subjectivity in the Democratic Republic of Congo: Why Do Lasting Peace and Justice Remain Elusive?', *International Journal on Minority and Group Rights* 23:2, 137–178.

Noor, M. et al. (2012) 'When Suffering Begets Suffering: The Psychology of Competitive Victimhood between Adversarial Groups in Violent Conflicts', *Personality and Social Psychology Review* 16(4): 351–374.

Omach, P. (2016) 'Civil Society Organizations and Local-Level Peacebuilding in Northern Uganda', *Journal of Asian and African Studies* 51(1): 77–96.

Pena, M. (2017) 'The Role of Intermediaries and Third Parties in Victim Participation' in K. Tibori-Szabó and M. Hirst (eds), *Victim Participation in International Criminal Justice: Practitioners' Guide*. The Hague: T.M.C. Asser Press/Springer, pp. 81–109.

Rothe D.L. (2014) 'Can an International Criminal Justice System Address Victims' Needs?' in D.L. Rothe, and D. Kauzlarich, (eds), *Towards a Victimology of State Crime*. New York: Routledge, pp. 238–249.

Shaw, R., Waldorf, L. and Hazan, P. (2010) *Localizing Transitional Justice: Interventions and Priorities after Mass Violence*. Stanford: Stanford University Press.

Stahn, C. (ed.) (2015) *The Law and Practice of the International Criminal Court*. Oxford: Oxford University Press.

TFV (2016) *Annual Report*, September.

Tibori-Szabó, K. et al. (2017) 'Communication between Victims' Lawyers and Their Clients' in K. Tibori-Szabó and M. Hirst (eds), *Victim Participation in International Criminal Justice: Practitioners' Guide*. The Hague: T.M.C. Asser Press/Springer, pp. 433–465.

Tonry, M. (2011) 'Punishment' in M. Tonry (ed.), *The Oxford Handbook of Crime and Criminal Justice*. Oxford: Oxford University Press, pp. 95–125.

Van den Wyngaert, C. (2011) 'Victims before International Criminal Courts: Some Views and Concerns of an ICC Trial Judge', *Case Western Reserve Journal of International Law* 44: 475–496.

Van Dijk, J. (2009) 'Free the Victim: A Critique of the Western Conception of Victimhood', *International Review of Victimology* 16: 1–33.

Van Ness, D.W. and Strong, K.H. (2015) *Restoring Justice: An Introduction to Restorative Justice*. Amsterdam: Anderson/Elsevier.

Vasiliev, S. (2009) 'Article 68 (3) and Personal Interests of Victims in the Emerging Practice of the ICC' in C. Stahn and G. Sluiter (eds), *The Emerging Practice of the International Criminal Court*. Leiden: Martinus Nijhoff, pp. 635–690.

Vasiliev, S. (2015) 'Victim Participation Revisited: What the ICC is Learning about Itself' in C. Stahn (ed.), *The Law and Practice of the International Criminal Court*. Oxford: Oxford University Press, pp. 1133–1202.

Walklate S. (2007) *Imagining the Victim of Crime*. Maidenhead: Open University Press.

Walklate S. (2011) 'Reframing Criminal Victimization: Finding a Place for Vulnerability and Resilience', *Theoretical Criminology* 15(2): 179–194.

Wemmers, J.-A. (2009) 'Victims and the International Criminal Court (ICC): Evaluating the Success of the ICC with Respect to Victims', *International Review of Victimology* 16: 211–227.

Wemmers, J.-A. and de Brouwer, A.-M. (2011) 'Globalization and Victims' Rights at the International Criminal Court' in R.M. Letschert and J. van Dijk (eds), *The New Faces of Victimhood Globalization, Transnational Crimes and Victim Rights*. Dordrecht: Springer.

Wolhuter, L., Olley, N. and Denham, D. (2009) *Victimology: Victimisation and Victims' Rights*. London/New York: Routledge/Cavendish.

Zappala, S. (2010) 'The Rights of Victims v. the Rights of the Accused', *Journal of International Criminal Justice* 8: 137–164.

CASE LAW

Cour Militaire (CM) – Orientale, *Affaire Bongi*, RPA 003/07, 28 July 2008.

The Prosecutor v. Jean-Pierre Bemba Gombo, Decision on common legal representation of victims for the purpose of trial, ICC-01/05-01/08-1005, 10 November 2010.

The Prosecutor v. Jean-Pierre Bemba Gombo, Order on the legal representation of victims previously represented by Me Assingambi Zarambaud, ICC-01/05-01/08-2964, 7 February 2014.

The Prosecutor v. Jean-Pierre Bemba Gombo, Judgment pursuant to Article 74 of the Statute, ICC-01/05-01/08-3343, 21 March 2016.

The Prosecutor v. Jean-Pierre Bemba Gombo, Decision on Sentence pursuant to Article 76 of the Statute, ICC-01/05-01/08-3399, 21 June 2016.

The Prosecutor v. Jean-Pierre Bemba Gombo, Judgment on the appeal of Mr Jean-Pierre Bemba Gombo against Trial Chamber III's 'Judgment pursuant to Article 74 of the Statute', ICC-01/05-01/08-3636-Red, 8 June 2018.

The Prosecutor v. Jean-Pierre Bemba Gombo, Appeals Chamber's Judgment dated 8 June 2018 on the reparations proceedings, ICC-01/05-01/08, 12 July 2018.

The Prosecutor v. Jean-Pierre Bemba Gombo, Final decision on the reparations proceedings, ICC-01/05-01/08-3653, 3 August 2018.

The Prosecutor v. Thomas Lubanga Dyilo, Judgment pursuant to Article 74 of the Statute, ICC-01/04-01/06, 12 March 2012.

The Prosecutor v. Thomas Lubanga Dyilo, Decision establishing the principles and procedures to be applied to reparations, ICC-01/04-01/06-2904, 7 August 2012.

The Prosecutor v. Thomas Lubanga Dyilo, Decision on the participation of victims in the appeals against Trial Chamber I's conviction and sentencing decisions, ICC-01/04-01/06 A 4, A 5, A 6, 13 December 2012.

The Prosecutor v. Thomas Lubanga Dyilo, Judgment on the appeal of Mr Thomas Lubanga Dyilo against his conviction, ICC-01/04-01/06 A 5, 1 December 2014, Annex 3.

The Prosecutor v. Thomas Lubanga Dyilo, Judgment on the appeals against the 'Decision establishing the principles and procedures to be applied to reparations' of 7 August 2012 with AMENDED order for reparations (Annex A) and public annexes 1 and 2, ICC-01/04-01/06-3129 and ICC-01/04-01/06-3129-AnxA, 3 March 2015.

The Prosecutor v. Thomas Lubanga Dyilo, Corrected version of the 'Decision Setting the Size of the Reparations Award for Which Thomas Lubanga Dyilo is Liable', ICC-01/04-01/06-3379-Red-Corr-tENG, 21 December 2017.

The Prosecutor v. Germain Katanga, Judgment pursuant to Article 74 of the Statute, ICC-01/04-01/07, 7 March 2014.

The Prosecutor v. Germain Katanga, Decision on Sentence pursuant to Article 76 of the Statute, ICC-01/04-01/07-3484, 23 May 2014.

The Prosecutor v. Germain Katanga, Order for Reparations pursuant to Article 75 of the Statute, ICC-01/04-01/07-3728, 24 March 2017.

The Prosecutor v. Bosco Ntaganda, Third decision on victims' participation in trial proceedings, ICC-01/04-02/06, 2 July 2015.

The Prosecutor v. Bosco Ntaganda, ICC-01/04-02/06, ICC-PIDS-CIS-DRC-02-014/19_Eng, updated July 2019.

The Prosecutor v. Ahmad Al Faqi Al Mahdi, Judgment and Sentence, ICC-01/12-01/15-171, 27 September 2016.

The Prosecutor v. Ahmad Al Faqi Al Mahdi, Reparations Order, ICC-01/12-01/15-236, 17 August 2017.

The Prosecutor v. Ahmad Al Faqi Al Mahdi, Public redacted version of 'Decision on Trust Fund for Victims' Draft Implementation Plan for Reparations', ICC-01/12-01/15-273-Red, 12 July 2018.

Tribunal de Grande Instance de Kinshasa/Kalamu, *Affaire Mputu Muteba et Consorts (Kimbanguistes case)*, RP 11.154/11.155/11.156, 17 December 2011.

Tribunal Militaire de Garnison (TMG) – Mbandaka, *Affaire dite BOKALA*, RP 101/006, 20 June 2006.

TMG Bunia, *Affaire KAHWA Panga*, RP 039/2006, 2 August 2006.

THE ROLE OF THE INTERNATIONAL CRIMINAL COURT IN AFRICA

The Epic Fails?

Max du Plessis and Christopher Gevers

1. INTRODUCTION

In writing about Africa and the International Criminal Court (ICC) over the past two decades, the temptation to allude to Epic narratives has been ever-present, and one in particular has haunted our collective reflections on the subject. We have written about 'stormy years', 'being caught between Scylla and Charybdis' and on more than one occasion, an early draft has had the phrase 'the Odyssey continues' lurking somewhere in the text, if not the title. Recently, employing Homer's Epic became more difficult, as the *Odyssey* appeared to be headed towards a precipitous and premature end when African states started making plans for their collective withdrawal from the Rome Statute.[1] While threats of a mass withdrawal have simmered – in the end only Burundi followed through (South Africa demurred) – there seems to be little hope of a rapprochement. In fact, recent developments in the Afghanistan situation suggest another storm might be on the horizon.

On reflection, in our writings at least, it has been unclear who was steering the ship: was the hero of the story the ICC navigating the waters (and avoiding the Siren calls) of international politics, or were African states navigating the waters of international law? In this chapter we want to focus specifically on the role that the ICC has played, not as hero but as protagonist, in Africa over the past two decades. We do so, jumping mythologies, with the intention of neither burying nor praising the ICC, but in order to reflect critically on the role it has played in the demise of this once promising relationship, and we consider whether the story might have turned out differently (or might yet still). For, while much of the blame is currently placed solely at the feet of African states and their hostility towards specific investigations (particularly against heads of state), this chapter aims to show that: (1) the fractures within this relationship have come about as a result of the actions (and *inactions*) of the ICC and its supporters; and (2) as far as African states' complaints are concerned, these were general concerns they had about the ICC that were present at its founding in 1998, and these concerns have come to be realised, for the worse, with each passing year. As such, the current situation might be characterised both as African states *falling out* with the ICC and as the ICC *falling into* patterns of behaviour that African states raised arguably legitimate concerns about, and thus sought to avoid, at Rome in 1998.

In this chapter we will consider the role that the ICC has played in Africa in light of the hopes and fears raised by African states at Rome regarding: the impartiality of the Prosecutor; the influence of the 'Great Powers'; the relationship between supranational and domestic prosecutions; and the Court's role in the pursuit of lasting peace and security. We begin by revisiting Rome to set out these concerns in more detail and end by revisiting Homer's Epic to consider whether we had the right 'hero' but the wrong story.

2. ROME REVISITED

Much has been written about African states 'astonishing enthusiasm' (Schabas 2013: 548) for, and participation in, the establishment of the ICC in Rome

[1] African Union, 'Withdrawal Strategy Document – Draft 2', 12 January 2017, para. 9.

in 1998 (see, for example, Maqungo 2000; Mochochoko 2005), and the fact that the first signatory to the Rome Statute was an African country (Senegal). However, less attention has been paid to the conditions African states placed on their support for the ICC's establishment or, in other words, the understandings under which they did so. Re-reading what we might optimistically call African states' *hopes* in 1998 or pessimistically call their *fears*, with not a small measure of hindsight, provides more insight into how the relationship unfolded or began to fall apart. While they varied in emphasis, four – let us agnostically call them 'concerns' – emerged from the collective and individual statements of African states to the plenary at Rome in 1998, namely: (1) the independence *and impartiality* of the Prosecutor; (2) the influence of the 'Great Powers' through the Security Council; (3) the relationship between supranational prosecutions and the protection of state sovereignty, as mediated by the principle of 'complementarity'; and (4) the relationship between the Court's work and the pursuit of peace.

These four concerns were succinctly set out by South Africa's delegate on behalf of the 16-member 'Southern African Development Community' on the opening day of the Rome Conference, who told the assembled diplomats, United Nations (UN) officials and non-governmental organisation (NGO) representatives that these African states desired that:

- the Prosecutor should be independent and have authority to initiate investigations and prosecutions on his or her own initiative *without interference from States or the Security Council*, subject to appropriate judicial scrutiny ... [and] [t]he independence of the Court must not be prejudiced by political considerations [Concern 1];
- the Court should contribute to furthering the integrity of States generally, as well as the *equality of States* within the general principles of international law [Concern 2];
- [the Court] should be an effective *complement to national criminal justice systems* ... [and] should also have competence in the event of the inability, unwillingness or unavailability of national criminal justice systems to prosecute those responsible for grave crimes under the Statute, *while respecting the complementary nature of its relationship with such national systems* [Concern 3]; and
- The Court [is] a necessary element for peace and security in the world ... and [its] establishment ... would not only strengthen the arsenal of measure to combat gross human rights gross human rights violations but would ultimately *contribute to the attainment of international peace* [Concern 4].[2]

2 As reported in *Rome Proceedings II*, (United Nations Diplomatic Conference of Plenipotentiaries on the Establishment of an International Criminal Court) Rome, 15 June–17 July 1998, p. 65.

In these four concerns, which were repeated elsewhere by other African states,[3] we can see the seeds of their disillusionment with the ICC today, as the fears underlying each of them have materialised – to a greater or lesser extent – since 1998, with little attempt to acknowledge or address them by the ICC or its supporters. In 1998, these fears themselves already had longer historical roots, based on African states' less than successful engagements with international courts (i.e. the International Court of Justice (ICJ)) and international criminal law (e.g. the Apartheid Convention) since independence, the 'burden of history in Africa's relationship with the international system' more broadly (Dersso 2016: 70) and the long shadow still cast by colonialism over international law (du Plessis 2003: 624–659).

This longer, tragic history was also the reason why 'Africa had a particular interest in the establishment of the Court', as was pointed out by the Organisation of African Unity (OAU) delegate at Rome in 1998,[4] and once again in the opening lines of the African Union's (AU) 2017 Withdrawal Strategy as the reason why African states 'initially saw the ICC as a beacon of emancipation – a solution for their continent's injustices'.[5]

3. FROM ROME TO RUINS

Placing African states' hopes *and fears* of what the ICC might become back into the story ought to dispel the problematic narrative that they were simply *naïve* at Rome in 1998. On the contrary, they were well aware of the potential shortcomings of the ICC, but supported it nonetheless (for reasons both noble and less so, no doubt). However, the *naïveté* trope might re-emerge insofar as African states hoped that it *might have been otherwise*. A determinist reading of subsequent events might suggest that they were the inevitable result of 'the political structures and uneven power relations that are embedded in the ICC's legal framework [that] have played out since the adoption of the Rome Statute in 1998' (Clarke et al. 2016: 10). On such a reading, *the writing was on the wall at Rome, and African states were naïve to think that it could be erased.*

Aside from cutting short our chapter, such a reading of events lets the Prosecutor (past and present), the Court and its (often naïve) supporters off

3 See Lesotho (*Rome Proceedings II*, p. 69), Tanzania (p. 74), Burkina Faso (p. 84), Namibia (p. 87), Swaziland (p. 108), Malawi (p. 108), Nigeria (p. 111), the Democratic Republic of the Congo (p. 112), Angola (p. 117), Burundi (p. 118), Egypt (p. 127), Benin (p. 128). The delegate from Lesotho noted that: 'In addition to strengthening the rule of law by providing certainty and consistency in international investigations and prosecutions' (p. 69).

4 As reported in *Rome Proceedings II*, p. 104.

5 AU, above n 1, para. 1.

the hook too easily. Not only have these largely legitimate concerns of African states (which were clearly articulated at the outset and have been repeated since) been simply ignored or problematically dismissed, but, as this section aims to show, they have materialised over the past two decades not purely by the mechanical operation of international law or only the unfolding of uneven international politics, but also by the actions and inactions of the ICC (and in some cases its supporters).

3.1. AN (IM)PARTIAL PROSECUTOR: SELECTION, NON-SELECTION AND PERCEPTION

To date, the ICC has only prosecuted Africans (and only two successfully).[6] While in 2016 the Prosecutor took the momentous step of formally opening an *investigation* outside of Africa (in respect of alleged international crimes committed in Georgia), it is yet to bring any cases in respect of that situation; all the remaining 10 situations and all the pending cases concern Africa and Africans. Reasonable people will disagree (as do *we*, in fact) on whether the Office of the Prosecutor (OTP) has 'targeted' African states, but there is minimal consensus (between us, at least) that: (1) the OTP has failed to pursue merit-worthy cases outside of Africa; and (2) the OTP has failed to adequately address the *perception* that it has targeted African states, compounding matters further.

3.1.1. Non-Selection and 'Slow-Walking' of Non-African Cases

Cases come before the ICC in one of three ways. First, in terms of Article 13(a) of the Rome Statute, the Prosecutor may pursue charges with respect to crimes within the jurisdiction of the ICC in situations where a state party, under Article 14, refers a situation to the Prosecutor for investigation. Second, in terms of Article 15, the Prosecutor may also investigate a situation on his/her own initiative (*proprio motu*), provided that the Pre-Trial Chamber of the ICC authorises the continuance of such investigation after being presented with the Prosecutor's motivation and supporting documents in this regard.

---

6 Both concern the situation in the DRC (see *Prosecutor v. Thomas Lubanga Dyilo* and *Jugement rendu en application de l'article 74 du Statut*, ICC-01/04-01/07-3436, 20 March 2014, and *Prosecutor v. Germain Katanga*, ICC-01/04-01/07, 27 March 2017). In addition, one person pleaded guilty (see *Prosecutor v. Ahmad Al Faqi Al Mahdi*, ICC-01/12-01/15, 27 September 2017), and four others were convicted of offences against the administration of justice. In contrast, six individuals (again, all Africans) were acquitted or had the charges against them dropped (namely Ngudjolo, Bemba, Ruto, Sang, Gbagbo and Blé Goudé – with appeals outstanding in respect of the latter two), and other prosecutions collapsed before going to trial (most infamously the case against Kenya's President Uhuru Kenyatta).

Somewhat ironically, it was with the not inconsiderable support of African states that the Prosecutor was given this significant power under the Rome Statute.[7] Third, the Security Council may refer a situation to the Prosecutor in terms of Article 13(b) of the Rome Statute, after which he/she may choose to investigate it and refer it to the Pre-Trial Chamber of the ICC, as set out in Article 15.

As Dugard points out, leaving aside Darfur and Libya, which were referred by the Security Council, the remaining situations being investigated and prosecuted by the ICC were *chosen* by the Prosecutor; as he/she was under no obligation to accept state referrals (including so-called 'self-referrals', such as in the Democratic Republic of the Congo (DRC), Uganda, the Central African Republic and Mali), such situations were therefore as much *selected* by the Prosecutor for investigation as the *proprio motu* investigations in Kenya, Côte d'Ivoire, Georgia and Burundi (Dugard 2013). Moreover, the current Prosecutor has taken the position that she is also under no obligation to accept Security Council referrals either, which means that her predecessor *chose* the Libyan and Sudanese situations as well.[8]

Be that as it may, no matter how often the Prosecutor and the ICC's defenders might repeat the mantra that the bulk of the ICC's cases arose from self-referrals by African states, this does not explain away the burning issue of the *non*-selection of other deserving cases outside of Africa (and there have been other deserving cases). In fact, the Prosecutor has directly and indirectly decided not to take on a number of non-African situations since 2002.

Perhaps the most obvious example of the *direct* refusal to take on a situation is the persistent refusal of the Prosecutor (both past and present) to take action in respect of crimes committed in or concerning Palestine. More than a decade ago, on 21 January 2009, Palestine made a declaration in terms of Article 12(3) of the Rome Statute recognising the jurisdiction of the ICC for the purpose of prosecuting international crimes committed in the territory of Palestine *since 1 July 2002*. The declaration came in the aftermath of Israel's attack on Gaza launched on 27 December 2008 (dubbed 'Operation Cast Lead'), which resulted in the deaths of 1,400 Palestinians, of which at least 850 were civilians, including 300 children and 110 women, and the wounding of over 5,000. The immediate question that arose was whether Palestine was a

---

7 The Southern African Development Community's 'Common Position' explicitly supported 'the independence of the Prosecutor, who should be able to initiate investigations and institute prosecutions on his or her own initiative and without influence from states or the Security Council, subject only to appropriate judicial scrutiny' (at p. 5). Similarly, the Dakar Declaration for the Establishment of the International Criminal Court, adopted in February 1998 by a number of African states, supported 'independence of the Prosecutor and his [*sic*] functions'.

8 See OTP, 'The ICC: A Response to African Concerns by Fatou Bensouda', Keynote Address at the Institute for Security Studies, 11 October 2012.

state for the purposes of the jurisdiction of the ICC under Article 12(1) of the Rome Statute, and so could make a declaration acceding to such jurisdiction in terms of paragraph 3 of the same Article. After three years of hand-wringing and debate over Palestine's status under international law (which included inviting leading international lawyers to participate in a roundtable discussion held by the OTP in October 2010), the Prosecutor decided that he could not in fact decide the issue as 'it [was] for the relevant bodies at the United Nations or the Assembly of States Parties to make the legal determination whether Palestine qualifies as a State for the purpose of acceding to the Rome Statute and thereby enabling the exercise of jurisdiction of the Court under article 12(1)'.[9]

This non-decision was met with dismay. Why had it taken the Prosecutor three years to come to such a brief and thinly supported conclusion? If it was that perfunctorily obvious to him when he issued the statement in April 2012, then why did he not arrive at the same conclusion three years earlier? Why did he not approach the Pre-Trial Chamber for a ruling on the question under Article 19(3) (as his successor has since done in respect of the alleged deportation of Rohingyas from Myanmar to Bangladesh)[10] or formally request the Assembly of States Parties (ASP) to consider it in terms of Article 112(2)(g) of the Rome Statute (as opposed to simply noting that that body '*could* ... in due course decide to address the matter')? As Dugard noted at the time, the only possible explanation for such a decision and its delay was that 'the Prosecutor lacks the strength to confront Israel, and thereby face the ire of the United States and many European states' (Dugard 2013). It was not just the Prosecutor who appeared reluctant: when 30 leading 'scholars and teachers of international law' sent a letter to the ASP requesting that it take up the Prosecutor's suggestion to consider the issue under Article 112(2)(g),[11] the President of the ASP allegedly 'suppressed the letter and kept its existence unknown to both the Bureau and the ASP itself' (ibid.).

In January 2015, Palestine tried again (notably, after being granted 'non-member observer state' status at the UN).[12] This time, for good measure, it submitted *both* a declaration under Article 12(3) accepting the ICC's jurisdiction and, a day later, it acceded to the Rome Statute. As a result, the Prosecutor announced that she was opening a preliminary examination into the situation in Palestine, noting that this was done 'as a matter of policy and

---

9 OTP, *Situation in Palestine*, 3 April 2012, para. 6. The Prosecutor added: 'The Rome Statute provides no authority for the Office of the Prosecutor to adopt a method to define the term "State" under article 12(3) which would be at variance with that established for the purpose of article 12(1).'

10 OTP, *Prosecution's Request for a Ruling on Jurisdiction under Article 19(3) of the Statute*, 9 April 2018.

11 Available at: https://www.ejiltalk.org/icc-assembly-of-states-parties-urged-to-decide-on-status-of-palestine.

12 See UNGA Resolution 16/19.

practice' whenever a '[state] referral or a *valid* declaration made pursuant to article 12(3) of the Statute' was received.[13] In doing so, the Prosecutor appeared to revise the terms of her office's previous *non-decision*, now claiming that it had been decided in April 2012 that Palestine was *not* a state as its 'status at the United Nations (UN) as an "observer entity" was determinative, since entry into the Rome Statute system is through the UN Secretary-General (UNSG), who acts as treaty depositary' (and hence its Article 12(3) declaration was retrospectively downgraded to a 'purported' rather than a 'valid' one).[14] However, as Palestine's status was now that of a 'non-member observer state', the Prosecutor decided that it could now 'lodge a declaration *validly* under article 12(3)' and sign up to the Rome Statute.[15]

Then, following three years of preliminary examination by the Prosecutor, which had not yet progressed past the initial *jurisdiction* phase,[16] in May 2018 Palestine *again* referred crimes committed within its territory to the Prosecutor, this time as *a state party* to the Rome Statute under Article 13(a) (therefore arguably making it more difficult for the Prosecutor to ultimately not select the situation).[17] Notwithstanding this extraordinary move, the Palestine situation remains firmly stuck in the preliminary examination stage,[18] after three attempted referrals by Palestine of the numerous international crimes committed on its territory, the first of which took place over a decade ago. Dugard's explanation for the Prosecutor's temerity continues to have purchase.

---

13 OTP, 'The Prosecutor of the International Criminal Court, Fatou Bensouda, Opens a Preliminary Examination of the Situation in Palestine', press release, 16 January 2015, ICC-OTP-20150116-PR1083.

14 Ibid.

15 The Prosecutor reiterated that: 'For the Office, the focus of the inquiry into Palestine's ability to accede to the Rome Statute *has consistently been the question of Palestine's* status *in the UN*, given the UNSG's role as treaty depositary of the Statute. The UNGA Resolution 67/19 is therefore determinative of Palestine's ability to accede to the Statute pursuant to article 125, and equally, its ability to lodge an article 12(3) declaration.'

16 When it comes to art. 12(3) referrals, the preliminary examination begins with the *subject-matter jurisdiction* phase (called Phase 2), followed by the *admissibility* phase and the *interests of justice* phase. See OTP, *Report on Preliminary Examination Activities 2017*, 4 December 2017, pp. 12–19, https://www.icc-cpi.int/itemsDocuments/2017-PE-rep/2017-otp-rep-PE_ENG.pdf.

17 While, as noted above, the Prosecutor is not bound to accept state referrals, in refusing to do so, there is some oversight by the Pre-Trial Chamber in the case of state referrals under art. 13(a), as the Court's jurisdiction is triggered by the referral itself. In contrast, when the Prosecutor decides to open an investigation using her *proprio motu* powers (which, in practice, she has considered art. 12(3) declarations to fall under), the Court's jurisdiction is only triggered once the Prosecutor has *formally* 'initiated an investigation' (i.e. decided to move beyond the preliminary examination phase).

18 At the time of writing, the Palestine situation was in the *admissibility* phase, with the *interests of justice* phase still to come. See OTP, *Report on Preliminary Examination Activities 2018*, 5 December 2018, pp. 63–70, https://www.icc-cpi.int/itemsDocuments/181205-rep-otp-PE-ENG.pdf.

This explanation also colours the Prosecutor (twice) refusing to open an investigation into Israel's 2010 attack on the Humanitarian Aid Flotilla bound for Gaza (*MV Mavi Marmara*), even though it concluded that 'the information available provides a reasonable basis to believe that war crimes were committed' by Israel during the attack.[19] In November 2014, the Prosecutor announced its refusal to open a formal investigation (following the referral by Comoros of the situation in May 2013). However, following a review application by Comoros, the Pre-Trial Chamber in July 2015 criticised that decision and asked the Prosecutor to reconsider it. After unsuccessfully appealing against the Pre-Trial Chamber's request to reconsider,[20] in November 2017 the Prosecutor issued a 'Final Decision' on the matter, in which she again refused to open an investigation. On both occasions, the Prosecutor argued that there was no reasonable basis to conclude that any potential case arising from the situation would be of sufficient gravity to be admissible. However, the Pre-Trial Chamber disagreed once again and in November 2018, it ordered the Prosecutor to open the investigation (an order she promptly appealed again).[21]

A similar pattern can be seen in the long-standing efforts of the former and present Prosecutor to 'not select' the situations in Iraq and Afghanistan. In 2006, after a preliminary examination into allegations of international crimes committed in Iraq by nationals of the UK (and other states parties), the Prosecutor decided that: (i) there was not sufficient evidence ('a reasonable basis') to support allegations of the targeting of civilians or clearly excessive attacks; and (ii) while there was sufficient evidence to support allegations of wilful killing and mistreatment of detainees, the limited number of victims meant that the admissibility requirement of 'gravity' had not been met.[22] The Prosecutor added further that while 'it was unnecessary to reach a conclusion on complementarity', he (at that stage the Prosecutor was a man) made a few tellingly cursory remarks to which we will return later (see section 3.3 below on complementarity).[23] Then, in May 2014, the current Prosecutor announced that she was once again opening a preliminary examination into crimes committed in Iraq by the UK armed forces between 2003 and 2008, based on a new communication received in 2014. In particular, she said that the new communication 'alleges a higher number of cases of ill-treatment of detainees and provides further details on the factual circumstances and the geographical

19 OTP, *Situation on Registered Vessels of Comoros, Greece and Cambodia: Article 53(1) Report*, 6 November 2014, para. 3.

20 The Prosecutor's appeal was dismissed on procedural grounds as inadmissible, and the merits were not considered. *Decision on the Admissibility of the Prosecutor's Appeal against the 'Decision on the Request of the Union of the Comoros to Review the Prosecutor's Decision Not to Initiate an Investigation'*, ICC-01/13-51 Appeals Chamber, 6 November 2015.

21 See OTP, above n 19, pp. 9–10.

22 Considering art. 53(1)(b) of the Rome Statute.

23 ICC, *OTP Response to Communications Received Concerning Iraq*, 7.

and temporal scope of the alleged crimes'.[24] However, four years later, this investigation remains in the preliminary phase; the Prosecutor is yet to open a formal investigation.[25]

Since it signed up to the Rome Statute in 2003, Afghanistan has continuously been the site of alleged international crimes at the hands of Afghan and foreign actors (in particular the US, but including other states). In January 2007, the Prosecutor publicly announced he had opened a preliminary examination into the situation. However, it took *almost seven years* for the preliminary examination to move beyond the initial jurisdiction phase.[26] Only in November 2017, more than a decade after announcing the preliminary examination, did the Prosecutor request permission from the Pre-Trial Chamber to officially open a formal investigation (*proprio motu*) into crimes committed on the territory of Afghanistan since 1 May 2003 (including crimes committed by US forces), as well as associated crimes committed on the territory of other states parties to the Statute since 1 July 2002 (including alleged torture by the Central Intelligence Agency (CIA)).[27]

Further delays followed, this time at the hand of the presidency (but without the public objection of the Prosecutor), when in March 2018, nearly four months after Pre-Trial Chamber III had begun considering the matter (and had already twice requested further information from the Prosecutor), the case was reassigned by the presidency to a newly constituted Pre-Trial Chamber II (following the election of new judges).[28] In April 2019, 12 years after the preliminary examination was made public, the Pre-Trial Chamber handed down its decision, refusing to allow the Prosecutor to open a formal investigation not for lack of evidence, but on the basis that it would not be in the 'interests of justice'.

What emerges from these examples is not only an *initial* strategy of non-selection of such situations, but, once they become unavoidable, a further strategy of 'slow-walk[ing] … preliminary examination[s] into oblivion … when superpowers are involved'.[29] Here, as Heller points out, the comparison between the progress of African and non-African situations through the different preliminary examination stages is particularly telling: consider the

---

24 OTP, *Prosecutor of the International Criminal Court, Fatou Bensouda, re-opens the preliminary examination of the situation in Iraq*, 13 May 2014.

25 See OTP, above n 19, pp. 9–10.

26 OTP, *Report on Preliminary Examination Activities 2013*, November 2013, p. 10, https://www.icc-cpi.int/OTP%20Reports/otp-report-2013.aspx.

27 Request, ICC-02/17-7-Conf-Exp, and public redacted version ICC-02/17-7-Red.

28 *Decision Assigning Judges to Divisions and Recomposing Chambers*, ICC-Pres-01/18 (16 March 2018).

29 Kevin J. Heller, 'The ICC in Palestine: Be Careful What You Wish For', *Justice in Conflict*, 2 April 2015, available at: https://justiceinconflict.org/2015/04/02/the-icc-in-palestine-be-careful-what-you-wish-for.

time it took the Afghanistan situation to proceed through the *jurisdiction* phase (seven years) compared to that of Guinea (four years) and Nigeria (three years). Even once permission to open a formal investigation is *requested* by the Prosecutor, different standards seem to apply. Compare the Pre-Trial Chambers' treatment of requests by the Prosecutor to open formal investigations in respect of Burundi and Afghanistan (submitted within months of each other in late 2017): a little over a month and a half later, the Burundi investigation was authorised,[30] whereas the Afghanistan authorisation decision was handed down *a year and a half* later.

Aside from the *direct* non-selection of cases, or their 'slow-walking', the Prosecutor has also managed to *indirectly* avoid situations outside of Africa through adopting a particular construction of the 'gravity' criterion. Notably, the Rome Statute does not enjoin the Prosecutor to consider gravity when selecting situations; the only two references to 'gravity' in the Rome Statute relate to the selection of *cases*.[31] However, not only has the OTP applied this criterion to the selection of *situations*, but in doing so, it has chosen to focus on *quantitative* gravity, which Heller argues has structurally led to both its almost exclusive focus on Africa and its failure to investigate non-African situations (Heller 2006: 34–35). Had it wished to, the OTP could have adopted a more multifaceted understanding of gravity that takes into account non-quantitative factors (i.e. systematicity, social alarm and state participation), one which, Heller argues, would 'greatly expand the number of situations that are viable candidates for investigation' and therefore would have 'naturally divert[ed] the OTP's attention from crimes committed in Africa' (Heller 2006: 35). Doing so, Heller noted at the time (in 2006), would have addressed the perception that the ICC was in fact the '*African* Criminal Court', but that perception, either then or now, remains unaddressed.

3.1.2. Perception

The first Prosecutor consistently responded to concerns about the court's African focus with the trope that his job was simply to 'apply the law' and that he '[would] not adjust [his] practices to political considerations' (Moreno-Ocampo 2008: 224; see also Nouwen and Werner 2011; and Kotecha 2018). Since leaving office, he has become defensive and more offensive, tweeting in 2017: 'African bias cover up African killers. Holocaust denial cover up Nazi crimes.' Despite some initial promise that her election might bring some much-needed diplomacy to

30 *Public Redacted Version of 'Decision Pursuant to Article 15 of the Rome Statute on the Authorization of an Investigation into the Situation in the Republic of Burundi'*, ICC-01/17-X-9-US-Exp, 25 October 2017 (made public on 9 November 2017).

31 See arts. 17 and 53 of the Rome Statute.

the OTP's relationship with African states,[32] little has changed under the current Prosecutor, who has for the most part repeated the line that 'political and extraneous considerations' are irrelevant to her decisions,[33] along with referring to the victims' interest (i.e. 'The [OTP] ... will go where the victims need us').[34] To date, there has been little to suggest either Prosecutor was willing to accede to African states' pleas to 'take [their] concerns seriously'.[35] In their approach, both Prosecutors have been encouraged by the attitude of the international criminal law community, which has become increasingly impervious to criticism *generally* (see Moyn 2017: 69) and dismissive of African states' concerns in particular.

This reticence has persisted despite growing calls from outside the Court and its supporters to take steps towards addressing these concerns. In 2013, the ASP held informal discussions during which there was 'broad agreement that the Assembly should consider looking into practical solutions consistent with the existing legal framework that would address concerns expressed by the African Union'.[36] During these discussions, which ultimately led to an amendment to the Rules of Procedure and Evidence (see Knottnerus 2014a), the participating African states broadly reiterated three of their four concerns from 1998, namely 'the exercise of prosecutorial discretion', 'the importance of the principle of complementarity and the fact that the [ICC] was a court of last resort' and 'the delicate balancing act ... [between] the fight against impunity on the one hand, and peace and stability on the other'.[37]

Even when the terms of the debate shifted to the more compromising language of the 'perception' of bias (see, in particular, the volume by Clarke, Knotterus and de Volder (2016)),[38] language which the AU had in fact employed at times from the outset,[39] the Prosecutor seemed reluctant to even concede

32 See OTP, above n 8.

33 Interview with Fatou Bensouda, *New African Magazine*, 28 January 2014.

34 'Fatou Bensouda: 'We Are Not against Africa', *New African*, 11 September 2012.

35 Benard Namunane, 'Why Africa Leaders Failed to Strike Deal on ICC in Ethiopia', *Daily Nation*, 13 October 2013.

36 ASP, Special segment as requested by the African Union: 'Indictment of Sitting Heads of State and Government and its Consequences on Peace and Stability and Reconciliation', Informal Summary by the Moderator (ICC-ASP/12/61), 27 November 2013, para. 8.

37 See ibid., paras. 9–10.

38 An edited volume which aims to move beyond what the editors call 'legalist or pragmatic solutions' to, and 'normative assessments' of, African states' concerns and rather 'explore and understand the different perceptions of the ICC in Africa': Clarke et al. 2016: 4.

39 In July 2008, following the Prosecutor's application for an arrest warrant against President Al Bashir, the AU's Peace and Security Council stressed 'the need for international justice to be conducted in a transparent and fair manner, in order to avoid any *perception of double standard*, in conformity with the principles of international law'. See AU Peace and Security Council, 'Communique', PSC/MIN/Comm(CXLII), 21 July 2008, para. 7. See also AU, above n 1, p. 1.

this much. The most considered discussion of the ICC's perception problem amongst African states from *within* the ICC came from the bench in the form of comments made by Judge Eboe-Osuji – now the President of the Court – in the *Kenyatta* case in 2013.[40]

Judge Eboe-Osuji's extended discussion of the ICC's perception problem amongst African states arose out of irritation, it seems, with the Prosecutor's repeated assertion that the partial exemption of Kenya's President and Deputy President from continuous presence at their trials 'would have a negative impact on the image of the Court'.[41] In response, Judge Eboe-Osuji pointed out that 'the empirical data points in the opposite direction: namely that *failure to grant the exemption* will have a negative impact on the image of the Court', and it is in this context that he turned to discuss African concerns about the ICC more generally.[42] Notably, he began his discussion by dismissing the facile distinction between law and politics, the first Prosecutor's mainstay, repeating the majority's observation that 'the view which insists that international law is capable of operating in a politically sterile environment implicates amazing naïveté as to *how life really works*'.[43] However, he went a step further, arguing that it also ignores 'how international law *as such* really works':[44] as the views of African leaders would amount to state practice in both *the formation of customary international law* and *the interpretation of treaties*, it was 'not only naïve for the judges and the prosecutor of this Court to ignore [them] ... but is also possibly wrong, as a matter of law, to do so'.[45] This was true, he added, not only in respect of the view of African states on the recusal of Uhuru Kenyatta, but the perception of the Court amongst African states more generally, as a result of the 'exclusively African content of the Court's current docket'.[46]

On the substance of African states' complaints, Judge Eboe-Osuji ultimately concluded that there were 'wholly legitimate reasons to explain the current content of the Court's docket'; however, in reaching this conclusion, he

40 'Separate Further Opinion of Judge Eboe-Osuji', *Prosecutor v. Uhuru Muigai Kenyatta*, ICC-01/09-02/11-830-Anx3-Corr, Trial Chamber V(b), 18 October 2013.

41 See ibid., p. 3; and OTP, *Prosecution's Observations on 'Defence Request Pursuant to Article 63(1) of the Rome Statute', Prosecutor v. Ruto and Sang*, ICC-01/09-01/11, 1 May 2013, para. 11.

42 In an earlier decision, he labelled this argument (made in respect of Kenyatta's Deputy President, William Ruto) 'an unpersuasive hyperbole with no hint of empirical support', pointed language of the sort generally reserved for the ICC's critics. See *Decision on Mr Ruto's Request for Excusal from Continuous Presence at Trial, Prosecutor v. Ruto and Sang*, ICC-01/09-01/11, 18 June 2013, para. 73.

43 *Decision on Defence Request for Conditional Excusal from Continuous Presence at Trial, Prosecutor v. Kenyatta*, ICC-01/09-02/11, 18 October 2013, para. 100 (own emphasis).

44 'Separate Further Opinion of Judge Eboe-Osuji', above n 40, para. 12.

45 Ibid., paras. 7–8, 13–14.

46 Ibid., para. 19.

rejected the Prosecutors' two common defences, namely: (i) 'the simplistic argument that most of the court's cases were referred to the Court by African leaders themselves'; and (ii) that 'African victims of the situations of which the Court is seised are [not] complaining that their plights are receiving the lion share of attention at the ICC'.[47] More importantly, for the present purposes, Judge Eboe-Osuji made two important observations regarding *how* these concerns should be addressed (presumably directed at the Prosecutor). The first was that:

> It is ... a matter of ordinary principles of politeness that people should be made to know that they have been listened to, when they have registered an anxious complaint and made a request. It helps to let them know that their request may not sit well, if that is the case, and why. To keep silent (in the face of an anxious complaint) might convey the unintended impression that their complaint is not important enough to be considered.

The second was that even 'wholly legitimate reasons' to explain the ICC's focus on Africa 'need to be made with some *emotional intelligence*'. To date, African states' concerns continue to be met with silence or, when addressed, without emotional intelligence. In fact, racially charged language has been employed in doing so, such as by dismissing '*emotionally* laden accusations of "neo-colonialism"', as against 'more *rationally* sustained arguments about the proper relationship between peace and justice' (van der Wilt 2011: 1066; see also Fanon 1986: 96–97), or tweets like '*African* bias cover up *African killers*. Holocaust denial cover up Nazi crimes' (see Gevers 2020).

Needless to say, this has done little for the ICC's perception problem on the continent, a problem that goes beyond 'principles of politeness', threatening to undermine the ICC's efficacy (and perhaps survival) in the long term. As Clarke et al. point out, perceptions of an international court 'can be an internal motivation for social actors to behave in a certain way' – such as for or against that institution – and so 'the perceptions of different audiences about the ICC may affect their behaviour towards the Court [which] ... in turn influences the Court's ability to achieve the objectives of the Rome Statute' (Clarke et al. 2016: 6–7). As far as states are concerned, there is no more important audience for the ICC than African states. As the AU's Panel of the Wise put it in 2011, 'imposing justice while ignoring legitimate African concerns may be detrimental to justice'.[48] Moreover, as Clarke et al. point out, in some senses 'reality is as good

47 Noting that 'African leaders are also entitled to press both the Court and the international community to ensure that victims of atrocities everywhere – not only in Africa – are extended the very justice that the ICC promises humanity'. Ibid., para. 21.

48 African Union Panel of the Wise, 'Peace, Justice, and Reconciliation in Africa: Opportunities and Challenges in the Fight against Impunity', *The African Union Series*, International Peace Institute, February 2013, p. 2.

as one's perception of reality', and so 'if we want to improve the functioning of international courts and alternative justice mechanisms, we need to take the perceptions of their effects more seriously, because "justice misperceived" can eventually turn into "justice denied"' (ibid.: 44). One gets the sense that we are nearing this point, and the Prosecutors' inaction has a big role to play in this.

3.2. THE SIREN CALL OF SECURITY COUNCIL POWERS

The 'non-selection' of cases by the Prosecutor has been compounded by the (less surprising) refusal of the Security Council to exercise its powers under the Rome Statute with a modicum of consistency (most notably by refusing to refer the situation in Syria to the ICC, even after 65 UN states signed a petition requesting it to do so). This much was anticipated by African states at Rome in 1998, who nevertheless grudgingly accepted the Security Council's role, notwithstanding the well-founded fear that its power would be exercised capriciously, perhaps in the hope that the Rome Statute might be a launchpad for broader Security Council reform (see du Plessis and Gevers 2009: 18–21). However, African states might not have anticipated just how central the Security Council would become to the ICC's work, not just through the referral of situations (which itself appeared unlikely in 1998), but also through the willingness of the Prosecutor and the ICC's supporters to operate within the shadow of its power (and politics) – or, as Schabas puts it, how the ICC would become 'shackled to the priorities of the Security Council, with all that this entails, including the veto', and '[march] in lock step with the permanent members' (Schabas 2013: 551).

For some time, African states have been trying to reform the Security Council[49] so that, in Nelson Mandela's words, it 'reflects the full tapestry of humankind' (Mandela 1993: 89; however, see also Graham 2012). Moreover, Africa's complaints in this regard are not going away: it bears the brunt of the current inequity, as it is 'the largest electoral bloc (28 percent) in the General Assembly, but is grossly underrepresented on the Security Council, with 20 percent of total council membership and no permanent seat' (Nadin 2016: 79). Given this considerable baggage and the prominent role it increasingly played in the ICC's work, for some time it was common, and appeared sufficient, to respond that African concerns were really all about the Security Council

[49] In 2005, African states adopted the 'Ezulwini Consensus', which, *inter alia*, called for 'not less than two permanent seats with … the right of veto' and five non-permanent seats. *The Common African Position on the Proposed Reform of the United Nations*, adopted by the African Union at the 7th Extraordinary Session 7–8 March 2005.

(as we did on more than one occasion; see du Plessis 2009; du Plessis and Gevers 2009: 180).

However, such a view overlooked how the Prosecutor and the ICC's supporters gradually, and at first perhaps unwittingly, gravitated towards the Siren calls of the Security Council's unrivalled powers. First, as discussed above, in 2005 the Prosecutor 'accepted' the referral of Darfur to the ICC, even when the terms of the referral appeared to encroach upon the Prosecutor's judicial mandate (by purporting to exclude from the ICC's jurisdiction nationals of states that were not party to the Rome Statute that take part in UN or AU operations in Sudan).[50] Second, as discussed below, the Prosecutor defined the terms of that 'judicial mandate' narrowly, leaving African states at the mercy of the Security Council when it came to 'non-judicial' reasons for deferring ongoing investigations in Darfur (see Akande, du Plessis and Jalloh 2010) and then Kenya (see Knotterus 2016). A 2007 OTP policy paper on the 'interests of justice' distinguished sharply between these and the 'interests of peace', noting that 'the latter falls within the mandate of other institutions' (i.e. the Security Council).[51] This was made specifically clear to African states by the new Prosecutor in 2012 – in a short-lived attempt at *rapprochement* – when she noted that 'the "interests of justice" must not be confused with the interests of peace and security, which fall within the mandate of other institutions, notably the UN Security Council and the African Union'.[52] Then, as the relationship between the two soured – in large measure due to disagreements over the Darfur proceedings – the Prosecutors repeatedly went to the Security Council to ask it to 'enforce' its decisions rather than approaching the AU and attempting to resolve the dispute.

The most recent example of the Prosecutor and the ICC's supporters' cosy relationship with the Security Council, and its insidious effects, concerns the ongoing debates about whether President al-Bashir enjoys immunity from arrest (debates that have become somewhat moot since his removal from office in an April 2019 coup). Since the Prosecutor requested a warrant for his arrest, academics have fiercely debated the status of al-Bashir's head of state immunity (see, for example, Akande 2009; and Gaeta 2009). A number of states refused to arrest him on the basis that he continued to enjoy such immunity and, as a result, these academic debates entered both domestic[53] and international courtrooms. The ICC's Pre-Trial Chambers has handed down no fewer than five

50 See SCR 1593 (2005), para. 6.

51 OTP, *Policy Paper on the Interests of Justice*, September 2007, p. 1.

52 OTP, above n 8.

53 See *Southern African Litigation Centre v. Minister of Justice and Constitutional Development and Others* [2015] ZAGPPHC 402; and *Minister of Justice and Constitutional Development and Others v. Southern African Litigation Centre and Others* 2016 (3) SA 317 (SCA).

decisions on the matter, which reached the same conclusion, albeit for different (and at times conflicting) reasons.[54]

As a result, when the issue came before the ICC Appeals Chamber in 2018, the Prosecutor was presented with a number of lines of reasoning to choose from in order to reach the conclusion that President al-Bashir does not enjoy immunity from arrest.[55] Tellingly, she settled on the argument that not only further legitimates the role of the Security Council under the Rome Statute, but also grants it extraordinary power beyond it (power that it did not even ask for). In brief, the Prosecutor reasoned that: (i) Security Council Resolution 1593 placed Sudan 'in a situation comparable to that of a State Party';[56] (ii) as such, by operation of Article 27(2), Sudan *itself* is precluded from asserting immunity in respect of President al-Bashir 'vis-à-vis the Court's request *to Sudan* for his arrest' (i.e. the *vertical effect* of Article 27(2)); and (iii) if Sudan *itself* cannot assert immunity vis-à-vis the Court, then 'it *must also* be precluded from asserting immunity vis-à-vis another State executing an arrest warrant issued by the Court' (i.e. the *horizontal effect* of Article 27(2)).[57]

In doing so, the Prosecutor chose to call *explicitly* for the expansion of the Security Council's powers under the Rome Statute by interpretation (African states' long-standing concerns about those notwithstanding), noting:

> [T]he AU argues that article 13(b) of the Statute does not expressly provide for the UN Security Council to have such a power. However, it overlooks that the Court may

---

54 See *Decision Pursuant to Article 87(7) on the Failure of Republic of Malawi to Comply with the Co-operation Request Issued by the Court with Respect to the Arrest and Surrender of Omar Hassan Ahmed Al Bashir: The Prosecutor v. Al Bashir*, ICC-02/05-01/09, Pre-Trial Chamber I, 12 December 2011; *Decision on the Non-compliance of the Republic of Chad with the Cooperation Requests Issued by the Court Regarding the Arrest and Surrender of Omar Hassan Ahmad Al-Bashir: The Prosecutor v. Al Bashir*, ICC-02/05-01/09, Pre-Trial Chamber I, 26 March 2013; *Decision on the Cooperation of the Democratic Republic of the Congo Regarding Omar Al Bashir's Arrest and Surrender to the Court: The Prosecutor v. Al Bashir*, ICC-02/05-01/09, Pre-Trial Chamber II, 9 April 2014; *Decision under Article 87(7) of the Rome Statute on the Non-compliance by South Africa with the Request by the Court for the Arrest and Surrender of Omar Al-Bashir: The Prosecutor v. Al Bashir*, ICC-02/05-01/09, Pre-Trial Chamber II, 6 July 2017; and *Decision under Article 87(7) of the Rome Statute on the Non-compliance by Jordan with Request by the Court for the Arrest and Surrender of Omar Al-Bashir: The Prosecutor v. Al Bashir*, ICC-02/05-01/09, Pre-Trial Chamber II, 11 December 2017.

55 As the Prosecutor herself noted: 'While the substance of the relevant obligations is clear in the Prosecution's view, it is undeniable that reasonable minds can at least vary (and even evolve) in their rationales for *why* this might be so; indeed, more than one of these explanations might be correct and even mutually reinforcing.' OTP, *Prosecution Response to the Observations of the African Union and the League of Arab States*, para. 2.

56 OTP Submission, para. 79, see generally paras. 64–95. See also *Prosecution Response to the Observations of the African Union and the League of Arab States*, paras. 29–32.

57 *Prosecution Response to the Observations of the African Union and the League of Arab States*, paras. 8–9.

> not simply interpret article 13(b) in isolation but in the context of the plenary powers of the UN Security Council under chapter VII of the UN Charter (which the AU seems to recognise), by virtue of article 21(1)(b) of the Statute. Other sources, such as the UN-ICC Relationship Agreement, are also instructive.[58]

Beyond the Rome Statute, the Prosecutor effectively endorsed the power of the Security Council to bind a state to a treaty to which it did not accede, and did so based on an expansive interpretation of the Security Council's powers and the terms of its resolutions. The same expansive interpretations have been used by the 'Great Powers' to extend their authority *generally* (to invade Libya), a practice to which African states have equally long-standing objections. Finally, in respect of the concern voiced by African states at Rome in 1998 (see section 3.3 below on complementarity), the effect of the Prosecutor's argument is the effective usurpation of the sovereignty of states by making them '*nothing more than the Court's agent* in executing the Court's arrest warrant', with domestic police and so on now acting under the 'enforcement jurisdiction … of the Court' (with the latter bearing no responsibility for the former).[59]

3.3. THE TROJAN 'WORKHORSE' OF COMPLEMENTARITY

The fear of an overzealous, sovereignty-usurping international court underpinned Africa states' insistence in 1998 that the ICC 'should be an effective *complement* to national criminal justice systems' and, as a result, there were significant safeguards included in the Rome Statute to address this concern. Chief among them was making the 'principle of complementarity' the ICC's organising principle, in terms of which the Court is required to take a back seat to domestic trials 'unless the State [concerned] is unwilling or unable genuinely to carry out the investigation or prosecution'.[60] Giving domestic prosecutions *primacy* over 'international' prosecutions was a deliberate choice at Rome to reverse the hierarchy that applied between the ad hoc Tribunals and domestic courts (where the former had primacy over the latter). This is not to say that the 'principle of complementarity' was without some risks; there was still a possibility of 'structures of inequality' (Clarke et al. 2016: 11) emerging in the application of the principle, particularly insofar as the *unable* exception to its application was concerned, which was more likely to apply to 'weaker' states. Nevertheless, at least as far as the text was concerned, it seemed to express a clear preference for domestic over international prosecutions.

---

58 Ibid., para. 30.
59 Ibid., para. 12.
60 Article 17(1)(a) of the Rome Statute.

However, uncertainty soon set in, as Megret and Sampson noted after the first decade of the Court's operation: 'One of the remarkable things about the … complementarity regime is how many of the things that the field thought it knew about it have turned out to be untrue; … how even the tidiest of schemes are put into flux' (Megret and Sampson 2013: 571–572). There were signs of trouble from the outset, when the first Prosecutor *solicited* a 'self-referral' from the DRC in 2004, notwithstanding the presumption that domestic proceedings were supposed to be the norm (perhaps *extorted* is more appropriate, given that the Prosecutor threatened to open his own *proprio motu* investigation if it did not refer the situation (Gaeta 2004: 949)). This was followed by another 'self-referral' by Uganda and the Central African Republic under similar conditions (Hall 2014: 1018). While this practice arguably did not violate the letter of the 'complementarity' principle, it certainly ran afoul of its spirit, as well as raising a number of policy concerns (see McAuliffe 2014: 281–285).

Matters got worse when Libya's new government sought to try Saif al-Islam Gaddafi domestically in 2012. Gaddafi was already subject to an ICC arrest warrant issued in June 2011 and he formally challenged the admissibility of the case on the basis of 'complementarity' (i.e. that Libya was both willing and able to try him).[61] While the Pre-Trial Chamber ultimately rejected Libya's complementarity challenge on the ground that it was *unable* to prosecute Gaddafi (mainly because the government did not actually have him in custody),[62] the challenge was opposed by many ICC supporters on the basis that Libya was apparently *too willing* to do so (see O'Donohue and Rigney 2012; Stahn 2012; Teitel 2012). In terms of this 'due process thesis', notwithstanding the text of the Rome Statute (see Heller 2006: 260–270), 'due process' was layered in as an additional requirement before domestic proceedings could displace the ICC under the principle of complementarity (for an earlier iteration, see Ellis (2002: 241)). In other words, 'states who wish to retain control over cases must ensure that trials adhere to international standards of due process … as found in international human rights instruments' (Megret and Sampson 2013: 574).

The difficulty with this argument being made in respect of Gaddafi was not only that it applied a *higher* standard of domestic proceedings than the text of the Rome Statute requires, but it also appeared to be applying a *doubled standard*: recall the casual manner in which the previous Prosecutor determined – in a sentence – that alleged war crimes in Iraq were being investigated by the relevant British authorities, thus displacing the ICC's

61 See *Motion on Behalf of the Government of Libya Requesting an Oral Hearing in Respect of its Admissibility Challenge Pursuant to Article 19 of the ICC Statute*, Pre-Trial Chamber I, 2 May 2012, para. 4.

62 *Decision on the Admissibility of the Case against Saif Al-Islam Gaddafi*, ICC-01/11-01, Pre-Trial Chamber I, 31 May 2013.

involvement. This was all the more galling as it recalled the recent experience of Rwanda with the ICTR, where that Tribunal transferred cases to France and the Netherlands without stringent due process guarantees or assessments, but it took five years for the Tribunal to transfer its first case to Rwanda, and only after Rwanda had created a special due process law applying solely to Article 11 *bis* transferees, abolished the death penalty and built a state-of-the-art prison (see Gevers 2016).

The ICC has helped to avoid further 'double standard' criticisms when it comes to complementarity by only pursuing cases in Africa (leaving nothing against which to compare the Africa-specific standard adopted in complementarity-based challenges by Kenya and Libya). Until this changes, it will remain a counterfactual debate. However, more concerning for African states is McAuliffe's suggestion that the Prosecutor's strategy of soliciting self-referrals and these debates over complementarity represent a broader strategy by the Court and its supporters to abandon the 'horizontal framework' contained in the Rome Statute ('rooted in State consent and deferential to the State's primacy of action regarding criminal prosecutions') in favour of a 'vertical framework [where] ... the Court enjoys priority over the national jurisdiction, incorporating notions of superior supranationality as an international body and implying a relationship of authority by intervening in the domain of domestic affairs' (McAuliffe 2014: 259–260; see further Megret 2010). Such a shift would be the realisation of the African states' fears expressed in Rome.

According to McAuliffe, since 1998 the ICC's gradual shift towards a vertical construction of its relationship to states represented a 'conscious choice' by the Court and its supporters to move away from the delicate balance struck at Rome between traditional statism and cosmopolitan supranationalism (McAuliffe 2014: 273). The reworking of 'complementarity' into so-called '*positive* complementarity' was central to this shift (see, for example, Stahn 2008). According to Stahn, by 2008, the 'classical vision of complementarity' (as 'an instrument to overcome sovereignty fears' of states and to 'remedy shortcomings or failures of domestic jurisdiction') had already been replaced by the 'positive' version, in terms of which 'complementarity is not only an instrument to monitor state action, but also a forum for *managerial interaction* between the Court and States' (ibid.: 88). According to McAuliffe, such arguments represent 'the tendency of scholars, activists, judges and lawyers in international criminal law to infer verticality or supranationality from the pure idea of international criminal justice on the basis of good faith but partial interpretations of texts agreed earlier by sovereignty-conscious States who would prefer a more horizontal relationship' (McAuliffe 2014: 256).

African states were among the most 'sovereignty-conscious' at Rome in 1998 – as a result of their complex relationship with sovereignty in the past (see generally Anghie 2005) and perhaps in the expectation that they would bear the brunt of an overzealous international court – and for that reason expressed their clear preference for a 'horizontal framework, rooted in State consent and deferential to the State's primacy of action regarding criminal prosecutions' (McAuliffe 2014: 261). This preference predictably grew as African states' other fears about the ICC appeared to be increasingly well founded. Placing this shift within the context of these broader concerns (and taking McAuliffe's thesis a step further), it might be argued that this 'creeping cosmopolitanism' has not been visited on Africa by chance; rather, it is the inevitable unfolding of the cosmopolitanism of international (criminal) lawyers (see Koskenniemi 2003) that was, for unrelated reasons, visited upon African states. And so, a longer historical arc brings the Court's 'creeping cosmopolitanism' and 'Africa problem' closer together.

Certainly, it stands to reason that the shift towards 'verticality or supranationality' would have been more difficult had its effects been felt by 'stronger states' (historically, politically and economically). In this regard, it is telling that the ICC's judges have recently begun to rein in the Prosecutor just as her investigations have begun to have such effects, not on the basis of complementarity, but on the terms often associated with it (i.e. 'the Court is not meant – or equipped – to address any and all … international crimes', has limited 'financial and human resources', and must manage 'victims' expectations').[63] Beyond weak and strong states, the gradual shift that empowers a global, largely Western elite (consisting not just of Court functionaries, but also of academics and NGO representatives) to 'oversee and manage' the anti-impunity efforts almost exclusively directed at African states has unnerving colonial parallels (particularly when taken together with the practices of the ICTR outlined above). The same is true of the over-emphasis on African states when it comes to interventions in the name of 'positive complementarity' – a secondary effect of this shift – such as 'capacity-building' and criminal law reform (see Gevers 2016).

3.4. A SEA CHANGE: FROM 'PEACE VERSUS JUSTICE' TO 'NO PEACE WITHOUT JUSTICE'

Finally, in 1998, African states hoped that the ICC would be 'a necessary *element* for peace and security in the world' and would 'ultimately *contribute to the attainment of international peace*', a framing that presumed that the 'justice' of the ICC would be one response amongst many to address conflict and attain 'peace', if not an instrument to that end. Ten years later, in July 2008,

[63] *Decision Pursuant to Article 15 of the Rome Statute on the Authorisation of an Investigation into the Situation in the Islamic Republic of Afghanistan*, Pre-Trial Chamber II, 12 April 2019, paras. 90, and 95–96.

the choice between these two possibly competing ends was sharply posed when the Prosecutor requested an arrest warrant for (then) President al-Bashir and the AU responded immediately by requesting the deferral of the proceedings, arguing that 'the search for justice should be pursued in a way that does not impede or jeopardize efforts aimed at promoting lasting peace'.[64] While the AU continually stressed the need to address 'in a mutually reinforcing manner the inter-linked issues of combating impunity and promoting peace',[65] from the outset the Prosecutor saw the matter more starkly (and simply): '[A] man committing genocide is standing in the way of justice, peace, and security for the Darfuris', he told the press in announcing his application for the arrest warrant.[66]

The distance between the views of African states and the ICC Prosecutors – which we might reductively call 'peace versus justice' and 'no peace without justice', respectively – raised in respect of Darfur, but by no means limited to it, sharpened over the coming months and years. Living in the present 'age of anti-impunity', the position of African states seems retrograde, or worse, but this was not the case in 1998, when the 'peace versus justice' debate was far more acceptable, including to many now anti-impunity-minded international lawyers (see Engle 2015). However, since 1998, the ground has shifted under the feet of African states, as the 'criminal turn' within the human rights movement more broadly has meant that 'the correlation between criminal prosecution and human rights has become so ingrained that expressing opposition to any particular international prosecution is sometimes seen as anti-human rights' (ibid.: 1118–1119). Tracing this 'criminal turn' within the human rights movement, and the ICC's role in it, is illuminating in many respects.

When the Prosecutor requested an arrest warrant for President al-Bashir in 2008, the AU responded immediately by establishing an independent High-Level Panel 'of distinguished Africans of high integrity, to examine the situation in depth'.[67] The Panel's detailed 144-page report (released in October 2009) adopted a balanced approach by reiterating that peace and justice were

---

64 AU Peace and Security Council, Communiqué, PSC/MIN/Comm(CXLII), 21 July 2008, paras. 3, 7, 11(i). The request was put before the Security Council by South Africa and Libya on 24 July 2008. See Security Council Report, 'Update Report No. 4: Sudan', 28 July 2008, https://www.securitycouncilreport.org/update-report/lookup_c_glkwlemtisg_b_4381649.php.

65 AU Peace and Security Council, above n 64, para. 11, arguing that 'the situation in Darfur is too serious and complex an issue to be resolved without recourse to an harmonized approach to justice and peace, neither of which should be pursued at the expense of the other' (see press release following the 3 July 2009 decision in *Sirte*).

66 OTP, *Prosecutor's Statement on the Prosecutor's Application for a Warrant of Arrest under Article 58 against Omar Hassan Ahmad Al Bashir*, 14 July 2008.

67 AU Peace and Security Council, Communiqué, PSC/MIN/Comm(CXLII), 21 July 2008, para. 11.

'inextricably linked', but cautioned that '[j]ustice with respect to Darfur *cannot be discussed in a vacuum*, but must be debated and decisions made within the context of the search for peace and accountability'.[68] Such debates and decisions, the report noted, were often more about *timing* (i.e. 'about which should come first between justice and peace')[69] than a hard choice between the two. This suggested that, in the case of Darfur, of the 'interconnected, mutually interdependent and equally desirable' objectives of peace, justice *and reconciliation*, 'the most urgent desire of the people of Darfur is to live in peace and security'.[70]

On this basis, the High-Level Panel took a measured approach in its recommendations, which concerned *both* peace and justice. Notably, while it framed its recommendations within the terms of the Rome Statute, it *did not* recommend the invocation of Article 16 seeking a deferral of the case before the ICC. Rather, it set out in detail its proposal for the establishment of a hybrid court (along the lines of the existing Special Court for Sierra Leone and the Extraordinary African Chambers in Senegal established to try Hissène Habré and others that came later),[71] despite the objections of supporters of the government, and simply noted that under the principle of complementarity, the ICC would be 'obliged to take consideration' of its establishment (along with other local 'effective justice measures'), which 'would also be of interest to the Security Council in reaching any decisions with respect to the situation in Darfur and the Sudan more generally'.[72] However, in its response, the AU endorsed the Panel's recommendations, but in doing so added the request for a deferral under Article 16 'in the interest of peace, justice and reconciliation'.[73]

The Prosecutor was less balanced and measured: in his December 2008 report to the Security Council, he asserted that 'justice will promote peace in Darfur'[74] and that '[a]s long as the arsonists are in charge, it does not matter how many fire-fighters you send … [t]here will never be enough'.[75] Then, in his

68 AU High-Level Panel on Darfur, 'Darfur: The Quest for Peace, Justice and Reconciliation', African Union Communiqué, Peace and Security Council, PSC/AHG/2 (CCVII), 29 October 2009, paras. 16 and 244.

69 AU High-Level Panel on Darfur, above n 68, para. 285.

70 Ibid., paras. 293–294.

71 See ibid., paras. 246–255.

72 Ibid., paras. 249 and 339.

73 PSC, *Communique of the 207th Meeting of the Peace and Security Council*, 29 October 2009, para. 5; *Decision on the Report of the Peace and Security Council on its Activities and the State of Peace and Security in Africa*, Assembly/AU/Dec.268(XIV) Rev.1, para. 16; and *Decision on the Report of the Second Meeting of States Parties to the Rome Statute on the International Criminal Court (ICC)* – Assembly/AU/Dec.270(XIV), para. 10, adopted by the Fourteenth Ordinary Session of the Assembly in Addis Ababa, Ethiopia on 2 February 2010.

74 OTP, *Eighth Report of the Prosecutor of the ICC to the UN Security Council Pursuant to UNSC 1593 (2005)*, 3 December 2008, para. 85.

75 OTP, *Statement to the United Nations Security Council on the Situation in Darfur, the Sudan, Pursuant to UNSCR 1593 (2005)*, 3 December 2008, p. 8.

June 2009 report, he drew sharper lines between his *purely 'judicial* mandate'[76] (under Resolution 1593) and the 'mandate of others'[77] who were responsible for: (i) 'the wider political and security process … in order to stop the violence *and prevent future crimes*' (the AU–UN mediators);[78] and (ii) 'promoting accountability and reconciliation at all levels … and in *preventing future crimes*'.[79] While he 'fully appreciated' the latter's importance, he made it clear that they would not interfere with '[t]he International Criminal Court … fulfilling its judicial mandate to factually and legally describe the crimes committed, and to prosecute its cases'[80] (although he promised to 'continue to inform all actors accordingly, allowing them to factor in the Office's activities … and the need to enforce the Court's decisions in their own planning').[81]

In his next report to the Security Council (notably, after the AU Panel had recommended that a hybrid court be established), the Prosecutor dug in further, drawing the line more sharply and narrowly, no longer between his exclusive mandate for 'justice' and others' for peace, security, reconciliation, etc., but *within* the mandate for justice: between his ongoing cases, which he said 'will be decided by the [ICC]',[82] and 'additional proceedings for other perpetrators as well as truth and reconciliation mechanisms',[83] which he was happy to leave to the AU's hybrid court and others (adopting, at best, Stahn's 'managerial division of labour' when it came to complementarity).[84] In the Prosecutor's mind, not only would justice not yield to peace, even temporarily, but the ICC's justice would not yield to domestic or regional courts (the 'classical' principle of complementarity notwithstanding).

These debates over the arrest warrant issued against President al-Bashir soon became enmeshed with larger issues, not only of the relationship between 'peace' and 'justice', but also of the relationship between African states (and the AU) and the ICC. The new Prosecutor certainly saw it that way when in 2012, shortly after coming into office, she gave a speech aimed at addressing African concerns, in which she notably chose to focus on '[r]econciling the independent role of the ICC Prosecutor with conflict resolution initiatives'.[85] She began by

---

76 OTP, *Statement to the United Nations Security Council on the Situation in Darfur, the Sudan, Pursuant to UNSCR 1593 (2005)*, 5 June 2009, paras. 15 and 37; and OTP, *Ninth Report of the Prosecutor of the International Criminal Court to the UN Security Council Pursuant to UNSCR 1593 (2005)*, 5 June 2009, paras. 19 and 30.

77 OTP, *Ninth Report*, above n 76, para. 19.

78 OTP, *Statement to the United Nations Security Council*, above n 76, para. 30.

79 Ibid., para. 35.

80 Ibid., para. 37.

81 Ibid, para. 19.

82 OTP, *Statement to the United Nations Security Council on the Situation in Darfur, the Sudan, Pursuant to UNSCR 1593 (2005)*, 4 December 2009, para. 18.

83 Ibid., para. 14.

84 See ibid., para 18.

85 OTP, above n 8.

drawing a now-familiar line between her mandate and 'the interests of peace and security, which falls within the mandate of other institutions, notably the UN Security Council *and the African Union*'. As she put it: 'The international community has put in place some clear divisions of responsibility. The UN Security Council is in charge of peace and security. The ICC is doing justice.'[86] However, she proceeded to blur these lines, noting that 'in the last ten years … [a] *criminal justice component* has been added to the toolbox of … international policy makers as they work to achieve peace and security' (i.e. Security Council referrals to the ICC). Furthermore, while it was the sole responsibility of the Security Council to decide when to employ it (as it concerned issues 'with which the Court and the … Prosecutor can[not] and should [not] be involved'), '[o]nce the Security Council takes *a political decision* to refer a situation to the Prosecutor, *the judicial process* begins', a process which cannot be stopped for non-judicial reasons (except, of course, by the Security Council under Article 16).

This 'new' approach by the Prosecutor (if that was what it was intended to be) amounted to the same inflexible outcome as her predecessor, save that, while the former Prosecutor was willing to share his *judicial* mandate, but not give up his cases, the new Prosecutor was willing to accept that the *peace and security* mandate now had a 'criminal justice component', but was equally unwilling to give up the cases that resulted from its exercise. In doing so, the new Prosecutor once again drew sharp, narrow lines: both in terms of what her mandate was (and was not) and how she would implement it. The former was between her mandate for justice and the Security Council's mandate for 'peace and security' (which, under the Rome Statute, was an exclusive one, notwithstanding her passing nod to the AU). The second concerned how she understood her mandate for justice and, in particular, the 'interests of justice' that the Rome Statute enjoined her to consider (see Article 53(1)(c) of the Rome Statute), which she defined narrowly. In particular, she stressed that 'the 'interests of justice' must not be confused with the interests of peace and security'[87] (see du Plessis and Gevers (2009) for an alternative interpretation), drawing on a 2007 policy that made the same distinction, but less definitively.[88] Notably, this narrow interpretation of the 'interests of justice' has recently been challenged

86 Ibid., noting: 'I should stress here that the "interests of justice" must not be confused with the interests of peace and security, which falls within the mandate of other institutions, notably the UN Security Council and the African Union. The Court and the Office of the Prosecutor itself are not involved in political considerations. We have to respect our legal limits. The prospect of peace negotiations is therefore not a factor that forms part of the Office's determination on the interests of justice.'

87 Ibid.

88 OTP, above n 51, p. 1. See, however, pp. 8–9 (noting that '[t]he concept of the interests of justice … should not be conceived of so broadly as to embrace *all issues* related to peace and security' and that art. 16 'does not displace the obligation of the Prosecutor to consider the interests of justice').

by the Pre-Trial Chamber in its Afghanistan decision, where it considered a number of 'non-judicial' factors in making its own assessment of the 'interests of justice'.

Nevertheless, the effect of the Prosecutors' approaches – both old and new – was a construction of the Rome Statute that left African states solely at the mercy of the Security Council (and the 'Great Powers') when it came to airing their concerns about the effects of the ICC's proceedings on peace, security and reconciliation (in Darfur and elsewhere), not only as sometimes competing ends, but even when it came to the question of 'sequencing' their pursuit. Notably, these concerns were present *before* the al-Bashir arrest warrant was issued (at least as early as Rome in 1998) and will likely outlast it.[89] In February 2019, following a 'widely consultative' process amongst 'AU Member States, transitional justice experts, practitioners, the academia, AU organs and victim groups, women rights experts and youths',[90] the AU's Heads of State and Government adopted the African Union Transitional Justice Policy (AUTJP).[91] The AUTJP is premised on the need to address 'peace, justice and reconciliation in a *holistic manner*', acknowledging that these are 'interrelated, interdependent and mutually reinforcing' goals, and the need to 'avoid *mechanistic* approaches'.[92] Moreover, it specifically recognises that while 'the prosecution of serious human rights violations is an important mechanism … it is imperative [to] … acknowledge that it [*sic*] role and significance may be limited in situations of mass violations'.[93] In doing so, the AUTJP's approach 'depart[s] sharply from the inordinate focus on retributive justice that dominates transitional debates *elsewhere*'.[94]

The AU's approach has no doubt been influenced in no small measure by growing frustration over the ICC Prosecutors' 'mechanistic' approach in respect of Darfur. The sharpest articulation of the link, and the frustration, is the 2014 op-ed co-authored by former South African President Thabo Mbeki (who was also the chairperson of the AU's High-Level Panel on Darfur). In the

89 African Union Panel of the Wise, above n 48, pp. ix, 2 and 5 (adding: 'Even where deeply divided countries have made short-term pragmatic concessions that privilege reconciliation and peace at the expense of justice, the purpose has ultimately been to strengthen institutions that diminish the persistence of impunity'). Notably, the report recommended that such a policy could draw on the 2009 AU High-Level Panel on Darfur's 2009 report.

90 Center for the Study of Violence and Reconciliation, 'Press Statement on Adoption of the African Union Transitional Justice Policy', 14 February 2019.

91 *Decision on the Draft Legal Instruments*, Assembly/AU/Dec.735(XXXII), adopted at the 32nd Ordinary Session of the Assembly of the African Union, 10–11 February 2019.

92 Ibid., pp. 6–8.

93 Ibid., p. 18 (adding that prosecution 'often only satisfies the need of some victims' and does not 'address the underlying political, socio-economic conditions which underlay the conflict or repression').

94 Ibid., p. 9.

2014 op-ed, entitled 'Courts Can't End Civil Wars' and co-authored with Mahmood Mamdani, Mbeki noted (Mbeki and Mamdani 2014):

> The conflict in South Sudan is only the latest instance where extreme violence has erupted after a breakdown of political order. But rather than prioritizing political reform, the international community tends to focus on criminalizing the perpetrators of violence. Since the end of the Cold War, the world has looked to the Nuremberg Trials as a model for closure in the wake of extreme violence; international criminal trials are the preferred response. This common sense should have come under scrutiny in recent months after a growing number of countries in the African Union advocated withdrawal from the ... [ICC]. Instead, the debate has focused on the motives of African leaders, not on the inadequacy of court trials as a response to politically driven mass violence.

As Mbeki and Mamdani pointed out, this 'common sense' preference for international criminal trials (which the AUTJP later labelled the 'the inordinate focus on retributive justice') was a recent one. At Rome in 1998, the 'inadequacy of court trials as a response to politically driven mass violence' (ibid.) was not the anathema it was by 2014. As Engle notes, in the 1990s 'human rights activists and international legal scholars [still] actively disagreed over whether justice (meaning criminal justice) should take priority over truth and peace, primarily in the context of transitional regimes' and there was a 'not uncommon understanding at the time that criminal prosecutions were in conflict with goals of truth and peace, as well as forgiveness' (Engle 2015: 1071 and 1087).

This was exemplified by South Africa's Truth and Reconciliation Commission (TRC), which was not only tolerated but also celebrated by international lawyers and NGOs. Notably, in support of their argument in 2014 that 'mass violence is ... driven by issues, not just perpetrators' (and that addressing it requires 'fixating less on perpetrators ... and being more alert to issues that drive continuous cycles of conflict'), Mbeki and Mamdani pointed to *inter alia* the negotiations to end apartheid in South Africa in the 1990s. Moreover, this was expressly acknowledged at Rome in 1998 (on account of the efforts by the South African delegation), where 'some regarded it as representative of an instance where the ICC should refrain from prosecution' (Engle 2015: note 58). Shortly after the adoption of the Rome Statute, Kofi Annan told a group of South African students that it was 'inconceivable that ... the Court would seek to substitute its judgement for that of a whole nation which is seeking the best way to put a traumatic past behind it and build a better future' (Annan 1998). There are obviously differences between the TRC and the situation in Darfur, but the point is that when the Rome Statute was adopted, it was at least possible to conceive of justice yielding to peace in certain circumstances (for Annan, in cases like South Africa, it was *inconceivable that it would not*).

However, since 1998, the 'turn to criminal law' by human rights advocates, institutions and courts has meant that the 'understanding of a dichotomous relationship between justice (meaning criminal justice), on [the] one hand, and truth, peace, and forgiveness, on the other', which was prevalent in the 1990s, has fallen away, and today 'most human rights advocates, institutions, and courts began to reject the dichotomies, seeing prosecutions as necessary to truth, and often to peace' (Engle 2015: 1090). In the contemporary human rights community, the obligation to prosecute atrocities has become absolute (ibid.: 1070) and 'the correspondence between criminal prosecution and human rights has become so ingrained that expressing opposition to any particular international prosecution is sometimes seen as anti-human rights' (ibid.: 1118–1119). Debates between 'peace and justice' have given way to the hardline 'no *lasting* peace without justice'[95] moniker that is dominant today.

The merits of this 'criminal turn' are discussed elsewhere (for some criticisms, see Engle (2015: 1119–1127)); for the present purposes, suffice it to point out that the current 'anti-impunity' position is the result of a shift in the relationship between 'peace' and 'justice' that has taken place since 1998 when the Rome Statute was enthusiastically supported by African states, and that African states have consistently resisted this shift (or at least its inflexibility). To the extent that the ICC Prosecutor and the Court's supporters are responsible for this shift (which, we suggest, they are to some degree), it is they who have moved away from African states' understanding of the Rome Statute in 1998, an understanding which, as Judge Eboe-Osuji noted (see section 3.1.2 above), is both politically and legally relevant, and should be taken into account. Regrettably, this has not been the case: when African states and leading African diplomats and academics have suggested a more dynamic and complex relationship between peace and justice, they have been either ignored or, according to Mbeki and Mamdani, their motives have been called into question.

4. CONCLUDING REMARKS: CORRECTING COURSE

In this chapter we have tried to outline the role that the ICC has played in the souring of its once-promising relationship with African states over the past two decades. Like Odysseus, the ICC has been navigating treacherous waters and seemingly omnipotent actors. Equally, like Odysseus, it has made decisions (and non-decisions) along the way that have made matters worse. It would be a brave onlooker who predicts where the story will go from here (and our own powers of prediction have failed in the past (see du Plessis and Gevers 2009), although we have correctly predicted that the ICC's African focus portends its downfall

95 See 'Declaration 1', adopted at the 2010 ICC Review Conference, Kampala, June 2010, https://asp.icc-cpi.int/iccdocs/asp_docs/Resolutions/RC-Decl.1-ENG.pdf.

(see du Plessis 2013)), but we make two closing remarks about the future of the ICC and its relationship with African states.

The first is that the Odyssey is far from over. In Homer's Epic, Odysseus' journey home to Ithaca took 10 years. In April 2019, 10 years after the ICC issued its arrest warrant, President al-Bashir was removed from office in a coup d'état and lost any claim he might have had to head of state immunity. This coincidence might leave the optimist to conclude that the ICC's travails are over – that they began and ended with President al-Bashir. However, leaving aside the question of whether now ex-President al-Bashir will be surrendered to the Court, as we have tried to demonstrate in this chapter, the ICC's problems extend beyond al-Bashir – rather, they can be traced back to the hopes and fears expressed by African states in Rome in 1998. The sum of their fears was that the ICC would come to mirror the worst iniquities of the international system, and there can be no clearer indication that this is the case than the recent decision of the Pre-Trial Chamber in respect of Afghanistan.

Twelve years after the Prosecutor first announced she was opening a preliminary investigation, the Pre-Trial Chamber decided that there was a reasonable basis to believe that international crimes had been committed in Afghanistan and that potential cases arising from the investigation would be admissible under Article 17, but that nevertheless opening a formal investigation was not in the 'interests of justice'. It did so on the basis of recent 'changes within the relevant political landscape' (i.e. increasing US hostility towards the ICC following the election of Donald Trump and direct threats to the Prosecutor and any others that facilitate the work of the ICC against the US or its ally Israel) that made it 'extremely difficult to gauge the prospects of securing meaningful cooperation from relevant authorities for the future' and the 'foreseeable absence of additional resources for the coming years in the Court's budget'.[96] For its critics, the ICC simply capitulated in the light of the political and economic costs of pursuing a case against a 'Great Power' at its first real attempt at doing so. Notably, the Pre-Trial Chamber handed down the decision one day *after* al-Bashir was deposed, a less than happy coincidence.

The second is that if the ICC is going to try to correct its course (and it is facing pressure from important quarters to do so),[97] then it would do well to learn from the failings of Odysseus, whose hubris and self-interest not only prolonged his voyage home, causing great suffering to his family, but ultimately led to the death of his entire crew (see Logan 1964: 34, 37). These moral failings resulted in a very different characterisation of Odysseus by Virgil in *The Aeneid*: in contrast to his heroic treatment by Homer, in Virgil's account

---

96 *Decision Pursuant to Article 15 of the Rome Statute*, above n 63, paras. 94–95.

97 See a recent op-ed by the first four Presidents of the ASP: Prince Zeid Raad Al Hussein, Bruno Stagno Ugarte, Christian Wenaweser and Tina Intelman, 'The International Criminal Court Needs Fixing', *The Atlantic Council*, 24 April 2019.

Odysseus was a 'double-talking', 'heartless schemer' (*The Aeneid* IX: 602; and II: 125). The allegation of 'double-talking' will likely resonate amongst some of the ICC's critics, and victims of atrocities in Afghanistan, Palestine and elsewhere, may feel that the ICC is a 'heartless schemer' that has not delivered on its promise to deliver justice. But even its supporters would struggle to resist the charge that the ICC has been increasingly acting out of self-interest (at least insofar as the Afghanistan decision is concerned). The claim of hubris is also likely to stick, as calls for the ICC and international criminal law to adopt a more modest assessment of their own ability have come from supporters and critics alike (see Stahn 2009: 259; Kendall and Nouwen 2016: 38–39). If the ICC does choose to correct its course, it should start with redressing its relationship with African states by taking their concerns seriously, if not out of a repudiation of the hubris of the past, then at least out of a recalibration of its 'self-interest' that recognises that it cannot survive without their support (particularly if it is to take on the US). If the ICC does not do so, it will likely suffer the fate of Odysseus in the retelling of the epic by Dante in *The Divine Comedy*, who, on account of his failings pointed out by Virgil, 'abort[ed] the *Odyssey* plot in mid-course and [left] the hero in the nether regions of the underworld' (Logan 1964: 44).

BIBLIOGRAPHY

Akande, D. (2004) 'International Law Immunities and the International Criminal Court', *Am. J. Int'l L* 98(3): 407–433.

Akande, D. (2009) 'The Legal Nature of Security Council Referrals to the ICC and its Impact on al-Bashir's Immunities', *JICJ* 7(2): 333–352.

Akande, D., du Plessis, M. and Jalloh, C. (2010) *Position Paper: An African Expert Study on the African Union Concerns about Article 16 of the Rome Statute of the ICC*. Pretoria: Institute for Security Studies.

Anghie, A. (2005) *Imperialism, Sovereignty and the Making of International Law*. Cambridge: Cambridge University Press.

Annan, K. (1998) Speech at the Witwatersrand University Graduation Ceremony, 1 September.

Bassiouni, C. (2005) *The Legislative History of the International Criminal* Court. New York: Ardsley.

Clark, R. (2001) 'Crimes against Humanity and the Rome Statute of the International Criminal Court' in M. Politi and G. Nesi (eds), *The Rome Statute of the International Criminal Court: A Challenge to Impunity*. Aldershot: Ashgate, pp. 75–93.

Clarke, K.M. (2009) *Fictions of Justice: The International Criminal Court and the Challenge of Legal Pluralism in Sub-Saharan Africa*. Cambridge: Cambridge University Press.

Clarke, K.M., Knottnerus, S. and de Volder, E. (eds) (2016) *Africa and the ICC: Perceptions of Justice*. Cambridge: Cambridge University Press, pp. 61–77.

Dersso, S. (2016) 'The ICC's Africa Problem: A Spotlight on the Politics and Limits of International Criminal Justice' in K.M. Clarke et al. (eds), *Africa and the ICC: Perceptions of Justice*, Cambridge: Cambridge University Press, pp. 61–77.

Dugard, J. (2013) 'Palestine and the ICC: Institutional Failure or Bias?', *Journal of International Criminal Justice* 11(3): 563–570.

Du Plessis, M. (2003) 'Historical Injustice and International Law: An Exploratory Discussion of Reparation for Slavery', *Human Rights Quarterly* 25(3): 624–659.

Du Plessis, M. (2008) 'The International Criminal Court and its work in Africa: Confronting the myths', ISS Paper 173, November.

Du Plessis, M. (2013) 'International Justice's Blind Spot: The ICC Should Prosecute beyond the Bounds of Africa', *The World Today*, June and July.

Du Plessis, M. and Gevers, C. (2009) 'Making Amend(ment)s: South Africa and the International Criminal Court from 2009 to 2010', *South African Yearbook of International Law* 34: 1–27.

Du Plessis, M. and Gevers, C. (2011) 'Another Stormy Year for the International Criminal Court and its Work in Africa', *South African Yearbook of International Law* 35: 163–180.

Ellis, M. (2002) 'The International Criminal Court and its Implication for Domestic Law and National Capacity Building', *Florida Journal of International Law* 15: 215–242.

Engle, K. (2015) 'Anti-impunity and the Turn to Criminal Law in Human Rights', *Cornell Law Review* 100: 1069–1127.

Fanon, F. (1986) *Black Skins, White Masks* (trans. Markmann, C.L.). London: Pluto Press.

Gaeta, P. (2004) 'The International Criminal Court and Complementarity: From Theory to Practice', *JICJ* 2: 949–952.

Gaeta, P. (2009) 'Does President Al Bashir Enjoy Immunity from Arrest?', *JICJ* 7: 315–332.

Gevers, C. (2016) 'Back to the Future?: civil society, the "turn to complementarity"', *Acta Juridica* 1: 95–126.

Gevers, C. (2020) 'Africa and International Criminal Law' in K. Heller, F. Megret, S. Nouwen, H. Ohlin and D. Robinson (eds), *The Oxford Handbook of International Criminal Law*. Oxford: Oxford University Press.

Graham, M. (2012) 'Foreign Policy in Transition: The ANC's Search for a Foreign Policy Direction during South Africa's Transition, 1990–1994', *The Roundtable* 101(5): 86–97.

Hall, C.K. (2014) 'Positive Complementarity in Action' in C. Stahn and M.M. El Zeidy (eds), *The International Criminal Court and Complementarity: From Theory to Practice*. Cambridge: Cambridge University Press, pp. 1014–1051.

Heller, K.J. (2006) 'The Shadow Side of Complementarity: The Effect of Article 17 of the Rome Statute on National Due Process', *Criminal Law Forum* 17: 255–280.

Kendall, S. and da Silva, C. (2016) 'Beyond the ICC: State Responsibility for the Arms Trade in Africa' in K.M. Clarke et al. (eds), *Africa and the ICC: Perceptions of Justice*. Cambridge: Cambridge University Press, pp. 407–436.

Kendall, S. and Nouwen, S. (2016) 'Speaking of Legacy: Towards an Ethos of Modesty at the International Criminal Tribunal for Rwanda', *Legal Studies Research Paper Studies, University of Cambridge*, Paper No. 20/2016, April.

Knottnerus, A.S. (2014a) 'Extraordinary Exceptions at the International Criminal Court: The (New) Rules and Jurisprudence on Presence at Trial', *Law and Practice of International Courts and Tribunals* 13: 261–285.

Knottnerus, A.S. (2014b) 'The Security Council and the International Criminal Court: The Unsolved Puzzle of Article 16', *The Netherlands International Law Review* 61: 195–224.
Koskenniemi, M. (2003) 'Legal Cosmopolitanism: Tom Franck's Messianic World', *NYU JILP* 35: 195–224.
Kotecha, B. (2018) 'The Art of Rhetoric: Perceptions of the International Criminal Court and Legalism', *Leiden Journal of International Law* 31(4): 939–962.
Logan, T.P. (1964) 'The Characterization of Ulysses in Homer, Virgil and Dante: A Study in Source and Analogues' *Annual Report of the Dante Society, with Accompanying Papers* 82: 19–46.
Mandela, N. (1993) 'South Africa's Future Foreign Policy', *Foreign Affairs* 72(5): 86–97.
Maqungo, S. (2000) 'The Establishment of the International Criminal Court: SADC's Participation in the Negotiations', *African Security Review* 9(1): 42–53.
Mbeki, T. and Mamdani, M. (2014) 'Courts Can't End Civil Wars', *New York Times*, 5 February.
McAuliffe, P. (2014) 'From Watchdog to Workhorse: Explaining the Emergence of the ICC's Burden-Sharing Policy as an Example of Creeping Cosmopolitanism', *Chinese Journal of International Law* 13: 259–296.
Megret, F. (2010) 'In Search of the "Vertical": Towards an Institutional Theory of International Criminal Justice's Core' in C. Stahn and L. Van der Herik (eds), *Future Perspectives on International Criminal Justice*. The Hague: TMC Asser Press, pp. 178–224.
Megret, F. and Samson, M.G. (2013) 'Holding the Line on Complementarity in Libya: The Case for Tolerating Flawed Domestic Trials', *J. Int'l Crim. Just.* 11: 571–589.
Mochochoko, P. (2005) 'Africa and the International Criminal Court' in E.A. Ankumah and E.K. Kwakwa (eds), *African Perspectives on International Criminal Justice*. Accra: Africa Legal Aid, pp. 241–258.
Moreno-Ocampo, L. (2008) 'The International Criminal Court: Seeking Global Justice', *Case Western Reserve Journal of International Law* 40: 215–225.
Moyn, S. (2017) 'Anti-impunity as Deflection of Argument' in K. Engle, Z. Miller and D. Davis (eds), *Anti-impunity and the Human Rights Agenda*. Cambridge: Cambridge University Press, pp. 68–94.
Nadin, P. (2016) *UN Security Council Reform*. New York: Routledge.
Nouwen, S. and Werner, W. (2011) 'Doing Justice to the Political: The International Criminal Court in Uganda and Sudan', *European Journal of International Law* 21: 941–965.
O'Donohue, J. and Rigney, S. (2012) 'The ICC Must Consider Fair Trial Concerns in Determining Libya's Application to Prosecute Saif al-Islam Gaddafi Nationally', *EJIL. Talk! Blog of the European Journal of International Law*, 8 June 2012, https://www.ejiltalk.org/the-icc-must-consider-fair-trial-concerns-in-determining-libyas-application-to-prosecute-saif-al-islam-gaddafi-nationally/.
Schabas, W.A. (2013) 'The Banality of International Justice', *JICJ* 11: 545–551.
Stahn, C. (2008) 'Complementarity: A Tale of Two Notions', *Criminal Law Forum* 19: 87–113.
Stahn, C. (2009) 'The Future of International Criminal Justice', *Hague Justice Journal* 4(3): 257–266.
Stahn, C. (2012) 'Libya, the International Criminal Court and Complementarity: A Test for Shared Responsibility', *JICJ* 10: 325–349.

Teitel, R. (2012) 'Local Injustice: Why We Shouldn't Forget about Saif Gaddafi', *I-CONnect Blog of the International Journal of Constitutional Law and Constitution Making*, 16 October 2012, http://www.iconnectblog.com/2012/10/local-injustice-why-we-shouldnt-forget-about-saif-gaddafi/.

Tladi, D. (2009) 'The African Union and the International Criminal Court: The Battle for the Soul of International Law', *South African Yearbook of International Law* 34: 57–69.

Van der Wilt, H. (2011) 'Universal Jurisdiction under Attack: An Assessment of African Misgivings towards International Criminal Justice as Administered by Western States', *JICJ* 9: 1043–1066.

Viljoen, F. (2005) 'A Human Rights Court for Africa, and Africans', *Brooklyn Journal of International Law* 30(1): 1–66.

CASE LAW

Decision on Defence Request for Conditional Excusal from Continuous Presence at Trial, Prosecutor v. Kenyatta, ICC-01/09-02/11, 18 October 2013.

Decision on Mr Ruto's Request for Excusal from Continuous Presence at Trial, Prosecutor v. Ruto and Sang, ICC-01/09-01/11, 18 June 2013.

Decision on the Admissibility of the Case against Saif Al-Islam Gaddafi, ICC-01/11-01, Pre-Trial Chamber I, 31 May 2013.

Decision on the Admissibility of the Prosecutor's Appeal against the 'Decision on the Request of the Union of the Comoros to Review the Prosecutor's Decision Not to Initiate an Investigation', ICC-01/13-51, Appeals Chamber, 6 November 2015.

Decision on the Cooperation of the Democratic Republic of the Congo Regarding Omar Al Bashir's Arrest and Surrender to the Court: The Prosecutor v. Al Bashir, ICC-02/05-01/09, Pre-Trial Chamber II, 9 April 2014.

Decision on the Non-compliance of the Republic of Chad with the Cooperation Requests Issued by the Court Regarding the Arrest and Surrender of Omar Hassan Ahmad Al-Bashir: The Prosecutor v. Al Bashir, ICC-02/05-01/09, Pre-Trial Chamber I, 26 March 2013.

Decision Pursuant to Article 15 of the Rome Statute on the Authorisation of an Investigation into the Situation in the Islamic Republic of Afghanistan, ICC-02/17-33, Pre-Trial Chamber II, 12 April 2019.

Decision Pursuant to Article 87(7) on the Failure of Republic of Malawi to Comply with the Co-operation Request Issued by the Court with Respect to the Arrest and Surrender of Omar Hassan Ahmed Al Bashir: The Prosecutor v. Al Bashir, ICC-02/05-01/09, Pre-Trial Chamber I, 12 December 2011.

Decision under Article 87(7) of the Rome Statute on the Non-compliance by South Africa with the Request by the Court for the Arrest and Surrender of Omar Al-Bashir: The Prosecutor v. Al Bashir, ICC-02/05-01/09, Pre-Trial Chamber II, 6 July 2017.

Decision under Article 87(7) of the Rome Statute on the Non-compliance by Jordan with Request by the Court for the Arrest and Surrender of Omar Al-Bashir: The Prosecutor v. Al Bashir, ICC-02/05-01/09, Pre-Trial Chamber II, 11 December 2017.

Minister of Justice and Constitutional Development and Others v. Southern African Litigation Centre and Others 2016 (3) SA 317 (SCA).

Motion on Behalf of the Government of Libya Requesting an Oral Hearing in Respect of its Admissibility Challenge Pursuant to Article 19 of the ICC Statute, ICC-01/11-01/11-132, Pre-Trial Chamber I, 2 May 2012.

Prosecutor v. Ahmad Al Faqi Al Mahdi, ICC-01/12-01/15, 27 September 2017.

Prosecutor v. Germain Katanga, ICC-01/04-01/07, 27 March 2017.

Prosecutor v. Ruto and Sang, ICC-01/09-01/11, 1 May 2013.

Prosecutor v. Thomas Lubanga Dyilo and *Jugement rendu en application de l'article 74 du Statut*, ICC-01/04-01/07-3436, 20 March 2014.

'Separate Further Opinion of Judge Eboe-Osuji', *Prosecutor v. Uhuru Muigai Kenyatta*, ICC-01/09-02/11-830-Anx3-Corr, Trial Chamber V(b), 18 October 2013.

Southern African Litigation Centre v. Minister of Justice and Constitutional Development and Others [2015] ZAGPPHC 402.

IS THE AFRICAN COURT ON HUMAN AND PEOPLES' RIGHTS WITH CRIMINAL JURISDICTION AN AFRICAN SOLUTION TO AN AFRICAN PROBLEM?

Jeremy Sarkin

1. INTRODUCTION

International criminal justice is facing trying times (Sirleaf 2016). It has many problems and faces many challenges (Hafetz 2017: 1133). This is particularly true of the International Criminal Court (ICC), which faces the wrath of the African Union (AU) as well as many African states because of its perceived bias towards African countries (Jalloh and Bantekas 2017). As a result, or maybe at least in part, the African Union intends to revolutionise (some say evolutionise (Abraham 2015)) the processes of dealing with criminal law by giving the African Court on Human and Peoples' Rights (ACHPR) criminal jurisdiction (Oehm 2018). This is groundbreaking because usually criminal law is exercised by states. The common view was that until more recent times, criminal jurisdiction was always a foundational aspect of a state's sovereign rights. However, there are many examples of states giving up that right to other bodies over the centuries. While the perception is that historically only states had the ability and the authority to enforce criminal law, to prosecute those suspects who violated the law and to implement criminal sanctions (Romano, Nollkaemper and Kleffner 2004: ix), international institutions have had that authority on occasion. However, states have not given up such authority to a regional institution; it is only in more recent times (since the 1990s) that some new international criminal institutions have been established with such a mandate.[1]

This is not the first time that international criminal jurisdiction has been exercised by a court. However, no international institution exercising criminal jurisdiction existed from the times of the Nuremburg and Tokyo trials in the 1940s until the International Criminal Tribunal for the former Yugoslavia was established in 1993. International judicial structures, characterised by the creation of the ICC, ad hoc criminal and hybrid tribunals, result in justice no longer being an exclusive and autonomous matter for states (Huneeus 2013: 1). However, no regional court has had criminal powers (Campbell 2018). Nonetheless, the move to give a regional body a criminal law mandate is in some ways a continuation of a trend to develop criminal processes external to states. The reformed African Court on Justice and Human Rights will become the first regional court with the ability to resolve cases concerning individual criminal charges (Huneeus 2013: 4). The idea of the revised mandate of the Court fits in with the philosophy of 'African solutions to African problems', a phrase coined by George Ayittey. However, this decision to give the African Court criminal jurisdiction has come under attack. It has been argued that the move to create such a court is for political reasons rather than to really impact the levels of crimes across the continent. Nevertheless, the Court may play a positive role and may add to the jigsaw of institutions that play a part in the process. Be that as it may, the ICC need not be 'the primary locus for combating impunity' (Mutua 2010: 7), but rather a means by which, through a system of collaboration between domestic and regional courts in conjunction with the ICC, egregious crimes may be addressed and long-term solutions implemented. In this vein, other mechanisms including the African Court with criminal jurisdiction can play their part. This is not new or novel, but part of a trend of giving more institutions supranational powers.

1 For a historical overview, see Rikhof (2014).

In fact, there has been a radical increase in the number of international courts and tribunals globally. The last century saw a dramatic increase in the number of such bodies (Buergenthal 2001: 267). More than 43 different types of international or regional courts were created in that period. Two of the interesting examples are the International Prize Court established by the terms of the Convention on an International Prize Court of 18 October 1907, wherein individuals were to be able to approach the court in relation to property, and the Central American Court of Justice, which was also established at the same time (Sarkin 2009: 14). Of the 43 international courts that have been established, at least 16 are still operating (Romano 2011). Today, there are more than 20 permanent international courts, compared to only six in 1990 (Alter 2014). In addition, about 125 adjudicative international institutions have come to the fore in the international and regional spheres. Some have called this the globalisation of courts, while it has been also called the justice cascade (Sikkink 2011). Specifically, there has been a mushrooming of such institutions (Kingsbury 2012) over the last three decades, so much so that this period has been termed the period of accountability (Meron 2018).

It is specifically the growth of criminal courts outside of the domestic context that can be seen. This is because there are often crimes or individuals that states will not or cannot prosecute. This was the reason behind the creation of the ad hoc tribunals (for Rwanda and the former Yugoslavia) and later on the ICC (Clarke, Knottnerus and de Volder 2016). Some states are unwilling or unable to deal with at least some of the cases that arose in their jurisdictions. These courts have been either international mechanisms or domestic courts with international features. Thus, criminal courts have been created outside of national processes at the international level, or those termed hybrid bodies that operate in the domestic context, but have both international and domestic characteristics. As a result, there are three types of international criminal courts operating today: a permanent court (the ICC), the two ad hoc tribunals (for Rwanda and the former Yugoslavia) and internationalised or 'hybrid' courts for such places as Cambodia, Kosovo, Sierra Leone, Timor-Leste and Bosnia (Alford 2000: 160). At the same time, there has been a shift from the use of global mechanisms towards the use of regional institutions (Alter 2014: 65). Many types of regional adjudicative processes have been developed. There are also another 80 'Quasi-Judicial, Implementation Control and other Dispute Settlement Bodies' that are in operation (Romano 2011). While there is trend towards regional institutions (Berry 2018), much of it for economic purposes and many with accountability mechanisms, this inclination towards institutional expansion and accountability does not extend to creating regional criminal courts (Burke-White 2003: 729). At present, no regional or even sub-regional criminal court can be found (Tiba 2015: 521), as no need for them has been apparent.

When it comes to institutions operating in Africa, a variety of institutions operate at the regional and sub-regional levels. There has also been a rapid increase in the number of courts operating in the region at the regional or sub-regional levels (Reinold 2019). Many are not operating optimally (Asare and Sekyere 2016), such as the East African Court of Justice (Possi 2018). There are also different AU institutions that operate to achieve a variety of objects, including the African Court and African Commission on Human and Peoples' Rights, the African Peer Review Mechanism, and the African Committee of Experts on the Rights and Welfare of the Child (ACERWC) (Sarkin 2011). A number of sub-regional institutions that have also come to the fore also have courts (Sarkin 2009b). None of these sub-regional courts has criminal jurisdiction. These courts, which have civil powers only, have been operating for a number of years and in some cases for decades. For example, the Economic Community of West African States (ECOWAS) Court has operated for many years (Happold and Radovi 2018; Alter, Helfer and McAllister 2013). However, some of these courts are not functioning. While there was a trend towards creating these courts and giving them expanded mandates, more recently there has been a reversal in such a tendency. This is because there has been something of a backlash or, some would say, a pushback against these courts (Madsen, Cebulak and Wiebusch 2018) across the region (Alter, Gathii and Helfer 2016). This resistance has occurred not only in Africa (Mälksoo 2016) but also elsewhere, including in the European court (Hofmann 2018). Many of these courts have faced state push back (Madsen et al. 2018) because of their decisions (Gathii 2014). Pushback has also occurred by the AU itself, specifically against the African Commission, but this has also affected the African Court (Daly and Wiebusch 2018). The court that suffered the most as a result of state resistance was the Southern African Development Community (SADC) Tribunal as a result of its robust decisions. It was first suspended and later had its jurisdiction to hear human rights cases removed (Sarkin 2016a).

These moves by states to reduce the role of various institutions (Murray and Long 2015), including tribunals and courts that have oversight over them, have similarly been at the heart of problems between the ICC and African states (Sarkin 2017). At the same time, struggles to try and limit oversight over African states are not confined to the role of the various courts, but also at the UN, the African Commission and elsewhere.

In this context, it is important to understand the expansion of the African Court to include criminal jurisdiction.[2] This will be the first regional criminal court in the world. However, it has been argued that regional human rights courts already deal with criminal matters. Thus, for example, the African

2 Interestingly, the African Court already examines criminal matters, but only as far as whether criminal laws and procedures in states comply with human rights obligations. See Possi (2017).

Court already deals with issues concerning the application of criminal law in countries and whether the criminal justice process in those countries complies with the African Charter and other international and regional instruments that the Court has a mandate to apply (Huneeus 2013). Nevertheless, the African Court will be unique in many ways, as exceptionally it will have not only criminal jurisdiction, but also a human rights focus, as well as a general international and regional law focus. Thus, it will have three areas of competence rather than only one. This will be a significant challenge for the Court.

This chapter seeks to understand the reasons for giving the African Court criminal jurisdiction and whether the creation of this court will achieve the goals articulated and even unarticulated. First, it reviews the process the regional system has adopted with regard to creating courts. It briefly reviews the historical development of institutions, including the African Court of Justice (AJ) and the ACHPR. The role of the African Court and why it is being reformed – first to merge with the ACJ and then to give it criminal jurisdiction – are examined. Thus, the process to adopt the Malabo Protocol is reviewed, as well as why the AU wishes the ACHPR to have criminal jurisdiction. The content of the Malabo Protocol is then reviewed to determine what the issues are concerning the jurisdiction, structure and role of the future Court that will have criminal jurisdiction, in addition to human rights and general international law jurisdiction. The crimes over which the Court will have jurisdiction are reviewed to determine what role it may play in dealing with the massive problems that exist in the region. The issue of who is given immunity from prosecution in the Malabo Protocol is discussed because this will be one of the most controversial features of the Court's jurisdiction, but also because it undermines Africa's claim that the Court will play the role it is envisaged to play; in this context, whether it will play a positive role and whether issues such as resources and capacity may undermine the role it could play are discussed.

2. FROM A HUMAN RIGHTS COURT ONLY TO A COURT ALSO WITH GENERAL INTERNATIONAL LAW AND CRIMINAL JURISDICTION

During the years of the Organisation of African Unity (OAU), there was no regional judicial adjudication mechanism (Okafor 2007). There was the African Commission and later other quasi-judicial bodies, but no judicial institution (Peter 1993). This was done deliberately in the process of establishing the African regional system in the 1960s, because at that stage a court was not desired (Naldi and Magliveras 1998: 431). For many years, there was opposition to the creation of such a court (Udombana 2000). It was argued in the OAU that appeasement and dialogue rather than court decisions were required.

The need to reform the OAU and to move to the AU brought with it a sense that a court or courts were needed for a range of reasons, including the sense that more judicial oversight was needed. (Sarkin 2017) As a result of these developments, two judicial institutions were crafted, not as part of the African Charter – wherein, for example, the African Commission has its legislative roots – but from new protocols (Evans and Murray 2008).

2.1. THE AFRICAN COURT OF JUSTICE

The African Court of Justice was established as part of the Constitutive Act of the African Union in 1999 (Akinseye-George 2001/2002). This Court was established to deal with disputes, interpret international law issues that arose and deal with difficulties arising from agreements that were entered into by states (van der Mei 2005). The Protocol of the Court of Justice of the African Union was agreed to by the AU in July 2003. It entered into force on 11 February 2009. Despite this, only 16 states have ratified the Protocol. However, the Court is not operational because the decision was taken early on that it was to merge with the ACHPR.

2.2. THE AFRICAN COURT ON HUMAN AND PEOPLES' RIGHTS

The ACHPR was established in terms of the Protocol to the African Charter on Human and Peoples' Rights on the Establishment of an African Court on Human and Peoples' Rights (Sarkin 2011). This Protocol was adopted by the member states of the then OAU in June 1998. The Protocol came into force on 25 January 2004. The entry into force of the Protocol occurred after the necessary 15 states ratified the instrument. Regardless, only eight of the 30 States Parties[3] to the Protocol have made the necessary declaration, as determined by the Protocol that recognises the competence of the Court to receive cases from non-governmental organisations (NGOs) and individuals.[4]

The African Court is established to oversee state compliance with various international human rights rules (Sarkin 2011). This enforcement role comprises the Court reviewing the actions of states to determine if they conform to the

---

3 The 30 states which have ratified the Protocol are: Algeria, Benin, Burkina Faso, Burundi, Cameroon, Chad, Comoros, Republic of the Congo, Côte d'Ivoire, Gabon, Gambia, Ghana, Kenya, Libya, Lesotho, Mali, Malawi, Mozambique, Mauritania, Mauritius, Nigeria, Niger, Rwanda, the Sahrawi Arab Democratic Republic, South Africa, Senegal, Tanzania, Togo, Tunisia and Uganda.

4 These states are: Benin, Burkina Faso, Côte d'Ivoire, Ghana, Mali, Malawi, Tanzania and Tunisia. Rwanda later withdrew its declaration giving access to NGOs and individuals. Recently some states have begun to withdraw their declarations.

requirements of various international laws. The Court has jurisdiction over matters presented to it concerning the African Charter, the Protocol and other applicable human rights instruments (Abass 2013a). The Court examines state conduct (in the wide sense) to determine whether that conduct is compliant with the various international human rights rules that are binding on the specific state in question. The Court must examine whether that action is legal or not and, if not, approve reparations designed to remediate the specific victims affected by the state's conduct. Even so, it ought to also try and promote deterrence against such conduct in the future. Whether this is a cornerstone of its work is uncertain. While the Court's decisions are meant to also be educative to others, including other states, whether the Court should push this role is also unclear. This role can and should be important regardless of whether the Court has criminal jurisdiction or not. Thus, the Court sets standards (whether clearly articulated or not) in a specific case that not only apply to that case, but that other states must also take note of and should follow the verdict in their own state. That is the case unless the decision is written in a way that makes it applicable only to the state that was before the Court. In any case, a limited application of the outcome applying to only one state is extremely rare. Almost all decisions should be applicable in all other African states. This is because all cases concern the interpretation of the African Charter and other instruments; thus, the decisions should be relevant to all states. The Court also issues reparations partly to compensate victims, but also as a means to counsel and warn other states that non-compliance has consequences. As such, a decision is not only meant to have an effect on the circumstances in the particular matter before the Court, but it is also meant to affect the circumstances in the other African countries. Hence, a case should not only affect those particular victims and that particular state, but is meant to have positive effects for similar victims who have been harmed in other states. Thus, those other states must also take steps to deal with the problems identified by the Court. In this fashion, the Court has an important role to play in its decisions for all states and all people in Africa rather than only for the country and the specific victims before it in a specific case.

What is clear is that reviewing state compliance can have constitutional and other legal repercussions for a state. The African Court can find a state to be non-compliant in many respects, including that the constitution of a state, the laws enacted by its parliament, and its regulations or other rules are not compatible with the human rights rules it is bound to follow. Similarly, the action taken by the state in other ways can also be found to be unlawful. When any of these matters are found to have occurred, the African Court can order the state to correct these matters, be they constitutional problems, laws, rules, actions or whatever has occurred in that state which is deficient from the position of the human rights rules that the state is bound to follow. Thus, the Court can order a state to do many things to deal with the problem, including constitutional changes, law reform, law annulment or any other steps to bring that state into compliance.

While some might argue that the Court is acting as an appellate court or as a constitutional court, it has stated that it is not. The Court emphasised in *Lohe Issa Konaté v. Burkina Faso* that: 'It is not an appellate jurisdiction to which decisions by national courts are referred.'[5] This view can be seen in cases dealing with criminal issues where, for example, the right to a fair trial have been adjudicated on. Thus, in *Christopher Jonas v. United Republic of Tanzania*, the Court found a breach of the right to free legal assistance under Article 7(1)(c) of the African Charter. In *Mohamed Abubakari v. United Republic of Tanzania*, the Court held that: 'An indigent individual under prosecution for a criminal offence has the special right to free legal assistance where the offence is serious and punishment prescribed by law severe.'[6] In the *Lohe Issa Konaté* case, the Court ordered the respondent state to '[e]xpunge from the Applicant's judicial records, all the criminal convictions pronounced against him'.[7] There have also been cases in which the Court dealt with the question of whether someone ought to be released from jail. Its decision in *Christopher Jonas* and *Mohamed Abubakari* to dismiss the applicants' application to be released is based on its stand in the *Alex Thomas* case. In this case, it stated that ordering '[t]he Applicant's release from prison can be made only under very specific and/or, compelling circumstances'.[8] In *Alex Thomas* and *Mohamed Abubakari*, the Court found that the applicants had not shown the exceptional circumstances that would call for their release. In *Alex Thomas*, Judges Elsie N. Thompson and Rafâa Ben Achour delivered a joint dissenting opinion where they reflected upon the Court's recognition that reopening the defence or the retrial would result in prejudice and result in a miscarriage of justice.

The critical point is that whatever one may see the African Court doing, it has already adjudicated on criminal law matters and has the power to make states change their laws, constitutions, conduct, processes or any other matter that does not conform to a human rights treaty or other law that the state is bound to follow. Thus, Alter notes that 'some scholars see … review of state acts as having a potential constitutional significance … Human rights law is often seen as a higher order legal obligation, so that the enforcement of international human rights agreements may be seen as largely analogous to constitutional review of state acts' (Alter 2013: 353). In fact, many have noted that international courts with human rights powers have a level of legal authority which is comparable to the constitutional and public law roles that

---

5 *Lohe Issa Konaté v. Burkina Faso*. Judgment on reparations of 3 June 2016, para. 24.

6 *Mohamed Abubakari v. United Republic of Tanzania*. Judgment of 3 June 2016, para. 139.

7 *Lohe Issa Konaté v. Burkina Faso*. Judgment on reparations of 3 June 2016.

8 *Alex Thomas v. United Republic of Tanzania*. Judgment of 20 November 2015, para. 157.

domestic courts have in many jurisdictions to strike down legislation or a range of matters to order a state to change its rules or conduct (Goldsmith and Levinson 2009). In fact, the European Court of Human Rights has often noted that the European Convention on Human Rights 'is a constitutional instrument of European public order (ordre public)'.[9] Thus, it recognises the constitutional effect of the instrument. However, it must be noted that the European and African systems are different, as is the relationship between national law and the interpretation of the Convention because of various factors, including the margin of appreciation, a particularly European concept that is usually applied to moral and ethical issues that may be viewed differently in the various countries in Europe. While the margin of appreciation ensures some degree of deference to the national system, it is seemingly not being relied on to the same extent anymore at the European Court, and in any case, this norm is not in existence in other regional arrangements. Also, a major difference is that, unlike the African and Inter-American Court of Human Rights, the European Court is not able to directly strike down national legislation. It is able to find violations of the Convention and leaves the remedial action to the national system. Critically, the contexts are different. The extensive and massive violations of human rights that have occurred in the Inter-American and African systems and the need to deal with these problems have been seen to be the reason why these systems do not apply any notions of margins of appreciation. Some have argued that the Inter-American Court acts as a 'continental constitutional court with powers to standardize the understanding of the Inter-American convention of human rights on the continent' (McGoldrick 2017: 361). Similarly, the African Court is tasked with ensuring respect across the continental for the rights in the African Charter and other human rights instruments that the state is bound to respect. As with the Inter-American Court, the African Court has the power and duty to homogenise the understanding of the various human rights instruments they apply in their work. The African Court is meant to ensure the systematic regional compliance with the human rights standards and norms that apply in the region and states.

Regardless, the African Court should be continually conscious of the great potential that its decisions may have in promoting a particular culture of human rights, as well as the methods used to respect, protect and promote them. It is true that it is contentious for the Court to order states to annul or amend their domestic laws. Such orders, which contribute greatly to advancing guarantees of non-repetition, are not an illegitimate encroachment upon the sovereignty of states if the conduct of the state is contrary to the content of the

[9] European Court of Human Rights in *Loizidou v. Turkey* (preliminary objections) [GC], 23 March 1995, no. 15318/89, §75.

Banjul Charter. This is a principle of international law. As has been noted by the Inter-American Court: '[A] State that has ratified a human rights treaty must make such amendments to its domestic legislation as may be necessary to ensure full compliance with the obligations undertaken.'[10]

Whatever one calls the powers of the African Court and whether one agrees with those powers, the fact is that such courts have such mandates because particular states have agreed to be bound by supranational instruments and, in particular, the African Charter. These states accept that a specific regional institution has the sole mandate to interpret this document (and others at times) and to make states comply with their interpretation. States accept the jurisdiction of these courts if they wish to by ratifying specific instruments. They thereby agree to be bound to the rulings, whether they like or agree with them or not. How one classifies the types of power that these courts have is irrelevant. The fact is simply that these courts have the powers to interpret, and states are bound to comply with the rulings emanating from the courts that examine and determine state compliance on human rights matters.

These issues are also relevant as far as extending the African Court's powers into criminal matters. This is because taking up this type of jurisdiction encroaches upon the usual authority of the state. Usually, it has been states that have criminal law powers. This has been eroded over time, especially over the last quarter of a century, during which time many international criminal courts have come into being.

When it comes to the benefits of such courts, it is important to note, as Ruti Teitel has, that: 'The domestic judiciary is … embedded within a particular political and constitutional system … the supranational rights institutions stand, by contrast, aloof from the domestic politics of transitional justice and … the politics of transitional constitutionalism' (Teitel 2015: 389). This is a crucial aspect understanding that many of the cases that go to such courts do not go to domestic courts because of the implications of such cases. Bearing this in mind, the implementation of a regional criminal court should not only encourage accountability within the state, but also contextualise the trial within the community. Furthermore, it should assist in the incorporation and utilisation of indigenous justice and healing practices to aid prosecution and ensure inter-generational healing. A regional criminal court could also offset political dynamics, as international criminal courts often fall victim to manipulation by those with more power (Hneeus 2012: 42). The critical issue will be how the Court takes up its criminal jurisdiction and how it exercises those powers. If the Court exercises these independently and for the good of the continent as a whole, it could have a significant impact.

---

10 *Bulacio v. Argentina* (Merits, Reparations and Costs). Judgment of 18 September 2003, para. 140.

2.3. MERGING THE AFRICAN HUMAN RIGHTS COURT AND THE AFRICAN COURT OF JUSTICE

The merger Protocol to combine the two courts was adopted on 1 July 2008. It required 15 ratifications to enter into force and to merge the African Human Rights Court and the African Court of Justice into a single court: the African Court of Justice and Human Rights (Kane and Motala 2009). However, as a result of an insufficient number of ratifications of the merger Protocol (Zschirnt 2018), the merged court has not come to fruition (Mngomezulu 2018). This does raise issues concerning the willingness of states to create and operationalise these Courts. On the one hand, states want to indicate their commitment to deal with problems in Africa, but on the other hand, they do not ratify the instruments that will allow oversight and scrutiny of what they are doing. As noted below, by far the majority of states do not permit individuals or groups to sue them for violations by not accepting the provision in the Protocol that would allow this.[11]

2.4. THE MALABO PROTOCOL

The Protocol to give the African Court criminal jurisdiction began with a first draft in 2008.[12] At the 23rd ordinary session in Malabo in June 2014, the African Heads of State and Governments adopted the Protocol on Amendments to the Protocol on the Statute of the African Court of Justice and Human Rights[13] (hereinafter the Malabo Protocol).[14]

The aim of the Protocol is to merge the African Court of Justice with the ACHPR, and add criminal jurisdiction to the Court. It would also change the name of the Court to the African Court of Justice and Human and Peoples' Rights.[15]

The entry into force of the combined court is regulated by Article 11 which provides that the Protocol and the annexed Statute will enter into force 30 days after the instruments of ratification have been deposited by at

11 On access and petitions, see Ssenyonjo (2013a).
12 On these historical origins, see Abass (2016: 11).
13 Malabo Protocol, adopted 27 June 2014, https://www.au.int/web/en/treaties/protocol-amendments-protocol-statute-african-court-justice-and-human-rights.
14 http://www.hrw.org/news/2014/11/13/statement-regarding-immunity-sitting-officials-expanded-african-court-justice-and-hu.
15 Article 8 of the Protocol on amendments to the protocol on the statute of the African Court of Justice and Human Rights, http://www.au.int/en/sites/default/files/PROTOCOL%20ON%20AMENDMENTS%20TO%20THE%20PROTOCOL%20ON%20THE%20AFRICAN%20COURT%20-%20EN_0.pdf.

least 15 Member States.[16] The Protocol has only 11 signatures and no ratifications from the 54 members of the AU. Thus, it looks as though the Court is a long way off from dealing with criminal cases when the number of ratifications is taken into account. It does not seem that the proposed Court will come into effect anytime soon. Abass has in fact questioned whether the threshold will even be reached (Abass 2016: 13). This is because there is a concern regarding the political will that is needed for the Malabo Protocol and the Court to actually succeed (Sirleaf 2016: 772). There are already many worrying indications of states lacking the commitment to hold individuals accountable for international crimes.

3. WHY THE MALABO PROTOCOL?

The process to develop a regional criminal court in Africa must be seen more as a political development than a legal one. It does emerge, at least in part, as a result of the squabble (Mbengue and McClellan 2018) between the AU and the ICC (Vilmer 2016). This dispute concerns the role played by the ICC (Mills and Bloomfield 2018), and its supposed bias towards African countries (Dembinski and Peters 2019) and because it is specifically targeting African leaders (Ssenyonjo 2013b). The timing of the request by the AU Assembly in 2009,[17] when it took the decision[18] to request the AU Commission and the African Commission on Human and Peoples' Rights to examine the consequences of giving the African Court jurisdiction to prosecute international crimes, including genocide, crimes against humanity and war crimes, took place at the same time as a decision was taken not to cooperate with the ICC (Mills and Bloomfield 2018). This was done after the AU Assembly's request to the Security Council, asking it to defer the ICC's investigation into Kenyan violence, was not acted upon by the Council. Therefore, it was decided to 'fast track the process of expanding the mandate of the African Court on Human and Peoples' Rights ... to try international crimes, such as genocide, crimes against humanity and war crimes'.[19] However, as will be discussed below, the Court will deal with many more crimes.

Even so, the development of the African criminal court process also emerges out of the fact that a number of countries outside of Africa, including

16 Ibid., art. 11(1).

17 At its summit held in Addis Ababa in February 2009.

18 Assembly/AU/Dec. 213(XII).

19 AU Assembly Decision on Africa's relationship with the International Criminal, 12 October 2013. Ext/Assembly/AU/Dec.1-4.

Belgium, France, Germany, Morocco and Spain, have been attempting to prosecute heads of states and some have indicted various African leaders and senior officials.[20] In this regard, the *Hissène Habré* case, in which the former President of Chad was prosecuted, must be considered (Marks 2004: 131). In this case, the AU finally and reluctantly agreed, after many years of attempts by Belgium and others, to have Habré held accountable for his violations committed in Chad before the Extraordinary African Chambers. Whether he ought to be tried in the African Court was considered by the Committee of Eminent African Jurists, established in 2006 at the Summit of the AU Heads of State and Government in Khartoum, Sudan.[21] The Committee found that neither the ACHPR nor the African Court of Justice had the requisite jurisdiction to prosecute him.[22] However, it did find that there existed 'the possibility of conferring criminal jurisdiction on the African Court of Justice to make the respect for human rights at national, regional and continental levels a fundamental tenet for African governance'.[23]

There are few who doubt the real motivations behind the plan to set up an African criminal court. Some see it as a way for African states to legitimately leave the ICC because they can attest to the fact they are leaving the Court not because of a lack of commitment to international justice, but because of the problems with the ICC. For some, the motivation behind the court is an attempt by African heads of state to shield themselves and their governments and senior state officials from accountability (Galvao Teles 2017: 66).

However, there is a tension here: there is a growing resistance from the AU and African states to robust oversight by the various mechanisms of international, regional and sub-regional bodies, including the African Court (Daly and Wiebusch 2018). At the same time, however, the AU seeks to limit the role of the ICC and give the regional court greater powers. However, the fact that few states ratify the Court's Protocols and when they do so are not doing so speedily shows the tension. Be that as it may, it needs to be understood that part of the thinking is to limit who the Court can indict. To give the Court powers over criminal law issues that are either beneficial to states or not is problematic from their point of view. Nonetheless, as has been noted generally and not specifically about dealing with crimes, regional human rights systems are 'only as strong and effective as the region's underlying unity and commitment to democracy and individual rights' (Bederman 2007: 226).

---

20 Including the Presidents of Angola, Burkina Faso, Côte d'Ivoire, Equatorial Guinea, Gabon, the Republic of the Congo, and Rwanda. A number of these processes occurred in 2009.

21 Assembly/AU/ Dec. 103 (VI), January 2006, at Khartoum, Sudan.

22 Report of the Committee of Eminent African Jurists on the Case of Hissène Habré, submitted to the Assembly of the African Union, Ordinary Session, July 2006, para. 26.

23 Ibid., para. 34.

4. THE JURISDICTION, STRUCTURE AND ROLE OF THE FUTURE COURT WITH CRIMINAL JURISDICTION

The future fully merged Court will have three sections: General Affairs (GA), Human and Peoples' Rights (HPR), and International Criminal Law (ICL),[24] with the latter consisting of three chambers: a Pre-Trial Chamber, a Trial Chamber and an Appellate Chamber.[25]

The General Affairs Section will be able to hear all cases that are submitted under Article 28 of the Statute of the African Court of Justice and Human and Peoples Rights, apart from those that fall under the other two sections:[26] the Human and Peoples' Rights Section will hear all human and peoples' rights cases,[27] and the International Criminal Law Section will deal with all cases relating to the crimes under the Court's jurisdiction.[28] The GA Section will have three judges, the HPR Section three judges, the Pre-Trial Chamber of the ICL one judge, its Trial Chamber three judges and the Appellate Chamber five judges.[29]

The Protocol provides that judges are to be impartial and independent, chosen from a group of people with 'high moral character', and who have the necessary qualifications to work in the 'highest judicial offices', are jurisconsults or have other recognised competence and experience in international law, international human rights law, international humanitarian law or international criminal law.[30] These judges are to be selected from lists of candidates who respectively have competence and experience in either: (a) international law; (b) international human rights law and international humanitarian law; or (c) international criminal law.[31] From these three lists, five judges are chosen from amongst the first two lists, and a further six from the last list.[32] States Parties that nominate candidates will choose the list on which their candidate will be placed.[33]

The lists are to be communicated by the Chairperson of the Commission to the Member States at least 30 days before the elections take place, which will happen during the Ordinary Session of the Assembly or of the Council.[34]

---

24 Annex to the Statute of the African Court of Justice and Human and Peoples Rights, art. 16(1).
25 Ibid., art. 16(2).
26 Ibid., art. 17(1).
27 Ibid., art. 17(2).
28 Ibid., art. 17(3).
29 Ibid., art. 10(1)–(5).
30 Ibid., art. 3.
31 Ibid., art. 4(1)(i)–(iv).
32 Ibid., art. 4(3).
33 Ibid., art. 4(2).
34 Ibid., art. 4(4).

Usefully, judges are elected for a single, non-renewable term of nine years, which will promote independence. To ensure rotation, five of the first elected judges will have their terms end after three years, another five will have their tenure end after six years.[35] Which judges fall into which category will be determined by drawing lots.[36] A president and vice-president will be chosen at the first ordinary session after the judges' election,[37] will serve for two-year periods and can be re-elected once.[38]

The Office of the Prosecutor shall have one Prosecutor and two Deputies.[39] They will be elected by the Assembly.[40] They will serve for seven (the Prosecutor, non-renewable)[41] and four (the Deputy Prosecutor, renewable once)[42] years respectively.

As far as its criminal jurisdiction is concerned, the Court will have authority over crimes that took place on a territory of a state,[43] when the person accused of the crime[44] or the victim[45] is a national of a state, or when non-nationals commit acts extraterritorially, but threaten a vital interest of that state.[46]

The Court will exercise its jurisdiction if the Prosecutor has a situation referred to him/her by a State Party,[47] by the Assembly of Heads of State and Government of the AU or by the Peace and Security Council of the AU,[48] or if the Prosecutor has initiated an investigation into such crimes in accordance with Article 46G.[49] Once a reasonable basis for proceeding exists, the Office establishes an investigation and must submit the investigation to a Pre-Trial Chamber.[50]

If a case is being investigated or prosecuted by a state that has jurisdiction over it, if a state has decided to not prosecute a person in a case over which it has jurisdiction, if the person accused has been tried for conduct that is the subject of a case before the Court or if the case is not of sufficient gravity, the case in question is inadmissible at the African Court.[51] If there is doubt

35 Ibid., art. 5(1).
36 Ibid., art. 5(2).
37 Ibid., art. 22(1).
38 Ibid., art. 22(2).
39 Ibid., art. 22A(1).
40 Ibid., art. 22A(2).
41 Ibid., art. 22A(3).
42 Ibid., art. 22A(4).
43 Ibid., art. 46E *bis* (2a).
44 Ibid., art. 46E *bis* (2b).
45 Ibid., art. 46E *bis* (2c).
46 Ibid., art. 46E *bis* (2d).
47 Ibid., art. 46F(1).
48 Ibid., art. 46F(2).
49 Ibid., art. 46F(3).
50 Ibid., art. 46G(3).
51 Ibid., art. 46H(2)(a)–(d).

over whether a state is unwilling to investigate or prosecute a specific case, the Court must determine if the person is being shielded, if there has been an unjustified delay in proceedings or if the proceedings are not being conducted in a manner that is impartial or independent.[52]

A very positive aspect of the Malabo Protocol is the adding of a Defence Office as a separate and independent organ of the Court, alongside the Presidency, the Office of the Prosecutor, and the Registry (Article 2(4)). It is a key addition because it shows the belief in the importance of equality of arms. This is a historical step forward – as defence counsel have often been overlooked and under-resourced in international criminal trials. Therefore, its inclusion in the Malabo Protocol is to be celebrated, especially the addition of 'adequate resourcing' for the counsel and the establishment of the position of 'Principal Defender' whose authority will be equal to the Prosecutor (du Plessis 2014: 201) A Trust Fund is to be established by the AU Assembly. This will be created for legal aid and assistance of victims of crimes or human rights violations and their families.[53] The money for the Trust Fund can be collected through fines or forfeiture when the Court orders this money or property to be transferred to the Fund.[54]

Another useful addition is the inclusion of a Victims' Office. While more recent tribunals have enhanced the role and status of victims, they are not always sufficiently protected and supported. Victims are vulnerable to intimidation, harassment, bribery and even assassination; therefore, there is a crucial need to protect victims and witnesses. For this reason, it is very positive that the Malabo Protocol has added such a unit. The Protocol further supports victims by requiring compensation and that reparations be made available to them (Sirleaf 2017: 88). Thus, it seems as though this type of protection is being taken seriously.

While there are useful aspects to the Protocol, overall there are problems with the drafting of it. In many places the document is not at all clear and its provisions have received many critical comments. It is accused of being drafted too simplistically and with an over-optimistic approach (Abass 2016: 13). There are several flawed provisions in the document that will most certainly curtail the Court's ability to actually prosecute some of the crimes. The Protocol has also been criticised for being subject to very limited public debate and consultations (du Plessis 2014: 199).[55] The drafting process was too rushed; therefore, it contains many errors and typographical problems (ibid.: 202). De la Rasilla del Moral (2017: 18) describes the document as containing

52 Ibid., art. 46H(3)(a)–(c).
53 Annex to the Statute of the African Court of Justice and Human and Peoples Rights, art. 46M(1).
54 Ibid., art. 46M(2).
55 https://fhr.org.za/index.php/latest_news/understanding-malabo-protocol.

'a series of drafting issues and "problematic features"'. Abass also states that the document contains a number of flawed provisions that will potentially curtail the Court's ability to prosecute international crimes, which he links to the combination of civil and criminal jurisdictions that is unprecedented internationally (Abass 2016: 14).

5. THE CRIMES OVER WHICH THE COURT WILL HAVE JURISDICTION

The Court will have jurisdiction over 14 crimes: genocide, crimes against humanity, war crimes, unconstitutional change of government, piracy, terrorism, mercenarism corruption, money laundering, trafficking in persons (Sana 2018), trafficking in drugs, trafficking in hazardous waste, illicit exploitation of natural resources (Abe and Ordor 2018) and the crime of aggression.[56] The Assembly, with the consent of the States Parties, may add crimes to this list.[57] There are no statutes of limitations applicable to any of the crimes within the jurisdiction of the Court.[58]

It is interesting to compare the fact that while the African Court will deal with 14 types of crime, the ICC, with many more judges and considerably more resources (although still significantly less than it needs; see O'Donohue 2013), has only dealt with three crimes, but will now deal with a fourth crime (aggression) (Sarkin and Almeida 2019). Thus, there is concern over the addition of 10 more crimes alongside the 'core' crimes that the African Court will deal with, besides its other two jurisdictional competencies.

It can be argued that such a long list of crimes also provides an opportunity to address crimes that often take place on the continent, but are not prosecuted. Expanded jurisdiction to address crimes against humanity, genocide and war crimes, but also other crimes of particular concern and relevance for African states could be very useful (Jalloh 2015: 5). The argumentation behind 'equalising' these crimes is that many of them have the capability to destabilise a country. There are several additions that are welcome because they are in line with the increasing recognition of sexual and gender-based violence when they are used as a weapon in conflicts. It may be that African states rely on the African Court to deal with these crimes and thus abdicate their responsibilities. This may result in very few of the 14 listed crimes being prosecuted by the Court and as a consequence by states.

---

56 Annex to the Statute of the African Court of Justice and Human and Peoples Rights, art. 28A(1)(1)–(14).

57 Ibid., art. 28A(2).

58 Ibid., art. 28A(3).

Thus, adding so many crimes to the Protocol could be perceived as 'an exciting opportunity' to tackle the crimes that are especially present on the continent, but for which there has been no accountability.

However, the large number of crimes that will fall under the Court's jurisdiction will probably have adverse effects. It will diminish the Court's effectiveness due to the level of complexity and the added work burden that will be added to the judges' responsibilities. A further problem is that many of the listed crimes are contentious. Usefully for the Court, the definitions of the core crimes of genocide, crimes against humanity and war crimes are widely agreed upon. The definitions of these are identical to those in the ICC Statute, although the other crimes contained in the Protocol are mainly new and unprecedented at the international or regional level. Such a wide jurisdiction over crimes leads to another problem: that of states having to domesticate whole new section of laws, which could potentially involves major rewrites of their national legislation. Still, some of the crimes use definitions that arise out of the national law of the state concerned. Thus, for terrorism, the Protocol provides that terrorism means any number of acts (de la Rasilla del Moral 2017: 9). Should the Protocol come into force, the Court will be the first regional court to have jurisdiction over the crime of 'terrorism' in peacetime (ibid.: 18). This could be a problematic crime and could be used as a political weapon against a government's opponents.

A useful addition contained in the Malabo Protocol is the fact that the Court can also address corporate responsibility rather than only individual criminal responsibility (Jalloh 2015: 5). This is particularly useful in the African context, because many corporations operating on the continent are foreign or multinationals, often avoiding prosecutions by arguing that the African states in which they are based have no jurisdiction to try them, irrespective of the harm they have caused. The liability of corporations is enhanced by the fact that many of the listed crimes have corporate elements to them (corruption, trafficking in hazardous waste, etc.). Thus, the Protocol sends a strong message that corporations will be held to the same standards as individuals.

The Malabo Protocol is the most comprehensive instrument regarding the crime of unconstitutional change of government, as set out in Article 28E (Manirakiza 2016: 88). Its addition is important because the use of coups and other processes that bring down democratically elected governments has been common on the continent (Abass 2016: 13). It is an issue that the AU has been attempting to deal with firmly, often by suspending the membership of such states from the AU. In this way, this is a useful type of crime to take up, but the problem will be at whom such cases are targeted. This type of crime has the potential to be used for political purposes and so scrutiny will be important. In so doing, the definition of what the criminal act is and when it ought to be used ought to be revisited (Mangu 2018).

6. IMMUNITY

One of the most problematic issues concerning the African Court's jurisdiction is the fact that the Court will not be able to prosecute heads of state and a variety of other state officials (Fombad and Kibet 2018). Article 46A *bis* of the Malabo Protocol deals with the immunity of heads of state and government, and state officials,[59] stating that: 'No charges shall be commenced or continued before the Court against any serving AU Head of State or Government, or anybody acting or entitled to act in such capacity, or other senior state officials based on their functions, during their tenure of office.'[60] It is not clear to whom and how many people this extends. The phrase 'or other senior state officials based on their functions' is very much a catch-all, with hardly any explanation as to what these functions would be (du Plessis 2014: 204; Abraham 2015: 14). Not surprisingly, it is considered to be the most controversial provision in the Protocol (Galvao Teles 2017: 67; du Plessis 2014: 203) because it could possibly lead to impunity. It is said that one of the biggest threats to sustainable peace in Africa is indeed impunity. Also problematic is the fact that the crimes in the Protocol could be used by states to limit the democratic space in their countries by attempting to get the legitimate conduct of its political opposition prosecuted. While the immunity provision is problematic, there will be many perpetrators who do not fall within the purview of this provision of the Malabo Protocol.

The African Court's provision of immunity for sitting heads of state or other state officials goes against the more recent consistent practice of international and hybrid criminal tribunals to hold officials responsible for serious crimes. However, the immunity provision is seen as being contrary to customary international law. While Abraham refers to immunity as having been banned by international criminal law and international human rights law, this is still not a position that is accepted by all, especially those in Africa. Regardless, the African Court immunity provision is a major setback for international justice (Abraham 2015: 14).

Du Plessis believes that the immunity clause was included because of the dual issue of the ongoing tension between the AU and the ICC over ensuring the protection of senior African leaders, and the belief that European prosecutors were specifically targeting African leaders along colonial lines (du Plessis 2014: 205). Abraham states that this provision is the primary reason for the establishment of the Court, referring to the supposedly dominant view among African leaders that people in such positions deserve absolute

59 See Malabo Protocol, art. 46A *bis*.

60 Article 46A *bis* of the Protocol on amendments to the protocol on the statute of the African Court of Justice and Human Rights.

immunity (Abraham 2015: 13). It is argued by those in favour of immunity that prosecuting sitting leaders will derail peace processes if they are prosecuted, but even if this is true, blanket immunity is overreaching, says du Plessis, who would be in favour of a provision that allows for the deferral of such cases (du Plessis 2014: 207). Participants in a meeting of experts discussing the Protocol were divided on the provision – some saw it as possibly contradicting the AU's Constitutive Act and even as a step backwards in the battle against impunity on the continent. Others maintained it to be a compromise that could ensure a better balance or sequencing of justice and peace (also referring to the temporary application of the provision: only while they are in office are they immune) (Jalloh 2015: 6).

7. WHY AFRICA MAY BENEFIT FROM A REGIONAL CRIMINAL COURT

The general academic attitude towards giving the African Court criminal jurisdiction is one of general scepticism and criticism. However, there is praise for some of the features of the proposed reformed Court.

One of the main reasons why having an African Court may be a positive feature is that it will allow crimes to be tried in, or at least be closer to, the region where these crimes were committed. The benefits of this are that investigations will have easier access to the evidence and witnesses (which is always a problem with international tribunals, which are often criticised for being located too far away from where the crimes took place). The proximity of the Court could also give victims and the inhabitants of Africa in general a greater sense of 'ownership' over trials and would facilitate greater interest and even participation.

The Malabo Protocol contains a number of important and welcome innovations that could be of assistance not just to Africa, but possible even for the whole international community (Nmehielle 2014). As Slye states, it may be able to 'identify a distinctly African conception of justice that is different from that found in other societies in the world' (Slye 2017: 234). Swigart (2017) has also argued that 'the African continent should instead be seen as the source of many innovative strategies for applying globally accepted legal principles at the local level'. Jalloh (2015: 5) in this vein also mentions that the Protocol adds a number of important advances, which could possibly have positive effects not just for Africa, but for the whole international community. Similarly, Van der Wilt (2016) applauds the expansion of the Court with a criminal chamber. Looking especially at modes of responsibility, he states that the Protocol, even if it is not yet in force, is promising because it shows that it understands the close connection 'between modes of criminal responsibility and the nature of specific crimes' (ibid.: 8). The Court could prove to be important to the future evolution of accountability for serious human rights violations in both Africa and the rest of the world (ibid.: 8). Establishing the Court could potentially fill the accountability gap that is created by states being unwilling or unable to prosecute criminals and could thus aid in ending impunity (Galvao Teles 2017: 66). As has been noted by Mazzeschi (2003: 339) 'the protection of human rights is, after all, the ultimate goal of the rules of international criminal law and humanitarian law'.

A variety of problems exist with the Malabo Protocol (Abass 2013a). However, Sirleaf believes that although it has its problems, the Protocol provides the African continent with an 'important, alternative vision of regional criminal justice' (2017: 72). It can be used as a 'gap-filler', which could act as the intermediary between national institutions that abuse human rights or fail to enforce them, and the international system that is unable to provide redress to individuals – it could lead to the ICC taking on the most severe situations, with the regional court stepping in for the other cases, which would not only reduce the ICC's workload, but could also reduce its expenses (ibid.: 87). Therefore, the Court could ensure that there is more accountability because there is an additional criminal jurisdiction institution focusing on Africa. What is clear is that for some, the decision to create the Court was influenced by a wish to improve the continent's experience with international criminal trials. If the Court were to work well and focus on serious international crimes, it could allow the ICC to focus on the most severe situations and invest its limited resources in other parts of the world (ibid.: 87). However, having an African criminal court would be worrying for the ICC. This is because the ICC may often lose the option of African States practising self-referral to it (Abass 2017: 13). According to Nel and Sibiya, the implementation of the African Criminal Court brings the AU one step closer to ensuring that the ICC will not prosecute Africans (2017: 97). Galvao Teles argues that the African Court should not weaken the ICC's contribution to criminal justice (2017: 67).

Creating a continental court that can adjudicate international crimes could advance international criminal justice in Africa and 'respond to the yearnings of ordinary Africans looking for justice whilst being sensitive to the unique African context' (Abraham 2015: 11). As Sirleaf (2017: 72) notes, the Malabo Protocol provides the Continent with 'an important, alternative vision of regional criminal justice'.

A reformed African Court with criminal jurisdiction could prove to be a valuable addition to the international criminal justice framework. A regional international criminal tribunal could help in terms of being closer to the crimes committed and thus have greater visibility and possibly assist in issues relating to deterrence and accountability. It could also give people greater familiarity with the Court, which at present is not very well known (Dinokopila 2017: 236). In this regard Galvao Teles (2017: 66) highlights the positive influence the Court could have on impunity for international crimes.

In fact, it can be argued that Africa needs such a court to prosecute the brutal crimes being committed against the innocent across the continent. This is because heinous violations of all descriptions are being perpetrated against men, women and children. Tens of thousands of women continue to be targeted for sexual crimes during conflicts, but also as part of their daily lives. Rape, sexual violence and sexual slavery are used daily across the continent as weapons of war. Bloody conflicts are playing out in the Central African Republic, South Sudan and Nigeria, and armed violence continues in the Democratic Republic of the Congo, Sudan and Somalia (Amnesty International 2015: 6). Hundreds of thousands of people have been displaced by armed conflict.

It should be noted and in fact highlighted that international and regional systems cannot be a panacea to solve these problems. They can play a part. They can promote the domestic applicability of human rights standards in trials. They can promote trials in the sense that, for example, the ICC's complementarity principle is in some ways a Sword of Damocles ensuring that states that do not take action against perpetrators or cannot do so will have such cases possibly taken up by the ICC. However, it needs to be remembered that international and regional courts are selective in terms of what cases they take on (Schabas 2015: 365). Overall, they take up very few cases. Their choices are based on a whole set of issues of which only one part is the domestic context of the state where the crimes took place (Smeulers, Weerdesteijn and Hola 2015). Thus, Smeulers, Weerdesteijn and Hola find that the ICC has taken on situations where the concerns are the gravest or the crimes are the most serious, but also note issues such as whether the situation in the country is a threat to international peace and security (ibid.: 28).

Issues that will cause difficulties for the reformed African Court and the ICC concern complementarity, as well as a potential overlap in cases. If the Court cooperates and works in a coherent way with the ICC, this could have a dramatic effect on the situation in Africa. The ICC can help the AU's initiatives to improve regional peace mechanisms, as long as they promote international criminal justice and are compatible with international human rights law (Ssekandi and Tesfay 2017: 25). The definitions used in the Malabo Protocol for these crimes are almost identical to those in the ICC Statute, which is perceived to be the latest advancement in international law.

However, there are likely to be tensions in the relationship between the ICC and the merged African Court. There are also potential problems regarding the relationship between the Court, sub-regional courts and national courts (Jalloh 2015: 6). The need for cooperation with the AU and African states are also likely to bring about a new set of challenges for the ACHPR. Very few states in Africa cooperate very meaningfully with the African Commission and the ACHPR already. Many have outstanding reports due and there is a further concern that many take a long time to respond to requests and do so often in limited ways. Thus, a key question will be whether there is the political will to support the Court. Another question will be whether states will always be willing to hand over those indicted by the Court. This will be tested when the Court wants to prosecute someone in an African country who is powerful. In those cases, will the state cooperate with the Court, especially if that person is close to the government?

Even if the processes work seamlessly, the ACHPR cannot be the solution to solving the continent's ills (Abatan and Spies 2016). The Court can only take up a handful of cases. But international and regional courts usefully promote states to take action themselves in relation to such types of cases. Simply by starting to investigate or even taking an interest in a domestic issue can often prod states into taking action. This can promote state compliance. The Court can play a role in promoting justice and reducing impunity (Sarkin 2016a). However, as stated above, the Court cannot be the panacea. The Court will undertake very few cases, so it will still be the domestic jurisdictions that have to handle the bulk of criminal cases. Whether they will do so is dependent on their political will and the resources available in all cases. Unfortunately, many states are selective in terms of what cases they take up (Hall 2010). However, the role of the Court will be dependent on many other actors in Africa. For instance, the AU has not been up to the challenge of doing what it should and could do. As such, it needs to be reformed to deal with human rights issues far more effectively. It cannot work on the margins of these issues as it has been doing thus far (Sarkin 2019). Its institutions need to change in order for it to have a greater role in relation to peace and security (Williams 2014), as well as a far more robust role when it comes to human rights matters. The human rights institutions need great support and greater independence (Sarkin 2018).

While Africans argue that the ICC unfairly targets the continent and African leaders, what is undeniable is that in many African countries, there is a peace and human rights deficit (Sarkin 2016b), which is disrupting the trend towards positive progress in levels of peace. (Sarkin 2017). These crises are severely affecting the human rights of people in those countries. Today, many humanitarian and human rights crises exist across the length and breadth of the continent. A democratic deficit and tremendous violations are occurring in countries such as Algeria, Angola, Burundi, the Central African Republic, Chad, the Democratic Republic of the Congo, Egypt, Equatorial Guinea, Eritrea, Ethiopia, Gabon, the Gambia, Libya, Mauritania, Rwanda, Somalia, South Sudan, Sudan, and Uganda. In this context, it is not surprising that on 10 December 2016, International Human Rights Day, the United Nations High Commissioner for Human Rights, Zeid bin Ra'ad al-Hussein, stated that:

> 2016 has been a disastrous year for human rights across the globe ... If the growing erosion of the carefully constructed system of human rights and rule of law continues to gather momentum, ultimately everyone will suffer.

While the African regional system has a range of institutions to address issues of peace and security as well as human rights problems, they are not having the necessary impact to avert the problems that exist. While it is true that institutions such as the Peace and Security Council, the African Commission on Human and Peoples' Rights, the African Court on Human and Peoples' Rights, the African Peer Review Mechanism and the African Committee on the Rights of the Child, as well as the various institutions in the sub-regional systems, are having some effect, many are not functioning, some are not functioning very well, some are under attack and some even have been dismembered (Sarkin 2016a). The role of these institutions needs urgent review in order to allow them to have greater impact on the situations occurring across the region (Sarkin 2019). While some of the problems concern budgeting and organisational matters, issues of independence and control by the AU dramatically affect the functioning of many of these bodies.

8. RESOURCES AND CAPACITY

A concern that may stymie the role of the reformed African Court is resources. Already the AU is having difficulty supporting its various institutions. The reason noted for the merger between the African Court of Justice and the ACHPR, as noted by the AU, was as follows: 'Underlying this decision was the concern at the growing number of AU institutions, which the AU could not afford to support.'[61] Thus, the funding needs of the two courts were seen to be a critical issue in relation to why the merger was needed. However, when the revised and revamped Court with criminal jurisdiction begins to function, it will be expensive to run. This is a perennial problem for such institutions (Ingadottir and Romano 2003). Underfunding has always been a problem for the institutions of the AU (Jalloh 2015: 6). The AU already has difficulties adequately funding its other institutions, especially the Commission and the Court. These institutions are underfunded and the Court is dependent on outside funding for various activities because its member states have for many years remained in arrears with their fees. Funding comes from the EU, the Deutsche Gesellschaft für Internationale Zusammenarbeit GmbH (GIZ) and the Macarthur Foundation, among others.

Adding a second and third chamber to the African Court is problematic because of the many additional costs that will come with it (Abraham 2015: 11). The budget is a major limitation on the work of the Court (Rao 1999: 404–406). The ACHPR had a budget of US$9 million; however, the cost for a single international criminal trial is estimated to be US$20,000,000 (du Plessis 2012),

61 http://en.african-court.org/index.php/faqs/frequent-questions#Criminal.

which is double the amount approved for the annual budget of the African Court and the Commission. However, the cost of prosecuting former Liberian President Charles Taylor at the Sierra Leonean Special Court was US$50 million (Abass 2013a). Abbas states that the cost of prosecuting one international crime could drain the annual budget of the Court. Huge financial resources are needed to bring such cases and whether Court will have these resources remains unknown, particularly when it is understood that groups that often fund such types of cases and these types of institution are unlikely to do so because they do not support what the Court will do.

Another problem that needs to be taken into account in the potential move to a court with three chambers is the capacity of the Court. This is a problem for many such courts (Cartier and Hoss 2014: 714–715). Already, with its relatively smaller workload, the Court has a backlog of cases. In fact, this backlog has been growing as more and more cases are filed before it. By the end of June 2016, the Court had received 101 cases, of which only 27 had been finalised. Significantly, the staff component of the Court is very small, with very few lawyers supporting the judges; by contrast, the ICC has over 1,300 staff members. The reformed African Court will need vast numbers of staff, especially those skilled and experienced in criminal law and criminal trials.

For these reasons, some ask whether the decision to cover international crimes is too ambitious and beyond the capacity of the African Court. In this regard, the number of judges assigned to the Court is low in order for it to function properly. While it depends on how many cases come to the Court and how many cases it decides to hear, if it is going to make an impact, it will need a bigger roster of judges in order to be able to adjudicate an increased number of cases.

The shortage of judges will more likely affect the international crimes section. While finding judges, prosecutors, investigators and defence counsel who possess the necessary expertise in and experience of international crimes to deal with all the crimes under the Court's jurisdiction will be difficult, there are such people who have experience from the other tribunals and elsewhere.

There is also concern about the political will that is needed in order for the Malabo Protocol and the Court that should come from it to succeed. There are already many worrying indications of states lacking the commitment to hold individuals accountable for international crimes. This fact is compounded by the general lack of signatures and ratifications to the Protocol.

9. CONCLUSION

At the end of the day, whether the move to give the African Court criminal jurisdiction is an African solution to an African problem depends on what the problem is. If the problem is the high level of human rights abuses as well as other types of crimes that are occurring, then the Court can play a part of the solution to this. However, if the allegation is that the Court is being reformed for political reasons then the Court may not be the solution to the problem. This is because the move to give the African Court criminal jurisdiction seemingly arises out of the political needs of the AU and African states that are no longer enamoured with the ICC (Nmehielle 2014). The expansion of the Court to deal with crimes may in fact be a subterfuge to address the criticism that when African states leave the ICC, they do so not because they are uncommitted to international justice, but rather because of their concerns with the way in which the ICC is being run. The establishment of the Court can be used to argue that the AU is committed to criminal justice and that African solutions are being used to deal with the needs of international criminal justice, which until now have been biased against Africans. If the Court is being reformed for political reasons, then its role actually will be limited.

Despite the problems that the new reformed African Court with criminal jurisdiction will face, there are potential benefits. Because of the massive human rights problems on the continent, there is a role that a regional criminal court can play in reducing these problems. Respect for human rights on the African continent needs to be improved dramatically. Many rights are regularly violated. The African human rights system, with its component parts, including the African Court, has an important role to play in promoting respect for rights across the continent. A criminal court can support this.

The reformed Court, if and when it comes into operation, which may still be a long way off, ought to be given a chance to play a key role in the fight against impunity that exists in Africa. Rather than trying to oppose the Court, a variety of international, regional and domestic role players could see the Court as a potential ally in the fight against impunity and accountability in Africa. The Court should be seen as another tool in the arsenal of international justice. For that reason, it could play a positive role if it chooses and takes on cases that promote accountability and the rule of law. This is crucially important as the Global Peace Index (GPI) indicates that the world has become less peaceful in more recent times, interrupting the increasing trend towards peace around the world. As a result, many more crimes and human rights violations are being committed. There is great inequality in levels of peace globally. The most peaceful countries are steadily improving their situation, while the least peaceful states continue to deteriorate, with increasing levels of violence and conflict. This has a particular bearing on Africa, where significantly more states are less peaceful and have many more violations (Williams 2008).

While the African Charter promotes human rights, it is not really understood or known about sufficiently on the continent. The rights it contains are not really respected, especially by certain states. The role of the Court is important in this sense, regardless of whether or not it has criminal jurisdiction. This is because part of the role of the Court is to promote respect in different ways.

The main one of these is through its judgments. While a judgment is relevant for the applicants and the case against the state it is brought against, its application has much wider effect. The decisions of the Court are also meant to educate others about what rights there are in Africa, what those rights mean in practice and what states are meant to do in relation to their obligations to these human rights. The Court interprets what the African Charter means in practice, what the duties of states are and how, legally speaking, states need to comply with the standards contained in the various human rights instruments to which they are subject. Thus, the Court must see each case as not only applying narrowly to the facts of the case in question, but also how the rights in the case need to be applied in all African countries. Thus, the Court should use judgments as an educational means for all Africans and, in particular, states. The reparations components of the judgments are not only relevant to the parties of the case, but are also a means to educate others about what will happen if rights are not respected. They are a way to acknowledge the harm suffered by victims and a means to allow these victims to be assisted in terms of dealing with what has occurred. Reparations are in part a way to punish a state for non-compliance – a means to try and ensure that states do not commit human rights abuses. Failing this, state will have to pay reparations. Thus, reparations are at times awarded in order to act as a deterrent so that in future, there will be a reluctance to commit such acts in the knowledge that there could be consequences to the state for doing so. Thus, finding a state responsible for violations is one way to prevent further violations, as states do not want to be found liable and thus the potential of being named can be a deterrent for some countries that are concerned about their reputation.

BIBLIOGRAPHY

Abass, A. (2013a) 'The Proposed International Criminal Jurisdiction for the African Court: Some Problematical Aspects', *Netherlands International Law Review* 60(1): 27–50.

Abass, A. (2013b) 'Prosecuting International Crimes in Africa: Rationale, Prospects and Challenges', *European Journal of International Law* 24(3): 933–946.

Abass, A. (2016) 'A Historical and Political Background to the Malabo Protocol' in G. Werle and M. Vormbaum (eds), *The African Criminal Court. A Commentary on the Malobo Protocol.* The Hague: T.M.C. Asser Press. International Criminal Justice Series 10, 11–28.

Abatan, E. and Spies, Y. (2016) 'African Solutions to African Problems?. The AU, R2P and Cote d'Ivoire', *South African Journal of International Affairs* 23(1): 21–38.

Abe, O. and Ordor, A. (2018) 'Addressing Human Rights Concerns in the Extractive Resource Industry in Sub-Saharan Africa using the Lens of Article 46(c) of the Malabo Protocol', *Law and Development Review* 11(2): 843–878.

Abraham, G. (2015) 'Africa's Evolving Continental Court Structures: At the Crossroads?' *Occasional Paper 209*, Governance and APRM Programme.

African Court on HPR 'Frequently Asked Questions: Does Court Deal Criminal Matters?', http://en.african-court.org/index.php/faqs/frequent-questions#Criminal.

African Union (2013) AU Assembly Decision on Africa's relationship with the International Criminal, Oct. 12, 2013. Ext/Assembly/AU/Dec.1–4.

African Union, Report of the Committee of Eminent African Jurists on the Case of Hissène Habré, submitted to the Assembly of the African Union, Ordinary Session, July 2006 para 26.

African Union, Annex to the Statute of the African Court of Justice and Human and Peoples Rights.

African Union, Article 46Abis protocol on amendments to the protocol on the statute of the African Court of Justice and Human Rights, http://www.au.int/en/sites/default/files/PROTOCOL%20ON%20AMENDMENTS%20TO%20THE%20PROTOCOL%20ON%20THE%20AFRICAN%20COURT%20-%20EN_0.pdf.

Akinseye-George, Y. (2001/2002) 'New Trends in African Human Rights Law: Prospects of an African Court of Human Rights', *University of Miami International and Comparative Law Review* 10: 159–175.

Alford, R.P. (2000) 'The Proliferation of International Courts and Tribunals: International Adjudication in Ascendance', *Am. Soc'y. Int'l L. Proc.* 94: 160–165.

Alter, K.J. (2013) 'The Multiple Roles of International Courts and Tribunals: Enforcement, Dispute Settlement, Constitutional and Administrative Review' in J.L. Dunoff and M.A. Pollack (eds), *International Law and International Relations: Synthesizing Insights from Interdisciplinary Scholarship*. Cambridge: Cambridge University Press, pp. 345–370.

Alter, K.J. (2014) *The New Terrain of International Law: Courts, Politics, Rights*. Princeton: Princeton University Press.

Alter, K.J., Gathii, J.T. and Helfer, L.R. (2016) 'Backlash against International Courts in West, East and Southern Africa: Causes and Consequences', *European Journal of International Law* 27: 293–328.

Alter, K.J., Helfer, L. and McAllister, J.R. (2013) 'A New International Human Rights Court for West Africa: The ECOWAS Community Court of Justice', *American Journal of International Law* 107(4): 737–779.

Alter, K.J. and Hooghe, L. (2016) 'Regional Dispute Settlement Systems' in T.J. Börzel and T. Risse (eds), *Oxford Handbook of Comparative Regionalism*. Oxford: Oxford University Press, pp. 538–558.

Amnesty International (2015) *Amnesty International World Report 2014/15*.

Amnesty International (2016) *Malabo Protocol, Legal and Institutional Implications of the Merged And Expanded African Court*, http://www.refworld.org/pdfid/56a9ddcf4.pdf.

Amnesty International (2017) *Counting Gains, Filling Gaps: Strengthening African Union's Response to Human Rights Violations Committed in Conflict Situations*.

Asare, B.E. and Sekyere, P. (2016) 'An Appraisal of Institutions of Global Governance: The Case of the African Human Rights System', *Journal of Pan African Studies* 9(1): 221–241.

Bederman, D.J. (2007) 'Diversity and Permeability in Transnational Governance', *Emory Law Journal* 57: 201–231.

Berry, D.S. (2018) 'Enforcement of Regional Economic Integration in the Caribbean: Treaty Enforcement by the Caribbean Court of Justice and Regimes for Enhanced Co-operation' in P. Butler, E. Lein and R. Salim (eds), *Integration and International Dispute Resolution in Small States*. New York: Springer International Publishing, pp. 61–86.

Buergenthal, T. (2001) 'Proliferation of International Courts and Tribunals: Is It Good or Bad?', *Leiden Journal of International Law* 14(2): 267–275.

Burke-White, W.W. (2003) 'Regionalization of International Criminal Law Enforcement: A Preliminary Exploration', *Texas International Law Journal* 38: 729–762.

Campbell, K. (2018) 'Building National and Regional Accountability for Conflict Related Sexual Violence: From Prosecutions in the Former Yugoslavia to the African Court of Justice and Human and Peoples' Rights', *International Human Rights Law Review* 7(2): 201–224.

Cartier, S. and Hoss, C. (2014) 'The Role of Registries and Legal Secretariats in International Judicial Institutions' in C.P.R. Romano, K.J. Alter and Y. Shany (eds), *The Oxford Handbook of International Adjudication*. Oxford: Oxford University Press, pp. 714–15.

Clarke, K.M., Knottnerus, A.S. and de Volder, E. (2016) *Africa and the ICC*. Cambridge: Cambridge University Press.

Daly, T.G. and Wiebusch, M. (2018) 'The African Court on Human and Peoples' Rights: Mapping Resistance against a Young Court', *International Journal of Law in Context* 14(2): 294–313.

De la Rasilla del Moral, I. (2017) 'An International Terrorism Court in the Age of International Adjudication', *Asian Yearbook of Human Rights and Humanitarian Law* 1: 76–108.

Dembinski, M. and Peters, D. (2019) 'The Power of Justice: How Procedural Justice Concerns Affect the Legitimacy of International Institutions', *Global Governance: A Review of Multilateralism and International Organizations* 25(1): 149–170.

Dinokopila, R.B. (2017) 'The Impact of Regional and Sub-regional Courts and Tribunals on Constitutional Adjudication in Africa' in C.M. Fombad (ed.), *Constitutional Adjudication in Africa*. Oxford: Oxford University Press, pp. 294–313.

Du Plessis, M. (2012) *Implications of the AU Decision to Give the African Court Jurisdiction over International Crimes*. Pretoria: Institute for International Security Studies.

Du Plessis, M. (2014) 'A New Regional International Criminal Court for Africa?', *SACJ* 2: 199–209.

Evans, M. and Murray, R. (2008) *The African Charter on Human and Peoples' Rights: The System in Practice 1986–2006*. Cambridge: Cambridge University Press.

Fombad, C.M. and Kibet, E. (2018) 'The Rule of Law in Sub-Saharan Africa: Reflections on Promises, Progress, Pitfalls and Prospects', *African Human Rights Law Journal* 18(1): 205–212.

Galvao Teles, P. (2017) 'The ICC at the Centre of an International Criminal Justice System: Current Challenges', *e-journal of International Relations* 8(1): 61–73.

Gathii, J. (2014) 'Mission Creep or a Search for Relevance: The East African Court of Justice's Human Rights Strategy', *Duke Journal of Comparative and International Law*, 24: 249–296.

Goldsmith, J., and Levinson, D. (2009) 'Law for States: International Law, Constitutional Law, Public Law', *Harvard Law Review* 122(7): 1791–1868.

Hafetz, J. (2017) 'Fairness, Legitimacy, and Selection Decisions in International Criminal Law', *Vanderbilt Journal of Transnational Law* 50: 1133–1171.

Hall, C.K. (2010) 'The Danger of Selective Justice: All Cases Involving Crimes under International Law Should Be Investigated and the Suspects, When There is Sufficient Admissible Evidence, Prosecuted' in M. Bergsmo (ed.), *Criteria for Prioritizing and Selecting Core International Crimes Cases*. Oslo: International Peace Research Institute (PRIO), pp. 171–181.

Happold, M. and Radović, R. (2018) 'The ECOWAS Court of Justice as an Investment Tribunal', *Journal of World Investment and Trade* 19(1): 95–117.

Hofmann, A. (2018) 'Resistance against the Court of Justice of the European Union', *International Journal of Law in Context* 14(2): 258–274.

Huneeus, A. (2013) 'International Criminal Law by Other Means: The Quasi-criminal Jurisdiction of Human Rights Courts', *American Journal of International Law* 107: 1–44.

Ingadottir, T. and Romano, C.P.R. (2003) 'The Financing of the International Criminal Court' in T. Ingadottir (ed.), *The International Criminal Court: Recommendation on Policy and Practice: Financing, Victims, Judges and Immunities*. New York: Transnational Publishing Inc., pp. 47–111.

Jalloh, C.C. (2015) 'International Justice, Reconciliation and Peace in Africa', *CODESRIA Policy Briefs* 1: 1–12.

Jalloh, C.C. and Bantekas, I. (eds) (2017) *The International Criminal Court and Africa*. Oxford: Oxford University Press.

Kane, I. and Motala, A.C. (2009) 'Creation of a New Court of Justice and Human Rights' in M. Evans and R. Murray (eds), *The African Charter on Human and Peoples' Rights: The System in Practice 1986–2006*. Cambridge: Cambridge University Press, pp. 406–440.

Kingsbury, B. (2012) 'International Courts: Uneven Judicialization in Global Order' in J. Crawford and M. Koskenniemi (eds), *Cambridge Companion to International Law*. Cambridge: Cambridge University Press, pp. 203–227.

Madsen, M.R., Cebulak, P. and Wiebusch, M. (2018) 'Backlash against International Courts: Explaining the Forms and Patterns of Resistance to International Courts', *International Journal of Law in Context* 14(2): 197–220.

Mälksoo, L. (2016) 'Russia's Constitutional Court Defies the European Court of Human Rights: Constitutional Court of the Russian Federation Judgment of 14 July 2015, no. 21-П/2015', *European Constitutional Law Review* 12: 377–395.

Malabo Protocol, adopted 27 June 2014, https://www.au.int/web/en/treaties/protocol-amendments-protocol-statute-african-court-justice-and-human-rights.

Mangu, A.M. (2018) 'The Role of the African Union and Regional Economic Communities in the Implementation of the African Charter on Democracy, Elections and Governance', *African Journal of Democracy and Governance* 5(3): 125–152.

Manirakiza, P. (2016) 'Insecurity Implications of Unconstitutional Changes of Government in Africa: From Military to Constitutional Coups', *Journal of Military and Strategic Studies* 17(2): 86–106.

Marks, S.P. (2004) 'The Hissène Habré Case: The Law and Politics of Universal Jurisdiction' in S. Macedo (ed.), *Universal Jurisdiction: National Courts and the Prosecution of Serious Crimes under International Law*. Philadelphia: University of Pennsylvania Press, pp. 131–167.

Mazzeschi, R.P. (2003) 'Reparation Claims by Individuals for State Breaches of Humanitarian Law and Human Rights: An Overview', *Journal of International Criminal Justice* 1: 339–347.

Mbengue, M.M. and McClellan, K. (2018) 'The ICC and Africa: Should the Latter Remain Engaged?' in Z. Yihdego, M.B. Hailu and F. Merso (eds), *Ethiopian Yearbook of International Law 2017*. New York: Springer, pp. 187–203.

McGoldrick, D. (2017) 'Affording states a margin of appreciation: comparing the European Court of Human rights and the Inter-American Court of Human Rights' in C. Buckley, A. Donald. and P. Leach (eds), *Towards Convergence in International Human Rights Law.* Leiden: Brill Nijhoff. pp. 323–365.

Meron, T. (2018) 'Closing the Accountability Gap: Concrete Steps toward Ending Impunity for Atrocity Crimes', *American Journal of International Law* 112(3): 433–451.

Mills, K. and Bloomfield, A. (2018) 'African Resistance to the International Criminal Court: Halting the Advance of the Anti-impunity Norm', *Review of International Studies* 44(1): 101–127.

Mngomezulu, B.R. (2018) 'Reflecting on the Pan-African Parliament: Prospects and Challenges', *Journal of African Union Studies* 7(2): 45–62.

Murithi, T. (2014) 'Between Political Justice and Judicial Politics: Charting a Way Forward for the African Union and the International Criminal Court' in G. Werle, L. Fernandez and M. Vormbaum, (eds), *Africa and the International Criminal Court*. The Hague: T.M.C. Asser Press/Springer, pp. 179–193.

Murray, R. and Long, D. (eds) (2015) *The Implementation of the Findings of the African Commission on Human and Peoples' Rights*. Cambridge: Cambridge University Press.

Mutua, M.W. (2010) *The International Criminal Court in Africa: Challenges and Opportunities.* Norwegian Peacebuilding Centre NOREF Working Paper.

Naldi, G.J. and Magliveras, K.D. (1998) 'Reinforcing the African System of Human Rights: The Protocol on the Establishment of a Regional Court of Human and Peoples' Rights', *Netherlands Quarterly of Human Rights* 16(4): 431–456.

Nel, M. and Ezrom Sibiya, V. (2017) 'Withdrawal from the International Criminal Court: Does Africa Have an Alternative?', *African Journal on Conflict Resolution* 17(1): 79–103.

Nmehielle, V.O. (2014) 'Saddling the New African Regional Human Rights Court with International Criminal Jurisdiction: Innovative, Obstructive, Expedient', *African Journal of Legal Studies* 7(1): 7–42.

O'Donohue, J. (2013) 'Financing the International Criminal Court', *International Criminal Law Review* 13: 269–296.

Oehm, F. (2018) 'From Nuremberg to Malabo: A Re-evaluation of the Tradition of Impunity of Economic Actors in International Criminal Law' in J. Nicholson (ed.), *Strengthening the Validity of International Criminal Tribunals*. Leiden: Brill, pp. 152–178.

Okafor, O.C. (2007) *The African Human Rights System, Activist Forces, and International Institutions.* Cambridge: Cambridge University Press.

Peter, C.M. (1993) 'The Proposed African Court of Justice: Jurisprudential, Procedural, Enforcement Problems and Beyond', *East African Journal of Peace and Human Rights* 1(2): 117–136.

Possi, A. (2017) 'It is Better That Ten Guilty Persons Escape Than That One Innocent Suffer: The African Court on Human and Peoples' Rights and Fair Trial Rights in Tanzania', *African Human Rights Yearbook* 1: 311–336.

Possi, A. (2018) 'An Appraisal of the Functioning and Effectiveness of the East African Court of Justice', *Potchefstroom Electronic Law Journal/Potchefstroomse Elektroniese Regsblad* 21(1): 2–42.

Ransdell, J. (2017) 'Power of the Purse: A Macro-survey of Recent Financing at International Criminal Courts and Tribunals with Special Emphasis on the International Criminal Court', *International Judicial Monitor*. Washington DC: International Judicial Academy.

Rao, S.R. (1999) 'Financing of the Court, Assembly of States Parties and the Preparatory Commission' in R.S. Lee (ed.), *The International Criminal Court: The Making of the Rome Statute*. The Hague: Kluwer Law, pp. 399–420.

Reinold, T. (2019) 'When is More More? The Proliferation of International Courts and Their Impact on the Rule of Law in Africa', *International Journal of Human Rights* 1–19.

Rikhof, J. (2014) 'Prosecution of International Crimes: A Historical and Empirical Overview', *Bergen Journal of Criminal Law and Criminal Justice* 2(2): 108–140.

Romano, C.P.R. (2011) 'A Taxonomy of International Rule of Law Institutions', *Journal of International Dispute Settlement* 2(1): 241–277.

Romano, C.P.R., Nollkaemper, A. and Kleffner, J.K. (2004) 'Preface' in C.P.R. Romano, A. Nollkaemper and J.K. Kleffner (eds), *Internationalized Criminal Courts and Tribunals*. New York: Oxford University Press, p. ix.

Sana, A.H. (2018) *Informing the Malabo Protocol Crime of Human Trafficking by Determining the Meaning of 'Appropriate and Effective Measures' under Article 4(2)(g) of the Maputo Protocol*. Doctoral dissertation, Strathmore University.

Sarkin, J. (2009a) 'The Origins of International Criminal Law: Its Connection to and Convergence with Other Branches of International Law', *Hague Justice Journal* 4(1): 5–41.

Sarkin, J. (2009b) 'The Role of the United Nations, the African Union and Africa's Sub-regional Organizations in Dealing with Africa's Human Rights Problems: Connecting Humanitarian Intervention and the Responsibility to Protect', *Journal of African Law* 53(1): 1–33.

Sarkin, J. (2011) 'The African Commission on Human and Peoples' Rights and the Future African Court of Justice and Human Rights: Comparative Lessons from the European Court of Human Rights', *South African Journal of International Affairs* 18(3): 281–293.

Sarkin, J. (2016a) 'A Critique of the Decision of the African Commission on Human and Peoples' Rights Permitting the Demolition of the SADC Tribunal: Politics versus Economics and Human Rights', *African Journal of International and Comparative Law* 24(2): 215–241.

Sarkin, J. (2016b) 'Is the African Union's Position on Non-indifference Making a Difference?: The Implementation of The Responsibility to Protect (R2P) in Africa in Theory and Practice', *Journal of African Union Studies* 5(1): 5–37.

Sarkin, J. (2017) 'Understanding the Changing Relationship of South Africa and the International Criminal Court: Towards a Culture of Greater Impunity in Africa?', *Revista Themis* XVIII(32): 7–33.

Sarkin, J. (2018) 'The Need to Reform the Political Role of the African Union (AU) in Promoting Democracy and Human Rights in Domestic States: Making States More Accountable and Less Able to Avoid Scrutiny at the United Nations and at the AU, Using Swaziland to Spotlight the Issues', *African Journal of International and Comparative Law* 26(1): 84–107.

Sarkin, J. (2019) 'Why the Role of the African Commission on Human and Peoples' Rights in Advancing Democratic Principles and Human Rights in African Countries Needs to

Be Reformed: An Examination Using the Lens of Swaziland/eSwatini', *Southern African Public Law* 34(2): 1–56.

Sarkin, J. and Almeida, J. (2019) 'Understanding the Activation of the Crime of Aggression at the International Criminal Court: Progress and Pitfalls', *Wisconsin International Law Review* 36(3): 518–551.

Schabas, W.A. (2015) 'Selecting Situations and Cases' in C. Stahn (ed.), *The Law and Practice of the International Criminal Court*. Oxford: Oxford University Press, pp. 365–381.

Sikkink, K. (2011) *The Justice Cascade: How Human Rights Prosecutions are Changing World Politics*. New York: WW Norton and Company.

Sirleaf, M.V.S. (2016) 'Regionalism, Regime Complexes, and the Crisis in International Criminal Justice', *Columbia Journal of Transnational Law* 54: 699–778.

Sirleaf, M.V.S. (2017) 'The African Justice Cascade and the Malabo Protocol', *International Journal of Transitional Justice* 11(1): 71–91.

Slye, R.C. (2017) 'Reflections on Africa and International Criminal Law' in *The Nuremberg Principles in Non-western Societies: A Reflection on their Universality, Legitimacy and Application*. Nuremburg: International Nuremberg Principles Academy.

Smeulers, A., Weerdesteijn, M. and Hola, B. (2015) 'The Selection of Situations by the ICC: An Empirically Based Evaluation of the OTP's Performance', *International Criminal Law Review* 15: 1–39.

Ssekandi, F. and Tesfay, N. (2017) 'Engendered Discontent: The International Criminal Court in Africa', *Geographic Journal of International Affairs* 18: 1–27.

Ssenyonjo, M. (2013a) 'Direct Access to the African Court on Human and Peoples' Rights by Individuals and Non-governmental Organisations: An Overview of the Emerging Jurisprudence of the African Court 2008–2012', *International Human Rights Law Review* 2(1): 17–56.

Ssenyonjo, M. (2013b) 'The Rise of the African Union Opposition to the International Criminal Court's Investigations and Prosecutions of African Leaders', *International Criminal Law Review* 13(2): 385–428.

Swigart, L. (2017) 'International Justice in Africa: Defining Authority and Localizing the Global', *iCourts Working Paper Series* 86: 1–35.

Tiba, F.K. (2015) 'Regional International Criminal Courts: An Idea Whose Time Has Come', *Cardozo Journal of Conflict Resolution* 17: 521–549.

Teitel, R. (2015) 'Transitional Justice and Judicial Activism: A Right to Accountability?', *Cornell International Law Journal* 48(2): 385–422.

Udombana, N.J. (2000) 'Towards the African Court on Human and Peoples' Rights: Better Late Than Never', *Yale Human Rights and Development Law Journal* 3: 45–111.

Van der Mei, A.P. (2005) 'The New African Court on Human and Peoples' Rights: Towards an Effective Protection Mechanism for Africa?', *Leiden Journal of International Law* 18(1): 113–129.

Van der Wilt, H.G. (2016) 'Expanding Criminal Responsibility in Transnational and International Organised Crime', *Groningen Journal of International Law* 4(1): 1–9.

Vilmer, J.B.J. (2016) 'The African Union and the International Criminal Court: Counteracting the Crisis', *International Affairs* 92(6): 1319–1342.

Williams, P.D. (2008) 'Keeping the Peace in Africa: Why African Solutions are Not Enough', *Carnegie Council for Ethics in International Affairs* 22(3): 309–329.

Williams, P.D. (2014) 'Reflections on the Evolving African Peace and Security Architecture', *Journal of African Security* 7(3): 147–162.
Zschirnt, S. (2018) 'Locking in Human Rights in Africa: Analysing State Accession to the African Court on Human and Peoples' Rights', *Human Rights Review* 19: 97–119.

CASE LAW

Alex Thomas v. United Republic of Tanzania. Judgment of 20 November 2015.
Bulacio v. Argentina (Merits, Reparations and Costs). Judgment of 18 September 2003.
Christopher Jonas v. United Republic of Tanzania. Judgment of 28 September 2017 (011/2015) [2017] AFCHPR 25.
Lohe Issa Konaté v. Burkina Faso. Judgment on reparations of 3 June 2016.
Loizidou v. Turkey (preliminary objections), ECtHR [GC], 23 March 1995, no. 15318/89.
Mohamed Abubakari v. United Republic of Tanzania. Judgment of 3 June 2016 (007/2013) [2013] AFCHPR 35.

HEAD OF STATE IMMUNITY IN THE AFRICAN CONTEXT

Godfrey Mupanga

1. INTRODUCTION

The position of state immunities since the *Pinochet* case[1] is one of the most confusing issues of customary international law. In recent times, two developments have thrown the law on state immunities into confusion and now threaten to turn the law on its head. These are the developments in international law on universal jurisdiction for crimes of international concern and the proliferation of regional and international judicial bodies with extensive jurisdiction over individuals.

1 *R v. Bow Street Metropolitan Stipendiary Magistrate ex parte Pinochet Ugarte (No. 3)* [2000] 1 AC 147, [1999] 2 All ER 97, [1999] 2 WLR 827.

It is well known now that the African Union (AU) has been on a collision course with the European Union (EU) over the use of universal jurisdiction by EU member states to bring to justice in their domestic courts African state officials accused of atrocity crimes in their home states. It is also well known now that since the International Criminal Court (ICC) issued a warrant for the arrest of Sudan's President, Omar al-Bashir, in 2009, the AU has raised concerns with the ICC over the perceived targeting of African state officials for prosecution. The AU has cited the immunity of an incumbent head of state as a possible bar to the prosecution of President al-Bashir by the ICC.

Mixing up perceived abuse of the principle of universal jurisdiction by European states to harass African leaders with the perceived targeting of African leaders by the ICC, the AU issued several resolutions, first asking the EU states to reconsider their employment of universal jurisdiction and the United Nations (UN) Security Council to exercise its powers under Article 16 of the Rome Statute to defer the prosecution of President al-Bashir (Jalloh 2010). The EU pointed out that the exercise of universal jurisdiction was a matter for its individual Member States and not for the regional body.[2] The UN Security Council, on the other hand, seems to have waved away the AU's request for a deferral of the case against President al-Bashir in a manner that the AU regarded as rather contemptuous.

The UN Security Council seems to have taken the same view with respect to the request for the deferral of the case against Kenyan President Uhuru Kenyatta and his deputy, William Samoei Ruto.[3] In later resolutions, as relationships between the AU on the one hand and the ICC and the Security Council on the other deteriorated, the AU increased its demands from Article 16 deferrals and suspension of the trials to a complete withdrawal of the Security Council referral of the situation in Darfur and a complete termination of the cases against President al-Bashir and Vice-President William Ruto.[4]

Clearly, it is the UN Security Council and certain European states that the AU had issues with. With the Security Council, it was the seemingly dismissive manner in which it dealt with the request for the deferral of the cases against Presidents al-Bashir and Uhuru Kenyatta and Vice-President Ruto that should have angered the AU. Yet the AU seems to have held this anger against the ICC. At an extraordinary session in October 2013, the AU Assembly expressed

2 'AU–EU Technical Ad Hoc Expert Group on the Principle of Universal Jurisdiction', Council of the European Union, 8672/1/09 REV 1, Brussels, 16 April 2009.

3 'Security Council Resolution Seeking Deferral of Kenyan Leaders' Trial Fails to Win Adoption, with 7 Voting in Favour, 8 Abstaining', Security Council, SC/11179, 7060th Meeting, 15 November 2013.

4 'Decision on the Progress Report of the Commission on the Implementation of Previous Decisions on the International Criminal Court', Doc. Assembly/AU/18(XX1V), Assembly/AU/Dec.547(XXIV), Assembly of the Union, Twenty-Fourth Ordinary Session, 30–31 January 2015, Addis Ababa, Ethiopia, para. 17(d) and (e).

concern over what it regarded as the 'politicisation and misuse of indictments against African leaders by [the] ICC'.[5] Furthermore, the report by the AU Commission on the implementation of the decisions of the AU Assembly on the ICC is quite revealing in terms of the extent of the anger that the AU directed at the ICC.[6] Even though the ICC was established to address individual criminal responsibility, the AU felt that 'Africa is being treated unfairly at the ICC'.[7] Consequently, the AU took the position 'to fight it [the ICC] to address the problem'.[8] But in doing so, the AU, like the proverbial grasshopper in the African fable, kicked its victim and lost its legs in the process.

In an attempt to ground its concerns and its fight against the ICC in law, the AU nailed its colours to the mast of head of state immunity. The AU also decided to take matters into its own hands by extending the jurisdiction of the African Court on Justice and Human and Peoples' Rights to cover crimes of international concern. Therefore, at its extraordinary session in October 2013, the AU Assembly decided, among other things, that 'to safeguard the constitutional order, stability and, integrity of Member States, no charges shall be commenced or continued before any International Court or Tribunal against any serving AU Head of State or Government or anybody acting or entitled to act in such capacity during their term of office'.[9] The AU Assembly also resolved to ask its member states that are parties to the Rome Statute to push for debate at the Assembly of States Parties the matter of indictment by the ICC of sitting African heads of state and government, and the effect that this phenomenon has on peace and stability in the continent.[10]

The resolutions of the AU Assembly over the AU's relationship with the ICC and their wording betray the anger and resentment that the AU has over the application of international criminal justice. The ICC has been the unfortunate target of this. The fight that the AU started with the global international criminal justice system represented by the ICC poses a threat to the progressive development of customary international law on state immunities. Since the decision of the House of Lords in the case of General Augusto Pinochet, customary international law on state immunities has been developing in a manner that fits with the global fight against impunity. For its part, the AU itself has publicly

5 'Decision on Africa's Relationship with the International Criminal Court (ICC)', Ext/Assembly/AU/Dec.1(Oct. 2013), Extraordinary Session of the Assembly of the African Union, 12 October 2013, Addis Ababa, Ethiopia.

6 Progress Report of the Commission on the Implementation of the Decisions of the Assembly of the African Union on the International Criminal Court, Executive Council, Twenty-Eighth Ordinary Session, 23–28 January 2016, EX.CL/952(XXVIII).

7 Ibid.

8 Ibid.

9 Ibid., para. 10(i).

10 Ibid., para. 10(vii).

displayed an aversion to impunity.[11] As the only regional organisation whose constitution views sovereignty as consisting more of responsibilities than of privileges and specifically enshrines the responsibility to protect, the general trajectory of the AU itself has been quite positive when it comes to fighting impunity for atrocity crimes.[12]

2. THE MALABO PROTOCOL

It was with much animosity and resentment of the emerging international criminal justice system, anchored by the ICC, and through a convoluted and dizzying process of protocols amending other amendment protocols of existing instruments, that in June 2014 the AU wound up with the Protocol on Amendments to the Protocol on the Statute of the African Court of Justice and Human and Peoples' Rights (hereinafter 'the Malabo Protocol').[13]

The Protocol on the Statute of the African Court of Justice and Human Rights merges the African Court of Justice, which is established under the Constitutive Act as an organ of the AU[14] but has hitherto not yet become functional, with the African Court on Human and Peoples' Rights,[15] which has been functional since November 2006. Effectively, therefore, the merged Court has not yet been established. The Protocol on the Statute of the African Court of Justice and Human and Peoples' Rights, which was adopted in Malabo, Equatorial Guinea in June 2014, seeks to expand the jurisdiction of the merged African Court of Justice and Human and Peoples' Rights to include a long list of international and transnational crimes.

Basically, the expanded African Court has jurisdiction over more offences than the ICC and all the ad hoc tribunals before it. It includes up to 14 crimes, most of which have never been prosecuted before by an international criminal

---

11 A permanent feature in all of the AU resolutions requesting UN Security Council deferral is the recitation of the AU's 'commitment to fight impunity in conformity with the provisions of Article 4(h) of the Constitutive Act of the African Union'. See African Union, *Decisions, Resolutions and Declarations of the Assembly of the Union*, Assembly/Au/Dec.397 (XVIII), para. 2.

12 One of the principles of the AU recorded in art. 4(h) of the Constitutive Act is that the AU has the right 'to intervene in a Member State pursuant to a decision of the Assembly in respect of grave circumstances, namely: war crimes, genocide and crimes against humanity'.

13 The complicated process of amendments is summarised in a report of Amnesty International, *Legal and Institutional Implications of the Merged and Expanded African Court* (London: Amnesty International, 2016), https://www.amnesty.org/download/Documents/AFR0130632016ENGLISH.PDF.

14 Articles 5(1)(d) and 18 of the Constitutive Act of the African Union.

15 The African Court on Human and Peoples' Rights was established by the Protocol to the African Charter on Human and Peoples' Rights on the Establishment of the African Court on Human and Peoples' Rights.

tribunal. In addition to the commonly known war crimes, genocide and crimes against humanity, the expanded African Court will have the jurisdiction to try crimes that include unconstitutional change of government, mercenarism, corruption, money laundering, trafficking in persons, trafficking in drugs, trafficking in hazardous waste and illicit exploitation of natural resources. A major concern that has been expressed by many is that the Court is overloaded.

Clearly, one of the issues that the AU has with the ICC over the enforcement of international criminal law and with European states over the application of universal jurisdiction is the question of immunity for high-ranking government officials. The AU has expressed concerns that the prosecution of Presidents al-Bashir and Kenyatta might jeopardise the prospects of finding lasting peace in Sudan and Kenya. Consequently, in the Malabo Protocol, the AU decided to correct this problem by including a clause that provides immunity from prosecution to sitting heads of state or any individuals acting as such during their tenure. Article 46A *bis* of the Malabo Protocol provides that: 'No charges shall be commenced or continued before the Court against any serving African Union Head of State or Government, or anybody acting or entitled to act in such capacity, or other senior state officials based on their functions, during their tenure of office.'

This chapter attempts to analyse the immunity clause of the Malabo Protocol with a view to establishing whether the clause is consistent with customary international law and the organising principles of the AU.

2.1. DISSONANCE WITH THE OBJECTS AND PURPOSES OF STATE IMMUNITIES

The notion of sovereignty entails that a state has authority over the people, property and events within its territory (de Than and Shorts 2012). A state may exercise jurisdiction over the people, property and events within its territory. A state may also lawfully exercise jurisdiction over disputes brought to the state for adjudication by agreement of the parties (ibid.). As an exception to the exercise of jurisdiction, customary international law recognises that certain people, things and events are entitled to immunity from the enforcement of municipal laws.

All states are presumed to be equal and sovereign. Therefore, a state's dignity would be affronted if it were required to submit to the jurisdiction of the courts of another state. Consequently, historically, states were granted immunity from the jurisdiction of the courts of other states in both criminal and civil disputes. Immunity is based on the principle of international law *par in parem no habet imperium*, which entails that an equal has no dominion over an equal.

The principle is in accordance with the international system of the 'sovereign equality of all' states envisaged under Article 2(1) of the UN Charter.

In the beginning, customary international law recognised absolute immunity for all activities of the state. There were no circumstances whatsoever where a national court could sit in judgment on a legal issue involving a foreign state or its government. Such issues were akin to those issues that are regarded as 'non-justiciable'. Once a defendant in a criminal or civil case was identified as a foreign state or a government of a foreign state, no domestic court would have any competence to assert jurisdiction over the case. Any action against such defendants was automatically barred in all national courts.[16]

Cases that illustrate the early practice of absolute immunity include *The Schooner Exchange v. McFaddon*,[17] *Parlement Belge*[18] and *Porto Alexandre*,[19] among others. In *The Schooner Exchange* case, Chief Justice Marshall of the US Supreme Court stated: 'The full and absolute territorial jurisdiction being alike the attribute of every sovereign, and being incapable of conferring extraterritorial power, would not seem to contemplate foreign sovereigns nor their sovereign rights as objects. One sovereign being in no respect amenable to another.'[20] The *Parlement Belge* case involved a vessel that was the property of the King of Belgium. In the *Porto Alexandre* case, the vessel in question had been requisitioned by Portugal for public purposes. Although in both cases the vessels were also used for commercial activities, the courts upheld the vessels' immunity. In both cases, the principle that a sovereign state could not be impleaded under any circumstances whatsoever before the courts of other states was upheld.

In medieval times, the concept of sovereignty made no distinction between the state and the personal sovereign. The ruler and the state were synonymous, and sovereignty was regarded as a personalised concept (Hillier 1998). From this conceptualisation of personalised sovereignty, the notion of head of state immunity arose as a derivative of state immunity. Consequently, early notions of immunity tended to vest this privilege in the personal sovereign, whose right to rule was regarded as flowing from God, the ultimate sovereign.

The divine right of kings as God's earthly representatives gave birth to the conflation of ruler and state and the political absoluteness of monarchs, which in turn begat the notion of absolute immunity for states and heads of state. The decline of monarchies and the rise of democracy diminished personal sovereignty and drew a distinction between the ruler and the state. It is said

16 *The Porto Alexandre* (1920) 1 ILR 146.
17 *The Schooner Exchange v. McFaddon* (1812) 7 Cranch 116.
18 *Parlement Belge* (1880) 5 PD 197.
19 *Porto Alexandre*, above n 16.
20 *The Schooner Exchange v. McFaddon*, above n 17, 137.

that immunity attaches to the state; it is not an individual right. Immunity is only extended to the head of state or high-ranking state officials who are the personification of the state. The immunity attaching to the state can therefore be waived by the state.

Before discussing the different types of immunity recognised under international law, it is necessary to stress the distinction between immunity and the concept of non-justiciability (de Than and Shorts 2012). A non-justiciable issue is one over which domestic courts are incapable of asserting jurisdiction. As a result, no judicial proceedings may be brought in the domestic courts over a non-justiciable issue. For example, under the traditional 'Act of State' doctrine, domestic courts refrain from sitting in judgment on political issues about how a foreign state has acted within its own territory (Robertson 1999). Immunity, on the other hand, applies to situations where the domestic courts ordinarily have jurisdiction over the matter, but due to the identity of one of the parties, the courts are prevented from exercising that jurisdiction.

This distinction is important in trying to understand the genesis of immunity as it is spelt out in Article 46A *bis* of the Malabo Protocol. A proper reading of the early decisions of the AU on the prosecution of African heads of state and other senior government officials tended to reveal an understanding of this distinction. Early AU decisions do not seem to suggest that President al-Bashir could not be prosecuted due to the immunity that he was entitled to, but that the time was not opportune for the prosecution. The emphasis on the reference to its commitment to ending impunity shows that the AU acknowledges that immunity does not mean impunity. Consequently, the operative part of the AU decisions before the extraordinary session of October 2013 did not suggest a termination of the proceedings altogether. The operative paragraph merely suggested a suspension of the prosecution for a period of one year to allow for the peace process to take precedence during that time.[21]

It is important to keep in mind that from the foregoing discussion, it is clear that the purpose of immunity is to preserve the dignity of sovereign states. Sovereign equality protects the dignity of states by preventing equals from

[21] See, for example, Decision on the Report of the 2nd Meeting of States Parties to the Rome Statute on the International Criminal Court (ICC) Doc.Assembly/AU/8(XIV), adopted at the 14th Ordinary Session of the Assembly, Addis Ababa, Ethiopia, 2 February 2010; Decision on the Implementation of the Decisions of the International Criminal Court, Doc.EX.CL639(XVIII); Decision on the Implementation of the Assembly Decisions on the International Criminal Court, Doc.Ex.CL/670(XIX), adopted at the 17th Ordinary Session, 30 June–1 July 2011; Decision on the Progress Report of the Commission on Implementation of the Assembly Decisions on the International Criminal Court (ICC), Doc.Ex.CL/710(XX), adopted at the 18th Ordinary Session, 29–30 January 2012, Addis Ababa, Ethiopia; Decision on the Jurisdiction, Justice and the International Criminal Court (ICC), Doc.Assembly/AU/13(XXI) adopted at the 21st Ordinary Session, 26–27 May 2013, Addis Ababa, Ethiopia.

subjecting themselves to the laws and justice institutions of others. Chief Justice Marshall regarded it as an obligation of the 'highest character' that a sovereign should 'not degrade the dignity of his nation by placing himself or its sovereign rights within the jurisdiction of another'.[22]

The nineteenth century and the first half of the twentieth century were characterised by industrialisation and the rise of socialist and communist states respectively. One of the consequences of industrialisation was the increased involvement of states in commerce. States that adopted communism and socialism also became more involved in commercial activities through nationalised firms and establishment of corporations wholly owned by the states. The increased involvement of states in commercial activities rendered the concept of absolute immunity obsolete (de Than and Shorts 2012). This led to the development of the doctrine of restrictive immunity, under which states grant immunity to foreign states for public or governmental acts of states (acts *jure imperii*), but not for private or commercial activities of the state (acts *jure gestionis*) (ibid.).

In the *Cristina* case,[23] Lord Macmillan expressed the view that immunity was essentially a concession to the dignity, equality and independence of foreign states. Where foreign sovereigns 'condescended to lay aside their dignity' by engaging in commercial activities, Lord Macmillan expressed reservations as to whether immunity should be extended in such circumstances.[24] Notable cases from different jurisdictions, including Austria, South Africa, Zimbabwe and Botswana, that went on to affirm the restrictive immunity approach include *Dralle v. Republic of Czechoslovakia*,[25] *Trendtex Trading Corporation Ltd. v. Central Bank of Nigeria*,[26] *Inter-Science Research and Development Services (Pty) Ltd v. Republica Popular de Mocambique*,[27] *Barker McCormac (Pvt) Ltd. v. Government of Kenya*,[28] *Bah v. Libyan Embassy*[29] and *International Committee of the Red Cross v. Sibanda and Another*.[30] In *Dralle v. Republic of Czechoslovakia*, the Supreme Court of Austria held that absolute immunity had lost its meaning and was no longer a rule of international law. In *Trendtex v. Central Bank of Nigeria*, the UK Court of Appeal held that restrictive immunity was a firmly established rule of customary international law.

22 *The Schooner Exchange v. Mcfaddon*, above n 17, 137.
23 *Compania Naviera Vascongado v. Steamship 'Cristina' and Persons Claiming and Interest Therein* [1938] AC 485.
24 Ibid., 498.
25 *Dralle v. Republic of Czechoslovakia* (1950) 17 ILR 165.
26 *Trendtex Trading Corporation Ltd. v. Central Bank of Nigeria* [1977] 2 WLR 356.
27 *Inter-Science Research and Development Services (Pty) Ltd v. Republica Popular de Mocambique* 1980 (2) SA 111.
28 *Barker McCormac (Pvt) Ltd. v. Government of Kenya* 1983 (4) SA 817 (ZS).
29 *Bah v. Libyan Embassy* 2006 (1) BLR 22 (IC).
30 *International Committee of the Red Cross v. Sibanda and Another* 2004 (1) ZLR 27.

Today most states have codified the qualified or restrictive approach to state immunity. In the US, codification of the restrictive approach to immunity was preceded by what is now commonly referred to as the 'Tate Letter' of 1952, which was issued by the State Department and confirmed that immunity would only be extended for public acts and not for private acts (Tate 1952; Jarvis 2015). It seems accurate to conclude, as the UK Court of Appeal stated in the *Trendtex* case, that restrictive immunity, under which immunity is granted for acts *jure imperii* but not for acts *jure gestionis*, is now a rule of customary international law.

The rule on restrictive immunity for sovereigns that 'condescend to lay aside their dignity' by being involved in commercial activity could be applied with even greater force to sovereigns that 'condescend to lay aside their dignity' by committing serious crimes of international concern that threaten international peace and security. Nothing could be more convincing than to argue that a sovereign that commits egregious human rights violations condemned as such by the entire international community thereby abrogates its sovereignty and therefore lays aside his dignity. Such a sovereign cannot be heard to complain that his dignity is affronted by being subjected to the jurisdiction if not of other states, then most certainly of courts or tribunals of an international character, for which their state has chosen to be a party or that are set up by the Security Council pursuant to its Chapter VII powers.

Under the 2004 UN Convention on Jurisdictional Immunities of States and Their Property, which has, however, not received sufficient signatures to date, it is clear that immunity relates to that of the state and its property from the 'jurisdiction of the courts of another state'.[31] By seeking to place incumbent state officials outside the reach of the African Court of Justice and Human Rights, which is an international court, the immunity clause of the Malabo Protocol misses the whole point of state immunity and thereby contradicts customary international law. The fact that African states that ratify the Protocol can claim immunity for their high-ranking state officials when they are arrested and detained in other states parties is a mockery of international criminal justice. The desirable position should be that ratification of the Protocol amounts to an unconditional waiver of any claims to immunity.

Another objective of the law on state immunities is to ensure the smooth conduct of diplomatic and inter-state relations. The Vienna Convention on Diplomatic Relations declares in its preamble that immunities are intended to ensure the efficient performance of diplomatic functions.[32] In the *Arrest Warrant* case, the International Court of Justice (ICJ) expressed the view that

---

31 See, for example, arts. 1 and 5 of the Convention on Jurisdictional Immunities of States and Their Property.

32 Vienna Convention on Diplomatic Relations, 18 April 1961, United Nations, *Treaty Series*, Vol. 500, p. 95.

immunities are extended not for the personal benefit of officials, but to ensure the effective performance of their official functions.[33] In exercising their diplomatic functions, high-ranking state officials such as heads of state often need to stay in communication with foreign governments. Frequently, there is a need to travel abroad to participate in international negotiations and inter-governmental meetings. State officials will be hindered in their functions if they are subjected to arrest and detention in foreign states. However, it is now questionable whether this purpose of immunity is still valid in view of the development and ready availability of communication technologies which mean that government officials do not necessarily have to travel abroad to conduct international relations. Consequently, as the purpose of state immunities continues to be eroded by developments in communication technologies, the AU would have been better advised to limit their application rather than expand them. In this respect, the immunity clause of the Malabo Protocol is inconsistent with the objects and purpose of state immunities under customary international law.

2.2. THE PURPOSE OF INTERNATIONAL CRIMINAL JUSTICE

By its very nature, international criminal justice is reserved for the most serious offences and individuals who bear the greatest responsibility for committing such offences. History shows that these egregious offences that qualify for prosecution under the international criminal justice system are usually committed by the most senior state officials purporting to act under the guise of their official duties.

Furthermore, under Article 46H of the Protocol on the Statute of the African Court of Justice and Human and Peoples' Rights as amended by the Malabo Protocol, the African Court exercises its jurisdiction on the basis of complementarity not only with national courts, but with regional economic courts as well. The fact that the AU foresees a possible situation in the future where courts established by regional economic communities will try individuals responsible for atrocity crimes on the African continent is something to celebrate. This kind of foresight fits in very well with the trajectory of the AU, which eschews impunity and strives for the rule of law and allocation of responsibility for atrocity crimes.

The concept of complementarity kicks in when a national court is unable or unwilling to prosecute. In most states, domestic laws allow for immunity for certain high-ranking state officials like the state president. Besides, it is usually

---

33 *Case Concerning the Arrest Warrant of 11 April 2000 (Democratic Republic of the Congo v. Belgium)* [2002] ICJ 1.

difficult to prosecute such people in national courts. In the circumstances, if sitting heads of state and other high-ranking officials are exempted from prosecution by the African Court of Justice and Human and Peoples' Rights, who then will prosecute them whenever they are accused of egregious crimes? Will this not lead to a situation where, in exercising its criminal jurisdiction, the African Court will end up dealing with low-level suspects and criminals?

2.3. INCONSISTENCY WITH CUSTOMARY INTERNATIONAL LAW

The immunity clause of the Malabo Protocol seems to contradict the current state of development of state immunity under customary international law. It is important to stress that immunity relates only to the enforcement of laws. Immunity has no bearing at all on the legal liability per se of a defendant. For this reason, it is often said that immunity does not mean impunity.

As we will see from the discussion below, immunity only leads to two possible outcomes. As will be apparent, none of these outcomes has the effect of exonerating the defendant from liability. First, accountability is delayed until such time that immunity can no longer avail the defendant. Second, immunity may also entail that accountability for international crimes is diverted to an appropriate court, before which head of state immunity may not be raised as a substantive or procedural bar to prosecution. What then is the current state of development of the customary international law of state immunity? It is necessary to make some general comments on some of the main aspects of the law.

2.4. FUNCTIONAL IMMUNITY (*RATIONE MATERIAE*) AND PERSONAL IMMUNITY (*RATIONE PERSONAE*)

Customary international law recognises two types of immunity: functional immunity (*ratione materiae*) and personal immunity (*ratione personae*) (Malanczuk 1997). Functional immunity is limited since it only applies to official acts carried out by state officials while in office; it does not cover acts of a personal nature, even if the acts are committed while in office. Functional immunity is substantive in nature. It continues to protect state officials from the jurisdiction of the courts of other states even after leaving office.

The rationale behind functional immunity derives from the sovereign equality of states. Since states are artificial legal persons, they can only act through their officials. Consequently, acts that are committed by state officials pursuant to their official capacities are regarded as acts of the state rather than as personal acts. Allowing domestic courts to exercise jurisdiction over acts of foreign officials would amount to exercising jurisdiction over the foreign state for which the officials acted. Therefore, functional immunity prevents domestic courts from enquiring into the acts of foreign states through proceedings against officials who carried out the acts (Akande 2004).

From these basic characteristics of functional immunity, it is clear that this type of immunity serves as a substantive bar to the exercise of jurisdiction by domestic courts over an incumbent head of state for acts committed while discharging his/her public functions. This type of immunity continues to apply even after the head of state has left office. Therefore, functional immunity protects both an incumbent and a former head of state from the jurisdiction of the courts of foreign states, provided that it can be shown that the acts were committed in the incumbent or former head of state's official capacity. The question that invariably arises is what amounts to official acts. Debate continues over the status of acts such as torture that, by definition, can only be committed by officials exercising public functions (Owie 2015; Zappala 2001). However, the preponderance of opinion seems to favour the view that even though by definition it can only be committed by public officials, torture and other acts that infringe upon *jus cogens* norms may not qualify as official acts. Therefore, head of state immunity does not cover such acts.[34]

Personal immunity, on the other hand, provides a procedural bar to proceedings in foreign courts. It applies to state officials while in office and covers both official acts and acts carried out in a private capacity before and after assumption of office. While the official remains in office, personal immunity is absolute. It ensures the total inviolability of state officials when travelling abroad.[35] It is irrelevant whether the visit is for official or private business. In *Republic of Austria v. Altman*,[36] Justice Breyer expressed the view that personal immunity 'is about a defendant's status at the time of suit, not about a defendant's conduct before the suit.'[37]

As it avails state officials while in office, the protection afforded by personal immunity only lasts during incumbency. Upon leaving office, the head of state or high-ranking state official sheds his/her personal immunity. Therefore, once the official vacates his/her position, he/she can be sued in domestic courts in criminal and civil proceedings for private acts that are not covered by functional immunity. In *Ex King Farouk of Egypt v. Christian Dior*,[38] the court

34 Sir Arthur Watts, 'Heads of State' in *Max Planck Encyclopedia of Public International Law* (Oxford: Oxford University Press, 2010), available at: http://opil.ouplaw.com/view/10.1093/law:epil/9780199231690/law-9780199231690-e1418?prd=EPIL.

35 *Case Concerning the Arrest Warrant of 11 April 2000 (Democratic Republic of the Congo v. Belgium)*, above n 33, paras. 70–71; *Case Concerning Certain Questions of Mutual Assistance in Criminal Matters (Djibouti v. France)* [2008] ICJ 177, para. 170.

36 *Republic of Austria v. Altman* 541 U.S. 677 (2004).

37 Ibid., 708.

38 *Ex King Farouk of Egypt v. Christian Dior* 24 ILR 228 (CA Paris, 1957).

held that while he remained king, King Farouk was protected by personal immunity from suit by Christian Dior for the cost of clothes that he had bought for his wife. However, once he lost his royal status, Christian Dior could sue for recovery of the debt incurred by him before his abdication as he was no longer entitled to claim immunity. In *Lafontant v. Aristide*,[39] a US District Court ruled that Jean-Bertrand Aristide was protected from suit in the US by immunity, even though he had been overthrown as President of Haiti and sent into exile following a coup. The finding of immunity rested on the fact that after the coup, the US government did not recognise the military government, but continued to recognise Aristide as head of state of Haiti.

Domestic courts have also upheld personal immunity for incumbent heads of state and other high-ranking state officials even where allegations of international crimes and breaches of *jus cogens* rules of international law are concerned. For example, in *Tachiona v. Mugabe*,[40] the court upheld the immunity of President Mugabe and his Minister of Foreign Affairs even though the suit sought redress for egregious violations, including torture, assault and execution, some of which were committed in personal capacities. The *Gaddafi* case involved the terrorist bombing of a French airliner, which caused the deaths of 156 passengers and 15 crew members. The French Court of Cassation held that the serious crimes related to terrorism that were being alleged against Colonel Gaddafi did not constitute an exception to the principle of the jurisdictional immunity of an incumbent foreign head of state.[41]

Personal immunity is similar to diplomatic immunity, which is governed by the 1961 Vienna Convention on Diplomatic Relations. In fact, it is sometimes said that some of the principles of personal immunity, such as inviolability, are imported from diplomatic immunity (Summers 2006).

3. THE EFFECT OF THE CASES OF PINOCHET, SLOBODAN MILOŠEVIC AND CHARLES TAYLOR[42]

At the turn of the twentieth century, a number of serving and former heads of state, including General Pinochet, Slobodan Miloševic and Charles Taylor, were arrested and accused of atrocity crimes. These arrests produced jurisprudence

---

39 *Lafontant v. Aristide* 844 F. Supp. 128 (E.D.N.Y. 1994).

40 *Tachiona v. Mugabe* 169 F. Supp. 2d 259 (S.D.N.Y. 2001).

41 *Gaddafi*, 125 ILR 490 (2001) (Court of Cassation, France).

42 *R v. Bow Street Stipendiary Magistrate and Others ex parte Pinochet Ugarte (Amnesty International and Others Intervening) (No. 3)* [1999] 2 All ER 97; *Prosecutor v. Slobodan Milošević*, Decision on Preliminary Motions, 8 November 2001; *The Prosecutor v. Charles Ghankay Taylor*, Case No. SCSL-2003-01-1, Decision on Immunity from Jurisdiction, 31 May 2004.

that has had a profound effect on the development of customary international law on the immunity of high-ranking state officials. In fact, the ICC Pre-Trial Chamber I has made reference to the increase in the number of incumbent or former heads of state prosecuted for international crimes to support the view that state immunity may not avail a defendant in cases prosecuted in international courts and tribunals.[43] In its Report on Jurisdictional Immunities of States and Their Property, the working group of the International Law Commission observed that national courts had in some cases shown sympathy towards the argument that states are not entitled to plead immunity where there has been a violation of human rights norms with the character of *jus cogens*.[44] In all the cases cited by the International Law Commission, the plea of sovereign immunity succeeded. However, most of the decisions were rendered prior to the cases of Pinochet, Milošević and Taylor.

One of the most enduring contributions of all these cases is that they confirmed that state immunity, which includes immunity of state officials, is still very much extant in customary international law. A sitting head of state, for example, enjoys personal immunity from the jurisdiction of foreign domestic courts. Sitting heads of state continue to enjoy absolute inviolability before national courts of foreign states, even when they are suspected of having committed acts that constitute atrocity crimes under international law.

The *Pinochet* case is a decision of a national court, but it has had a tremendous impact on the development of customary international law of state immunity. Before this case, no former head of state had ever been required to submit to the criminal justice process of a friendly state that he/she was visiting in order to answer criminal charges arising from acts committed in the former head of state's state (Robertson 1999). Yet the House of Lords held that a former head of state could not rely on state immunity to avoid court proceedings where that former head of state is accused of breaches of international law prohibitions with *jus cogens* status, such as torture. This is because systematic torture can never be regarded as a legitimate state function.

---

43 *The Prosecutor v. Omar Hassan Ahmad Al Bashir*, ICC-02/05-01/09, Decision Pursuant to Article 87(7) of the Rome Statute on the Failure by the Republic of Malawi to Comply with the Cooperation Requests Issued by the Court with Respect to the Arrest and Surrender of Omar Hassan Ahmad Al Bashir, 12 December 2011.

44 *Al-Adsani v. UK*, Application No. 35763/97, Strasbourg, 21 November 2001, (1999) 2 *Yearbook of the International Law Commission* 155; International Law Commission, Draft Articles on Jurisdictional Immunities of States and Their Property [1991] 2(2) *Yearbook of the International Law Commission* 12; UN Doc. A/46/10 (1991); *Controller and Auditor General v. Sir Ronald Davidson* [1996] 2 New Zealand Law Reports 278; *Princz v. Federal Republic of Germany* 26 F 3d 1166 (DC Cir. 1994), 1176–1185; *Siderman de Blake v. Republic of Argentina* 965 F 2d 699 (9th Cir. 1992); *Argentine Republic v. Amerada Hess Shipping Corporation* 488 US 428 (1989); *Saudi Arabia v. Nelson* 507 U.S. 349 (1993).

The case of Charles Taylor before the Special Court for Sierra Leone established the point that the nature of a court or tribunal can determine whether the accused person has immunity or not. In this case, whether Taylor was protected by head of state immunity was dependent on whether the Special Court for Sierra Leone was a national or international court.[45] According to the Court, the distinction between national and international courts is important because immunity flows from the principle of sovereign equality of states, which prevents one state from sitting in judgment on another state's conduct. Since the principle of sovereign equality – the basis of the concept of immunity – is not implicated in proceedings by international tribunals, immunity has no place in a prosecution by an international tribunal, which is not an organ of any state.[46]

The Court ruled that the since the Special Court for Sierra Leone was an international court, Charles Taylor did not enjoy any immunity before this court. In any case, at the time that the case was argued, Taylor had ceased to be head of state. 'The immunity *ratione personae* which he claimed had ceased to attach to him.'[47]

What then can we make of the current state of the development of state immunity under customary international law? Geoffrey Robertson's comment on the absolute nature of personal immunity of diplomats, which, I argue, applies with equal force to heads of state, aptly captures the sequence of application of functional immunity and personal immunity. Robertson (1999) writes that absolute personal immunity lasts from the time of assumption of office to the time the official vacates the official position. 'Thereafter, however, they shed that total immunity and wear its undergarment: immunity *ratione materiae*, covering only their actions done in the course of official duties.'[48]

Therefore, from this discussion, we can conclude that a sitting head of state is entitled to absolute immunity and may not be impleaded in the courts of other states for both criminal and civil wrongs, the seriousness of the allegations notwithstanding. However, once the head of state leaves office and becomes a former head of state, he/she loses the protection of personal immunity and becomes entitled only to the protection afforded by functional immunity. Only acts committed in the former head of state's official capacity are protected by functional immunity. As the case of former King Farouk of Egypt referred to above shows, the former head of state becomes liable for all acts committed in his/her private capacity.

---

45 *The Prosecutor v. Charles Ghankay Taylor*, above n 42, para. 49.
46 Ibid., para. 51.
47 Ibid., para. 59.
48 Ibid.

As the case of Pinochet shows, upon shedding immunity *ratione personae*, a former head of state cannot seek the protection of immunity *ratione materiae* for acts that breach an international law prohibition that has achieved *jus cogens* status, such as the prohibition of torture committed systematically for policy reasons, since such acts can never be regarded as legitimate state functions. It seems that other egregious violations, such as genocide, that have also achieved *jus cogens* status dissolve the functional immunity that a former head of state might otherwise be entitled to under customary international law.

Clearly, the African Court of Justice and Human Rights has the status of an international court. There is no room at all for arguing that the African Court may be regarded as a domestic court. In the circumstances, applying the rule established by the Special Court for Sierra Leone in the *Charles Taylor* case, there cannot be any question of immunity as between the African Court and any sitting or former head of state. This rule was confirmed by the ICJ in the *Arrest Warrant* case between Belgium and the Democratic Republic of the Congo. This then is one of the problems with the immunity clause of the Malabo Protocol. By purporting to offer blanket immunity to high-ranking state officials, including immunity for criminal responsibility before the African Court of Justice and Human and Peoples' Rights, Article 46A *bis* of the Malabo Protocol contradicts what appears to be the current state of development of customary international law on state immunities.

Furthermore, following the recent developments in customary international law of state immunities discussed above and the ratification of the Rome Statute, a significant number of African states, including Kenya and South Africa, adopted domestic legislation to implement the letter and spirit of the Rome Statute. Such domestic legislation tends to reflect the position that there can be no question of immunity before international courts for sitting or former heads of state. Indeed, the courts in Kenya and South Africa have found that President Omar al-Bashir, a sitting head of state, does not enjoy immunity from prosecution by the ICC for atrocity crimes.[49] These states will face insurmountable difficulties in trying to spell out state immunity when they adopt legislation to domesticate their obligations under the Malabo Protocol. Attempting to reconcile the approach to immunity under the Rome Statute on the one hand and the Malabo Protocol on the other will present serious difficulties.

The conviction held by African governments that European states were abusing universal jurisdiction and that the ICC was targeting African leaders

[49] *Kenya Section of the International Commission of Jurists v. Attorney-General & Minister of State for Provincial Administration and Internal Security* [2011] eKLR; *Southern African Litigation Centre v. Minister of Justice and Constitutional Development & 11 Others*, Case No. 27740/2015, Gauteng High Court, Pretoria; *The Minister of Justice and Constitutional Development v. The Southern African Litigation Centre* [2016] ZASCA 17.

motivated the AU to consider empowering the African Court of Justice and Human and Peoples' Rights with jurisdiction to try crimes of international concern. Clearly, one of the issues that the AU currently has with the ICC over the prosecution of African leaders and European states over the application of universal jurisdiction is the question of immunity for high-ranking government officials. As the case of al-Bashir shows, the approach that the ICC and some states have taken on the issue of immunity of incumbent heads of non-ICC states in domestic legal systems of ICC states parties is problematic. Consequently, the Malabo Protocol seeks to correct this problem by including a clause that provides blanket immunity from prosecution to sitting heads of state or any individuals acting as such during their tenure.

By wording the immunity clause in the manner that it did, the AU seems to have overcorrected what it understands to be the anomaly in the approach of the ICC. As argued elsewhere in this chapter, the correct position of immunity under customary international law should be that sitting heads of state are not immune to prosecution as such for crimes of international concern; rather, immunity for sitting heads of state may apply to exclude proceedings in domestic courts. The immunity clause gives credence to the suspicions held by many that the AU's axe to grind with the European states over the application of universal jurisdiction and with the ICC is really about shielding high-ranking government officials from being held accountable for atrocity crimes (Jalloh and Elias 2015).

Yet, in its trajectory, the AU has been about accountability for violations of human rights. The oft-quoted Article 4(h) of the Constitutive Act of the AU recognises the right of the AU to intervene in any member state in cases of grave circumstances that include crimes of international concern, namely war crimes, genocide and crimes against humanity. Furthermore, in all resolutions on the work of the ICC in Africa, the AU clearly shows that it forswears impunity. A blanket immunity that purports to exclude incumbent high-ranking state officials from the jurisdiction of the African Court of Justice and Human Rights is clearly inconsistent with this trajectory of the AU and its organising principles.

4. THE SPECTRE OF BREACHING VIENNA CONVENTION OBLIGATIONS

Most AU members that are not parties to the Rome Statute have nevertheless appended their signatures to it. It is trite that, under Article 18 of the Vienna Convention on the Law of Treaties, a state that signs a treaty pending ratification has an obligation to act in ways that do not defeat the letter and spirit of the treaty. Specifically, a state that has signed, but not ratified, a treaty is under an obligation to 'refrain from acts which would defeat the object and purpose' of that treaty.[50]

The approach to state immunities under the Rome Statute regime is spelt out in Articles 27(2) and 98(1). Obviously, the Rome Statute applies to states that have ratified it. Very carefully crafted, the provisions of Articles 27(2) and 98(1) are addressed to the ICC. In its wording under Articles 27(2) and 98(1), the Rome Statute portrays an understanding of head of state immunity that is consistent with the position of customary international law. Article 27(2) makes it clear that immunities due to the official capacity of a person shall not bar the ICC from exercising jurisdiction over the person. Pursuant to this article, immunity may not avail a sitting head of state of a state party indicted or prosecuted by the ICC, which is an international tribunal. Article 98(1), on the other hand, states that unless it has obtained a waiver of immunity, the ICC may not request a state's cooperation in the surrender of a suspect if such a request would lead the state to 'act inconsistently with its obligations under international law with respect to the State or diplomatic immunity'.

If we accept that Rome Statute states parties consent and voluntarily submit to the jurisdiction of the ICC, thereby foregoing any claims to immunity, in theory, the effect of Article 98(1) is that the ICC is precluded from requesting states to arrest a sitting head of state of a non-party, for example, which would inevitably involve bringing the head of state before the domestic legal system of another state. Such a situation would be contrary to customary international law, which continues to protect the inviolability of sitting heads of states and to prevent them from being dragged before domestic legal systems. AU members that have signed the Rome Statute are obliged to refrain from acts and behaviour that would contradict its objectives and purpose. By signing or ratifying the Malabo Protocol with the immunity clause in its current wording, the AU member states raise the spectre of deliberately acting in a way that might defeat the objects and purpose of the Rome Statute.

It may be important to note that AU member states that signed the Rome Statute assumed an obligation to refrain from acts that would defeat its objects before they assumed any obligations under the Malabo Protocol. Yet Article 26 of the Vienna Convention on the Law of Treaties, which provides for the *pacta sunt servanda rule*, entails that states that ratify both the Rome Statute and the Malabo Protocol must honour their obligations under both treaties. Each of the treaties should be enforced by the parties. Faced with conflicting obligations, African states that ratify both instruments will have to breach of the two, thereby falling foul of the *pacta sunt servanda* doctrine.

---

50 Vienna Convention on the Law of Treaties, concluded at Vienna on 23 May 1969, United Nations Treaty Series, Vol. 1155, No. 18232, 1980.

5. SUGGESTIONS FOR REFORM

5.1. CONFLATING IMMUNITY AS A MATTER OF SUBSTANTIVE LAW AND IMMUNITY AS A PROCEDURAL MATTER

The Malabo Protocol suffers from poor draftsmanship. One of the biggest problems of the immunity clause of the Malabo Protocol arising from this poor draftsmanship is that it conflates immunity as a matter of substantive law and immunity as a procedural matter. Yet, as we have argued elsewhere in this chapter, immunity only applies as a matter of adjectival law. In the *Arrest Warrant* case, the ICJ stated that the presence of immunity does not necessarily mean the absence of jurisdiction and vice versa.[51] I would recommend that an amendment be effected to the immunity clause of the Statute of the African Court of Justice and Human and Peoples' Rights in a way that deals with state immunities at two separate stages.

The first stage relates to the relationship between the accused person and the African Court of Justice and Human and Peoples' Rights. Here, immunity may be raised in relation to the question of the criminal liability of the defendant before the Court. As between the accused person and the Court, the issue of immunity is dealt with as a matter of substantive law. At this level, it can safely be said that customary international law does not allow immunity to excuse high-ranking government officials, including a sitting head of state, since the African Court of Justice and Human and Peoples' Rights is an international court. Article 27(2) of the Rome Statute provides a good example of how the matter can be tackled at this level as a matter of substantive law.

The second stage should deal with immunity as a matter of procedural law. In this respect, the Rome Statute could allow for immunity where the court asks states for cooperation in the arrest, extradition and surrender of high-ranking state officials facing charges before the court. As between a defendant entitled to immunity and a third state, immunity may apply unless the state for which the defendant is an official has waived the immunity. Much like Article 98(1) of the Rome Statute, such a clause would serve as a procedural fix that fits in neatly with the trajectory of the AU. Such a procedural fix would have the effect of increasing the comfort levels of AU states that genuinely eschew impunity, but are not yet ready for the jettisoning of customary law immunities altogether (Jakobsen 2005).

---

51 *Case Concerning the Arrest Warrant of 11 April 2000*, above n 33, para. 59.

5.2. LACK OF PRECISION IN THE DEFINITION OF 'SENIOR STATE OFFICIALS'

Possibly also arising from poor draftsmanship is the open-ended nature of the list of people who may qualify as senior state officials who might then be entitled to immunity in Article 46A *bis*. Immunity under this article is extended to serving heads of state, heads of government and acting heads of state and heads of government, and 'other senior state officials'. Amnesty International has decried the lack of precision in the definition of 'senior state officials' and the lack of an exhaustive list of individuals who may qualify as 'senior state officials'.

Having regard to state practice and decisions that include the *Arrest Warrant* and *Pinochet* cases, it seems that senior state officials that are automatically entitled to immunity include the head of state or head of government, senior cabinet members and foreign and defence ministers.[52] In addition to diplomatic and consular agents that are covered by the Vienna Convention on Diplomatic Relations, the ICJ added 'certain holders of high-ranking office in a state, *such as* the Head of State, Head of Government and Minister for Foreign Affairs'.[53] The use of the words 'such as' suggests that the ICJ does not prefer a closed list of senior officials entitled to state immunity (Akande and Shah 2010).

Similarly, the 2004 UN Convention on Jurisdictional Immunities of States and Their Property defines the term 'state' as including simply 'representatives of the state acting in that capacity'. No attempt is made in this instrument to make the list of officials who are entitled to immunity exhaustive. There are obvious benefits to keeping the list open-ended. It allows the courts some discretion at any given time to determine, on the facts of each case, whether immunity may be extended to the official in question. This allows the courts to develop the law on officials that are entitled to immunity in an organic way.

However, closing the list of official positions that are entitled to immunity allows for certainty, which is an important ingredient of the rule of law. The fact that everyone knows in advance the positions that are entitled to immunity limits the possibilities for abuse by government officials who may have the right to suggest to courts the foreign officials that are entitled to immunity. An amendment to Article 46A *bis* that includes an exhaustive list of senior state officials to whom immunity may be extended would remove any uncertainty and resolve the discomfort that many people have with the immunity clause of the Malabo Protocol.

---

52 *Arrest Warrant of 11 April 2000 (Democratic Republic of Congo v. Belgium)* [2002] ICJ Rep 3; *R v. Bow Street Magistrates ex parte Pinochet Ugarte (No. 3)* [2000] 1 AC 147 (HL).

53 Ibid., para. 53.

BIBLIOGRAPHY

Akande, D. (2004) 'International Law Immunities and the International Court', *American Journal of International Law* 98: 407–433.
Akande, D. and Shah, S. (2010) 'Immunities of State Officials, International Crimes, and Foreign Domestic Court', *European Journal of International Law* 21: 815–852.
De Than, C. and Shorts, E. (2012) *International Criminal Law and Human Rights*. London: Sweet & Maxwell.
Hillier, T. (1998) *Sourcebook on Public International Law*. London: Cavendish Publishing.
Jakobsen, M. (2005) *Immunity versus Impunity? Reconciling Articles 27(2) and 98(1) of the Rome Statute*. RGSL Working Papers No. 23, Riga Graduate School of Law, Riga, Latvia.
Jalloh, C.C. (2010) 'Universal Jurisdiction, Universal Prescription? A Preliminary Assessment of the African Perspectives on Universal Jurisdiction', *Criminal Law Forum* 21: 1–65.
Jalloh, C.C. and Elias, O. (eds) (2015) *Shielding Humanity: Essays in International Law in Honour of Judge Abdul G. Koroma*. Leiden: Brill Nijhoff.
Jarvis, R.M. (2015) 'The Tate Letter: Some Words Regarding its Authorship', *American Journal of Legal History* 55: 465–472.
Malanczuk, P. (1997) *Akehurst's Modern Introduction to International Law*, 7th edn. London: Routledge.
Robertson, G. (1999) *Crimes Against Humanity: The Struggle for Global Justice*. London: Allen Lane, Penguin Press.
Salvatore Zappala, S. (2001) 'Do Heads of State in Office Enjoy Immunity from Jurisdiction for International Crimes? The Ghaddafi Case before the French Cour de Cassation', *European Journal of International Law* 12: 595–612.
Summers, M.A. (2006) 'Immunity or Impunity? The Potential Effect of Prosecutions of State Officials for Core International Crimes in States Like the United States That are Not Parties to the Statute of the International Criminal Court', *Brooklyn Journal of International Law* 31: 463–493.
Tate, J.B. (1952) 'Changed Policy Concerning the Granting of Sovereign Immunity to Foreign Governments', *Department of State Bulletin* 26: 984–985.
Udoka Owie, U. (2015) 'The Pinochet Case: Expounding or Expanding International Law', *International Journal of International Law* 2: 158–174.

CASE LAW

Al-Adsani v. UK, Application No. 35763/97, Strasbourg, 21 November 2001.
Argentine Republic v. Amerada Hess Shipping Corporation 488 US 428 (1989).
Arrest Warrant of 11 April 2000 (Democratic Republic of Congo v. Belgium) [2002] ICJ Rep 3.
Bah v. Libyan Embassy 2006 (1) BLR 22 (IC).
Barker McCormac (Pvt) Ltd. v. Government of Kenya 1983 (4) SA 817 (ZS).
Case Concerning Certain Questions of Mutual Assistance in Criminal Matters (Djibouti v. France) [2008] ICJ 177.
Case Concerning the Arrest Warrant of 11 April 2000 (Democratic Republic of the Congo v. Belgium) [2002] ICJ 1.

Compania Naviera Vascongado v. Steamship 'Cristina' and Persons Claiming and Interest Therein [1938] AC 485.

Controller and Auditor General v. Sir Ronald Davidson [1996] 2 New Zealand Law Reports 278.

Dralle v. Republic of Czechoslovakia (1950) 17 ILR 165.

Ex King Farouk of Egypt v. Christian Dior 24 ILR 228 (CA Paris, 1957).

Gaddafi, 125 ILR 490 (2001) (Court of Cassation, France).

International Committee of the Red Cross v. Sibanda and Another 2004 (1) ZLR 27.

Inter-Science Research and Development Services (Pty) Ltd v. Republica Popular de Mocambique 1980 (2) SA 111.

Kenya Section of the International Commission of Jurists v. Attorney-General & Minister of State for Provincial Administration and Internal Security [2011] eKLR.

Lafontant v. Aristide 844 F. Supp. 128 (E.D.N.Y. 1994).

Parlement Belge (1880) 5 PD 197.

Princz v. Federal Republic of Germany 26 F 3d 1166 (DC Cir. 1994).

Prosecutor v. Slobodan Milošević, Case No. IT-99-37-PT, Decision on Preliminary Motions, 8 November 2001.

R v. Bow Street Stipendiary Magistrate and Others ex parte Pinochet Ugarte (Amnesty International and Others Intervening) (No. 3) 1 AC 147, [1999] 2 All ER 97, [1999] 2 WLR 827.

Republic of Austria v. Altman 541 U.S. 677 (2004).

Saudi Arabia v. Nelson 507 U.S. 349 (1993).

Siderman de Blake v. Republic of Argentina 965 F 2d 699 (9th Cir. 1992).

Southern African Litigation Centre v. Minister of Justice and Constitutional Development & 11 Others, Case No. 27740/2015, Gauteng High Court, Pretoria.

Tachiona v. Mugabe 169 F. Supp. 2d 259 (S.D.N.Y. 2001).

The Minister of Justice and Constitutional Development v. The Southern African Litigation Centre [2016] ZASCA 17.

The Porto Alexandre (1920) 1 ILR 146.

The Prosecutor v. Charles Ghankay Taylor, Case No. SCSL-2003-01-1, Decision on Immunity from Jurisdiction, 31 May 2004.

The Prosecutor v. Omar Hassan Ahmad Al Bashir, ICC-02/05-01/09, Decision Pursuant to Article 87(7) of the Rome Statute on the Failure by the Republic of Malawi to Comply with the Cooperation Requests Issued by the Court with Respect to the Arrest and Surrender of Omar Hassan Ahmad Al Bashir, 12 December 2011.

The Schooner Exchange v. McFaddon (1812) 7 Cranch 116.

Trendtex Trading Corporation Ltd. v. Central Bank of Nigeria [1977] 2 WLR 356.

INDEX

www.ingramcontent.com/pod-product-compliance
Ingram Content Group UK Ltd.
Pitfield, Milton Keynes, MK11 3LW, UK
UKHW051926100926
8556IPUK00022B/1398

9 781780 689074